# Artificial Intelligence and Cognitive Science

*Conceptual Issues*

Series Editors

Andy Clark and Josefa Toribio
*Washington University*

# Series Contents

# Cognitive Architectures in Artificial Intelligence

*The Evolution of Research Programs*

Edited with an introduction by

Andy Clark and Josefa Toribio
*Washington University*

Routledge
Taylor & Francis Group

NEW YORK AND LONDON

First published by Garland Publishing, Inc

This edition published 2011 by Routledge
711 Third Avenue, New York, NY 10017
2 Park Square, Milton Park, Abingdon, Oxon, OX14 4RN

**Library of Congress Cataloging-in-Publication Data**

Cognitive architectures in artificial intelligence : the evolution of
research programs / edited with introductions by Andy Clark and
Josefa Toribio.
     p.  cm. — (Artificial intelligence and cognitive science ; 2)
     Includes bibliographical references.
     ISBN 0-8153-2769-2 (alk. paper)
     1. Artificial intelligence—Data processing. 2. Cognition.
3. Computer architecture. I. Clark, Andy, 1957–  . II. Toribio,
Josefa. III. Series.
Q336.C658  1998
006.3—dc21                      98-27060
                                   CIP

**Publisher's Note**
The publisher has gone to great lengths to ensure the quality of this reprint
but points out that some imperfections in the original may be apparent.

# Contents

# Introduction

## Mental Bedrock?

The first volume in this series presents a collection of seminal papers introducing, challenging, and defending a computational approach to the study of mind and cognition. The present volume examines the three main research programs that have sprung, directly or indirectly, from those original seeds. These are the programs of classical cognitive science and physical symbols system theory, of connectionism (artificial neural networks), and of autonomous agent theory and artificial life.

At issue in the debate between these three research programs is the nature of what we shall term "mental bedrock," namely, the type and level of systemic organization that best explains cognitive phenomena. Each research program has a distinctive vision of the nature and shape of this mental bedrock. For the classicist, it consists in a body of atomic symbols and combinatorial and transformative rules. For the connectionist, it consists in the use of finer-grained representational elements and of a "vector-transformation" style of processing and retrieval. With autonomous agent theory, things became more complex as part of the agenda is to focus attention on a more basic range of tasks — those requiring robust real-world activity and real-time response. Relative to such tasks, the explanatory bedrock is shifted to the subtle mixtures of bodily biomechanics, environmental opportunities, and neural processing strategies that together underpin adaptive success.

In this brief introduction we shall comment on each research program in turn, sketching distinctive claims and characteristic problems, and locating various papers according to their role in this burgeoning dialectical web.

First up to bat is, of course, classical cognitive science and its theoretical expression in the physical symbol-system hypothesis. This is the idea, beautifully explained by Allen Newell in the opening paper, that all intelligence depends on the presence of physical stuff arranged so as to meet the following conditions: It must support a set of atomic symbols — physical patterns that can be combined to yield complex expressions; it must support a wide range of such patterns and expressions, as well as a set of manipulative processes that create, copy, modify, and delete expressions according to stored instructions, which are themselves just more expressions; and some of the expressions must relate consistently to a wider world of real objects. A physical symbol system (see also Newell and Simon 1981, p. 40–42) is thus any system in which inner tokens can be created, destroyed, and manipulated in these distinctive ways, and in which the tokens can be interpreted as the physical vehicles of specific contents.

The best way to get to grips with the physical symbol-system hypothesis is to examine the details of the best empirical work characteristic of the approach. The paper by Rosenbloom et al. provides an accessible yet substantial introduction to a leading (indeed, *the* leading) exemplar of such work — the SOAR architecture.

SOAR is a large-scale, ongoing collaborative project that applies the basic ideas of the physical symbol-systems hypothesis in the context of a general-purpose, multifaceted, reasoning engine. All of SOAR's long-term knowledge is stored using a uniform representational format (known as a production memory) in which knowledge is rendered as condition-action structures ('productions') of the form "if X then do Y." When solving a problem, SOAR accesses this memory store, moving into working memory everything that looks relevant to the problem at hand. It then reasons by generating a series of subgoals whose combined satisfaction would solve the problem either by achieving the subgoals directly or by decomposing them into a sequence of further subgoals (and so on). Successful sequences of subgoals can be "chunked" together and retained as a new problem-solving unit for future use.

SOAR has been successfully deployed in domains such as computer configuration, algorithm design, medical diagnosis, tic-tac-toe playing, and many more. Four key commitments seem to characterize the project, and I think it is fair to view these commitments as part and parcel of the physical symbol-systems approach considered as a distinctive practical hypothesis meant to guide empirical research. The commitments are:

1. To use a symbolic code as the primary means of storing long-term knowledge.

2. To analyze reasoning as the capacity to successfully search a symbolic problem-space.

3. To explain human intelligence as the operation of a small set of basic mechanisms of reasoning and learning (as evidenced in the use of a single mode of knowledge encoding and learning).

4. To pitch the computational story at, or close to, the level of conscious, deliberate thought (as evidenced in the talk of SOAR as targeting the "cognitive band," Rosenbloom et al., this volume) in which thoughts flow in a (relatively) slow, serial sequence. See, however, Newell (this volume) for a four-level decomposition of the cognitive band itself (hence the caveat "or close to" in the above formulation).

The three remaining papers in section one offer a variety of critiques of the SOAR style approach, and (more generally) of the physical symbol-system ideas upon which it is built. The common ground of the three critiques concerns the biological, psychological, and neurophysiological implausibility of some of SOAR's central commitments and assumptions. Norman, while praising SOAR as a compelling benchmark in artificial intelligence, argues that several central assumptions look to be biologically and neurophysiologically suspect — especially the assumptions concerning uniform modes of representation, memory, and learning. By way of contrast, Norman points to the idea of multiple memory systems in psychology, and to connectionist work in learning and knowledge representation. Dennett likewise worries about biological plausibility, accusing SOAR of a kind of rationalistic "hyperfunctionalism" that ignores the roles of evolutionarily basic mechanisms of pleasure and pain while stressing "business-like efficiency" and emotionally disengaged reason. Michael Arbib, in the final paper of the section, notes that work in neuroscience (on vision, memory, and action) seems to eschew neat symbolic representations in favor of messier, distributed patterns that act as "partial representations." More positively, Arbib purposes a new kind of 'mental bedrock' in which cognitive and neural levels of description are bridged using a vocabulary of functionally defined 'schemas' (see Arbib, this volume). One crucial feature is that the contents of the multiple, 'partial representations' that Arbib posits are unlikely to directly match the elements of our abstract understanding of a problem domain. In a rather clear sense, the spirit of symbol-system artificial intelligence is to go straight for the jugular and directly to recapitulate the space of conscious, deliberative reason using language-like internal representations and a set of logical operations. The common goal of much work in the competing paradigms, by contrast, is to somehow coax semantically sensible behavior from a seething mass of hard-to-manage parallel interactions between distributed and more semantically opaque inner elements and resources.

Another major criticism of symbol-system artificial intelligence is, of course, that it seems inappropriate as a model of fast, fluent, everyday action (as opposed to slow, deliberate reason). Thus Dreyfus and Dreyfus (1988) (reprinted in volume one of this series) argue that everyday skilled performances (such as driving, playing tennis, even chess playing) are not, and could not be, supported by any finite set of symbolically coded rules, facts, or propositions, but depend rather on a process of "holistic similarity recognition" better modeled using connectionist resources. A related worry was recently raised by the computer scientist Barbara Hayes-Roth, who issued the following "friendly challenge":

> Give us "Agent-SOAR" [a system capable of] operating continuously, selectively perceiving a complex unpredictable environment, noticing situations of interest. Show us how it . . . makes the best use of dynamic but limited resources under real-time constraints (Hayes-Roth 1994, p. 96).

(This general challenge can, however, be leveled equally at work in both the classical and the connectionist paradigms, as we shall later see.)

Section two introduces the major alternative to a symbolic, SOAR-style approach, in the form of connectionism (sometimes called parallel distributed processing or artificial neural networks). The section begins with a thorough introduction to the alternative vision in the form of Paul Churchland's treatment of connectionist and classical views of theories. As a thumbnail sketch, connectionist models consist of many simple (vaguely "neuron-like") processors, linked in parallel by a large number of weighted connections. The simple processors (known as 'units') are sensitive only to local influences. They take inputs from a small group of 'neighbors' and pass outputs (modified by unit-firing functions and connection weights) to other units. In such systems knowledge is not encoded in stored symbol strings but in the long-term weights and gross unit architecture. Moreover, such systems are typically not programmed but trained, by exposure to repeated exemplars of a target input-output function and the use of an automated learning routine. Finally, the kind of knowledge representation often developed is, as Churchland stresses, a type of *prototype*-based encoding. Specific contents are expressed as patterns of unit activation, and similar contents get expressed by related, but not identical patterns. The system learns the typical coactivated feature sets that correspond to specific objects, processes, or events and treats these as "hot spots" in a kind of articulated, high-dimensional representation space (for details, see sections four and five of the paper by Churchland). In these networks, the basic processing operations are defined over numerical vectors and information-retrieval emerges as a species of vector-completion given a partial vector as cue. The networks exhibit nice properties such as generalization (the capacity to deal sensibly with novel inputs on the basis of similarity to stored knowledge) and graceful degradation (the capacity to behave sensibly given noisy or degraded inputs or following structural damage).

The most influential early objection to connectionism was framed by Fodor and Pylyshyn (1988) and concerned the issue they dubbed "systematicity." The key observation is that the cognitive capacities of human agents are deeply interanimated: If you are capable of having the thought that John loves Mary, you are capable of having the systematically related thought that Mary loves John. And if you can also think about Fred, you can think that Fred loves Mary, and so on. The best explanation of such an interanimated set of potential thoughts, according to Fodor and Pylyshyn, is to posit a set of inner symbols and procedures for combining and recombining them. Connectionism, insofar as it does not posit such discrete, recombinable symbolic elements, is unable (so it is argued) to properly account for the observed systematicity of thought. The paper by Paul Smolensky takes up this issue and develops a connectionist rejoinder. It is followed by a skeptical response from Fodor and McLaughlin. Of course, the debate does not stop there: For more contributions, see e.g., van Gelder (1990), Chalmers (1990), Davies (1991), and Dennett (1991). But I propose instead to point at another set of issues, ones that will help to set the scene for our third and final paradigm.

Consider, once again, the issues of biological and evolutionary plausibility. Three species of biologically based critique of (much, not all) connectionist research strike me as especially telling.

The first concerns the use of artificial tasks and the choice (Dennett 1991) of input and output representations. Typical early models retained much of the classical vision of cognitive tasks as thin fragments of human competence, defined as state transitions in which artificial codes stand for salient environmental features. Thus, for example, a connectionist net might be trained to learn an artificial grammar (Elman 1991), or to decide when blocks will balance on a movable fulcrum (Plunkett and Sinha 1991). The latter case looks more concrete until you realize that the input is a coded representation and the output is not real motor action but just the relative activity of two units interpreted so that equal activity indicates an expectation of balance and excess activity indicates a prediction of overbalancing. Such abstractly coded renditions of a problem space make for good, neat, experiments. But it is not clear (as we shall see) that cognitive science can now afford to thus abstract away from the real world poles of perception and action, and from the extra issues involved in pressing multiple kinds of adaptive response from a single agent.

The second (related) issue concerns scaling up. Typical experiments use dramatically reduced versions of real-world problems. Biological neural nets, by contrast, must cope with very high-dimensional sensory inputs, which may be relevant to multiple problems and hence require active sorting and routing of signals (see Churchland and Sejnowski 1992, p. 125 and Karmiloff-Smith 1992). Solutions that work well in smaller spaces often fail dismally when confronted with more complex data.

Finally, the neural verisimilitude of most such simulations is pretty minimal. Real neuronal assemblies exhibit many additional properties, such as nonlocal effects (caused by chemical diffusion over a whole population of cells, etc.), continuous-time processing, multiple activation functions, and highly recurrent connectivity. Second generation connectionism added recurrency into the models (see e.g., Elman 1991). Third generation work in "dynamical connectionism" adds further features from the above list, as well as the use of noise, time-delays, and analog signaling, and is thus exploring an ever-richer space of possible system dynamics (see Wheeler 1994, Port and van Gelder 1995, and Clark 1997a).

Early connectionist research, nonetheless, played a truly crucial role in the expansion of our computational horizons. It showed how to solve complex problems without the use of a standard, symbol-manipulating substrate. But we must now tune and expand the connectionist perspective. Tuning involves the incorporation of additional dynamical properties such as those mentioned previously. Expansion involves the use, at least at times, of a different research methodology — one geared to the study of whole, simple systems, able to move and act in a real or simulated environment. These twin foci (richer dynamics and agent-environment interaction systems) form the theoretical core of our third and final (for now) take on mental bedrock — artificial life and autonomous agent theory.

The section opens with a short, and in many ways prophetic, squib written by Daniel Dennett back in 1978. Here, Dennett asks why cognitive science doesn't try to model whole but simpler creatures instead of "sub-subsystems with artificially walled-off boundaries." Dennett's vision started to become flesh (well — metal, rubber, silicon) in the mid-to-late 1980s with the advent of research programs such as Rodney Brook's mobile robot (mobot) laboratory. Brooks (whose paper follows Dennett's in this volume) aims to create mobile robots whose task is to achieve some goal in a real-world setting. Such robots include Genghis — a robot insect capable of negotiating an obstacle-strewn room — and Herbert (Connell 1989) — a Coke can collecting robot that functions in the changing and complex environment of the MIT media lab. What is theoretically important here is Brooks' commitment to the use of what he terms a "subsumption architecture." Such an architecture short-circuits what Malcolm, Smithers, and Hallam (1989) nicely dub the sense-think-act cycle of traditional approaches. Instead of having powerful sensing capacities that deliver rich streams of data to a kind of central planner capable of symbolic reasoning, the subsumption approach exploits a bag of relatively autonomous behavior-producing models ("layers"). Each layer constitutes a complete route from input to action, and inter-layer communication is by simple signals ("turn me on," "turn me off") rather than by complex message-passing. In the robot Herbert, for example, one layer controlled obstacle avoidance, another controlled table-spotting, a third controlled can-grasping, etc. Part of what Brooks and others are calling into question is thus the need for rich, integrated internal-world models, internal symbol-passing communication, and the use of symbolic knowledge representations.

Nonetheless, despite the (misleading) title of Brooks' paper, "Intelligence without Representation," Brooks himself does not mean to deny that some interpretable inner states play a role in the production of behavior. He is not opposed to a kind of "minimal representationalism" — only to the use of the kinds of rich, symbolic data-structure familiar from work in classical cognitive science. That said, Brooks also explicitly distinguishes his work from connectionist approaches, insisting that the architectures he is studying are much more special purpose, and stressing the importance of real, robotically embodied, action-taking.

Van Gelder's paper makes a broader case against both representational and computational vocabularies, arguing that certain features of biological cognition will better reward analysis using the mathematical and geometric tools of dynamical systems theory (see the exposition in the text). At the heart of van Gelder's argument are the observations that real *timing* is crucial for biological problem solving, and that much of our daily activity involves processes of continuous circular causation, in which some feature X both affects and is affected by some feature Y, which (simultaneously) both affects and is affected by X. This complex relationship (think of two jazz musicians improvising), it is suggested, cannot be adequately analyzed by thinking of one item *representing* the other (too linear, too one-way), and is better captured using the alternate tools of dynamical analysis (but see Clark, in press-a).

Many people working in real-world robotics do, for whatever reason, prefer to use the kinds of analytic tool championed by van Gelder (see e.g., Beer 1995). But it is a rather open question whether we should see such tools as direct competitors with notions such as internal representation and computation, or instead as offering additional and complementary modes of systemic analysis. Van Gelder explores both options, while the short paper by Clark raises some doubts about the more radical vision. (For a longer treatment of these issues see Clark (1997a), (1997b) and (in press-a).)

The most pressing problem for work in real-world robotics remains, however, the most obvious one: Will such representation-sparse, 'bag-of-tricks' models ever be able to explain the kinds of advanced cognitive phenomena that set the original agenda for the sciences of the mind? Such phenomena include, for example, the capacity to reason off-line (to plan next year's family vacation, to assess various possible courses of action and choose one, and to think about the distal, absent, and nonexistent) and the capacity to entertain abstract ideas (e.g., to regard an action as charitable, or as morally suspect). Certainly, it is not prima facie evident exactly how representation-free or representation-sparse successes in domains such as wall-following bear on the issue of (the mechanistic underpinnings of) advanced reason.

The dialectic is complex, however, insofar as part of the radical agenda is to somewhat marginalize the kinds of "advanced" cognition just described and to suggest that the bulk of daily, skilled behavior (natural intelligence) depends on the kinds of strategy studied by Brooks, Beer, van Gelder, and others. In the closing paper, Margaret Boden attempts, in part, to reconcile these competing visions by carefully analyzing the notion of autonomy as it applies to real and artificial creatures. Boden's discussion draws usefully on work in several of the paradigms represented in this volume, and adds a valuable discussion of one further dimension of work in artificial life, namely, work on emergence and collective effects (see e.g., the discussion of flocking behavior as the emergent product of multiple individuals each following three simple rules).

At the end of the day then, the precise relations between the various approaches explored in this volume remains unclear. The most vigorous proponents of each approach typically depict it as, indeed, an account of mental bedrock — a distinctive and exclusive vision of the type or level of systemic organization best suited to the task of explaining mind and cognition. But given the wide variety of phenomena studied by the sciences of the mind and the different interests of philosophers, psychologists, and neuroscientists (to name but three), it seems equally possible that a mixed bag of analytic tools, computational architectures, and types of model will be required. What is now most urgently needed, I suspect, is a better understanding of the evolutionary and developmental bridges that link low-level, on-line, reactive behavior, and something more like 'off-line,' advanced reason (for some thoughts, see Clark and Grush in press). In seeking to understand such bridges we will be forced (I believe) to think harder about the variety of ways in which internal dynamics might be used to replicate salient external or bodily dynamics without gross real-world action, the many ways in which environmental structures and resources can actively complement on-board biological processing (so as to press maximal benefit from inner routines), and — perhaps most importantly — the way public language and written text transform the computational spaces negotiated by human thought (see e.g., Clark 1998; in press-b; and Dennett 1991, ch. 7-9). The future shape of cognitive science will surely depend on the success or failure of each paradigm's attempt to build bridges between fluent, real-time behavior and advanced reason.

Andy Clark and Josefa Toribio

## References

Beer, R. (1995). "A Dynamical Systems Perspective on Agent-Environment Interaction." *Artificial Intelligence* 72: 173–215.
Chalmers, D. (1990). "Syntactic Transformations on Distributed Representation." *Connection Science* 2: 53–62.
Churchland, P., and Sejnowski, T. (1992). *The Computational Brain*. Cambridge: MIT Press.
Clark, A. (1997a). *Being There: Putting Brain, Body and World Together Again*. Cambridge: MIT Press.
Clark, A. (1997b). "The Dynamical Challenge." *Cognitive Science* 21(4): 461–81.
Clark, A. (1998). "Magic Words: How Language Augments Human Computation." In P. Carruthers (ed.), *Language and Thought*. Cambridge: Cambridge University Press.
Clark, A. (in press-a). "Time and Mind." *Journal of Philosophy*.
Clark, A. (in press-b). "Where Brain, Body and World Collide." *Daedalus*.
Clark, A., and Grush, R. (in press). "Towards a Cognitive Robotics." *Adaptive Behavior*.
Connell, J. (1989). *A colony architecture for an artificial creature* (Technical Report No. II 5 1). MIT AI Laboratory.
Davies, M. (1991). "Concepts, Connectionism, and the Language of Thought." In W. Ramsey, S. Stich, and D. Rumelhart (eds.), *Philosophy and Connectionist Theory* (pp. 229–58). New Jersey: Erlbaum.
Dennett, D. (1991). "Mother Nature versus the Walking Encyclopedia." In W. Ramsey, S. Stich, and D. Rumelhart (eds.), *Philosophy and Connectionist Theory* (pp. 21–30). New Jersey: Erlbaum.
Dennett, D. (1991). *Consciousness Explained*. New York: Little Brown and Co.

Dreyfus, H., and Dreyfus, S. (1986). *Mind over Machine*. New York: Free Press.

Elman, J. (1991). "Representation and Structure in Connectionist Models." In G. Altman (ed.), *Cognitive Models of Speech Processing*. Cambridge: MIT Press.

Fodor, J., and Pylyshyn, Z. (1988). "Connectionism and Cognitive Architecture: A Critical Analysis." *Cognition* 28: 3–71.

Hayes-Roth, B. (1994). "On Building Integrated Cognitive Agents," Review of Allen Newell's *Unified Theories of Cognition*. In W. Clancey, S. Smoliar, and M. Stefile (eds.), *Contemplating Minds*. Cambridge: MIT Press.

Karmiloff-Smith, A. (1992). *Beyond Modularity: A Developmental Perspective on Cognitive Science*. Cambridge: MIT Press/Bradford Books.

Malcolm, C., Smithers, T., and Hallam, J. (1989). *An Emerging Paradigm in Robot Architecture*. Edinburgh: Edinburgh University Department of Artificial Intelligence.

Newell, A. and Simon, H. (1981). "Computer Science as Empirical Inquiry." In J. Haugeland (ed.), *Mind Design*. Cambridge: MIT Press.

Plunkett, K. and Sinha, C. (1991). "Connectionism and Developmental Theory." *Psykologisk Skriftserie Aarhus* 16: 1–34.

Port, R., and van Gelder, T. (eds.). (1995). *Mind as Motion: Dynamics, Behavior, and Cognition*. Cambridge: MIT Press.

van Gelder, T. (1990). "Compositionality: A Connectionist Variation on a Classical Theme." *Cognitive Science* 14: 355–84.

Wheeler, M. (1994). "From Activation to Activity." *Artificial Intelligence and the Simulation of Behavior (AISB) Quarterly* 87: 36–42.

COGNITIVE SCIENCE 4, 135–183 (1980)

# Physical Symbol Systems*

ALLEN NEWELL

*Carnegie-Mellon University*

On the occasion of a first conference on Cognitive Science, it seems appropriate to review the basis of common understanding between the various disciplines. In my estimate, the most fundamental contribution so far of artificial intelligence and computer science to the joint enterprise of cognitive science has been the notion of a *physical symbol system*, i.e., the concept of a broad class of systems capable of having and manipulating symbols, yet realizable in the physical universe. The notion of *symbol* so defined is internal to this concept, so it becomes a hypothesis that this notion of symbols includes the symbols that we humans use every day of our lives. In this paper we attempt systematically, but plainly, to lay out the nature of physical symbol systems. Such a review is in ways familiar, but not thereby useless. Restatement of fundamentals is an important exercise.

## 1. INTRODUCTION

The enterprise to understand the nature of mind and intelligence has been with us for a long time. It belongs not to us alone, who are gathered at this conference, nor even to science alone. It is one of the truly great mysteries and the weight of scholarship devoted to it over the centuries seems on occasion so oppressively large as to deny the possibility of fundamental progress, not to speak of solution.

Yet for almost a quarter century now, experimental psychology, linguistics, and artificial intelligence have been engaged in a joint attack on this mystery

*This research was sponsored by the Defense Advanced Research Projects Agency (DOD), ARPA Order No. 3597, Monitored by the Air Force Avionics Laboratory Under Contract F33615-78-C-1551.

The views and conclusions contained in this document are those of the author and should not be interpreted as representing the official policies, either expressed or implied, of the Defense Advanced Research Projects Agency, or the U.S. Government.

Herb Simon would be a co-author of this paper, except that he is giving his own paper at this conference. The key ideas are entirely joint, as the references indicate. In addition, I am grateful to Greg Harris, John McDermott, Zenon Pylyshyn, and Mike Rychener for detailed comments on an earlier draft.

that is fueled by a common core of highly novel theoretical ideas, experimental techniques, and methodological approaches. Though retaining our separate disciplinary identities. we have strongly influenced each other throughout this period. Others have been involved in this new attack, though not so centrally—additional parts of computer science and psychology, and parts of philosophy, neurophysiology, and anthropology.

Our communality continues to increase. In consequence, we are engaged in an attempt to bind our joint enterprise even more tightly by a common umbrella name, *Cognitive Science*, a new society, and a new series of conferences devoted to the common theme—the outward and institutional signs of inward and conceptual progress. On such an occasion, attempts to increase our basis of mutual understanding seem to be called for.

In my own estimation (Newell & Simon, 1976), the most fundamental contribution so far of artificial intelligence and computer science to this joint enterprise has been the notion of a *physical symbol system*. This concept of a broad class of systems that is capable of having and manipulating symbols, yet is also realizable within our physical universe, has emerged from our growing experience and analysis of the computer and how to program it to perform intellectual and perceptual tasks. The notion of symbol that it defines is internal to this concept of a system. Thus, it is a hypothesis that these symbols are in fact the same symbols that we humans have and use everyday of our lives. Stated another way, the hypothesis is that humans are instances of physical symbol systems, and, by virtue of this, mind enters into the physical universe.

In my own view this hypothesis sets the terms on which we search for a scientific theory of mind. What we all seek are the further specifications of physical symbol systems that constitute the human mind or that constitute systems of powerful and efficient intelligence. The physical symbol system is to our enterprise what the theory of evolution is to all biology, the cell doctrine to cellular biology, the notion of germs to the scientific concept of disease, the notion of tectonic plates to structural geology.

The concept of a physical symbol system is familiar in some fashion to everyone engaged in Cognitive Science—familiar, yet perhaps not fully appreciated. For one thing, this concept has not followed the usual path of scientific creation, where development occurs entirely within the scientific attempt to understand a given phenomenon. It was not put forward at any point in time as a new striking hypothesis about the mind, to be confirmed or disconfirmed. Rather, it has evolved through a much more circuitous root. Its early history lies within the formalization of logic, where the emphasis was precisely on separating formal aspects from psychological aspects. Its mediate history lies within the development of general purpose digital computers, being thereby embedded in the instrumental, the industrial, the commercial and the artificial—hardly the breeding ground for a theory to cover what is most sublime in human thought.

The resulting ambivalence no doubt accounts in part for a widespread proclivity to emphasize the role of the *computer metaphor* rather than a *theory of information processing*.

The notion of symbol permeates thinking about mind, well beyond attempts at scientific understanding. Philosophy, linguistics, literature, the arts—all have independent and extensive concerns that focus on human symbols and symbolic activity. Think only of Cassirier or Langer or Whitehead in philosophy. Consider semantics, concerned directly with the relation between linguistic symbols and what they denote, or Jung, in a part of psychology remote from experimentation and tight theory. These are vast realms of scholarship, by any reckoning.

I cannot touch these realms today in any adequate way. Perhaps, I can let one quote from Whitehead stand for them all:

> After this preliminary explanation we must start with a definition of symbolism: The human mind is functioning symbolically when some components of its experience elicit consciousness, beliefs, emotions, and usages, respecting other components of its experience. The former set of components are the "symbols", and the later set constitute the "meaning" of the symbols. The organic functioning whereby there is transition from the symbol to the meaning will be called "symbolic reference". (1927, pp. 7–8)

This statement, from over fifty years ago, has much to recommend it. Let it serve as a reminder that the understanding of symbols and symbolism is by no means brand new. Yet the thread through computer science and artificial intelligence has made a distinctive contribution to discovering the nature of human symbols. Indeed, in my view the contribution has been decisive.

The notion of a physical symbol system has been emerging throughout the quarter century of our joint enterprise—always important, always recognized, but always slightly out of focus as the decisive scientific hypothesis that it has now emerged to be.

For instance, recall the rhetoric of the fifties, where we insisted that computers were *symbol manipulation machines* and not just *number manipulation machines*. The mathematicians and engineers then responsible for computers insisted that computers only processed *numbers*—that the great thing was that instructions could be translated into numbers. On the contrary, we argued, the great thing was that computers could take instructions and it was incidental, though useful, that they dealt with numbers. It was the same fundamental point about symbols, but our aim was to revise opinions about the computer, not about the nature of mind.

Another instance is our ambivalence toward list processing languages. Historically, these have been critically important in abstracting the concept of symbol processing, and we have certainly recognized them as carriers of theoretical notions. Yet we have also seen them as *nothing but* programming languages, i.e., as nothing but tools. The reason why AI programming continues to be done almost exclusively in list processing languages is sought in terms of ease of programming, interactive style and what not. That Lisp is a close approximation to a pure symbol system is often not accorded the weight it deserves.

Yet a third instance can be taken from our own work. When we laid out the notion of physical symbol system in our book on human problem solving (Newell & Simon, 1972), we did this as an act of preparation, not as the main point. We focussed the theory on how people solved problems, given that they were symbol manipulation systems. Even when, a little later, we chose to focus on the physical symbol system hypothesis per se (Newell & Simon, 1976), it was in the context of receiving an award and thus we described it as a conceptual advance that had already transpired.

A fourth and final instance is the way information processing systems are presented in cognitive psychology. Even in the best informed presentations (e.g., Clark & Clark, 1977; Lindsay & Norman, 1977; Rumelhart, 1977) there is little emphasis on symbolic functioning per se. When concern is expressed about the adequacy of information processing notions for psychology (e.g., Neisser, 1976), the role of symbolic functioning is not addressed. There are some very recent exceptions to this picture (Lachman, Lachman, & Butterfield, 1979). But some of these (Allport, 1979; Palmer, 1978) seem to view such developments as rather new, whereas I see them as having been the taproot of the success in Artificial Intelligence right from the start almost twenty-five years ago.

In sum, it seems to me, a suitable topic for this conference is to attempt, systematically but plainly, to lay out again the nature of physical symbol systems. All this will be in some ways familiar, but I hope far from useless. Restatement of fundamentals is an important exercise. Indeed, I can take my text from Richard Feynman. He is speaking of Fermi's law of optics, but it applies generally:

> Now in the further development of science, we want more than just a formula. First we have an observation, then we have numbers that we measure, then have a law which summarizes all the numbers. But the real *glory* of science is that we can find a way of thinking such that the law is *evident*. (1963, p. 26)

Physical symbol systems are becoming for us simply *evident*. But they are our *glory*, and it is fitting that we should understand them with a piercing clarity.

And so, if you cannot stand what I say here as science, then take it as celebration.

## 1.1 Constraints on Mind

Let me provide a general frame for the paper. The phenomena of mind have arisen from a complex of aspects of the physical universe, localized strikingly (though possibly not exclusively) in us humans. We scientists, trying to discern

4

the physical nature of mind, can cast these aspects as a conjunction of constraints on the nature of mind-like systems. Then our discovery problem is that of finding a system structure that satisfies all these constraints. In trying to make that discovery, we can use any tactics we wish. The constraints themselves are simply desiderata and have no privileged status.

There is no magic list of constraints that we can feel sure about. Their choice and formulation is as much a step in the discovery process as solving the constraint satisfaction problem after positing them. However, it is easy to list some candidate constraints that would find general acknowledgement. Figure 1 presents a baker's dozen.

These constraints are far from precisely defined. Operationalizing the notion of self-awareness poses difficult problems, however critical it seems as a requirement. Even what constitutes the brain is open, moving over the last thirty years from an essentially neural view to one that includes macromolecular mechanisms as well. Not all the constraints are necessarily distinct. Conceivably, human symbolic behavior and linguistic behavior could be the same, as could development and learning. Not all constraints are necessarily independent. To be a neural system implies being a physical system, though there can be reasons to consider the more general constraint separately. Some of the constraints are familiar back to Aristotle, others are recent additions. Who would have thought to add the concern with robustness under error if computers and their programs had not exhibited the sort of brittle, ungraceful degradation that we have all come to know so well.

What seems clear is that, when we finally come to know the nature of mind in humans, it will be seen to satisfy all of these constraints (and others that I have neglected to list). And when we finally come to know the nature of intelligence generally, it will be seen how its variety arises from a release from some of these constraints.

Our difficulty, as scientists, is that we cannot solve for systems that satisfy

1. Behave as an (almost) arbitrary function of the environment (universality).
2. Operate in real time.
3. Exhibit rational, i.e., effective adaptive behavior.
4. Use vast amounts of knowledge about the environment.
5. Behave robustly in the face of error, the unexpected, and the unknown.
6. Use symbols (and abstractions).
7. Use (natural) language.
8. Exhibit self-awareness and a sense of self.
9. Learn from its environment.
10. Acquire its capabilities through development.
11. Arise through evolution.
12. Be realizable within the brain as a physical system.
13. Be realizable as a physical system.

Figure 1. Constraints on Mind.

such simultaneous constraints. Indeed, we cannot usually do better than to generate on one constraint and test on the others. Thus, particular constraints are taken by various groups of scientists as the frame within which to search for the nature of mind. One thinks of Ashby (1956) and his formulation in terms of general differential equation systems, which is to say, basically physically realizable systems. Or the endeavor of those working in the fifties on self-organizing systems to work within neuron-like systems (Yovits & Cameron, 1960; Yovits, Jacobi, & Goldstein, 1962). Or the emergence of a sociobiology that works primarily from evolutionary arguments (Wilson, 1975). And, of course, both the neurophysiologists and the linguists essentially work from within their respective disciplines, which correspond to constraints in our list. Artificial intelligence works from within the digital computer—sometimes, it seems, even from within Lisp. However, the computer is not one of these constraints, though strongly associated with the first item, and my purpose is not to identify particular constraints with particular disciplines. The constraints are conceptual aspects of the nature of the human mind, and they must all be taken into account in the final analysis, whatever the starting point.

Which constraint forms a preferred basis from which to conduct the search for the nature of mind? Most important, a constraint must provide a *constructive* definition of a class of systems. Otherwise, search within it cannot occur, because it will not be possible to generate candidates whose properties can then be explored. Several of the constraints have real difficulty here—development and learning, robustness, real-time operation. For instance, we simply have no characterization of all systems that show development; all we can do is pose a system described within some other class and ask about its developmental characteristics. The constraint of development must remain primarily a test, not a generator. On the other hand some constraints, such as using language, do very well. The formalisms for grammars provide potent generative bases.

The strength of a constraint, or its distinctiveness with respect to mind, also weighs in the balance, however difficult the assessment of such a characteristic. For example, one real problem with the evolution constraint is that we know it gives rise to an immense diversity of systems (organisms). It is not clear how to get it to generate systems that are shaped at all to mind-like behavior. Again, linguistics has fared much better in this regard. For linguistics has appeared, until recently, to be distinctively and uniquely human. As a last example, one major argument against the universal machines of logic and computer science has always been that universality had been purchased at the price of total inefficiency, and a class which relied on such an aspect seemed irrelevant to real systems.

But such considerations are only preferences. Our joint scientific enterprise demands that substantial groups of scientists focus on all these constraints and their various combinations. It demands that new constraints be discovered and added to the list, to provide new ways from which to seek the true nature of mind.

My focus on physical symbol systems in this paper certainly amounts to an argument for taking one particular class of systems as the base—as the generator—for the search for mind. This class appears to satisfy jointly at least two of the constraints in the list—*universality* and *symbolic behavior*—and to give good evidence of being able to be shaped to satisfy other constraints as well, while still remaining usefully generative. But, as the discussion should make clear, this is just an argument over scientific tactics—over the right way to go about untying the great puzzle knot that is the mind. On the matter of scientific substance, we need to understand all we can about all the aspects represented in these constraints.

## 1.2. Plan

Let me preview what I intend to do, so as to be as plain and straightforward as possible.

To present the notion of a physical symbol system, I introduce a specific example system. This permits a concrete discussion of the key property of universality, the first constraint on our list. With this concept in hand, I generalize the example system to the class of all physical symbol systems. This makes it evident that systems that satisfy the constraint of universality also are capable of a form of symbolic behavior. The Physical Symbol System Hypothesis states in essence that this form of symbolic behavior is all there is; in particular, that it includes human symbolic behavior. I turn briefly to the question of system levels, which allows the placement of the symbol level within the larger frame of physical systems. With all these elements on the table, I then discuss some issues that are important to understanding the notion of physical symbol system and the hypothesis, and their roles in cognitive science.

So far I have been careful always to refer to a *physical* symbol system, in order to emphasize two facts. First, such a system is realizable in our physical universe. Second, its notion of symbol is *a priori* distinct from the notion of symbol that has arisen in describing directly human linguistic, artistic and social activities. Having been clear about both of these, we can drop the adjective, except when required to emphasize these two points.

As already stated, the fundamental notion of a physical symbol system presented here is not novel scientifically. Even the formulation presented does not differ in any important way from some earlier attempts (Newell & Simon, 1972; Newell & Simon, 1976). I am engaged in restatement and explication. The details and the tactics of the formulation are new and I hope thereby to make matters exceptionally clear and to highlight some important features of such systems. Still, it does not follow that the notion of physical symbol system and the particular hypothesis about it are accepted by all, or accepted in exactly the form that is given here.

## 2. SS: A PARADIGMATIC SYMBOL SYSTEM

Figure 2 lays out our example symbol system schematically. We will call it SS (Symbol System) for short. It is a machine which exists in an environment consisting of *objects*, distributed in a space of *locations*. We can imagine the objects having some sort of structure and dynamics, and doing their individual and interactive thing in this space.

SS consists of a *memory*, a set of *operators*, a *control*, an *input*, and an *output*. Its inputs are the objects in certain locations; its outputs are the modification or creation of the objects in certain (usually different) locations. Its external behavior, then, consists of the outputs it produces as a function of its inputs. The larger system of environment plus SS forms a closed system, since the output objects either become or affect later input objects. SS's internal state consists of the state of its memory and the state of the control; and its internal behavior consists of the variation in this internal state over time.

The memory is composed of a set of *symbol structures*, $\{E_1, E_2, \ldots E_m\}$, which vary in number and content over time. The term *expression* is used interchangeably with *symbol structure*. To define the symbol structures there is given a set of abstract *symbols*, $\{S_1, S_2, \ldots S_n\}$. Each symbol structure is of a given *type* and has some number of distinguished *roles*, $\{R_1, R_2, \ldots\}$. Each role contains a symbol, so if we take the type as understood implicitly and the roles as the successive positions on the paper, we could write an expression as:

$$(S_1 \ S_2, \ldots S_n)$$

If we wanted to show the roles and the type explicitly we could write:

$$(\text{Type: T } R_1:S_1 \ R_2:S_2, \ldots R_n:S_n)$$

The roles (and their number) are determined by the *type*, of which there can be a large variety. The same symbol, e.g., $S_k$, can occupy more than one role in a structure and can occur in more than one structure. By the *content* of an expression is meant simply the symbols associated with the roles of the expression.

SS has ten operators, each shown as a separate box in the figure. Each operator is a machine that takes one or more symbols as input and produces as output some symbol (plus possibly other effects) as a result. The behavior that occurs when an operator and its inputs combine is called an *operation*. The details of the behavior of the system come from these operations, which we will go over in a moment.

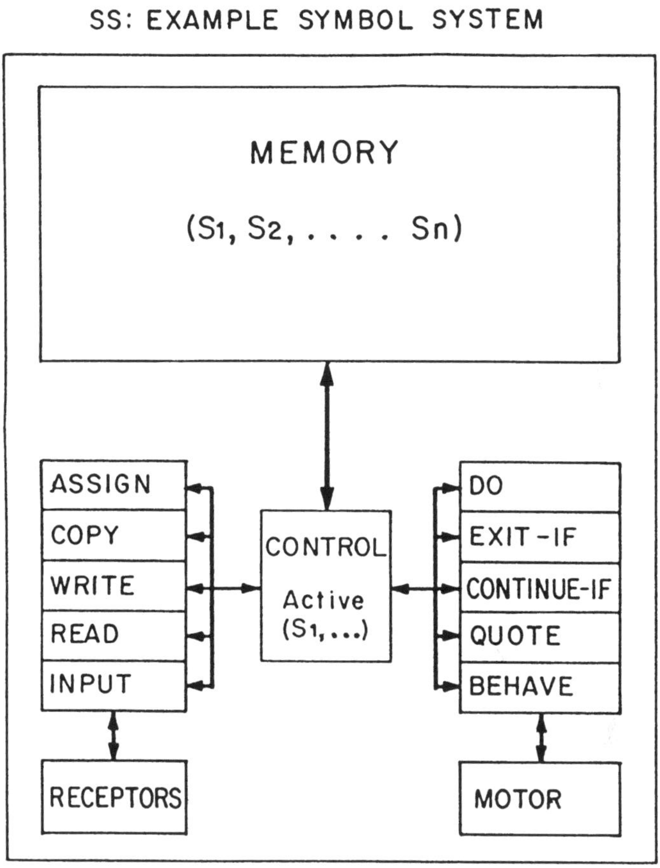

## SS: EXAMPLE SYMBOL SYSTEM

Figure 2. Structure of SS, a Paradigmatic Symbol System.

The behavior of the system is governed by the control. This is also a machine; its inputs include the operators: It has access to their inputs and outputs and can evoke them. It also has as an input the symbol for a single expression, which is called the *active* expression. The behavior of the control consists of the continual *interpretation* of whatever expression is active. If this specifies an operation to be performed, then the control will bring the input symbols to the input locations of the indicated operator and then evoke the operator to produce the result, i.e., it will effect the combining of data and operators. The control also determines which expression shall become active next, so that the behavior of the total system runs on indefinitely. We will describe the control in detail after discussing the operators.

| | |
|---|---|
| **Assign** symbol S₁ to the same entity as symbol S₂<br>Produces S₁ with new assignment | (assign S₁ S₂) |
| **Copy** expression E (create new symbol)<br>Produces newly created expression and symbol | (copy E) |
| **Write** S₁ at role R₁,. . . in expression E<br>Produces the modified expression<br>nil is the same as doesn't exist | (write E R₁S₁ . . .) |
| **Read** symbol at role R of E<br>Produces the expression or nil | (read R E) |
| **Do** sequence S₁ S₂ S₃ . . .<br>Produces the expression produced by last S₁. | (do S₁ S₂ . . .) |
| **Exit** sequence if the prior result is E<br>Produces prior expression | (exit-if E) |
| **Continue** sequence if the prior result is E<br>Produces prior expression | (continue-if E) |
| **Quote** the symbol S<br>Produces S without interpretation | (quote S) |
| **Behave** externally according to expression E<br>Produces feedback expression | (behave E) |
| **Input** according to expression E<br>Produces new expression or nil | (input E) |

Figure 3. Operators of SS.

Figure 3 lists the operations of SS. There exists a type of symbol structure, which we will call a *program*, which has roles corresponding to an operator and the inputs appropriate to that operator. These program expressions are shown in the figure at the right.

**Assign** a symbol. This establishes a basic relationship between a symbol and the entity to which it is assigned, which we call *access*. While it lasts (i.e., until the assignment is changed) any machine (i.e., the ten operators and the control) that has access to an occurrence of this symbol in an expression has access to the assigned entity. If a machine has access to an expression, then it can obtain the symbols in the various roles of the expression and it can change the symbols in these roles. Symbols can be **assigned** to entities other than expressions, namely, to operators and roles. Access to an operator implies access to its inputs, outputs, and evocation mechanism. Access to a role of a given type implies access to the symbol at that role for any expression of the given type and access to write a new symbol at that role.

**Copy** expression. This adds expressions and symbols to the system. The new expression is an exact replica of the input expression, i.e., the same type and the same symbols in each role. A new symbol is created along with the new expression (a necessity for gaining access to the expression).

10

**Write** an expression. This creates expressions of any specified content. It does not create a new expression (**copy** does that), but modifies its input expression. What to **write** is specified by giving the roles and the new symbols that are to occupy these roles. **Write** permits several symbols to be written with a single operation; it could as well have permitted only one. For example, given a type with roles R₁, R₂, etc., in order, and given an expression (X Y Z), [**write** (X Y Z) R₁ A R₃ C] produces a modified expression (A Y C).

**Write** establishes a symbol at a given role whether or not there was a symbol at that role before, and independent of what symbols exist at other roles. **Writing** nil at a role effectively deletes it.

**Read** the symbol at a specific role. This obtains the symbols that comprise an expression, given that the expression has been obtained. It is possible that no symbol exists for a given role; in this case **read** produces the symbol nil. (Thus it can be seen why **writing** nil at a role effectively deletes it.)

**Do** sequence. This makes the system do arbitrary actions, by specifying that it do one thing after another. There are an unlimited number of input roles, one for each element in the sequence. The last expression produced during such a sequence is taken to be the result of the sequence. All the expressions produced by earlier items in the sequence are ignored. Of course, actions may have taken place along the way (often referred to as side effects), e.g., assignment of symbols.

**Exit-if** and **Continue-if**. The system behaves conditionally by continuing or exiting (terminating) the execution of a sequence. A conditional operator tests if the expression produced at the immediately preceding step of the sequence is the same as its input expression. It then takes a specific control action. For example, [**do** . . . A (**exit-if** A) . . .] would exit, i.e., would not complete the rest of the sequence. If symbols A and B designate different expressions, then [**do** . . . B (**continue-if** A) . . .] would also exit. The output of the operator is the expression tested, which then becomes the output of the sequence if there is termination.

**Quote** a symbol. The control automatically interprets every expression that becomes active. This operator permits it to not interpret a given expression, but to treat its symbol as the final result.

**Behave** externally. There exists some collection of external behaviors controllable by SS. Symbol structures of some type exist that instruct the organs that produce this external behavior. It will be enough to have an operator that evokes these expressions. Execution of the operator will produce some expression that provides feedback about the successful accomplishment (or failure) of the external operation.

**Input** from environment. Inputs from the external environment enter the system by means of newly created expressions that come to reside in the memory. These inputs occur when the **input** operator is evoked; there may be different channels and styles of input, so that **input** takes an expression as input to specify this. The input expressions are processed when **input** is evoked, since the resulting expression is interpreted by the control, though presumably the new expressions are not of type program, but some type related to describing the external environment.

11

Interpret the active expression:

> If it is not a program:
> Then the result is the expression itself.

> If it is a program:
> Interpret the symbol of each role for that role;
> Then execute the operator on its inputs;
> Then the result of the operation is the result.

Interpret the result:

> If it is a new expression:
> Then interpret it for the same role.

> If it is not a new expression:
> Then use as symbol for role.

Figure 4. Operation of SS's Control.

The operation of the control is shown in Figure 4. The control continuously interprets the active expression. The result of each interpretation is ultimately a symbol, though other actions (i.e., side effects) may have occurred during the act of interpretation, which are also properly part of the interpretation.

Control interprets the active expression by first determining whether it is a program symbol structure. Thus the control can sense a structure's type. If it is not a program, then the result of the interpretation is just the symbol itself (i.e., the symbol is treated as data).

If the active expression is a program, then the control proceeds to execute the operation specified by the program. However, the actual symbols in the program at the roles for the operator and its inputs must themselves be interpreted. For these symbols might not be the operator and inputs, respectively, but programs whose interpretations are these symbols. Thus, the control interprets each symbol in the program until it finally obtains the actual symbols to be used for the operator and the inputs. Then, it can actually get the operation performed by sending the input symbols to the appropriate operator, evoking it, and getting back the result that the operator produces.

Control then interprets the result (as arrived at through either of the routes above). If it is a new expression, then it proceeds to interpret it. If it is not new, then it finally has obtained the symbol.

The control has the necessary internal machinery to interpret each operator or input symbol in a program until it obtains the symbol finally to be used for each role in the program. This will be the one that is finally not a program type of structure. The control remembers the pending interpretations and the results produced so far that are still waiting to be used. The normal way to realize all this in current technology is with a pushdown stack of contexts; but all that is specified here is end result of interpretation, not how it is to be accomplished.

We now have an essentially complete description of one particular symbol system. To generate a concrete (and particular) behavioral trajectory, it is only necessary to provide an *initial* condition, consisting of the set of initial expressions in the memory and the initial active expression. The system behaves in interaction with the environment, but this is accounted for entirely by the operation of the **input** and **behave** operators. The operation of these two operators depends on the total environment in which the system is embedded. They would normally be given by definite mechanisms in the external structure of the system and the environment, along with a set of laws of behavior for the environment that would close the loop between output and input. From a formal viewpoint the operation of these two operators can just be taken as given, providing in effect a *boundary* condition for the internal behavior of the system.

This type of a machine is certainly familiar to almost everyone in Cognitive Science, at least in outline. The virtue of SS over others that might be even more familiar is that it is designed to aid understanding the essential features of symbols and symbolic behavior. There are no irrelevant details of SS's structure. Each operator (and also the control) embodies a generalized function that is important to understanding symbolic systems.

The expository virtues of SS aside, it remains a garden variety, Lisp-ish sort of beast.

## 3. UNIVERSALITY

That our example symbol system is garden variety does not keep it from being a variety of a very remarkable genus. Symbol systems form a class—it is a class that is characterized by the property of *universality*. We must understand this remarkable property before we can generalize appropriately from our paradigmatic symbol system to a characterization of the entire class.

Central to universality is flexibility of behavior. However, it is not enough just to produce any output behavior; the behavior must be *responsive* to the inputs. Thus, a universal machine is one that can produce an arbitrary input–output function; that is, that can produce any dependence of output on input.

Such a property is desirable for an adaptive, intelligent system which must cope with environments whose demands are not known at the time the system is designed. Indeed, this property heads the constraints in Figure 1. Being able to produce *any* behavior in response to a situation is neither absolutely necessary nor hardly sufficient for success. But the more flexibility the better; and if behavior is too unresponsive, the system will fail against its environment. Almost all purposive behavior shows intricate dependence on the environment, i.e., shows the flexible construction of novel input-output functions—an animal circling its prey, a person in conversation with another, a player choosing a chess move, a student solving a physics exercise, a shopper bargaining with a seller, and on and on. This was the classic insight of Cybernetics—systems appeared

13

*purposive* when their behavior was dependent on the environment so as to attain (or maintain) a relationship; and *feedback* was necessary to obtain this dependence with a changing environment. The formulation here separates the ability to produce the dependence (universality) from the way such a ability can be used to produce purposiveness, the latter residing in the rationality constraint in Figure 1.

The property of universality cannot be quite so simply defined. Four difficulties, in particular, must be dealt with.

The first difficulty is the most obvious. Any machine is a prisoner of its input and output domains. SS, our example system, presents an abstract machine-centered view, so that the external world is pretty much what is seen by the machine. But this is deceptive. Machines live in the real world and have only a limited contact with it. Any machine, no matter how universal, that has no ears (so to speak) will not hear; that has no wings, will not fly. Thus universality will be relative to the input and output channels. Such a consideration is alleviated in theoretical discussions by the simple expedient of considering only abstract inputs and outputs. It can be alleviated in the real world by providing transducers that encode from one input–output channel to another. Thus, being able to produce any function between two given domains permits inducing any function between two other domains if the domains are hooked up appropriately.[1] But this interface limit must always be remembered.

The second difficulty is also obvious. In the physical world there are limits—limits to the speed of components, to spatial and energy sensitivity, to material available for memory, to reliability of operation, to name just the more obvious. To state a tautology: No system can behave beyond its physical limits. Thus, the universality of any system must be taken relative to such physical implementation limits.

The third difficulty is more serious. A machine is defined to be a system that has a specific determined behavior as a function of its input. By definition, therefore, it is not possible for a single machine to obtain even *two* different behaviors, much less any behavior. The solution adopted is to decompose the input into two parts (or aspects): one part (the *instruction*) being taken to determine which input-output function is to be exhibited by the second part (the *input-proper*) along with the output. This decomposition can be done in any fashion—for instance, by a separate input channel or by time (input prior to a starting signal being instruction, afterward being input-proper). This seems like an innocent arrangement, especially since the input-proper may still be as open as desired (e.g., all future behavior). However, it constitutes a genuine limitation on the structure of the system. For instance, the instruction must have enough capacity to specify all of the alternative functions. (If the instruction to a machine consists only of the setting of a single binary toggle switch, then the machine

---

[1]The internal domains must have enough elements to permit discrimination of the elements of the external domains, a condition which Ashby (1956) called the *Law of requisite variety*.

cannot exhibit three different input-output behaviors.) Most important, the basic decomposition into two parts has far-reaching consequences—it guarantees the existence of symbols.

The fourth difficulty is the most serious of all. There appears to be no way that a universal machine can behave literally according to *any* input–output function, if the time over which the behavior is to occur is indefinitely extended (e.g., the entire future after some period of instruction). This is the import of the discovery of *noncomputable* functions, which is an important chapter in the theory of computing machines (Brainerd & Landweber, 1974; Minsky, 1967). The difficulty is fundamentally that there are too many functions—too many ways to have to instruct a machine to behave.

This can be appreciated directly by noting that each instruction to the machine, no matter how complex, is simply a way of naming a behavior. Thus, a machine cannot produce more distinct behaviors than it can have distinct instructions. Let the number of possible instructions be K. The number of behaviors is the number of input–output functions, so if there are M possible inputs and N possible outputs, then the number of behaviors is $N^M$ (i.e., the assignment of one of the N possible outputs for each of the M inputs). Thus, K instructions must label $N^M$ behaviors. If K, M, and N are all in the same range, then $N^M$ is going to be *very* much bigger than K. Now, as time is permitted to extend indefinitely into the future, all three possibilities (K, M, and N) will grow to become countably infinite. But, although K (the number of instructions) grows to be countably infinite, $N^M$ (the number of functions to be labeled) grows much faster to become uncountably infinite. In sum, there simply are not enough possible instructions to cover all the functions that must be named.

If all possible functions cannot be attained, then some way must be found to describe which can and which cannot. Therein lies a further difficulty. Suppose a descriptive scheme of some sort is used, in order to say that a given machine can realize functions of certain descriptions and not functions of other descriptions. What do we know then about the functions that are not describable by the given scheme? We have confounded the properties of the descriptive scheme with the properties of the machine. Indeed, the suspicion might arise that a connection exists between descriptive schemes and machines, so that this difficulty is part and parcel of the main problem itself.

The solution has been to take the notion of a machine itself as the keystone. Direct description of behavior is abandoned, and in its place is put *the behavior produced by such and such a machine*. For any class of machines, defined by some way of describing its operational structure, a machine of that class is defined to be universal if it can behave like any machine of the class. This puts simulation at the center of the stage; for to show a given input–output behavior is to simulate a machine that shows that input–output behavior. The instructional input to the machine must now be some means of describing any arbitrary machine of the given class. The machine whose universality is being demonstrated must take that input and behave identically to the machine described by its input, i.e., it must simulate the given machine.

The notion of universality thus arrived at is *relative*, referring only to the given class of machines. Universal machines could exist for classes of machines, all right, but the input–output functions encompassed by the whole class could still be very limited. Such a universal machine would be a big frog in a small pond of functions.

The next step is to attempt to formulate very large classes of machines, by means of general notions of mechanism, in order to encompass as wide a range of input–output functions as possible. (The input and output domains are always taken to be intertranslatable, so the relevant issue is the functional dependence of output on input, not the character of the inputs and outputs taken separately.) Another important chapter in the theory of computing (Brainerd & Landweber, 1974; Minsky, 1967) has shown that all attempts to do this lead to classes of machines that are equivalent in that they encompass in toto exactly the same set of input–output functions. In effect, there is a single large frog pond of functions no matter what species of frogs (types of machines) is used. But the frog pond is just a pond; it is not the whole ocean of all possible functions.

That there exists a most general formulation of machine and that it leads to a unique set of input–output functions has come to be called *Church's thesis* after Alonzo Church, the logician who first put forth this claim with respect to one specific formulation (recursive functions) (Church, 1936). Church's statement is called a *thesis* because it is not susceptible fo formal proof, only to the accumulation of evidence. For the claim is about ways to formalize something about the real world, i.e., the notion of machine or determinate physical mechanism. Self-evidently, formal proof applies only after formalization. The most striking evidence has been the existence of different maximal classes of machines, derived from quite different formulations of the notion of machine or procedure, each of which turns out to be capable of producing exactly this same maximal set of functions.

A large zoo of different formulations of maximal classes of machines is known by now—Turning machines, recursive functions, Post canonical systems, Markov algorithms, all varieties of general purpose digital computers, most programming languages (viewed as specifications for a machine). As a single neutral name, these classes are interchangebly called the *effectively computable procedures* and the functions that can be attained by the machines are called the *computable* functions.

These maximal classes contain universal machines, i.e., machines that, if properly instructed through part of their input, can behave like any other machine in the maximal class. But then they can produce all the input-output functions that can be produced by any machine, however defined (i.e., in any other maximal class). It is these machines that are usually referred to as universal machines. From now on this is what we shall mean by *universal*. The proofs of the existence of these universal machines are also part of this early great chapter in the theory of logic and computers.

SS, our paradigmatic symbol system, is universal. Thus, it has as much flexibility as it is possible to obtain. It is useful to show that SS is universal. It is easy to do and its demonstration will make the notion transparent and keep it from accruing any mystery. Having the demonstration will also provide us with an example of a program in SS, which will clarify any confusing points in its definition. We will also be able to use this demonstration to support several points about general symbol systems when we examine them in the next section.

To show that SS is universal, all we need to show is that it can simulate any member of a class of machines already known to be a maximal class. Let us choose the class of Turing machines: It is simple, classical, and everyone knows that it is a formulation of a maximal class.

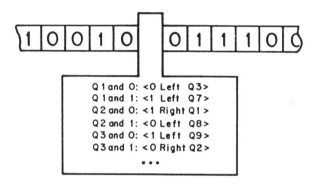

Figure 5. Simulation of Arbitrary Turing Machine by SS.

At the top, Figure 5 shows a classical one-tape Turing machine. There is a single unending tape, with each cell holding a 0 or a 1. There is a control, which has a single reading head at a given cell of the tape. The control is in one of a finite set of states, Q1, Q2 . . . ,Qn. For the control to be in a particular state implies it will do the following things:

It will read the symbol on the tape, i.e., detect whether it is 0 or 1.

It will write a symbol on the tape, either a 0 or 1 (as determined by the state and the symbol read).

It will move the tape head one square, either to the left or the right (as determined by the state and the symbol read).

It will change itself to be in a new state (as determined by the state and the symbol read).

Instead of going to a new state, the machine may come to a halt.

Nothing is said about what sorts of physical arrangements are used to create the set of states for a given Turing machine and make it behave in the way specified. But we can write down for each state what it *will* do, and we have done this in Figure 5 for a couple of states (Q1, Q2, etc.) For each state we have two entries, depending on whether the tape cell has a 0 or a 1: the symbol to be written on the tape (either a 0 or a 1); whether to move left or right; and the state to go to. If a special next state, *halt*, is given, the machine halts.

Any machine built to behave this way is a Turing machine. Turing machines differ only in the number of states they have and in what happens at each state, within the limits described above. However, the class of all Turing machines is very large—by using enough states (and it may take a very large number) the input–output behavior of *any* physical mechanism can be approximated as closely as required. It is one of these maximal class of machines, even though a Turing machine's moment by moment behavior seems very restricted.

The bottom of Figure 5 gives the program in SS that simulates an arbitrary Turing machine. The Turing machine itself must be represented. This is done entirely within the memory of SS, rather than in terms of the external input and output interfaces of SS. For any reasonable **input** and **behave** operators this extra translation would be straightforward. The representation uses three types of symbol structures, one for the tape cell and the other two for the state of the Turing machine control. The tape cell has three roles: *Content* holds the tape-symbol, either 0 or 1; *left* holds the symbol for the tape cell to the left; and *right* holds the symbol for the tape cell to the right. The Turing machine state *has* two roles: *if-0* to hold the specifications for what to do if the tape cell holds 0; and *if-1* for what to do if the tape holds 1. Each specification (the third symbol structure type) has three roles: *Content* holds the tape-symbol to be written, either 0 or 1; *move* holds the direction to move the tape, either *left* or *right*; and *next* holds the symbol for the next state to go to.

There is a single program expression, called TM, which accomplishes the simulation. TM consists of **doing** a sequence of six subprograms, each of which accomplishes one step of the basic definition. There is a symbol T for the current tape cell under the head, a symbol S for the current state of the Turing machine control, and a symbol A for the actions specified by the state (which will be different depending on the tape symbol). The program is shown as a single nested expression with many subexpressions. This is simply for convenience of reading; it does not indicate any additional properties of SS. Complex subexpressions are constructed entirely through the use of assignment. In each case what occurs in an expression is a symbol, which is assigned to the subexpression. Thus, the actual representation of TM is:

TM: [do TM1 TM2 TM3 TM4 TM5 TM]

TM1: [do TM11 TM12 TM13]

TM11: [read content T]

TM12: [continue-if 0]

TM13: [assign A TM131]

TM131: [read if-0 S]

TM2: . . .

And so on through the whole expression.

Let us take up the steps of TM in order.

1. The first step reads the symbol on the tape and if it is 0 assigns the symbol A to be the actions specified in case 0 occurs, i.e., the substructure at if-0.
2. The second step similarly assigns A to be the actions specified at if-1, if 1 is the tape symbol. (Only one of the two possible assignments to A will occur, since they are mutually exclusive.)
3. The third step writes the symbol specified via A into the tape-cell. This is a simple transfer of a symbol; it even occupies the same role in both structures, i.e., content.
4. The fourth step moves the tape left or right by using the symbol specified via A as the role symbol to extract the left or right link from the tape-cell.
5. The fifth step is to assign S to be the next state as specified via A.
6. The sixth and final step is to do TM again, which repeats the entire interpretation, now on the changed values of T and S.

This demonstration of universality is transparent, because the universality of some given system (here, Turing machines) has already been established, and the system itself (here, SS) has reasonable properties as a programming system.

Of course, it is necessary that the program be correct. In fact, two bugs exist in the present version. One arises because we didn't take care of halting. This requires more conventions: The Turing machine halts if the symbol *halt* occurs for the next state; then TM should exit and return to whatever program executed it, with the current tape cell (T) as output. The other bug arises because the tape for a Turing machine is of indefinite extent, while the representation of the tape in SS necessarily consists of only a finite number of symbol structures, one for each cell. It is necessary for the simulation to extend the tape in either direction, if it runs off an end. Again, by convention, the symbol *tape-end* occurring in a tape cell at either *left* or *right* will indicate the end of the tape.

```
TM-Exec: [do TM T]
TM: [do
         [do [read content T] [continue-if 0] [assign A [read if-0 S]]]
         [do [read content T] [continue-if 1] [assign A [read if-1 S]]]
         [write T content [read content A]]
         [assign T [do [read [read move A] T]
                       [continue-if tape-end]
                       [assign New-T [copy T]]
                       [write New-T content 0 [read [read move A] other ] T]
                       [write T [read move A] New-T]
                       New-T]]
    [assign S [read next A]]
    [exit-if halt]
    TM]
    other: [right:left left:right]
```

Figure 6. Correct Simulation of Arbitrary Turing Machine by SS.

Just for completeness, a correct version of the program appears in Figure 6. To correct the first bug, a top level program TM-Exec is defined, which simply executes TM and, when it is done, outputs T. Correspondingly, TM now tests if the new S is halt and exits if it is. For the other bug, TM senses whether the next tape cell is the symbol tape-end and, if so, extends the tape. This occurs en passant within the expression for moving the tape, [**assign** T [**read** [**read** move A] T]], by performing the regular operation within a **do**-sequence where it can continue if tape-end is found. It then creates a new tape cell (calling it New-T) and links it up in the several ways necessary. It ends by handing the new cell (as New-T) to the **assign** operator, just as if that cell had been found initially.

## 4. GENERAL SYMBOL SYSTEMS

We can now describe the essential nature of a (physical) symbol system. We start with a definition:

*Symbol systems* are the same as *universal machines*.

It may seem strange to *define* symbol systems to be universal machines. One would think that symbol systems should be defined to be that class of systems that *has* symbols according to some abstract characterization. Then it would be a fundamental theoretical result that symbol systems are universal. However this way is not open to us, without a certain amount of scientific legerdemain. The fact is that we do not have an independent notion of a symbol system that is precise enough to counterpoise to a universal machine, and thus subsequently to prove their equivalence. Instead, we have *discovered* that universal machines always contain within them a particular notion of symbol and symbolic behavior, and that this notion provides us for the first time with an adequate abstract characterization of what a symbol system should be. Thus, tautalogically, this notion of symbol system, which we have here called *physical symbol system*, is universal.

Does not SS, the machine we have just defined, provide a paradigmatic example that could be suitably generalized to define the class of symbol systems? True, SS was put together precisely to bring out the essential properties of symbols. Alas (for such an enterprise), SS and all its kindred have emerged simply as *reformulations* of the concept of universal machines. Historically, we are genuinely in the position of discoverers, not inventers. For analytic purposes we can certainly now propose axiomatic formulations of symbol systems and prove their equivalence to universal machines. But I prefer an exposition that emphasizes the dependence, rather than the independence, of the notion of (physical) symbol system on the notion of universal machines.

Thus, our situation is one of defining a symbol system to be a universal machine, and then taking as a hypothesis that this notion of symbol system will prove adequate to all of the symbolic activity this physical universe of ours can exhibit, and in particular all the symbolic activities of the human mind. In regard to our list of constraints of mind in Figure 1, two seemingly separate constraints (universality and using symbols) have been satisfied by a single class of systems.

We can now proceed to the essential nature of symbols and symbolic behavior in universal systems and to their generality. Note, however, that universal machines provide a peculiar situation with respect to what is essential. Every universal machine exhibits in some form all the properties of any universal machine. To be sure, differences exist among universal machines—in primitive structure, in processing times, in sensitivities, and in processing reliabilities. Though important—even critical—for some aspects of the phenomena of mind, these differences are not critical for the nature of symbols. Thus, when we focus on certain properties, we are providing an emphasis, rather than separating what cannot in truth be separated.

We start with a discussion of designation and interpretation. Then we go through the operators of SS. Though defined as specific operators for a specific machine, each corresponds to a general functional capability. Each operator thus raises the question of the necessity of this functional capability to a symbol system and also of the forms that it can take in alternative implementations while still accomplishing the essential function.

## 4.1. Designation

The most fundamental concept for a symbol system is that which gives symbols their symbolic character, i.e., which lets them stand for some entity. We call this concept *designation*, though we might have used any of several other terms, e.g., *reference*, *denotation*, *naming*, *standing for*, *aboutness*, or even *symbolization* or *meaning*. The variations in these terms, in either their common or philosophic usage, is not critical for us. Our concept is wholly defined within the structure of a symbol system. This one notion (in the context of the rest of a symbol system) must ultimately do service for the full range of symbolic functioning.

Let us have a definition:

> *Designation:* An entity X designates an entity Y relative to a process P, if, when P takes X as input, its behavior depends on Y.

There are two keys to this definition. First, the concept is grounded in the behavior of a process. Thus, the implications of designation will depend on the nature of this process. Second, there is action at a distance: The process behaves as if inputs, remote from those in it in fact has, effect it. This is the symbolic aspect, that having X (the symbol) is tantamount to having Y (the thing designated) for the purposes of process P.

The symbols in SS satisfy this definition of designation. There are a set of processes (the operators and the control) to which symbols can be input, and when so input the processes behave as a function, not of the symbols themselves, but of what the symbols have been assigned to—what, therefore, they designate.

The question of what symbolization implies in SS can only be worked out by understanding the nature of these processes, which can now be called *symbolic processes*. That these processes taken together are sufficient for attaining universality states the biggest implication. That this universality is attained only because of the existence of symbols provides the conceptual knot that makes the notion deep.

In SS, the second aspect of the definition is provided by the mechanism of *access*, which is part of the primitive structure of SS. It provides remote connections of specific character, as spelled out in describing **assign**. This specification is generated by enumerating for each of the ten operators plus the control the precise access needed to carry out their specified operations. Exactly these and no other forms of access are needed. This access is needed to exactly three types of entities: symbol structures, operators, and roles in symbol structures. Thus, *access* is no homunculus, providing that this finite set of primitive properties can be realized in physical mechanisms. We already know, through our experience with digital computers, that this is not only possible but eminently practical.

The great magic comes because this limited capability for accessing supports a general capability for designation. The set of processes must be expanded to include programs, and their inputs must be taken to include expressions. Then, for any entity (whether in the external world or in the memory), if an expression can be created at time T that is dependent on the entity in some way, processes can exist in the symbol system that, at some later Time T', take that expression as input and, behaving according to the recorded structure, behave in a way dependent on the entity. Hence these expressions designate the entity.

An important transitive law is illustrated in this, in which if X designates Y and Y designates Z, then X designates Z. In the case in point, there is first the acquisition which, through access to the actual external structure, creates a structure in the memory of the system that depends on this external entity; then the preservation of that memory structure through time yields a memory structure at some later time that still depends on the object; finally, the access associated with the internal symbol makes that structure available to a process, which then behaves accordingly, impressing it on still another entity and instantiating the relation of designation.

Because of the universality of symbol systems, the scope of this capability for designation is wide open and hardly yet explored. To repeat an earlier remark, the power of a designatory capability depends entirely on the symbolic processes to which it is coupled. If these processes are restricted enough, the total system may be able to accomplish little; if they are universal, then the total system may be able to do all that is required in human symbolization.

This general symbolic capability that extends out into the external world depends on the capability for acquiring expressions in the memory that record features of the external world. This in turn depends on the **input** and **behave** operators, whose details have not been described, but which limit access to the external world in some fashion. Such limits do not affect the capability of the symbol system to designate arbitrary entities, though they might limit the extent to which such capabilities could be utilized by a given system.

Designation is at the heart of universality. For one machine to behave as an arbitrary other machine, it must have symbols that designate that other. Once the input of the to-be-universal machine is separated into two parts, one of which is an instruction about something outside the machine (to wit, the other machine), there is no way out from generating some symbolic capability. That this symbolic capability should be general enough to encompass all notions of symbolic action derives (if indeed it is true) from the scope of what was to be symbolized, namely any input–output function. But the kernel of the notion of symbols arrived by the single act of getting a machine to act like something other than what it is.

A distinctive feature of SS is taking the general capability for symbols and access as central. Most formalizations of the notion of universal machine (all but those such as Lisp that stem from the work in artificial intelligence) take as central a more primitive capability for accessing, reflecting an interest in showing how universality can be build up by a machine. For instance, the Turing machine has symbols for the states of the control. These have the property of access, but are fixed and unchangeable—symbols cannot be created or reassigned. They do not provide the indefinitely extendable symbol system that is required for universality, but only some of the machinery for it. The indefinitely extendable symbol system is constructed as an addressing scheme on the (indefinitely extendable) tape. The construction is made possible by the tape movement operators, which provide the primitive accessing capability.

The underlying physical mechanism for obtaining access is some sort of switching mechanism that opens up a path between the process and the thing accessed. There are a wide variety of such switching mechanisms, but they are closely related to *search*. If the medium is recalcitrant, e.g., the Turing machine tape, the symbol system is implemented through a linear search of the tape and a match of a finite set of tape-symbols that serves to address the expression accessed. In more perspicuous media, i.e., a preorganized addressing switch for a random access memory, the implementation takes features from the symbol token (the address) and uses them to construct a direct path to the requisite location.

The usual formulations of universal machines also tend to use the term *symbol* for the alphabet of distinctive patterns that can occur in the memory medium (e.g., the 0 and 1 tape symbols for our Turing machine). As defined, these entities are not symbols in the sense of our symbol system. They satisfy only part of the requirements for a symbol, namely being the tokens in expressions. It is of course possible to give them full symbolic character by programming an accessing mechanism that gets from them to some data structure. Table look-up mechanisms provide one scheme. Actually, the alphabet of such symbols is usually quite small (e.g., only two for our version of a Turing machine), so they operate more like letters, i.e., the elements out of which a genuine set of symbols can be constructed.

## 4.2. Interpretation

The term *interpretation* is taken here in the narrow sense it has acquired in computer science:

> *Interpretation:* The act of accepting as input an expression that designates a process and then performing that process.

All the behavioral flexibility of universal machines comes from their ability to create expressions for their own behavior and then produce that behavior. Interpretation is the necessary basic mechanism to make this possible. The general designatory capabilities of symbol systems underly the ability to create the designating expressions in the first place. Although little can be said about exact boundaries, some *interior milieu* must exist within which the symbol system can freely and successfully interpret expressions. Given this, obtaining other performances according to specification can be compromised in various ways, e.g., by error, by indirect and shared control, or whatever.

The symbols that designate operators are absolutely essential, and no quantity of symbols for expressions or roles can substitute for them. These are the symbols that have an external semantics wired into them—which finally solve Tolman's problem of how his rats, lost in thought in their cognitive maps, could ever behave. The number of such symbols can be shrunk by various encodings and parametrizations, but it cannot vanish. Equally (and more likely for real systems), the number can be much larger and the decomposition can be radically different than for SS.

The control exhibits a basic tripartite decomposition of the total processes of the machine, which can be indicated by (*control* + (*operators* + *data*)). Behavior is composed by one part, the control, continually bringing together two other parts, the operators and the data, to produces a sequence of behavior increments (i.e., the operation formed by the application of the operator to the data). This will be recognized as familiar from every computer, programming language, and mathematical system.[2] This structure can be taken as an essential organizational feature of all symbolic systems.

This organization implies a requirement for *working memory* in the control to hold the symbols for the operator and data as they are selected and brought together. Our description of SS in Figure 2 shows only the place for the active symbol and for the input and output symbols for the operators. This is the tip of the iceberg; perusal of Figure 4 shows that additional working memory is needed. What memory will vary with the type of universal machine, but some is always implied by the act of decomposition. Thus working memory is an invariant feature of symbol systems.

However, many things about the control of SS are not invariant at all over different types of universal symbol systems. One must be careful to treat SS as a frame for describing *functional* capabilities, abstracting away from many of its structural features. Three examples of this are:

SS's control requires an unbounded amount of memory (essentially a pushdown stack) because the nesting of programs can be indefinitely extended. This is inessential, though it makes for simplicity. Normally control is a fixed machine with fixed memory; and regular memory (which is unbounded) is used according to some memory management strategy to handle excessive embedding.

SS has a serial control, i.e., a single control stream. This is inessential, though it also makes for simplicity. There may be multiple control streams of all sorts. The **input** and **behave** operators may both be evoked and operate in parallel. There may be multiple controls, a few or many, functionally specialized or all equivalent, and interconnected in a variety of ways. The parallel units may themselves be universal machines, or limited controllers, or only operators. Under some conditions the resulting processing aggregate is not universal, under many it is.

SS is a totally reliable system, nothing in its organization reflecting that its operators,

---

[2]Mathematics exhibits the application of operator to data, i.e., function to argument, while leaving the control indeterminate, i.e., in the hands of the mathematician.

control or memory could be erroful. This is inessential, though it again makes for simplicity. As was noted earlier, universality is always relative to physical limits, of which reliability is one. Once fundamental components are taken as having probabilities of failure, then ultimate performance is necessarily probabilistic. If failure probabilities are significant, the system organization can include counteracting features, such as checking, redundant processing, and redundant memory codes. Up to a point universality can be maintained as a practical matter; at some point it is lost.

All of these complexities are important in themselves, and some of them lie behind other constraints in Figure 1. They do not seem of the essence in understanding the nature of symbolic capability.

## 4.3. Assign: Creating Designations

The function of the **assign** operator is to create a relation of access, hence of designation, between a symbol and an entity. It is, of course, limited to the access relations supported by the underlying machinery of SS: between SS's symbols and SS's expressions, roles, and operators.

**Assign** implies several important properties:

At any time, a symbol designates a single entity.
Many symbols can designate the same entity.
A symbol may be used to designate any entity.

SS provides absolute and uniform adherence to these properties, but this is not necessary. For instance, from SS's simulation of a Turing machine, it can be seen that the requirements for multiple assignment and reassignment of a symbol to an arbitrary entity are needed only for the small set of working symbols used in the TM program (T, S, and A). All the other symbols (content, **do**, TM, . . .) can have fixed assignments. From this, the more general capability can be built up—which is what programming the simulation demonstrates.

The situation here generally applies. Small amounts of the requisite capabilities can be parlayed into the full-flecged capability. The minimal conditions are rarely interesting from a theoretical view, though successful elimination of an entire functional capability can be revealing. Minimal basic capabilities often imply gross inefficiencies and unreliabilities. Typical is the additional level of interpretation, if simulation is used to recover the additional capabilities (as in our example). Thus, symbol systems that satisfy additional constraints of Figure 1 are likely to satisfy pervasively such properties as those above.

It is often observed that the symbols of formal systems are totally abstract, whereas symbols as used by humans often have information encoded into the symbol itself, i.e., that is not arbitrary what a symbol is used for. The word for not being happy is "unhappy," in which some knowledge about what the word designates is available from an analysis of the word itself. In plane geometry small letters (a, b, . . .) are sides of triangles and capital letters (A, B, . . .) are their opposite angles. In general, the use (and usefulness) of *encoded names* has no bearing on the basic nature of symbol systems. Encoded names can be taken to be abstract symbols with bound expressions that provide the information in the encoded name. Thus, one expression has been granted a preferred access status. Though the assignment of symbols to entities has been limited, this will have an effect only if no freely assignable symbols remain as part of the system.

## 4.4 Copy: Creating New Memory

By applying **copy** whenever needed, SS obtains both an unbounded supply of expressions (hence of memory) and of symbols. That **copy** creates a copy is unessential, although by doing so it accomplishes a sequence of **reads** and **writes**. The essential aspect is obtaining the new expression and the new symbol. Neither can be dispensed with.

One of the few necessary conditions known for universal machines is:

A universal machine must have an unbounded memory.

The classical machine hierarchy of finite state machines, pushdown automata, linear bounded automata and Turing machines, expresses the gradation of capability with limitations in memory (Hopcroft & Ullman, 1969). Though essential, the condition of unboundedness is of little import, since what counts is the structure of the system. In all cases, the structure of the unbounded memory must eventually become uniform. Ultimately, SS has just a supply of undifferentiated *stuff* out of which to build expressions; the Turing machine has just a supply of undifferentiated tape cells. Thus, for every machine with unbounded memory, there are machines with identical structure, but bounded memory, that behave in an identical fashion on all environments (or problems) below a certain size or complexity.

The unimportance of actual unboundedness should not be taken to imply the unimportance of large memory. The experience in AI is everlastingly for larger effective memories (i.e., memories with adequately rapid access). A key element in list processing was the creation of dynamic memory, which effectively removed the memory limit problem from the operation of the system, while, of course, not removing it absolutely (i.e., available space eventually runs out). It is no accident that humans appear to have unbounded long-term memory. Thus, rather than talk about memory being actually unbounded, we will talk about it being *open*, which is to say available up to some point, which then bounds the performance, both qualitatively and quantitatively. *Limited*, in opposition to open, will imply that the limit is not only finite, but small enough to force concern. Correspondingly, *universal* can be taken to require only sufficiently open memory, not unbounded memory.

Symbols themselves are not memory; only expressions are. Though in SS symbols and expressions come into existence together, they are independent and could have separate **create** operators. Many symbols may be assigned to a single expression and many expressions may have the same symbol (over time) or may be unsymbolized and be accessible through other means. Symbols are the patterns in the symbol structure that permit accessing mechanisms to operate. Having an open number of symbols, but only a limited amount of memory, is not sufficient for a universal machine. On the other hand, with only a limited set of symbols, but an open supply of expressions, it is possible to create an open set of symbols. The use of a limited alphabet to create words is paradigmatic. However, just the anatomy of alphabets and words does not reveal the key issue, which is the construction of an accessing mechanism that makes the words behave like symbols, i.e., designate.

SS actually has an open supply of expressions of each type (and exactly what types exist was not specified). As might be expected, only a single source of openness is needed, providing it is not peculiarly tucked away, as in a pushdown stack. Further, SS's definition does not specify whether expressions themselves are limited or whether some of them can be open. This is again an unessential issue, as long as at least one open source is available for construction of whatever facilities are needed. The creation of an open structure type, the *list*, out of an open set of expressions of a limited structure type, the *pair* consisting of a *symbol* and a *link*, is paradigmatic. Though conceptually simple, such a construction was a major step in creating appropriate symbol systems.

### 4.5 Write: Creating Arbitrary Expressions

Another obvious, but important, necessary capability of a universal machine is:

> A universal machine must be able to create expressions of arbitrary character.

SS does this through a single uniform operator, **write**, though there are indefinitely many complex and indirect ways of attaining the result. To be unable to create an expression, by any means at all, would imply a failure to be universal (e.g., to simulate a machine that did produce that expression as an output).

In the usual way of specifying universal machines, particular representations are used for the expressions, e.g., the Turing tape or Lisp lists. Much of the idiosyncracy of such systems arises from the need to encode all structures of interest into this fixed structure. SS has remained general on this score, admitting only a basic capability for having expressions with distinct roles. Thus, we simply defined a new data type for each entity we needed to discuss,—programs, tape cells, and machine states.

It is unclear how to state the fundamental capability provided by expressions, but easy enough to exhibit it in simple and paradigmatic form. It is not enough to have only symbols. Expressions permit more than one symbol to be brought together in a way that is not determined wholly by the symbols, but provides additional structure, hence discriminability. This is what SS has in the roles—actually, in the association from the role symbol to its content symbol. There are an indefinite number of ways to provide such added structure to yield symbol expressions.

In SS's scheme, the symbols for roles are *relative* symbols. They differ in this respect from the symbols for expressions or operators, which are *absolute*. Given the symbol *move*, which designates the role in the tape-cell of the Turing machine, the process that takes roles as input, namely, **write** and **read**, can access the appropriate location in any tape-cell expression. Thus, role symbols are functions of one input (the expression), and akin to operators. These relative role symbols can be replaced by absolute symbols that uniquely designate the locations in particular expressions, though an additional operator is required to obtain these location symbols. This is the standard recourse in common programming languages, which provide *addresses* of list cells and array cells. Thus, all symbols can be absolute, with all context dependence relegated to a limited set of operators.

## 4.6. Read: Obtaining Symbols in Expressions

**Read** is the companion process to **write**, each being necessary to make the other useful. **Read** only obtains what was put into expressions by **write** at an earlier time; and a **write** operation whose result is never **read** subsequently might as well not have happened.[3]

The **read-write** coupling emphasises another necessary principle of symbol systems:

> Memory must be stable.

Though much less investigated than the question of amount of memory, this principle is of the same character. In so far as memory is unreliable, the ability of the symbol system to deliver a given input-output function is jeopardized. Such a limitation does not destroy the functional character of a symbol system; it only modulates it. Of course, different systems behave differently under unreliability, and systems can be designed to mitigate the effects of unreliability. Such considerations are outside the bounds of the paper (though they show up as one of the constraints in Figure 1).

In SS the reading operator was defined in the classical way, namely, a local operator whose scope was a given expression. This provides no global access to the memory. Indeed, SS is totally dependent on the initial data structures to

---

[3]This is too strong: The read operator is not the only process that reads expressions; control at least reads programs; and if the expression might have been read but wasn't because of a contingency in the environment, then the write operator still would have been useful, analogous to insurance that is never cashed.

provide linkages around the memory. A more global accessing operator could also be given:

> **Find** the expression that matches roles          (**find** R₁ S₁ . . .)
> Produces the expression or nil

In SS, attention must be paid to constructing access links to the new expressions created by **copy**; this is usually done by virtue of their symbols occurring in other expressions that are being built. Given other processing organizations, such as ones with parallel activity, then a **find** operation would be necessary, since the access links could not exist for **read** to suffice as a retrieval mechanism.

Such a global operator cannot as it stands replace the local one, since it identifies expressions by content, not by role in some other expression. However, versions can be created to combine both functions.

### 4.7 Do: Integrating and Compositing Action

To be able to describe behavior in expressions, the behavior must be decomposed, whether for a description indirectly as a machine that generates the behavior, or any other type of description. All such decompositions involve both primitives and combining schemes. For SS, doing a sequence of operations is the combining operation. It reflects directly a necessary requirement on decomposition:

> Universal machines must be able to determine the future independent of the past.

Looked at in terms of a prespecified input–output function, it is only necessary that the future beyond the point of instruction be open. But if new instructional input is permitted at any time (the realistic version of the flexibility constraint), then any commitment for the entire future can be a genuine restriction of flexibility. Instruction following such a commitment might require its undoing.

Other forms of decomposition exist besides the pure *time-slice* scheme used by SS (and also by existing digital computers and programming languages), in which each operator specifies completely what happens in the next time increment, leaving complete freedom of specification beyond. For instance, the commitments of the past could decay in some way, rather than cease abruptly; the future action, although still free to be anything, could be taken from a different base line in some way. Little is known about such alternative decompositions in terms of providing universal instructable behavior.

**Do** as an operator can be eliminated, because its essential function is also performed by the control. Interpreting the arguments of an operator prior to executing that operator (which corresponds to function composition) provides the essentials of a time decomposition. Thus, the function would still be provided, even though the **do** operator itself were eliminated.

## 4.8 Exit-if and Continue-if: Converting Symbols to Behavior

One of the most characteristic features of programming languages is the existence of conditional operators, the **in-then-else** of Algol-like languages, the
**branch on zero** of machine languages, or the **conditional expression** of Lisp.
These operators seem to contain the essence of making a decision. Beside embodying the notion of data dependence in pure form, they also are unique in
embodying the conversion from symbols to behavior. They would appear to be a
functional requirement for universality. They do not seem so much deeply implicated in the concept of symbols itself, but rather associated with the system that
operates with symbols.

However, it has been known since the earliest formulations of universal
machines that such conditionals are not uniquely required. The requirement is to
be able to compose all functions, and many other primitive functions provide the
essential combinative services. For example, the minimum function is often
used. It can be seen that taking the minimum of a set of elements effects a
selection, thus making a decision. But the minimum function has no special
symbol-to-behavior character; it has the same form as any other function.

Thus, conditionals are a convenience in SS. They can be dispensed with
and the same work done by **assign, copy, write, read** and **do**. A simple way to
show this is to write the simulation of the Turing Machines without using the
conditionals. The universality of SS is shown by this program; hence the universality can be attained by whatever limited means are sufficient to accomplish this
simulation. Figure 7 shows this simulation without the conditional. This corre-

```
TM-Exec: [do [assign [quote Next-step] [quote TM]] TM T]
TM: [do
          [assign 0 [read if-0 S]]
          [assign 1 [read if-1 S]]
          [assign A [read content T]]
          [write T content [read content A]]
          [assign T [read [read move A] T ]]
          [assign S [read next A]]
          Next-step]
tape-end: [do
          [assign New-T [copy T]]
          [write New-T content 0 [read [read move A] other ] T]
          [write T [read move A] New-T]
          New-T]
other: [right:left left:right]
halt: [assign [quote Next-step] nil]
```

Figure 7. Elimination of Conditional Operators from Simulation of Turing Machine.

sponds to the completely correct simulation of Figure 6, so that all places where conditionals originally occurred are covered.

It is instructive to understand the basic device in Figure 7. Conditionality is the dependence of behavior on data. The data in the simulation are symbols. Hence, each possible data symbol can be assigned whatever is to be the case if that data symbol is encountered. The symbol that actually occurs and is accessed brings with it the behavior to be taken.

There are three places where conditionals must be removed. The first is taking appropriate action, depending on 0 or 1. For this, 0 is assigned the action specifications for 0, and 1 the action specifications for 1. Then accessing the symbol that actually occurs in the tape cell, via (**read** content T), obtains the action specification as a function of the occurring state. This is assigned to the temporary working symbol, A, and the program can proceed as before.

The second place is sensing the end of the tape. Here, the symbol tape-end is assigned to be the program that extends the tape. Due to the recursive interpretation of control, accessing tape-end leads to the interpretation of this program, which then fixes up the tape en passant. Thus, the main program, TM, never has to deal with the problem explicitly.

The third place is exiting on halt. This is a little tricky, because a symbol (halt) must be converted to a permanent change of behavior (exiting the infinite loop of TM). The final step of TM, which is the recursive step to repeat TM, is made into a variable symbol, Next-step. This is assigned to be TM in TM-Exec, so that if nothing changes this symbol, TM, will be repeated, just as before. The symbol halt is assigned to a program that assigns Next-step to be nil. Thus, if halt is encountered, this program is executed, making TM into a straight-line program, which will then exit. It is necessary to use **quote** in the **assignments** of program symbols (Next-step and TM), or they would be executed inadvertently.

This style of programming illustrates an important relativity of view. From the perspective of the program there is no choice and no decision; it simply puts one foot in front of the other so to speak. From the perspective of the outside observer a choice is being made dependent on the data. The views are reconciled when it is seen that the program is constructing its own path, laying down each next step just in front of itself, like a stepping-stone, and then stepping onto it.

## 4.9 Quote: Treating Processes as Data

All universal systems contain a distinction between operators and data (i.e., arguments). To create its own procedures, a system must distinguish some expressions as data at one time (when creating or modifying them) and as program at another time (when interpreting them). This is a genuine contextual effect, since the expression is to be same in either case. This is only a binary distinction, and it can be achieved in many ways: by having a program memory as distinct from a data memory, with a transfer operation to activate the program; by marking the program so the control will not interpret it and then removing the mark to activate it; by having an **execute** operator that only interprets under deliberate command; or by having a **quote** operator that inhibits interpretation on command. For SS, since its control cycle is to interpret everything, the **quote** command is the natural choice.

However, as Figure 5 again shows by producing the simulation without the use of **quote**, this operator does not imply an additional primitive functional requirement. What Figure 5 actually shows is that if a symbol system is willing to operate in indirect simulation mode, the distinctions can be introduced by data conventions. This is because the control of the system now becomes programmable.[4]

## 4.10. Behave and Input: Interacting with the External World

**Behave** and **input** have played a muted role in the exposition of SS, only because the emphasis has been on the basic functional requirements for symbolization and for universality. These capabilities must exist in some interior system, and thus can be illustrated there, without involving the interaction with the external world.

**Behave** and **input** imply an extension of the basic access mechanism, beyond the operators, roles and expressions, as described above. The symbols that are operands in **behave** must access in some way the effector mechanisms. These symbols can be viewed simply as additional operators which haven't been specified because there was no need to. **Input**, on the other hand, requires its output symbols to reflect an invariant relation to the state of the external environment (via states of the receptor mechanism). The invariance doesn't have to be perfect; it can even change over time (though not too rapidly). But without some reliable transduction from external structure to symbols, the symbol system will not be able to produce reliable functional dependence on the external environment.

General symbol systems include unlimited elaborations on **behave** and **input**. In particular, versions of these operators need not link to a genuine external world, but simply to other components of the total system that provide additional computational devices. These may be integral to the actual operation of the system in practice. Such additional facilities do not destroy the capability for symbolic action. The only requirement is that they be symbolizable, i.e., have symbols that evoke them and symbols that reflect their behavior.

## 4.11. Symbol Systems Imply Universality

The notion of universality has been expressed to reveal how it contains a notion

---

[4]The quotes can likewise be removed from Figure 7 by rewriting the TM program so it is a nonprogram data structure that is interpreted by an SS program.

of symbol and symbol system. Though at the beginning of the section I claimed it was inappropriate to act as if we had an independent characterization of symbol system; it is now certainly useful to extract from the current formulation what a symbol system might be, independent of the notion of universality. For instance, this might lead to interesting variants of symbol systems that are not universal in some important way (i.e., in some way other than physical limits).

Consider the following generalized characterization of the notions involved in physical symbol systems:

Symbols as abstract types that express the identity of multiple tokens.

Expressions as structures containing symbol tokens.

Designation as a relation between a symbol and the entities it symbolizes.

Interpretation as realizing the designations of expressions.

Operations of assigning symbols, and copying, reading, and writing expressions.

These notions all seem fundamental to symbolic functioning. It is difficult to envision a notion of symbol that does not embody some version of these capabilities, and perhaps much more besides. These notions are too vague to actually define symbolic functioning. For instance, the statement about designation does not describe the properties of the relation, e.g., between the word "cat" and the animal cat. The statement about interpretation leaves entirely open what symbolic activity is actually about—it could easily hide a homunculus. Still, these might form the thematic kernel from which to precipitate independent characterizations of symbols.

In particular, there exists an instantiation of these notions that regains the formulation of a physical symbol system. The chief additional ingredient (abstracted away in generating the list above) is a notion of symbolic *processing*. Designation is given a primitive basis primarily in the accessing of other expressions. Interpretation is given a formulation involving only expressions that designate symbolic processing. Assigning, copying, reading, and writing are taken as specific processing functions; in particular, reading is taken only as the ability to obtain constituent symbols. These particularities would no doubt be included in some fashion in any instantiation of the general notion of symbols stated above. However, the instantiation for physical symbol systems is still highly special, and much is missing: designation of external entities, wider ranges of interpretive activity, and so on.

Yet, as we have seen, this process-oriented instantiation of these notions is by itself sufficient to produce universality. No embedding of the symbol system into a larger processing system with other capabilities is required, though sufficient freedom from physical limitations (i.e., sufficient memory, reliability, etc.) must exist. In the preceding discussion, the operations of **exit-if, continue-if,** do, **quote**, and **find** were shown to be collectively unnecessary to achieve universality. Thus, the operations that appear inherently involved in symbolic processing (**assign, copy, read, write,** and **interpret**) are collectively sufficient to produce universality. No augmentation with any nonsymbolic processing machinery is required. Although the argument was carried through on a particular system, SS, it applies generally to the functional capabilities themselves.

A novel feature of physical symbol systems is the approach to symbolic function, not just by processing, but by *internal* symbolic processing. The primitive symbolic capabilities are defined on the symbolic processing system itself, not on any external processing or behaving system. The prototype symbolic relation is that of access from a symbol to an expression, not that of naming an external object. Thus, it is an implication of the formulation, not part of its definition, that the appropriate designatory relations can be obtained to external objects (via chains of designation). Because of this, the exact scope of that designatory capability is left open, implicit in the ramifications of universality.

Thus, we are lead finally to the following hypothesis:

> Any reasonable symbol system is universal (relative to physical limitations).

It is important to distinguish symbol systems that are computationally limited because of physical constraints or limited programs and data from symbol systems that fall short of providing universality because of structural limitations. The hypothesis refers to the latter.

Despite this hypothesis, one might still want to formulate a notion of symbol system that was not also universal, even though it would be limited. One general path might be to deny the process base. But this seems unfruitful, since symbol systems must ultimately be used by processing systems, and this path simply keeps the processing implications off stage. The addition of a processing base would very likely simply convey universality. Another possibility is to consider systems with many symbol systems, each ranging over severely limited domains with limited intercommunication. These could violate some aspects of assignment, so that genuinely limited systems might emerge. But, in general, looking for a more limited conception of symbolic system, in order to get something conceptually independent of universality, does not seem particularly rewarding. This seems especially the case in trying to understand the human mind, which surely exhibits extreme flexibility even though it must cope with some stringent physical limitations.

## 5. THE PHYSICAL SYMBOL SYSTEM HYPOTHESIS

Having finally made clear the nature of a physical symbol system, the major hypothesis can be stated explicitly (Newell & Simon, 1976):

*Physical Symbol System Hypothesis:* The necessary and sufficient condition for a physical system to exhibit general intelligent action is that it be a physical symbol system.

*Necessary* means that any physical system that exhibits general intelligence will be an instance of a physical symbol system.

*Sufficient* means that any physical symbol system can be organized further to exhibit general intelligent action.

*General intelligent action* means the same scope of intelligence seen in human action: that in real situations behavior appropriate to the ends of the system and adaptive to the demands of the environment can occur, within some physical limits.

The hypothesis takes as given the identity of symbol systems and universal systems, and asserts their connection to rationality, a concept which did not enter into their formulation. The hypothesis implicitly asserts that physical symbol systems cover human symbol systems, since general intelligence includes human intelligence. It can be taken as also asserting the essential role of human symbols in human rational behavior, if that cannot be taken for granted.

The hypothesis implies that symbol systems are the appropriate class within which to seek the phenomena of mind. However, it does not mention *mind* explicitly, but rather the notion of general intelligent action. It thereby implicitly takes general intelligence to be the key to the phenomena of mind. Given the democracy of the constraints in Figure 1, this may seem a little presumptuous. If so, it is not a presumption that makes a substantial difference in the short term. The systems that satisfy all of the constraints will undoubtedly be a highly distinctive subclass of those that satisfy only the three involved in the hypothesis—universality, symbols, and rationality. This distinctiveness could well include phenomena of mind that would make the total class appear quite unmind-like. That possibility does not affect the tactical issue of approaching the phenomena of mind via this class of systems.

The statement of necessity is straightforward. A general intelligent system, whatever additional structures and processes it may have, will contain a physical symbol system. It will be possible to find what serves as symbols and as expressions; and to identify what processes provide the functions that we have enumerated and discussed. The variability of realization discussed in the next section may make these structures and processes far from obvious, but they will exist.

The statement of sufficiency requires a little care. A universal system always contains the potential for being any other system, if so instructed. Thus, a universal system can become a generally intelligent system. But it need not be one. Furthermore, instructability does not imply any ability at self-instruction, so that there may be no way to transform such a system into one that is generally intelligent, i.e., no external agent with the capability to successfully instruct it need be available. Given the nature of universality, this sufficient condition does not have much bite; it is the necessary condition which carries the strong implications.

The notion of general intelligence can only be informally circumscribed, since it refers to an empirical phenomenon. However, the intent is clear—to cover whatever will come to be called intelligent action as our understanding of the phenomenon increases. The term *general* excludes systems that operate only in circumscribed domains. If the domain is narrow enough, considerable intellectual power may be possible from systems that are not physical symbol systems. Thus, a specific enumeration algorithm for chess that achieved master level, but was realized directly in hardware in a way that avoided the full capabilities of a symbol system, would not provide a counterexample to the hypothesis. General intelligence implies that within some broad limits anything can become a task. It would suffice to ask if the given narrow algorithm could also accept other novel tasks; and on this it would, per hypothesis, fail.

All real systems are limited: To be generally intelligent does not imply the ability to solve or even formulate all problems. We have used the phrase *physical limits* to indicate the effects of underlying limits to speed, memory size, reliability, sensitivity, etc. The existence of such limits implies the possibility of quibbles in assessing the hypothesis, if the limits are so stringent as to deny a system any reasonable scope for positive performance. The formulation above does not attempt to be precise enough to deal with such quibbles.

## 5.1. Why Might the Hypothesis Hold?

That the hypothesis refers to rationality, rather than more generally to phenomena of mind, is not just a rhetorical preference. The hypothesis is based on the empirical evidence of the last twenty years in artificial intelligence. That evidence specifically relates to rational goal-directed behavior, and not to the other constraints (though some evidence exists touching one or two others). Thus, the hypothesis really must be cast in this narrower form.

It is important to understand that the hypothesis is empirical and rests on this body of experience. Artificial intelligence has made immense progress in developing machines that perceive, reason, solve problems, and do symbolic tasks. Furthermore, this has involved the deliberate use of symbol systems, as witnessed in the development and exploitation of list processing. This use of symbolic computation distinguishes artificial intelligence from most other enterprises within computer science (though not all). These advances far outstrip what has been accomplished by other attempts to build intelligent mechanisms, such as the work in building robots driven directly by circuits, the work in neural nets, or the engineering attempts at pattern recognition using direct circuitry and analogue computation.[5] There is no space in this paper to review the evidence for this, which covers the development of an entire field over almost a quarter century. Reverence to the most recent textbooks will have to suffice (Nilsson, 1980; Winston, 1977).

Given our present understanding of intelligent programs, an analysis can be made of why symbol systems play a necessary role in general intelligent action. Again, there is no space to do more than outline this analysis here. There seem to be three main points.

1. A general intelligent system must somehow embody aspects of what is to be attained prior to attainment of it, i.e., it must have *goals*. Symbols that designate the situation to be attained (including that it is to be attained, under what conditions, etc.) appear to be the only candidate for doing this. It might seem an alternative to build goal-orientation into the structure of the system at design time (as is often done in programs that have a single fixed task, such as playing a game). However, this does not suffice for a general intelligence facing an indefinite sequence of novel and sufficiently diverse goal situations.

2. A general intelligent system must somehow consider candidate states of affairs (and partial states) for the solutions of these goals (leading to the familiar search trees). Symbols in a symbol system appear to be the only way to designate these, especially as the diversity and novelty of the states and partial states increase without bound.

3. An intelligent system must fashion its responses to the demands of the task environment. As the diversity of tasks expand, i.e., as the intelligence becomes general, there would seem to be no way to avoid a flexibility sufficient to imply universality and hence symbols.

The backbone of the above argument is: (1) rationality demands designation of potential situations; (2) symbol systems provide it; (3) only symbol systems can provide it when sufficient novelty and diversity of task are permitted. This latter aspect is analogous to standard arguments in linguistics concerning the implications of generation of novel sentences.

## 6. REALIZATIONS AND SYSTEM LEVELS

Symbol systems, as described, are abstract. We now need to consider their realization in our physical universe. The key to this is our experience with the construction of digital computers. That current digital technology involves a hierarchy of levels is well known and appreciated. However, it is part of the story of symbol systems and needs to be recounted briefly.

A standard set of levels has emerged as digital computers have been developed. These levels are levels of *description*, since it is always the same physical system that is being described. Each level consists of characteristic

---

[5]The term *direct* is used as a shorthand to indicate that the systems do not use digital computers as a major component.

components that can be connected together in characteristic fashion to form systems that process a characteristic medium. The different descriptions form a sequence of levels, because the components, connections and media of one level, are defined in terms of systems at the next lower level.

The bottom-most level starts with the description of the physical devices in electronic terms. It is usually called the *device* level. Above this is the *circuit* level, which consists of electrical currents and voltages, traveling in wires. Above that is the *logic* level, in which there occur registers containing bits, with transfer paths between them and various logical functions occurring when bits pass through functional units. Operation here is entirely parallel, as it is at all lower levels. The next level is the *program* level which contains data structures, symbols (or variables), addresses, and programs. Operation is sequential, consisting of control streams produced by interpreters, though concurrent control streams may exist. This is the level of the symbol system as it occurs in digital computers. Above the programming level is the level of gross anatomy, the so-called *PMS (Processor-Memory-Switch)* level. Here there is simply a medium, called data or information, which flows along channels called links and switches and is held and processed by units called memories, processors, controls, and transducers. It is the level at which you order a computer system from the manufacturer.

Each of these levels provides a complete description of a system, i.e., one in which the present state of the machine plus the laws of behavior of the system (at that level) determine the entire trajectory of the system through time.[6]

Although apparently only a way of describing the physical world, each level in fact constitutes a *technology*. That is, any description of a system can be realized physically, because physical techniques exist for creating the required components and assembling them according to the description. Circuits of any description can be built; so also logic circuits, and programs with any data types and routines. At the PMS level, computer configurations can be ordered with various combinations of memory boxes, disks, and terminals. And so on. (Limits do exist to the realizability of arbitrary descriptions, e.g., the number of nested expressions in a programming language or the fanout in a logic circuit technology; these complicate, but do not destroy, the technological character of a level.) Thus, these levels of description do not exist just in the eye of the beholder, but have a reality in this combinative characteristic in the real world. The levels are not arbitrary and cannot be created at will, just by an act of analysis. On the other hand, there is no persuasive analysis yet that says this particular set of levels is necessary or unique and could not be replaced by a quite different set.

From the prior discussion of symbol systems we should be prepared for the existence of an indefinitely wide variety of symbol systems. Such variety stems from all the different forms of operators, controls, memories, and symbol-

---

[6]The top level (PMS) is often an exception, for behavioral laws are not usually formulated for it.

structures that still add up to universal symbolic capability. The logic level structure that creates a particular symbol system is called the *architecture*. Thus, there is an indefinite variety of architectures. Indeed, they are so diverse that we have no reasonable characterizations of the class of all architectures.

What we had no right to expect is the immense variety of physical ways to realize any fixed symbol system. What the generations of digital technology have demonstrated is that an indefinitely wide array of physical phenomena can be used to develop a digital technology to produce a logical level of essentially identical character. If evidence must be quoted for this, it comes in the form of the *architecture family*, achieved first by IBM in the mid-sixties with System/360 and now provided by most manufacturers, whereby many implementations exist for a given architecture, trading cost for speed and memory capacity. Programs that run on one implementation also run on the other. Furthermore, these implementations are not all planned for in advance, but as brand new technologies gradually come into existence at the device level, new implementations of the existing architecture are created.

Thus the picture that emerges is a series of levels of technology, with a many-many mapping between levels—each level giving rise to an immense diversity of systems at the next higher level, and each system at a given level being realizable by an immense diversity of organizations at the next lower level.

That humans are physical symbols systems implies that there exists a physical architecture that supports that symbol system. The relatively gross facts about the nervous system reveal some natural candidates for the levels of organization at which technologies do exist. The neural level surely constitutes a technology. So also does the macromolecular level (in fact, several technologies may exist there). It is possible to be mistaken about the levels, given the potentiality at the macromolecular level, as seen, for instance, in the immune system. But such uncertainty does not destroy the essential picture:

> There must exist a neural organization that is an architecture—i.e., that supports a symbol structure.

Furthermore, the immense diversity of lower level technologies that can lead to an architecture certainly enhances the chance that a biological based architecture could have evolved.

This is a genuine prediction on the structure of the nervous system and should ultimately inform the attempt to understand how the nervous system functions. It does not appear to have done so, though from time to time the suggestion has even been made directly (Newell, 1962). In fact, I know of no discussion of the issue in the neuroscience literature.

The reasons for this lack of attention by the neurosciences lie beyond the present paper. Some of the considerations are evident in Geschwind's paper at this conference (Geschwind, 1980), where emphasis is placed on the special-purpose computational systems that seem to be available in the organism, even to doubting that any general purpose mechanisms exist. As the present exposition should make clear, the requirement for universal symbolic functioning is not incompatible with extensive special-purpose computational structure. It implies neither that everything must be done through programming a small set of primitive facilities nor that the symbol system occur as an isolated component. To take SS (or similar examples of formally defined universal systems) as implying such properties fails to appreciate the actual functional requirements they express.

The levels structure of physical implementation, and our experience with it for digital technologies, leads to understanding how one level can be *sealed off* from its lower level during normal operation. This is the phenomenon of not being able to identify *under normal conditions* the technology in which a computer is implemented, if access is available only to the behavior at the symbolic level. This sealing off produces an effect in which the symbolic behavior (and essentially rational behavior) becomes relatively independent of the underlying technology. Applied to the human organism, this produces a physical basis for the apparent irrelevance of the neural level to intelligent behavior. The neural system is not in fact irrelevant—its operation supports the symbolic level. But it does so in a way that normally hides most of its properties, realizing instead a symbol system with properties of its own.

The phrase *under normal conditions* is essential to the above characterization. Errors of all sorts that occur at lower levels typically propagate through to higher levels (here, the symbolic level) and produce behavior that is revealing of the underlying structures. Likewise, simply forcing a system against the physical limits of its behavior reveals details of the underlying technologies. Given a stop watch, the freedom to specify the tasks to be performed on a computer, and a system that is not designed to deceive, much can be learned of the lower levels of implementation. Similarly, if the system uses large subsystems of special computational character, these too may reveal themselves.

This entire story of technological system levels, and the many-many relationship of systems on the symbol level to architectures that support it, is an important part of the current knowledge about symbol systems. Like the link to rational behavior (as expressed in the basic hypothesis), it is primarily empirically based.

## 7. DISCUSSION

With the basic story now before us, a few issues can be touched on to make sure that the notion of symbol system and the hypothesis are correctly understood.

### 7.1. Knowledge and Representation

Two terms intimately related to symbolic behavior have not appeared in the discussion so far: *representation* and *knowledge*. Both have rather clear meanings within the concept of physical symbol system, especially in the practice of artificial intelligence. However, formal theories of these concepts are relatively chaotic, with little agreement yet. Still, it is useful to indicate the sense of these notions, albeit briefly.

Representation is simply another term to refer to a structure that designates:

> X *represents* Y if X designates aspects of Y, i.e., if there exist symbol processes that can take X as input and behave as if they had access to some aspects of Y.

The qualitification to aspects of Y, rather than just Y, simply reflects language usage in which X can be said to represent a complex object Y without being faithful (i.e., designating) all aspects of Y.

Representation is sometimes formulated in terms of a mapping from aspects of Y to aspects of X. Implicit in this formulation is that something can be done with X, i.e., that processes exist that can detect the aspects of X that are images of aspects of Y. Hence the whole forms a designatory chain.

Representation is also sometimes formulated in terms of a data structure with its associated *proper* operations. This view emphasizes the coupling of the static structure (what is often simply called *the* representation) and the processing that defines what can be encoded into the structure, what can be retrieved from it and what transformations it can undergo with defined changes in what is represented. This view suppresses the function of the memory structure (i.e., what it represents) in favor of the essential mechanics, but it comes to exactly the same thing as the formulation in terms of designation.

The term representation focuses attention on the image of the distal object in the symbolic structure which represents it. The analysis of universality and symbols, as presented here, focuses on the adequacy of constructing functions from the distal object to the behavior of the system, which works through the representations as an intermediate structure. Such a presentation leaves undeveloped the structure of descriptive schemes, with the corresponding questions of efficiency and usefulness. We saw a reason for this in the initial formulation of universality, where it was important to avoid confounding the limitations of descriptive schemes for possible functions with what functions could actually be produced by a machine.

Existing work, mostly stemming from the analysis of formal logic, confirms that the class of systems described here (i.e., universal symbol systems) is also the class of systems with general powers of representation or (equivalently) description. The representational range of all first order predicate calculi is the same and corresponds to universal systems (when one asks what functions can be described in the logic). An important chapter in logic was the demonstration that set theory, perhaps the most useful descriptive scheme developed in mathematics, was formulable in first order logic, thus becoming simply another alternative descriptive scheme, not one capable of describing a different range of entities and situations. Higher order logics (which progressively remove restrictions on the domains of variables in logical formula) do not extend the expressive range. Modal notions, such as *possibility* and *necessity*, long handled axiomatically in a way that made their relationship to standard logic (hence universal symbol systems) obscure, now appear to have an appropriate formulation within what is called *possible world semantics* (Hintikka, 1975; Kripke, 1972), which again brings them back within standard logic. The continuous functions that naturally occur in the world (hence, must be represented) are produced by systems of limited energy. Hence, they must be of limited frequency (i.e., limited *bandwidth*) and have, by the so-called *sampling theorem*, adequate finite discrete representations.

The above rapid transit through some basic theoretical results on representation is meant to indicate only two things: First, some general things are known about representation; and second, representation is intimately tied to symbol systems. Much more is known in empirical and practical ways about representation, especially from investigations of artificial intelligence systems. However, no adequate theory of representation exists for questions of efficiency, efficacy, and design—the level at which most interesting issues arise.

Knowledge is the other term that has not figured as prominently in our discussion as might have been expected. It is a competence-like notion whose nature can be indicated by the slogan formula:

$$\text{Representation} = \text{Knowledge} + \text{Access}$$

Given a representation, making use of it requires processing to produce other symbolic expressions (or behavior). Although it is possible for a symbolic structure to yield only a small finite number of new expressions, in general there can be an unbounded number. Consider what can be obtained from a chess position, or from the axioms of group theory, or from a visual scene. Further, to obtain most of these new expressions requires varying amounts of processing. Thus, it is theoretically useful to separate analytically the set of potential expressions that a representation can yield from the process of extracting them, i.e., the access to them. Knowledge is this abstract set of all possible derived expressions.

This notion, which corresponds to the set of all implications of a set of propositions, has a history in philosophy as a candidate for the definition of knowledge. It has seemed unsatisfactory because a person could hardly be said to know all the implications of a set of propositions. However, its position within an explicit processing theory presents quite a different situation. Here, having knowledge is distinguished from having it available for any particular use, and in a principled way that depends on the details of the processing system. This formulation in fact corresponds to the actual use of the term in artificial intelligence, where it is necessary to talk about what is available in a data structure that could be extracted by more or different processing.

43

## 7.2. Obstacles to Consideration

The basic results we have been reviewing have been with us for twenty years in one guise or another. Some attitudes about them have grown up that are obstacles to their correct interpretation. These are worth mentioning, at least briefly:

*The Turing Tar Pit.* The phrase is Alan Perlis'.[7] The view is that all distinctions vanish when considering systems simply as universal machines (i.e., as Turing machines), since all systems become equivalent. Therefore, general results about universality cannot be of interest to any real questions. On the contrary, the question of interest here is precisely what structure provides flexibility. The discovery that such flexibility requires symbols is a real one. The Turing Tar Pit only traps the unwary who already live within the world of universal symbol systems, which of course computer scientists do.

*The computer as tool kit.* The universality of the digital computer means it can be used to simulate and build models for any system of interest, from chemical processing plants to traffic control to human cognition. Therefore, its role and significance are no different for cognitive science than for any other science or engineering. On the contrary, it is the structure of the digital computer itself (and the theoretical analysis of it) that reveals the nature of symbolic systems. When the computer, as a general purpose tool, is used to simulate models of mind, these are models of symbol systems (though of different architectures than that of the computer being used as tool).

*The requirement for unbounded memory.* Universality implies unbounded memory. All real systems only have bounded memory. Therefore, the property of universality cannot be relevant to the understanding of intelligent mechanisms. On the contrary, as we emphasized earlier, the structural requirements for universality are not dependent on unbounded memory, only whether the absolute maximal class of input–output functions can be realized. Symbol systems are still required if universality is demanded over any sufficiently large and diverse class of functions.

*The ignoring of processing time.* Universality requires no restraint on processing time. Indeed, simulations run indefinitely slower than what they simulate. But time and resource limits are of the essence of intelligent action. Therefore, universality results are of little interest in understanding intelligence. On the contrary, the requirement for symbol systems remains with the additon of physical limits, such as real time (or reliability, sensitivity, . . .). The objection confuses necessary and sufficient conditions. The real question is what is the subclass of symbol systems that also satisfies the real time constraint. This is sufficiently important to the general argument of this paper that we take it up below in more detail.

*The requirement for experimental identification.* An experimental science of behavior can only be concerned with what it can identify by experimental operations. Universal machines (and various general representations) mimic each other and are indistinguishable experimentally. Therefore, they are not of interest to psychology. On the contrary, if humans have this chameleon-like character (which it appears they do), then it is the basic task of psychology to discover ways to discern it

[7]Some readers may be unacquainted with the famous Tar Pits of La Brea, California, which trapped and sucked down innumerable prehistoric animals without distinction—large and small, fierce and meek.

experimentally, however difficult. Without downplaying these difficulties, the objection overstates the lack of identifiability in the large (i.e., in the face of sufficiently wide and diverse contexts and varieties of measurement).

*The uniform nature of symbol systems.* General symbol systems imply a homogeneous set of symbols, in which everything is done by uniform mechanisms. But physiology and anatomy show clearly that the nervous system is filled with computational systems of immense specialization (and evolution affirms that this is how it would be). Therefore, humans (and other animals) cannot have symbol systems. On the contrary, this objection inducts the wrong attributes from existing computer architectures. The functional properties we have summarized are what is important. These can be realized in an immense diversity of schemes, including ones that are highly parallel and full of special mechanisms.

*The discrete nature of symbols.* Symbol systems are ultimately just a collection of bits—of yes's and no's. Such a discrete representation cannot possibly do justice to the nature of phenomenal experience, which is continuous and indefinitely rich. On the contrary, there is good reason not to trust the intuition about the relation of phenomenal reality and discreteness. On the side of constructed systems, speech and vision recognition systems begin to show adequate ways in which continuous environments can be dealt with. On the side of the human, the discrete cellular nature of biological systems (and below that of molecular structure) gives pause on the anatomical side; as does the sampled-data character of the visual system on the behavioral side. However, nothing to speak of is known about "continuous" symbol systems, i.e., systems whose symbols have some sort of continuous topology.

*The computer metaphor.* The computer is a metaphor for the mind. Many metaphors are always possible. In particular, new technologies always provide new ways to view man. Therefore, this metaphor too will pass, to be replaced by a metaphor from the next technology. On the contrary, though it is surely possible and sometimes fruitful to use the computer metaphorically to think about mind, the present development is that of a scientific theory of mind, not different in its methodological characteristics from scientific theories in other sciences. There has been an attempt in the philosophical literature to take *metaphor* as a metaphor for all theory and science (Black, 1962), a view well represented by Lakoff (1980) at this conference. Like all metaphors, it has its kernel of truth. But the sign is wrong. The more metaphorical, the less scientific. Again, the more metaphors the better, but the more comprehensive the theory of a single phenomenon, the better. *Computational metaphor* does not seem a happy phrase, except as a rhetorical device to distance theoretical ideas flowing from the computer and keep them from being taken seriously as science.

## 7.3. The Real-Time Constraint

A brief discussion of the constraint that processing occurs in real time may serve to clarify the role of symbol systems in the total endeavor to understand the phenomena of mind.

No doubt, living in real time shapes the nature of mind, and in more ways than we can imagine at present. For instance, it produces the existential dilemma that gives rise to search as a pervasive feature of all intelligent activity. Limited processing resources per unit time continually must be committed *now* without further ado—the opportunity to spend *this now* already slipping past. Imperfect present knowledge always produces imperfect commitments, which leads to (still imperfect) corrective action, which cascades to produce combinatorial search.

As noted earlier, such considerations do not remove the need for symbols. Intelligent activity in real time cannot be purchased by foregoing symbols. Rather, those symbol systems that can perform adequately in real time become the focus of interest in the search for a theory of mind. How would one seek to discover such a class? One way—though only one—is to work within the class of symbol systems to find architectures and algorithms that are responsive to the constraints of real time.

An example is the intensive explorations into the nature of multiprocessing systems. This is being fueled much more generally by computer science interests, driven by the advances in technology which provide increasingly less expensive processing power. The range of such explorations is extremely broad, currently, and much of it appears remote from the interests of cognitive science. All of it assumes that the total systems will be general purpose computers (though with interesting twists of efficiency and specialization). It will add up eventually to a thorough understanding of the space, time, and organization trade-offs that characterize computers that operate under severe time constraints.

Another example, somewhat closer to home, are the so called *production systems* (Waterman & Hayes-Roth, 1978), which consist of a (possibly very large) set of condition-action rules, with continuous parallel recognition of which rules are satisfied in the present environment and selection of one (or a few) of the satisfied rules for action execution. There are several reasons for being interested in such systems (Newell, 1973; Newell, 1979). However, a prime one is that they are responsive to the real-time constraint. The parallel recognition brings to bear, at least potentially, all of the knowledge in the system on the present moment when a decision must be made. Such systems are also universal symbol systems. They would have done as well as SS for illustrating the nature of symbols, save for the confusion engendered by their also exhibiting aspects responsive to other constraints.

The point of both examples (and others that could have been given) is not the particular contributions they might make individually. Rather, they illustrate the ability to explore classes of systems that are responsive to additional constraints by developing subclasses of architectures within the class of universal symbol systems. That the space of all universal symbol systems contains vast regions of systems inappropriate to some of the other conditions of mind-like systems is irrelevant. More precisely, it is irrelevant if the larger class is a suitable base for further analysis and exploration—which is exactly what current experience in computer science attests.

## 8. CONCLUSION

Let us return to our general problem of discovering the nature of mind, and the decomposition of that problem into a dozen constraints (Figure 1). We now have a class of systems that embodies two of the constraints: universality and symbolic behavior. Furthermore, this is a *generative* class. It is possible to construct systems which are automatically within the class. Thus this class can be used to explore systems that satisfy yet other constraints. Indeed, that is exactly the twenty-five-year history of artificial intelligence—an explosion of exploration, all operating from within the class of systems that were automatically universal and symbolic. The generative character comes through clearly in this history as the initial versions of digital computers were shaped via the development of list-processing to also bring their general symbolic character to the fore.

This class of universal–symbolic systems is now tied to a third constraint, rationality. That is what the Physical Symbol System Hypothesis says. Unfortunately, the nature of rational action is not yet well enough understood to yield general generative formulations, to permit exploring other constraints within a constructive framework that automatically satisfies the rationality constraint (as well as the universality and symbolic behavior constraints). Major attempts in artificial intelligence still start from basic symbolic capability and posit their own idiosyncratic processing organization for attaining rational behavior. However, some parts of the puzzle are already clear, such as the notion of goal and goal hierarchies, and the concept of heuristic (i.e., knowledge controlled) search. Thus, we may not be too far away from the emergence of an accepted generative class of systems that are universal-symbol and also rational. The excitement that rippled through the artificial intelligence world at the beginning of the seventies when the so-called planning languages first came on the scene (Hewitt, 1971; Rulifson, Derksen, & Waldinger, 1972) stemmed in large part because it seemed that this step had been taken. We didn't quite make it then, but experience keeps accumulating.

This phenomenon continues: Discovering that it is possible to shape new subclasses that satisfy additional constraints on our list. We discussed briefly the real-time constraint. We did not discuss, but could have, progress with respect to a few of the other constraints (though by no means all), e.g., linguistics or vast knowledge—not just general progress, but progress in shaping a generative class of systems that automatically by construction satisfies the constraint.

I end by emphasizing this evolution of generative classes of systems that satisfy successively more constraints in our list, because it can stand as a final bit of evidence that we are on the right track—that symbol systems provide us with the laws of qualitative structure within which we should be working to make fundamental progress on the problem of mind. It is one more sign, coupled with

47

the rich web of concepts illustrated in the prior pages, of the scientific fruitfulness of the notion of a physical symbol system.

Francis Crick, in his Danz lectures *Of Molecules and Men*, discusses the problem of how life could have arisen:

> [This] really is the major problem·in biology. How did this complexity arise?
>
> The great news is that we know the answer to this question, at least in outline. I call it news because it is regrettably possible in very many parts of the world to spend three years at a university and take a university degree and still be largely ignorant of the answer to this, our most fundamental problem. The answer was given over a hundred years ago by Charles Darwin and also by A. R. Wallace. Natural selection, Darwin argued, provides an "automatic" mechanism by which a complex organism can survive and increase in both number and complexity. (1966, p. 7)

For us in Cognitive Science, the major problem is how it is possible for mind to exist in this physical universe. The great news, I say, is that we know, at least in outline, how this might be. I call it news because, though the answer has been with us for over twenty years, it seems to be not to be widely recognized. True, the answer was discovered indirectly while developing a technological instrument; and key steps in its evolution occurred while pursuing other scientific goals. Still, there remains no reason not to face this discovery, which has happened to us collectively.

## REFERENCES

Allport, D. A. Conscious and unconscious cognition: A computational metaphor for the mechanism of attention and integration. In Nilsson, L. G. (Ed.), *Perspectives on Memory Research*, Hillsdale, N.J.: Erlbaum, 1979.

Ashby, W. R. *Introduction to cybernetics*. New York: Wiley, 1956.

Black, M. *Metaphors and models*. Ithaca, NY: Cornell University, 1962.

Brainerd, W. S., & Landweber, L. H. *Theory of computation*. New York: Wiley, 1974.

Church, A. An unsolvable problem of elementary number theory. *The American Journal of Mathematics*, 1936, *58*, 345–363.

Clark, H., & Clark, E. *The Psychology of language: An introduction to psycholinguistics*. New York: Harcourt, Brace, Jovanovich, 1977.

Crick, F. *Of molecules and men*. Seattle, WA: University of Washington Press, 1966.

Feynman, R. P., Leighton, R. B., & Sands, M. *The Feynman lectures in physics*. New York: Addison Wesley, 1963.

Geschwind, N. Neurological knowledge and complex behaviors. In Norman, D. A. (Ed.), *La Jolla Conference on Cognitive Science*, Program in Cognitive Science, UCSD, 1979.

Hewitt, C. *Description and Theoretical Analysis (using Schemata) of Planner: A language for proving theorems and manipulating models in a robot*. PhD thesis, MIT, January, 1971.

Hintikka, J. *The Intentions of intentionality and other new models for modality*. Dordrecht, Holland: Reidel, 1975.

Hopcroft, J. E., & Ullman, J. D. *Formal languages and their relation to automata*. Reading, MA: Addison-Wesley, 1969.

Kripke, S. Semantical analysis of modal logic II. In Addision, J. W., Henkin, L. & Tarski, A. (Ed.), *The Theory of Models*, Amsterdam: North Holland, 1972.

Lachman, R., Lachman, J. L., & Butterfield, E. C. *Cognitive psychology and information processing: An introduction*. Hillsdale, NJ: Erlbaum, 1979.

Lakoff, G. Toward an experientialist philosophy: The case from literal metaphor. In Norman, D. A. (Ed.), *La Jolla Conference on Cognitive Science*. Program in Cognitive Science, UCSD, 1979.

Lindsay, P. H., & Norman, D. A. *Human information processing: An introduction to psychology*. *2nd Ed.* New York: Academic, 1977.

Minsky, M. *Computation: finite and infinite machines*. Englewood Cliffs, NJ: Prentice-Hall, 1967.

Neisser, U. *Cognition and reality*. San Francisco: Freeman, 1976.

Newell, A. Discussion of the session on integration in information in the nervous system. In *Proceedings of the International Union of Physiological Sciences, III*, International Union of Physiological Sciences, 1962.

Newell, A. Production systems: Models of control structures. In W. C. Chase, (Ed.), *Visual information processing*, New York: Academic, 1973.

Newell, A. Harpy, production systems and human cognition. In R. Cole, (Ed.), *Perception and Production of Fluent Speech*, Hillsdale, N.J.: Erlbaum, 1980.

Newell, A., & Simon, H. A. *Human problem solving*. Englewood Cliffs, NJ: Prentice-Hall, 1972.

Newell, A. & Simon, H. A. Computer science as empirical inquiry: Symbols and search. *Communications of the ACM*, 1976, *19*(3), 113–126.

Nilsson, N. *Principles of artificial intelligence*. Palo Alto, CA: Tioga, 1980.

Palmer, S. E. Fundamental aspects of cognitive representation. In Rosch, E. & Lloyd, B. B. (Ed.), *Cognition and Categorization*, Hillsdale, N.J.: Erlbaum, 1978.

Rulifson, J. F., Derksen, J. A.; & Waldinger, R. J. *QA4: A procedural calculus for intuitive reasoning*. Technical Report 73, Artificial Intelligence Center, Stanford Research Institute, 1972.

Rumelhart, D. E. *Introduction to human information processing*. New York: Wiley, 1977.

Waterman, D. A., & Hayes-Roth, F. (Eds.). *Pattern directed inference systems*. New York: Academic, 1978.

Whitenead. *Symbolism: Its meaning and effect*. New York: Macmillan, 1927.

Wilson, E. O. *Sociobiology: The new synthesis*. Cambridge, MA: Harvard University Press, 1975.

Winston, P. *Artificial intelligence*. Reading, MA: Addison-Wesley, 1977.

Yovits, M. C. & Cameron, S. (Eds.). *Self organizing systems*. New York: Pergamon, 1960.

Yovits, M. C., Jacobi, G. T., & Goldstein, G. D. (Eds.). *Self organizing systems 1962*. Washington, DC: Spartan, 1962.

Artificial Intelligence 47 (1991) 289–325
Elsevier

# A preliminary analysis of the Soar architecture as a basis for general intelligence

Paul S. Rosenbloom*

*Information Sciences Institute, University of Southern California, 4676 Admiralty Way, Marina del Rey, CA 90292-6695, USA*

John E. Laird

*Department of Electrical Engineering and Computer Science, University of Michigan, Ann Arbor, MI 48109, USA*

Allen Newell

*Department of Computer Science, Carnegie-Mellon University, Pittsburgh, PA 15213, USA*

Robert McCarl

*Department of Electrical Engineering and Computer Science, University of Michigan, Ann Arbor, MI 48109, USA*

Received May 1989

*Abstract*

Rosenbloom, P.S., J.E. Laird, A. Newell and R. McCarl, A primary analysis of the Soar architecture as a basis for general intelligence, Artificial Intelligence 47 (1991) 289–325.

In this article we take a step towards providing an analysis of the Soar architecture as a basis for general intelligence. Included are discussions of the basic assumptions underlying the development of Soar, a description of Soar cast in terms of the theoretical idea of multiple levels of description, an example of Soar performing multi-column subtraction, and three analyses of Soar: its natural tasks, the sources of its power, and its scope and limits

## Introduction

The central scientific problem of artificial intelligence (AI) is to understand what constitutes intelligent action and what processing organizations are

* Much of the work on this article was done while the first author was affiliated with the Knowledge Systems Laboratory, Department of Computer Science, Stanford University.

capable of such action. Human intelligence—which stands before us like a holy grail—shows to first observation what can only be termed *general intelligence*. A single human exhibits a bewildering diversity of intelligent behavior. The types of goals that humans can set for themselves or accept from the environment seem boundless. Further observation, of course, shows limits to this capacity in any individual—problems range from easy to hard, and problems can always be found that are too hard to be solved. But the general point is still compelling.

Work in AI has already contributed substantially to our knowledge of what functions are required to produce general intelligence. There is substantial, though certainly not unanimous, agreement about some functions that need to be supported: symbols and goal structures, for example. Less agreement exists about what mechanisms are appropriate to support these functions, in large part because such matters depend strongly on the rest of the system and on cost-benefit tradeoffs. Much of this work has been done under the rubric of AI tools and languages, rather than AI systems themselves. However, it takes only a slight shift of viewpoint to change from what is an aid for the programmer to what is structure for the intelligent system itself. Not all features survive this transformation, but enough do to make the development of AI languages as much substantive research as tool building. These proposals provide substantial ground on which to build.

The Soar project has been building on this foundation in an attempt to understand the functionality required to support general intelligence. Our current understanding is embodied in the Soar architecture [22, 26]. This article represents an attempt at describing and analyzing the structure of the Soar system. We will take a particular point of view—the description of Soar as a hierarchy of levels—in an attempt to bring coherence to this discussion.

The idea of analyzing systems in terms of multiple levels of description is a familiar one in computer science. In one version, computer systems are described as a sequence of levels that starts at the bottom with the device level and works up through the circuit level, the logic level, and then one or more program levels. Each level provides a description of the system at some level of abstraction. The sequence is built up by defining each higher level in terms of the structure provided at the lower levels. This idea has also recently been used to analyze human cognition in terms of levels of description [38]. Each level corresponds to a particular time scale, such as $\sim 100$ msec. and $\sim 1$ sec., with a new level occurring for each new order of magnitude. The four levels between $\sim 10$ msec. and $\sim 10$ sec. comprise the cognitive band (Fig. 1). The lowest cognitive level—at $\sim 10$ msec.—is the symbol-accessing level, where the knowledge referred to by symbols is retrievable. The second cognitive level—at $\sim 100$ msec.—is the level at which elementary deliberate operations occur; that is, the level at which encoded knowledge is brought to bear, and the most elementary choices are made. The third and fourth cognitive levels—at $\sim 1$ sec.

| Rational Band | . . . | |
|---|---|---|
| | ~10 sec. | Goal attainment |
| Cognitive Band | ~1 sec. | Simple operator composition |
| | ~100 msec. | Elementary deliberate operations |
| | ~10 msec. | Symbol accessing |
| Neural Band | . . . | |

Fig. 1. Partial hierarchy of time scales in human cognition.

and ~10 sec.—are the simple-operator-composition and goal-attainment levels. At these levels, sequences of deliberations can be composed to achieve goals. Above the cognitive band is the rational band, at which the system can be described as being goal oriented, knowledge-based, and strongly adaptive. Below the cognitive band is the neural band.

In Section 2 we describe Soar as a sequence of three cognitive levels: the memory level, at which symbol accessing occurs; the decision level, at which elementary deliberate operations occur; and the goal level, at which goals are set and achieved via sequences of decisions. The goal level is an amalgamation of the top two cognitive levels from the analysis of human cognition.

In this description we will often have call to describe mechanisms that are built into the architecture of Soar. The architecture consists of all of the fixed structure of the Soar system. According to the levels analysis, the correct view to be taken of this fixed structure is that it comprises the set of mechanisms provided by the levels underneath the cognitive band. For human cognition this is the neural band. For artificial cognition, this may be a connectionist band, though it need not be. This view notwithstanding, it should be remembered that it is the Soar architecture which is primary in our research. The use of the levels viewpoint is simply an attempt at imposing a particular, hopefully illuminating, theoretical structure on top of the existing architecture.

In the remainder of this paper we describe the methodological assumptions underlying Soar, the structure of Soar, an illustrative example of Soar's performance on the task of multi-column subtraction, and a set of preliminary analyses of Soar as an architecture for general intelligence.

## 1. Methodological assumptions

The development of Soar is driven by four methodological assumptions. It is not expected that these assumptions will be shared by all researchers in the field. However, the assumptions do help explain why the Soar system and project have the shapes that they do.

The first assumption is the utility of focusing on the cognitive band, as opposed to the neural or rational bands. This is a view that has traditionally been shared by a large segment of the cognitive science community; it is not, however, shared by the connectionist community, which focuses on the neural band (plus the lower levels of the cognitive band), or by the logicist and expert-systems communities, which focus on the rational band. This assumption is not meant to be exclusionary, as a complete understanding of general intelligence requires the understanding of all of these descriptive bands.[1] Instead the assumption is that there is important work to be done by focusing on the cognitive band. One reason is that, as just mentioned, a complete model of general intelligence will require a model of the cognitive band. A second reason is that an understanding of the cognitive band can constrain models of the neural and rational bands. A third, more applied reason, is that a model of the cognitive band is required in order to be able to build practical intelligent systems. Neural-band models need the higher levels of organization that are provided by the cognitive band in order to reach complex task performance. Rational-band models need the heuristic adequacy provided by the cognitive band in order to be computationally feasible. A fourth reason is that there is a wealth of both psychological and AI data about the cognitive band that can be used as the basis for elucidating the structure of its levels. This data can help us understand what type of symbolic architecture is required to support general intelligence.

The second assumption is that general intelligence can most usefully be studied by not making a distinction between human and artificial intelligence. The advantage of this assumption is that it allows wider ranges of research methodologies and data to be brought to bear to mutually constrain the structure of the system. Our research methodology includes a mixture of experimental data, theoretical justifications, and comparative studies in both artificial intelligence and cognitive psychology. Human experiments provide data about performance universals and limitations that may reflect the structure of the architecture. For example, the ubiquitous power law of practice— the time to perform a task is a power-law function of the number of times the task has been performed—was used to generate a model of human practice [39, 55], which was later converted into a proposal for a general artificial learning mechanism [27, 28, 61]. Artificial experiments—the application of implemented systems to a variety of tasks requiring intelligence—provide sufficiency feedback about the mechanisms embodied in the architecture and their interactions [16, 51, 60, 62, 73]. Theoretical justifications attempt to provide an abstract analysis of the requirements of intelligence, and of how various architectural mechanisms fulfill those requirements [38, 40, 49, 54, 56]. Comparative studies, pitting one system against another, provide an evaluation of how well the respective systems perform, as well as insight about how the capabilities of one of the systems can be incorporated in the other [6, 50].

---

[1] Investigations of the relationship of Soar to the neural and rational bands can be found in [38, 49, 56].

The third assumption is that the architecture should consist of a small set of orthogonal mechanisms. All intelligent behaviors should involve all, or nearly all, of these basic mechanisms. This assumption biases the development of Soar strongly in the direction of uniformity and simplicity, and away from modularity [10] and toolkit approaches. When attempting to achieve a new functionality in Soar, the first step is to determine in what ways the existing mechanisms can already provide the functionality. This can force the development of new solutions to old problems, and reveal new connections—through the common underlying mechanisms—among previously distinct capabilities [53]. Only if there is no appropriate way to achieve the new functionality are new mechanisms considered.

The fourth assumption is that architectures should be pushed to the extreme to evaluate how much of general intelligence they can cover. A serious attempt at evaluating the coverage of an architecture involves a long-term commitment by an extensive research group. Much of the research involves the apparently mundane activity of replicating classical results within the architecture. Sometimes these demonstrations will by necessity be strict replications, but often the architecture will reveal novel approaches, provide a deeper understanding of the result and its relationship to other results, or provide the means of going beyond what was done in the classical work. As these results accumulate over time, along with other more novel results, the system gradually approaches the ultimate goal of general intelligence.

## 2. Structure of Soar

In this section we build up much of Soar's structure in levels, starting at the bottom with memory and proceeding up to decisions and goals. We then describe how learning and perceptual-motor behavior fit into this picture, and wrap up with a discussion of the default knowledge that has been incorporated into the system.

### 2.1. Level 1: Memory

A general intelligence requires a memory with a large capacity for the storage of knowledge. A variety of types of knowledge must be stored, including declarative knowledge (facts about the world, including facts about actions that can be performed), procedural knowledge (facts about how to perform actions, and control knowledge about which actions to perform when), and episodic knowledge (which actions were done when). Any particular task will require some subset of the knowledge stored in the memory. Memory access is the process by which this subset is retrieved for use in task performance.

The lowest level of the Soar architecture is the level at which these memory phenomena occur. All of Soar's long-term knowledge is stored in a single production memory. Whether a piece of knowledge represents procedural, declarative, or episodic knowledge, it is stored in one or more productions. Each production is a condition-action structure that performs its actions when its conditions are met. Memory access consists of the execution of these productions. During the execution of a production, variables in its actions are instantiated with values. Action variables that existed in the conditions are instantiated with the values bound in the conditions. Action variables that did not exist in the conditions act as generators of new symbols.

The result of memory access is the retrieval of information into a global working memory. The working memory is a temporary memory that contains all of Soar's short-term processing context. Working memory consists of an interrelated set of objects with attribute-value pairs. For example, an object representing a green cat named Fred might look like (object o025 ^name fred ^type cat ^color green). The symbol o025 is the identifier of the object, a short-term symbol for the object that exists only as long as the object is in working memory. Objects are related by using the identifiers of some objects as attributes and values of other objects.

There is one special type of working memory structure, the preference. Preferences encode control knowledge about the acceptability and desirability of actions, according to a fixed semantics of preference types. Acceptability preferences determine which actions should be considered as candidates. Desirability preferences define a partial ordering on the candidate actions. For example, a better (or alternatively, worse) preference can be used to represent the knowledge that one action is more (or less) desirable than another action, and a best (or worst) preference can be used to represent the knowledge that an action is at least as good (or as bad) as every other action.

In a traditional production-system architecture, each production is a problem-solving operator (see, for example, [42]). The right-hand side of the production represents some action to be performed, and the left-hand side represents the preconditions for correct application of the action (plus possibly some desirability conditions). One consequence of this view of productions is that the productions must also be the locus of behavioral control. If productions are going to act, it must be possible to control which one executes at each moment; a process known as conflict resolution. In a logic architecture, each production is a logical implication. The meaning of such a production is that if the left-hand side (the antecedent) is true, then so is the right-hand side (the consequent).[2] Soar's productions are neither operators nor implications. Instead, Soar's productions perform (parallel) memory retrieval. Each produc-

---

[2] The directionality of the implication is reversed in logic programming languages such as Prolog, but the point still holds.

tion is a retrieval structure for an item in long-term memory. The right-hand side of the rule represents a long-term datum, and the left-hand side represents the situations in which it is appropriate to retrieve that datum into working memory. The traditional production-system and logic notions of action, control, and truth are not directly applicable to Soar's productions. All control in Soar is performed at the decision level. Thus, there is no conflict resolution process in the Soar production system, and all productions execute in parallel. This all flows directly from the production system being a long-term memory. Soar separates the retrieval of long-term information from the control of which act to perform next.

Of course it is possible to encode knowledge of operators and logical implications in the production memory. For example, the knowledge about how to implement a typical operator can be stored procedurally as a set of productions which retrieve the state resulting from the operator's application. The productions' conditions determine when the state is to be retrieved—for example, when the operator is being applied and its preconditions are met. An alternative way to store operator implementation knowledge is declaratively as a set of structures that are completely contained in the actions of one or more productions. The structures describe not only the results of the operator, but also its preconditions. The productions' conditions determine when to retrieve this declarative operator description into working memory. A retrieved operator description must be interpreted by other productions to actually have an affect.

In general, there are these two distinct ways to encode knowledge in the production memory: procedurally and declaratively. If the knowledge is procedurally encoded, then the execution of the production reflects the knowledge, but does not actually retrieve it into working memory—it only retrieves the structures encoded in the actions. On the other hand, if a piece of knowledge is encoded declaratively in the actions of a production, then it is retrievable in its entirety. This distinction between procedural and declarative *encodings* of knowledge is distinct from whether the knowledge is declarative (represents facts about the world) or procedural (represents facts about procedures). Moreover, each production can be viewed in either way, either as a procedure which implicitly represents conditional information, or as the indexed storage of declarative structures.

## 2.2. Level 2: Decisions

In addition to a memory, a general intelligence requires the ability to generate and/or select a course of action that is responsive to the current situation. The second level of the Soar architecture, the decision level, is the level at which this processing is performed. The decision level is based on the memory level plus an architecturally provided, fixed, decision procedure. The decision level proceeds in a two phase elaborate-decide cycle. During elaboration, the memory is accessed repeatedly, in parallel, until quiescence is reached; that is, until no more productions can execute. This results in the retrieval into working memory of all of the accessible knowledge that is relevant to the current decision. This may include a variety of types of information, but of most direct relevance here is knowledge about actions that can be performed and preference knowledge about what actions are acceptable and desirable. After quiescence has occurred, the decision procedure selects one of the retrieved actions based on the preferences that were retrieved into working memory and their fixed semantics.

The decision level is open both with respect to the consideration of arbitrary actions, and with respect to the utilization of arbitrary knowledge in making a selection. This openness allows Soar to behave in both plan-following and reactive fashions. Soar is following a plan when a decision is primarily based on previously generated knowledge about what to do. Soar is being reactive when a decision is based primarily on knowledge about the current situation (as reflected in the working memory).

## 2.3. Level 3: Goals

In addition to being able to make decisions, a general intelligence must also be able to direct this behavior towards some end; that is, it must be able to set and work towards goals. The third level of the Soar architecture, the goal level, is the level at which goals are processed. This level is based on the decision level. Goals are set whenever a decision cannot be made; that is, when the decision procedure reaches an impasse. Impasses occur when there are no alternatives that can be selected (*no-change* and *rejection* impasses) or when there are multiple alternatives that can be selected, but insufficient discriminating preferences exist to allow a choice to be made among them (*tie* and *conflict* impasses). Whenever an impasse occurs, the architecture generates the goal of resolving the impasse. Along with this goal, a new *performance context* is created. The creation of a new context allows decisions to continue to be made in the service of achieving the goal of resolving the impasse—nothing can be done in the original context because it is at an impasse. If an impasse now occurs in this subgoal, another new subgoal and performance context are created. This leads to a goal (and context) stack in which the top-level goal is to perform some task, and lower-level goals are to resolve impasses in problem solving. A subgoal is terminated when either its impasse is resolved, or some higher impasse in the stack is resolved (making the subgoal superfluous).

In Soar, all symbolic goal-oriented tasks are formulated in problem spaces. A problem space consists of a set of states and a set of operators. The states represent situations, and the operators represent actions which when applied to states yield other states. Each performance context consists of a goal, plus roles for a problem state, a state, and an operator. Problem solving is driven by decisions that result in the selection of problem spaces, states, and operators for their respective context roles. Given a goal, a problem space should be selected in which goal achievement can be pursued. Then an initial state should be selected that represents the initial situation. Then an operator should be selected for application to the initial state. Then another state should be selected (most likely the result of applying the operator to the previous state). This process continues until a sequence of operators has been discovered that transforms the initial state into a state in which the goal has been achieved. One subtle consequence of the use of problem spaces is that each one implicitly defines a set of constraints on how the task is to be performed. For example, if the Eight Puzzle is attempted in a problem space containing only a slide-tile operator, all solution paths maintain the constraint that the tiles are never picked up off of the board. Thus, such conditions need not be tested for explicitly in desired states.

Each problem solving decision—the selection of a problem space, a state, or an operator—is based on the knowledge accessible in the production memory. If the knowledge is both correct and sufficient, Soar exhibits highly controlled behavior; at each decision point the right alternative is selected. Such behavior is accurately described as being algorithmic or knowledge-intensive. However, for a general intelligence faced with a broad array of unpredictable tasks, situations will arise—inevitably and indeed frequently—in which the accessible knowledge is either incorrect or insufficient. It is possible that correct decisions will fortuitously be made, but it is more likely that either incorrect decisions will be made or that impasses will occur. Under such circumstances search is the likely outcome. If an incorrect decision is made, the system must eventually recover and get itself back on a path to the goal, for example, by backtracking. If instead an impasse occurs, the system must execute a sequence of problem space operators in the resulting subgoal to find (or generate) the information that will allow a decision to be made. This processing may itself be highly algorithmic, if enough control knowledge is available to uniquely determine what to do, or it may involve a large amount of further search.

As described earlier, operator implementation knowledge can be represented procedurally in the production memory, enabling operator implementation to be performed directly by memory retrieval. When the operator is selected, a set of productions execute that collectively build up the representation of the result state by combining data from long-term memory and the previous state. This type of implementation is comparable to the conventional implementation of an operator as a fixed piece of code. However, if operator implementation knowledge is stored declaratively, or if no operator implementation knowledge is stored, then a subgoal occurs, and the operator must be implemented by the execution of a sequence of problem space operators in the subgoal. If a declarative description of the to-be-implemented operator is available, then these lower operators may implement the operator by interpreting its declarative description (as was demonstrated in work on task acquisition in Soar [61]). Otherwise the operator can be implemented by decomposing it into a set of simpler operators for which operator implementation knowledge is available, or which can in turn be decomposed further.

When an operator is implemented in a subgoal, the combination of the operator and the subgoal correspond to the type of deliberately created subgoal common in AI problem solvers. The operator specifies a task to be performed, while the subgoal indicates that accomplishing the task should be treated as a goal for further problem solving. In complex problems, like computer configuration, it is common for there to be complex high-level operators, such as Configure-computer which are implemented by selecting problem spaces in which they can be decomposed into simpler tasks. Many of the traditional goal management issues—such as conjunction, conflict, and selection—show up as operator management issues in Soar. For example, a set of conjunctive subgoals can be ordered by ordering operators that later lead to impasses (and subgoals).

As described in [54], a subgoal not only represents a subtask to be performed, but it also represents an introspective act that allows unlimited amounts of meta-level problem-space processing to be performed. The entire working memory—the goal stack and all information linked to it—is available for examination and augmentation in a subgoal. At any time a production can examine and augment any part of the goal stack. Likewise, a decision can be made at any time for any of the goals in the hierarchy. This allows subgoal problem solving to analyze the situation that led to the impasse, and even to change the subgoal, should it be appropriate. One not uncommon occurrence is for information to be generated within a subgoal that instead of satisfying the subgoal, causes the subgoal to become irrelevant and consequently to disappear. Processing tends to focus on the bottom-most goal because all of the others have reached impasses. However, the processing is completely opportunistic, so that when appropriate information becomes available at a higher level, processing at that level continues immediately and all lower subgoals are terminated.

## 2.4. Learning

All learning occurs by the acquisition of chunks—productions that summarize the problem solving that occurs in subgoals [28]. The actions of a chunk represent the knowledge generated during the subgoal; that is, the results of the subgoal. The conditions of the chunk represent an access path to this knowledge, consisting of those elements of the parent goals upon which the results depended. The results of the subgoal are determined by finding the elements generated in the subgoal that are available for use in subgoals—an element is a result of a subgoal precisely because it is available to processes outside of the subgoal. The access path is computed by analyzing the traces of the productions that fired in the subgoal—each production trace effectively states that its actions depended on its conditions. This dependency analysis yields a set of conditions that have been implicitly generalized to ignore irrelevant aspects of the situation. The resulting generality allows chunks to transfer to situations other than the one in which it was learned. The primary system-wide effect of chunking is to move Soar along the space-time trade-off by allowing relevantly similar future decisions to be based on direct retrieval of information from memory rather than on problem solving within a subgoal. If the chunk is used, an impasse will not occur, because the required information is already available.

Care must be taken to not confuse the power of chunking as a learning mechanism with the power of Soar as a learning system. Chunking is a simple goal-based, dependency-tracing, caching scheme, analogous to explanation-based learning [4, 36, 50] and a variety of other schemes [55]. What allows Soar to exhibit a wide variety of learning behaviors are the variations in the types of subgoals that are chunked; the types of problem solving, in conjunction with the types and sources of knowledge, used in the subgoals; and the ways the chunks are used in later problem solving. The role that a chunk will play is determined by the type of subgoal for which it was learned. State-no-change, operator-tie, and operator-no-change subgoals lead respectively to state augmentation, operator selection, and operator implementation productions. The content of a chunk is determined by the types of problem solving and knowledge used in the subgoal. A chunk can lead to skill acquisition if it is used as a more efficient means of generating an already generatable result. A chunk can lead to knowledge acquisition (or knowledge level learning [5]) if it is used to make old/new judgments; that is, to distinguish what has been learned from what has not been learned [52, 53, 56].

## 2.5. Perception and motor control

One of the most recent functional additions to the Soar architecture is a perceptual-motor interface [75, 76]. All perceptual and motor behavior is mediated through working memory; specifically, through the state in the top problem solving context. Each distinct perceptual field has a designated attribute of this state to which it adds its information. Likewise, each distinct motor field has a designated attribute of the state from which it takes its commands. The perceptual and motor systems are autonomous with respect to each other and the cognitive system.

Encoding and decoding productions can be used to convert between the high-level structures used by the cognitive system, and the low-level structures used by the perceptual and motor systems. These productions are like ordinary productions, except that they examine only the perceptual and motor fields, and not any of the rest of the context stack. This autonomy from the context stack is critical, because it allows the decision procedure to proceed without waiting for quiescence among the encoding and decoding productions, which may never happen in a rapidly changing environment.

### 2.6. Default knowledge

Soar has a set of productions (55 in all) that provide default responses to each of the possible impasses that can arise, and thus prevent the system from dropping into a bottomless pit in which it generates an unbounded number of content-free performance contexts. Figure 2 shows the default production that allows the system to continue if it has no idea how to resolve a conflict impasse among a set of operators. When the production executes, it rejects all of the conflicting operators. This allows another candidate operator to be selected, if there is one, or for a different impasse to arise if there are no additional candidates. This default response, as with all of them, can be overridden by additional knowledge if it is available.

One large part of the default knowledge (10 productions) is responsible for setting up operator subgoaling as the default response to no-change impasses on operators. That is, it attempts to find some other state in the problem space to which the selected operators can be applied. This is accomplished by generating acceptable and worst preferences in the subgoal for the parent problem space. If another problem space is suggested, possibly for implementing the operator, it will be selected. Otherwise, the selection of the parent problem space in the subgoal enables operator subgoaling. A sequence of operators is then applied in the subgoal until a state is generated that satisfies the preconditions of an operator higher in the goal stack.

Another large part of the default knowledge (33 productions) is responsible for setting up lookahead search as the default response to tie impasses. This is accomplished by generating acceptable and worst preferences for the *selection* problem space. The selection problem space consists of operators that evaluate the tied alternatives. Based on the evaluations produced by these operators, default productions create preferences that break the tie and resolve the impasse. In order to apply the evaluation operators, domain knowledge must exist that can create an evaluation. If no such knowledge is available, a second impasse arises—a no-change on the evaluation operator. As mentioned earlier,

---

If there is an impasse because of an operator conflict
and there are no candidate problem spaces available
then reject the conflicting operators.

---

Fig. 2. A default production.

the default response to an operator no-change impasse is to perform operator subgoaling. However, for a no-change impasse on an evaluation operator this is overridden and a lookahead search is performed instead. The results of the lookahead search are used to evaluate the tied alternatives.

As Soar is developed, it is expected that more and more knowledge will be included as part of the basic system about how to deal with a variety of situations. For example, one area on which we are currently working is the provision of Soar with a basic arithmetical capability, including problem spaces for addition, multiplication, subtraction, division, and comparison. One way of looking at the existing default knowledge is as the tip of this large iceberg of background knowledge. However, another way to look at the default knowledge is as part of the architecture itself. Some of the default knowledge—how much is still unclear—must be innate rather than learned. The rest of the system's knowledge, such as the arithmetic spaces, should then be learnable from there.

## 3. Example: multi-column subtraction

Multi-column subtraction is the task we will use to demonstrate Soar. This task has three advantages. First, it is a familiar and simple task. This allows the details of Soar not to be lost in the complexities of understanding the task. Second, previous work has been done on modeling human learning of subtraction in the Sierra architecture [71]. Our implementation is inspired by the Sierra framework. Third, this task appears to be quite different from many standard search-intensive tasks common in AI. On the surface, it appears difficult to cast subtraction within the problem-space framework of Soar—it is, after all, a procedure. One might also think that chunking could not learn such a procedure. However, in this example, we will demonstrate that multi-column subtraction can be performed by Soar and that important parts of the procedure can be learned through chunking.

There exist many different procedures for performing multi-column subtraction. Different procedures result in different behaviors, both in the order in which scratch marks—such as borrowing notations—are made and in the type of mistakes that might be generated while learning [72]. For simplicity, we will demonstrate the implementation of just one of the many possible procedures. This procedure uses a borrowing technique that recursively borrows from a higher-order column into a lower-order column when the top number in the lower-order column is less than the bottom number.

### 3.1. A hierarchical subtraction procedure

One way to implement this procedure is via the processing of a goal hierarchy that encodes what must be done. Figure 3 shows a subtraction goal

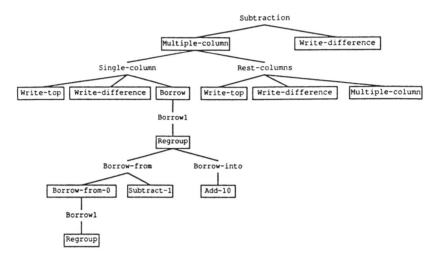

Fig. 3. A goal hierarchy for multi-column subtraction.

hierarchy that is similar to the one learned by Sierra.[3] Under each goal are shown the subgoals that may be generated while trying to achieve it. This Sierra goal hierarchy is mapped onto a hierarchy of operators and problem spaces in Soar (as described in Section 2). The boxed goals map onto operators and the unboxed goals map onto problem spaces. Each problem space consists of the operators linked to it from below in the figure. Operators that have problem spaces below them are implemented by problem solving in those problem spaces. The other operators are implemented directly at the memory level by productions (except for multiple-column and regroup, which are recursive). These are the primitive acts of subtraction, such as writing numbers or subtracting digits.

The states in these problem spaces contain symbolic representations of the subtraction problem and the scratch marks made on the page during problem solving. The representation is very simple and direct, being based on the spatial relationships among the digits as they would appear on a page. The state consists of a set of columns. Each column has pointers to its top and bottom digits. Additional pointers are generated when an answer for a column is produced, or when a scratch mark is made as the result of borrowing. The physical orientation of the columns on the page is represented by having "left" and "right" pointers from columns to their left and right neighbors. There is no inherent notion of multi-digit numbers except for these left and right relations between columns. This representation is consistent with the operators, which

---

[3] Sierra learned a slightly more elaborate, but computationally equivalent, procedure.

treat the problem symbolically and never manipulate multi-digit numbers as a whole.

Using this implementation of the subtraction procedure, Soar is able to solve all multi-column subtraction problems that result in positive answers. Unfortunately, there is little role for learning. Most of the control knowledge is already embedded in the productions that select problem spaces and operators. Within each problem space there are only a few operators from which to select. The preconditions of the few operators in each problem space are sufficient for perfect behavior. Therefore, goals arise only to implement operators. Chunking these goals produces productions that are able to compute answers without the intermediate subgoals.[4]

### 3.2. A single-space approach

One way to loosen up the strict control provided by the detailed problem-space/operator hierarchy in Fig. 3, and thus to enable the learning of the control knowledge underlying the subtraction procedure, is to have only a single subtraction problem space that contains all of the primitive acts (writing results, changing columns, and so on). Figure 4 contains a description of the

---

- *Operators*:
  **Write-difference:** If the difference between the top digit and the bottom digit of the current column is known, then write the difference as an answer to the current column.
  **Write-top:** If the lower digit of the current column is blank, then write the top digit as the answer to the current column.
  **Borrow-into:** If the result of adding 10 to the top digit of the current column is known, and the digit to the left of it has a scratch mark on it, then replace the top digit with the result.
  **Borrow-from:** If the result of subtracting 1 from the top digit in the current column is known, then replace that top digit with the result, augment it with a scratch mark and shift the current column to the right.
  **Move-left:** If the current column has an answer in it, shift the current column left.
  **Move-borrow-left:** If the current column does not have a scratch mark in it, shift the current column left.
  **Subtract-two-digits:** If the top digit is greater than or equal to the lower digit, then produce a result that is the difference.
  **Subtract-1:** If the top digit is not zero, then produce a result that is the top digit minus one.
  **Add 10:** Produce a result that is the top digit plus ten.
- *Goal Test*: If each column has an answer, then succeed.

Fig. 4. Primitive subtraction problem space.

---

[4] This work on subtraction was done in an earlier version of Soar that did not have the perceptual-motor interface described in Section 2. In that version, these chunks caused Soar to write out all of the column results and scratch marks in parallel—not very realistic motor behavior. To work around this problem, chunking was disabled for goals in this task during which environmental interactions occurred.

problem space operators and the goal test used in this second implementation. The operators can be grouped into four classes: the basic acts of writing answers to a single column problem (write-difference, write-top); borrow actions on the upper digits (borrow-into, borrow-from); moving from one column to the next (move-left, move-borrow-left); and performing very simple arithmetic computations (subtract-two-digits, subtract-1, add-10). With this simple problem space, Soar must learn the subtraction procedure by acquiring control knowledge that correctly selects operators.

Every operator in the subtraction problem space is considered for every state in the space. This is accomplished by having a production for each operator that generates an acceptable preference for it. The conditions of the production only test that the appropriate problem space (subtraction) is selected. Similar productions existed in the original implementation, except that those productions also contained additional tests which ensured that the operators would only be considered when they were the appropriate ones to apply.

In addition to productions which generate acceptable preferences, each operator has one or more productions which implement it. Although every operator is made acceptable for every state, an operator will actually be applied only if all of the conditions in the productions that implement it are satisfied. For example, write-difference will only apply if the difference between the top and bottom numbers is known. If an operator is selected, but the conditions of the productions that implement it are not satisfied, an impasse arises. As described in Section 2, the default response to this type of impasse is to perform operator subgoaling.

Figure 5 shows a trace of Soar's problem solving as it performs a simple two-column subtraction problem, after the learning of control knowledge has been completed. Because Soar's performance prior to learning on this problem is considerably more complicated, it is described after this simpler case. The

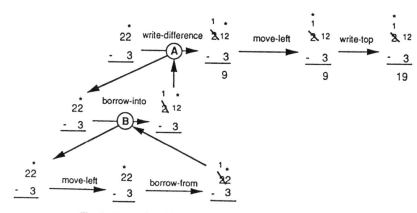

Fig. 5. Trace of problem solving after learning for 22 − 3.

top goal in this figure is to have the result of subtracting 3 from 22. Problem solving in the top goal proceeds from left to right, diving to a lower level whenever a subgoal is created in response to an impasse. Each state is a partially solved subtraction problem, consisting of the statement of the subtraction problem, a ∗ designating the current column, and possibly column results and/or scratch marks for borrowing. Operator applications are represented by arrows going from left to right. The only impasses that occur in this trace are a result of the failure of operator preconditions—a form of operator no-change impasse. These impasses are designated by circles disrupting the operator-application arrows, and are labeled in the order they arise (A and B). For example, impasse A arises because write-difference cannot apply unless the lower digit in the current column (3) is less than the top digit (2).

For impasse A, operator subgoaling occurs when the subtraction problem space is selected in the subgoal. The preconditions of the write-difference operator are met when a state has been generated whose top digit has been changed from 2 to 12 (by borrowing). Once this occurs, the subgoal terminates and the operator applies, in this case writing the difference between 12 and 3. In this implementation of subtraction, operator subgoaling dynamically creates a goal hierarchy that is similar to the one programmed into the original implementation.

### 3.3. Performance prior to learning

Prior to learning, Soar's problem solving on this task is considerably more complicated. This added complexity arises because of an initial lack of knowledge about the results of simple arithmetic computations and a lack of knowledge about which operators should be selected for which states. Figure 6

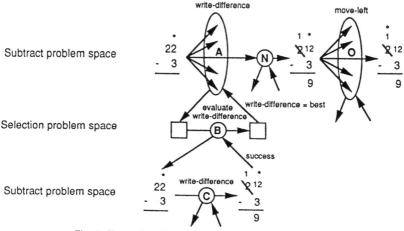

Fig. 6. Trace of problem solving before learning for 22 − 3.

shows a partial trace of Soar's pre-learning problem solving. Although many of the subgoals are missing, this small snapshot of the problem solving is characteristic of the impasses and subgoals that arise at all levels.

As before, the problem solving starts at the upper left with the initial state. As soon as the initial state is selected, a tie impasse (A) arises because all of the operators are acceptable and there are no additional preferences that distinguish between them. Default productions cause the selection space to be selected for this impasse. Within this space, operators are created to evaluate the tied operators. This example assumes that evaluate-object(write-difference) is selected, possibly based on advice from a teacher. Then, because there is no knowledge available about how to evaluate the subtraction operators, a no-change impasse (B) occurs for the evaluation operator. More default productions lead to a lookahead search by suggesting the original problem space (subtraction) and state and then selecting the operator that is being evaluated. The operator then applies, if it can, creating a new state. In this example, an operator subgoal impasse (C) arises when the attempt is made to apply the write-difference operator—its preconditions are not satisfied. Problem solving continues in this subgoal, requiring many additional impasses, until the write-difference operator can finally be applied. The lookahead search then continues until an evaluation is generated for the write-difference operator. Here, this happens shortly after impasse C is resolved. The system was given the knowledge that a state containing an answer for the current column is a (partial) success—such states are on the path to the goal. This state evaluation is then converted by default productions into an evaluation of "success" for the operator, and from there into a best preference for the operator. The creation of this preference breaks the operator tie, terminating the subgoals, and leading to the selection of the preferred operator (write-difference). The overall behavior of the system during this lookahead search is that of depth-first search—where backtracking occurs by subgoal termination—intertwined with operator subgoaling. Once this search is completed, further impasses (N) arise to actually apply the selected operator, but eventually, a solution is found.

One way in which multi-column subtraction differs from the classic AI search tasks is that the goal test is underspecified. As shown in Fig. 4, the goal test used here is that a result has been generated for each column of the problem. This determines whether some answer has been given for the problem, but is inadequate to determine whether the correct answer has been generated. The reason for this is that when solving a subtraction problem, the answer is in general not already available. It is theoretically (and practically) possible to use an addition procedure to test whether the subtraction procedure has generated the correct result. However, that corresponds to a deliberate strategy of "checking your work", rather than to the normal procedural goal test of determining whether the sequence of steps has been completed.

One consequence of having an underspecified goal test is that the combination of the problem space and goal test are not sufficient to ensure correct performance. Additional knowledge—the control knowledge which underlies the subtraction procedure—must also be provided in some form. VanLehn provided Sierra with worked-out examples which included the order in which the primitive external actions were to be performed [71]. The approach that we have taken is to provide advice to Soar [12] about which task operators it should evaluate first in the selection problem space. This ensures that the first answer generated during the lookahead search is the correct one.

## 3.4. *Learning in subtraction*

When chunking is used during subtraction problem solving, productions are created which reproduce the results of the subgoals in similar future situations. For the subgoals created because of tie impasses, the chunks create best preferences for the operators that led to the solution. These chunks essentially cache the results of the lookahead searches. A set of such chunks corresponds to a plan (or procedure)—they determine at every step what should be done—thus chunking converts Soar's behavior from search into plan (or procedure) following. When Soar is rerun on the same problem, the tie impasses do not arise and the solution is found directly, as in Fig. 5.

One important issue concerning the chunked productions is their generality. Does Soar only learn chunks that can apply to the exact same problem, or are the chunks general enough so that advice is no longer needed after a few subtraction problems have been completed? The answer is that the learned control chunks are quite general—so general that only one or two are required per operator. Once these chunks are acquired, Soar is able to solve perfectly all multi-column subtraction problems that have a positive answer. One sample control chunk for the borrow-into operator is shown in Fig. 7. Similar chunks are learned for each of the other major operators.

One reason for this generality is that operator subgoaling leads to a fine-grained goal hierarchy. There are a large number of relatively simple goals having to do with satisfying the preconditions of an operator. Because the problem solving for these goals is relatively minimal, the resulting chunks are quite general. A second reason for the generality of the learning is that the

---

If the super-operator is write-difference,
  and the bottom digit is greater than the top digit,
then make a best preference for borrow-into.

---

Fig. 7. A control chunk for borrow-into.

control chunks do not test for the specific digits used in the problems—if such tests were included, the chunks would transfer to many fewer problems.[5]

Though the control chunks that are learned are quite general, many specialized implementation chunks are also learned for the simple arithmetic operators. For example, the set of chunks that are eventually learned for the subtract-two-digits operator comprise a partial subtraction table for one- and two-digit numbers. Conceivably, these chunks could have been learned before multi-column subtraction is ever attempted—one may imagine that most of these simple digit manipulations are learned during earlier lessons on addition and single-column subtraction. Alternatively, these chunks can continue to be acquired as more multi-column subtraction problems are solved. The control chunks would all be acquired after a few trials, but learning of arithmetic knowledge would continue through later problems.

## 4. Analysis of Soar

There are a variety of analyses that could be performed for Soar. In this section we take our cue from the issues provided by the organizers of the 1987 Workshop on the Foundations of Artificial Intelligence [14]. We examine the set of tasks that are natural for Soar, the sources of its power, and its scope and limits.

### 4.1. Natural tasks

What does it mean for a task to be natural for an architecture? To answer this question we first must understand what a task is, and then what it means for such a task to be natural. By "task" we will mean any identifiable function, whether externally specified, or completely internal to the system. Computer configuration and maneuvering through an obstacle course are both tasks, and so are inheritance and skill acquisition. One way to define the idea of naturalness for a combination of a task and architecture is to say that a task is natural for an architecture if the task can be performed within the architecture without adding an extra level of interpretation within the software. This definition is appealing because it allows a distinction to be made between the tasks that the architecture can perform directly and those that can be done, but for which the architecture does not provide direct support. However, applying

---

[5] Chunking would include tests for the digits if their specific values were examined during the lookahead searches. However, the actual manipulation of the numbers is performed by the simple arithmetic operators: add-10, subtract-1 and subtract-two-digits. Before an operator such as write-difference is applied, an operator subgoal is created in which subtract-two-digits is selected and applied. The chunk for this subgoal reproduces the result whenever the same two digits are to be subtracted, eliminating the need for subtract-two-digits in such situations in the future. In the following lookahead searches, only pointers to the digits rather than the actual digits are ever tested, thereby leading to control chunks that are independent of the actual digits.

70

this definition is not without its problems. One problem is that, for any particular task, it is possible to replace the combination of an interpreter and its interpreted structures with a procedure that has the same effect. Some forms of learning—chunking, for example—do exactly this, by compiling interpreted structures into the structure of the interpreter. This has the effect of converting an unnatural task implementation into a natural one. Such a capability causes problems for the definition of naturalness—naturalness cannot be a fixed property of the combination of a task and an architecture—but it is actually a point is favor of architectures that can do such learning.

A second problem is that in a system that is itself built up in levels, as is Soar, different tasks will be performed at different levels. In Soar, tasks can be performed directly by the architecture, by memory retrieval, by a decision, or by goal-based problem solving. A task is implemented at a particular level if that level and all lower levels are involved, but the higher levels are not. For example, consider the task of inheritance. Inheritance is not directly implemented by the Soar architecture, but it can be implemented at the memory level by the firing of productions. This implementation involves the memory level plus the architecture (which implements the memory level), but not the decision or goal levels. Alternatively, inheritance could be implemented at the decision level, or even higher up at goal level. As the level of implementation increases, performance becomes more interpretive, but the model of computation explicitly includes all of these levels as natural for the system.

One way out of this problem is to have pre-theoretic notions about the level at which a particular task ought to be performable. The system is then natural for the task if it can be performed at that level, and unnatural if it must be implemented at a higher level. If, for example, the way inheritance works should be a function of the knowledge in the system, then the natural level for the capability is at the memory level (or higher).

In the remainder of this section we describe the major types of tasks that appear to us to be natural in Soar. Lacking any fundamental ways of partitioning the set of all tasks into principled categories, we will use a categorization based on four of the major functional capabilities of Soar: search-based tasks, knowledge-based tasks, learning tasks, and robotic tasks. The naturalness judgments for these task types are always based on assumptions about the natural level of implementation for a variety of subtasks within each type of task. We will try to be as clear as possible about the levels at which the subtasks are being performed, so that others may also be able to make these judgments for themselves.

### 4.1.1. Search-based tasks

Soar performs search in two qualitatively different ways: within context and across context. Within-context search occurs when Soar "knows" what to do at every step, and thus selects a sequence of operators and states without going into a subgoal. If it needs to backtrack in within-context search, and the states in the problem space are internal (rather than states of the outside world), it can do so by reselecting a previously visited state. Within-context search corresponds to doing the task, without lookahead, and recovering if anything goes wrong. Across-context search occurs when the system doesn't know what to do, and impasses arise. Successive states in the search show up in successively lower contexts. Backtracking occurs by terminating subgoals. Across-context search corresponds to lookahead search, hypothetical scenario generation, or simulation.

Various versions of Soar have been demonstrated to be able to perform over 30 different search methods [21, 25, 26]. Soar can also exhibit hybrid methods—such as a combination of hill-climbing and depth-first search or of operator subgoaling and depth-first search—and use different search methods for different problem spaces within the same problem.

Search methods are represented in Soar as method increments—productions that contain a small chunk of knowledge about some aspect of a task and its action consequences. For example, a method increment might include knowledge about how to compute an evaluation function for a task, along with the knowledge that states with better evaluations should be preferred. Such an increment leads to a form of hill climbing. Other increments lead to other search methods. Combinations of increments lead to mixed methods.

The basic search abilities of making choices and generating subgoals are provided by the architecture. Individual method increments are at the memory level, but control occurs at the decision level, where the results of all of the method increments can be integrated into a single choice. Some search knowledge, such as the selection problem space, exists at the goal level.

### 4.1.2. Knowledge-based tasks

Knowledge-based tasks are represented in Soar as a collection of interacting problem spaces (as are all symbolic goal-oriented tasks). Each problem space is responsible for a part of the task. Problem spaces interact according to the different goal-subgoal relationships that can exist in Soar. Within each problem space, the knowledge is further decomposed into a set of problem space components, such as goal testing, state initialization, and operator proposal [77]. These components, along with additional communication constructs, can then be encoded directly as productions, or can be described in a high-level problem space language called TAQL [77], which is then compiled down into productions. Within this overall problem space organization, other forms of organization—such as object hierarchies with inheritance—are implementable at the memory level by multiple memory accesses. Task performance is represented at the goal level as search in problem spaces.

Several knowledge-based tasks have been implemented in Soar, including the R1-Soar computer configuration system [51], the Cypress-Soar and Designer-Soar algorithm design systems [60, 62], the Neomycin-Soar medical diagnosis system [73], and the Merl-Soar job-shop scheduling system [16].

These five knowledge-based systems cover a variety of forms of both construction and classification tasks. Construction tasks involve assembling an object from pieces. R1-Soar—in which the task is to construct a computer configuration—is a good example of a construction task. Classification tasks involve selecting from among a set of objects. Neomycin-Soar—in which the task is to diagnose an illness—is a good example of a classification task.[6] In their simplest forms, both construction and classification occur at the decision level. In fact, they both occur to some extent within every decision in Soar—alternatives must be assembled in working-memory and then selected. These capabilities can require trivial amounts of processing, as when an object is constructed by instantiating and retrieving it from memory. They can also involve arbitrary amounts of problem solving and knowledge, as when the process of operator-implementation (or, equivalently, state-construction) is performed via problem solving in a subgoal.

### 4.1.3. Learning tasks

The architecture directly supports a form of experiential learning in which chunking compiles goal-level problem solving into memory-level productions. Execution of the productions should have the same effect as the problem solving would have had, just more quickly. The varieties of subgoals for which chunks are learned lead to varieties in types of productions learned: problem space creation and selection; state creation and selection; and operator creation, selection, and execution. An alternative classification for this same set of behaviors is that it covers procedural, episodic and declarative knowledge [56]. The variations in goal outcomes lead to both learning from success and learning from failure. The ability to learn about all subgoal results leads to learning about important intermediate results, in addition to learning about goal success and failure. The implicit generalization of chunks leads to transfer of learned knowledge to other subtasks within the same problem (within-trial transfer), other instances of the same problem (across-trial transfer), and other problems (across-task transfer). Variations in the types of problems performed in Soar lead to chunking in knowledge-based tasks, search-based, and robotic tasks. Variations in sources of knowledge lead to learning from both internal and external knowledge sources. A summary of many of the types of learning that have so far been demonstrated in Soar can be found in [61].

The apparent naturalness of these various forms of learning depends primarily on the appropriateness of the required problem solving. Towards the natural end of the spectrum is the acquisition of operator selection productions, in

---

[6] In a related development, as part of an effort to map the Generic Task approach to expert system construction onto Soar, the Generic Task for classification by establish-refine has been implemented in Soar as a general problem space [17].

which the problem solving consists simply of a search with the set of operators for which selection knowledge is to be learned. Towards the unnatural end of the spectrum is the acquisition of new declarative knowledge from the outside environment. Many systems employ a simple store command for such learning, effectively placing the capability at the memory level. In Soar, the capability is situated two levels further up, at the goal level. This occurs because the knowledge must be stored by chunking, which can only happen if the knowledge is used in subgoal-based problem solving. The naturalness of this learning in Soar thus depends on whether this extra level of interpretation is appropriate or not. It turns out that the problem solving that enables declarative learning in Soar takes the form of an understanding process that relates the new knowledge to what is already known. The chunking of this understanding process yields the chunks that encode the new knowledge. If it is assumed that new knowledge should always be understood to be learned, then Soar's approach starts to look more natural, and verbatim storage starts to look more inappropriate.

### 4.1.4. Robotic tasks

Robotic tasks are performed in Soar via its perceptual-motor interface. Sensors autonomously generate working memory structures representing what is being sensed, and motor systems autonomously take commands from working memory and execute them. The work on robotics in Soar is still very much in its infancy; however, in Robo-Soar [30], Soar has been successfully hooked up to the combination of a camera and a Puma arm, and then applied to several simple blocks-world tasks.[7] Low-level software converts the camera signal into information about the positions, orientations and identifying characteristics of the blocks. This perceptual information is then input to working memory, and further interpreted by encoding productions. Decoding productions convert the high-level robot commands generated by the cognitive system to the low-level commands that are directly understood by the controller for the robot arm. These low-level commands are then executed through Soar's motor interface.

Given a set of operators which generate motor commands, and knowledge about how to simulate the operators and about the expected positions of blocks following the actions, Robo-Soar is able to successfully solve simple blocks-world problems and to learn from its own behavior and from externally provided advice. It also can make use of a general scheme for recovering from incorrect knowledge [23] to recover when the unexpected occurs—such as when the system fails in its attempt to pick up a triangular prism—and to learn to avoid the failure in the future. Robo-Soar thus mixes planning (lookahead

---

[7] The work on Robo-Soar has been done in the newest major release of Soar (version 5) [24, 63], which differs in a number of interesting ways from the earlier versions upon which the rest of the results in this article are based.

search with chunking), plan execution and monitoring, reactivity, and error recovery (with replanning). This performance depends on all of the major components of the architecture, plus general background knowledge—such as how to do lookahead search and how to recover from errors—and specific problem spaces for the task.

## 4.2. Where the power resides

Soar's power and flexibility arise from at least four identifiable sources. The first source of power is the universality of the architecture. While it may seem that this should go without saying, it is in fact a crucial factor, and thus important to mention explicitly. Universality provides the primitive capability to perform any computable task, but does not by itself explain why Soar is more appropriate than any other universal architecture for knowledge-based, search-based, learning, and robotic tasks.

The second source of power is the uniformity of the architecture. Having only one type of long-term memory structure allows a single, relatively simple, learning mechanism to behave as a general learning mechanism. Having only one type of task representation (problem spaces) allows Soar to move continuously from one extreme of brute-force search to the other extreme of knowledge-intensive (or procedural) behavior without having to make any representational decisions. Having only one type of decision procedure allows a single, relatively simple, subgoal mechanism to generate all of the types of subgoals needed by the system.

The traditional downside of uniformity is weakness and inefficiency. If instead the system were built up as a set of specialized modules or agents, as proposed in [10, 34], then each of the modules could be optimized for its own narrow task. Our approach to this issue in Soar has been to go strongly with uniformity—for all of the benefits listed above—but to achieve efficiency (power) through the addition of knowledge. This knowledge can either be added by hand (programming) or by chunking.

The third source of power is the specific mechanisms incorporated into the architecture. The production memory provides pattern-directed access to large amounts of knowledge; provides the ability to use strong problem solving methods; and provides a memory structure with a small-grained modularity. The working memory allows global access to processing state. The decision procedure provides an open control loop that can react immediately to new situations and knowledge; contributes to the modularity of the memory by allowing memory access to proceed in an uncontrolled fashion (conflict resolution was a major source of nonmodularity in earlier production systems); provides a flexible control language (preferences); and provides a notion of impasse that is used as the basis for the generation of subgoals. Subgoals focus the system's resources on situations where the accessible knowledge is inadequate; and allow flexible meta-level processing. Problem spaces separate control from action, allowing them (control and action) to be reasoned about independently; provide a constrained context within which the search for a desired state can occur; provide the ability to use weak problem solving methods; and provide for straightforward responses to uncertainty and error (search and backtracking). Chunking acquires long-term knowledge from experience; compiles interpreted procedures into non-interpreted ones; and provides generalization and transfer. The perceptual-motor system provides the ability to observe and affect the external world in parallel with the cognitive activity.

The fourth source of power is the interaction effects that result from the integration of all of the capabilities within a single system. The most compelling results generated so far come about from these interactions. One example comes from the mixture of weak methods, strong methods, and learning that is found in systems like R1-Soar. Strong methods are based on having knowledge about what to do at each step. Because strong methods tend to be efficient and to produce high-quality solutions, they should be used whenever possible. Weak methods are based on searching to make up for a lack of knowledge about what should be done. Such methods contribute robustness and scope by providing the system with a fall-back approach for situations in which the available strong methods do not work. Learning results in the addition of knowledge, turning weak methods into strong ones. For example, in R1-Soar it was demonstrated how computer configuration could be cast as a search problem, how strong methods (knowledge) could be used to reduce search, how weak methods (subgoals and search) could be used to make up for a lack of knowledge, and how learning could add knowledge as the result of search.

Another interesting interaction effect comes from work on abstraction planning, in which a difficult problem is solved by first learning a plan for an abstract version of the problem, and then using the abstract plan to aid in finding a plan for the full problem [41, 57, 70, 69]. Chunking helps the abstraction planning process by recording the abstract plan as a set of operator-selection productions, and by acquiring other productions that reduce the amount of search required in generating a plan. Abstraction helps the learning process by allowing chunks to be learned more quickly—abstract searches tend to be shorter than normal ones. Abstraction also helps learning by enabling chunks to be more general than they would otherwise be—the chunks ignore the details that were abstracted away—thus allowing more transfer and potentially decreasing the cost of matching the chunks (because there are now fewer conditions).

### 4.3. Scope and limits

The original work on Soar demonstrated its capabilities as a general problem solver that could use any of the weak methods when appropriate, across a wide range of tasks. Later, we came to understand how to use Soar as the basis for knowledge-based systems, and how to incorporate appropriate learning and perceptual-motor capabilities into the architecture. These developments increased Soar's scope considerably beyond its origins as a weak-method problem solver. Our ultimate goal has always been to develop the system to the point where its scope includes everything required of a general intelligence. In this section we examine how far Soar has come from its relatively limited initial demonstrations towards its relatively unlimited goal. This discussion is divided up according to the major components of the Soar architecture, as presented in Section 2: memory, decisions, goals, learning, and perception and motor control.

### 4.3.1. Level 1: Memory

The scope of Soar's memory level can be evaluated in terms of the amount of knowledge that can be stored, the types of knowledge that can be represented, and the organization of the knowledge.

*Amount of knowledge.* Using current technology, Soar's production memory can support the storage of thousands of independent chunks of knowledge. The size is primarily limited by the cost of processing larger numbers of productions. Faster machines, improved match algorithms and parallel implementations [13, 65, 66] may raise this effective limit by several orders of magnitude over the next few years.

*Types of knowledge.* The representation of procedural and propositional declarative knowledge is well developed in Soar. However, we don't have well worked-out approaches to many other knowledge representation problems, such as the representation of quantified, uncertain, temporal, and episodic knowledge. The critical question is whether architectural support is required to adequately represent these types of knowledge, or whether such knowledge can be adequately treated as additional objects and/or attributes. Preliminary work on quantified [43] and episodic [56] knowledge is looking promising.

*Memory organization.* An issue which often gets raised with respect to the organization of Soar's memory, and with respect to the organization of production memories in general, is the apparent lack of a higher-order memory organization. There are no scripts [59], frames [33], or schemas [1] to tie fragments of related memory together. Nor are there any obvious hierarchical structures which limit what sets of knowledge will be retrieved at any point in time. However, Soar's memory does have an organization, which is derived from the structure of productions, objects, and working memory (especially the context hierarchy).

What corresponds to a schema in Soar is an object, or a structured collection of objects. Such a structure can be stored entirely in the actions of a single production, or it can be stored in a piecemeal fashion across multiple productions. If multiple productions are used, the schema as a unit only comes into existence when the pieces are all retrieved contemporaneously into working memory. The advantage of this approach is that it allows novel schemas to be created from fragments of separately learned ones. The disadvantage is that it may not be possible to determine whether a set of fragments all originated from a single schema.

What corresponds to a hierarchy of retrieval contexts in Soar are the production conditions. Each combination of conditions implicitly defines a retrieval context, with a hierarchical structure induced by the subset relationship among the combinations. The contents of working memory determines which retrieval contexts are currently in force. For example, problem spaces are used extensively as retrieval contexts. Whenever there is a problem solving context that has a particular problem space selected within it, productions that test for other problem space names are not eligible to fire in that context. This approach has worked quite well for procedural knowledge, where it is clear when the knowledge is needed. We have just begun to work on appropriate organizational schemes for episodic and declarative knowledge, where it is much less clear when the knowledge should be retrieved. Our initial approach has been based on the incremental construction, via chunking, of multi-production discrimination networks [53, 56]. Though this work is too premature for a thorough evaluation in the context of Soar, the effectiveness of discrimination networks in systems like Epam [7] and Cyrus [19] bodes well.

### 4.3.2. Level 2: Decisions

The scope of Soar's decision level can be evaluated in terms of its speed, the knowledge brought to bear, and the language of control.

*Speed.* Soar currently runs at approximately 10 decisions/second on current workstations such as a Sun4/280. This is adequate for most of the types of tasks we currently implement, but is too slow for tasks requiring large amounts of search or very large knowledge bases (the number of decisions per second would get even smaller than it is now). The principal bottleneck is the speed of memory access, which is a function of two factors: the cost of processing individually expensive productions (the *expensive chunks* problem) [67], and the cost of processing a large number of productions (the *average growth effect* problem) [64]. We now have a solution to the problem of expensive chunks which can guarantee that all productions will be cheap—the match cost of a production is at worst linear in the number of conditions [68]—and are working on other potential solutions. Parallelism looks to be an effective solution to the average growth effect problem [64].

*Bringing knowledge to bear.* Iterated, parallel, indexed access to the contents of long-term memory has proven to be an effective means of bringing knowledge to bear on the decision process. The limited power provided by this process is offset by the ability to use subgoals when the accessible knowledge is inadequate. The issue of devising good access paths for episodic and declarative knowledge is also relevant here.

*Control language.* Preferences have proven to be a flexible means of specifying a partial order among contending objects. However, we cannot yet state with certainty that the set of preference types embodied in Soar is complete with respect to all the types of information which ultimately may need to be communicated to the decision procedure.

### 4.3.3. Level 3: Goals

The scope of Soar's goal level can be evaluated in terms of the types of goals that can be generated and the types of problem solving that can be performed in goals. Soar's subgoaling mechanism has been demonstrated to be able to create subgoals for all of the types of difficulties that can arise in problem solving in problem spaces [21]. This leaves three areas open. The first area is how top-level goals are generated; that is, how the top-level task is picked. Currently this is done by the programmer, but a general intelligence must clearly have grounds—that is, motivations—for selecting tasks on its own. The second area is how goal interactions are handled. Goal interactions show up in Soar as operator interactions, and are normally dealt with by adding explicit knowledge to avoid them, or by backtracking (with learning) when they happen. It is not yet clear the extent to which Soar could easily make use of more sophisticated approaches, such as non-linear planning [2]. The third area is the sufficiency of impasse-driven subgoaling as a means for determining when meta-level processing is needed. Two of the activities that might fall under this area are goal tests and monitoring. Both of these activities can be performed at the memory or decision level, but when they are complicated activities it may be necessary to perform them by problem solving at the goal level. Either activity can be called for explicitly by selecting a "monitor" or "goal-test" operator, which can then lead to the generation of a subgoal. However, goals for these tasks do not arise automatically, without deliberation. Should they? It is not completely clear.

The scope of the problem solving that can be performed in goals can itself be evaluated in terms of whether problem spaces cover all of the types of performance required, the limits on the ability of subgoal-based problem solving to access and modify aspects of the system, and whether parallelism is possible. These points are addressed in the next three paragraphs.

*Problem space scope.* Problem spaces are a very general performance model. They have been hypothesized to underlie all human, symbolic, goal-oriented behavior [37]. The breadth of tasks that have so far been represented in problem spaces over the whole field of AI attests to this generality. One way of pushing this evaluation further is to ask how well probem spaces account for the types of problem solving performed by two of the principal competing paradigms: planning [2] and case-based reasoning [20].[8] Both of these paradigms involve the creation (or retrieval) and use of a data structure that represents a sequence of actions. In planning, the data structure represents the sequence of actions that the system expects to use for the current problem. In case-based reasoning, the data structure represents the sequence of actions used on some previous, presumably related, problem. In both, the data structure is used to decide what sequence of actions to perform in the current problem. Soar straightforwardly performs procedural analogues of these two processes. When it performs a lookahead search to determine what operator to apply to a particular state, it acquires (by chunking) a set of search control productions which collectively tell it which operator should be applied to each subsequent state. This set of chunks forms a procedural plan for the current problem. When a search control chunk transfers between tasks, a form of procedural case-based reasoning is occurring.

Simple forms of declarative planning and case-based reasoning have also been demonstrated in Soar in the context of an expert system that designs floor systems [47]. When this system discovers, via lookahead search, a sequence of operators that achieves a goal, it creates a declarative structure representing the sequence and returns it as a subgoal result (plan creation). This plan can then be used interpretively to guide performance on the immediate problem (plan following). The plan can also be retrieved during later problems and used to guide the selection of operators (case-based reasoning). This research does not demonstrate the variety of operations one could conceivably use to modify a partial or complete plan, but it does demonstrate the basics.

*Meta-level access.* Subgoal-based problem solving has access to all of the information in working memory—including the goal stack, problem spaces, states, operators, preferences, and other facts that have been retrieved or generated—plus any of the other knowledge in long-term memory that it can access. It does not have direct access to the productions, or to any of the data structures internal to the architecture. Nonetheless, it should be able to indirectly examine the contents of any productions that were acquired by chunking, which in the long run should be just about all of them. The idea is to reconstruct the contents of the production by going down into a subgoal and retracing the problem solving that was done when the chunk was learned. In this way it should be possible to determine what knowledge the production cached. This idea has not yet been explicitly demonstrated in Soar, but research on the recovery from incorrect knowledge has used a closely related approach [23].

The effects of problem solving are limited to the addition of information to

---

[8] The work on Robo-Soar also reveals Soar's potential to exhibit reactive planning [11]. The current version of Soar still has problems with raw speed and with the unbounded nature of the production match (the expensive chunks problem), but it is expected that these problems will be solved in the near future.

working memory. Deletion of working memory elements is accomplished by a garbage collector provided by the architecture. Productions are added by chunking, rather than by problem solving, and are never deleted by the system. The limitation on production creation—that it only occurs via chunking—is dealt with by varying the nature of the problem solving over which chunking occurs [56]. The limitation on production deletion is dealt with by learning new productions which overcome the effects of old ones [23].

*Parallelism.* Two principal sources of parallelism in Soar are at the memory level: production match and execution. On each cycle of elaboration, all productions are matched in parallel to the working memory, and then all of the successful instantiations are executed in parallel. This lets tasks that can be performed at the memory level proceed in parallel, but not so for decision-level and goal-level tasks.

Another principal source of parallelism is provided by the motor systems. All motor systems behave in parallel with respect to each other, and with respect to the cognitive system. This enables one form of task-level parallelism in which non-interfering external tasks can be performed in parallel. To enable further research on task-level parallelism we have added the experimental ability to simultaneously select multiple problem space operators within a single problem solving context. Each of these operators can then proceed to execute in parallel, yielding parallel subgoals, and ultimately an entire tree of problem solving contexts in which all of the branches are being processed in parallel. We do not yet have enough experience with this capability to evaluate its scope and limits.

Despite all of these forms of parallelism embodied in Soar, most implementations of the architecture have been on serial machines, with the parallelism being simulated. However, there is an active research effort to implement Soar on parallel computers. A parallelized version of the production match has been successfully implemented on an Encore Multimax, which has a small number (2–20) of large-grained processors [66], and unsuccessfully implemented on a Connection Machine [15], which has a large number (16 K–64 K) of small-grained processors [9]. The Connection Machine implementation failed primarily because a complete parallelization of the current match algorithm can lead to exponential space requirements. Research on restricted match algorithms may fix this problem in the future. Work is also in progress towards implementing Soar on message-passing computers [65].

### 4.3.4. Learning

In [61] we broke down the problem of evaluating the scope of Soar's learning capabilities into four parts: when can the architecture learn; from what can the architecture learn; what can the architecture learn; and when can the architecture apply learned knowledge. These points are discussed in Section 4.1, and need not be elaborated further here.

One important additional issue is whether Soar acquires knowledge that is at the appropriate level of generalization or specialization. Chunking provides a level of generality that is determined by a combination of the representation used and the problem solving performed. Under varying circumstances, this can lead to both overgeneralization [29] and overspecialization. The acquisition of overgeneral knowledge implies that the system must be able to recover from any errors caused by its use. One solution to this problem that has been implemented in Soar involves detecting that a performance error has occurred, determining what should have been done instead, and acquiring a new chunk which leads to correct performance in the future [23]. This is accomplished without examining or modifying the overgeneral production; instead it goes back down into the subgoals for which the overgeneral productions were learned.

One way to deal with overspecialization is to patch the resulting knowledge gaps with additional knowledge. This is what Soar does constantly—if a production is overspecialized, it doesn't fire in circumstances when it should, causing an impasse to occur, and providing the opportunity to learn an additional chunk that covers the missing case (plus possibly other cases). Another way to deal with overspecialized knowledge is to work towards acquiring more general productions. A standard approach is to induce general rules from a sequence of positive and negative examples [35, 45]. This form of generalization must occur in Soar by search in problem spaces, and though there has been some initial work on doing this [48, 58], we have not yet provided Soar with a set of problem spaces that will allow it to generate appropriate generalizations from a variety of sets of examples. So, Soar cannot yet be described as a system of choice for doing induction from multiple examples. On the other hand, Soar does generalize quite naturally and effectively when abstraction occurs [69]. The learned rules reflect whatever abstraction was made during problem solving.

Learning behaviors that have not yet been attempted in Soar include the construction of a model of the environment from experimentation in it [46], scientific discovery and theory formation [31], and conceptual clustering [8].

### 4.3.5. Perception and motor control

The scope of Soar's perception and motor control can be evaluated in terms of both its low-level I/O mechanisms and its high-level language capabilities. Both of these capabilities are quite new, so the evaluation must be even more tentative than for the preceding components.

At the low-level, Soar can be hooked up to multiple perceptual modalities (and multiple fields within each modality) and can control multiple effectors. The critical low-level aspects of perception and motor control are currently done in a standard procedural language outside of the cognitive system. The resulting system appears to be an effective testbed for research on high-level aspects of perception and motor-control. It also appears to be an effective testbed for research on the interactions of perception and motor control with other cognitive capabilities, such as memory, problem solving, and learning. However, it does finesse many of the hard issues in perception and motor control, such as selective attention, shape determination, object identification, and temporal coordination. Work is actively in progress on selective attention [74].

At the high end of I/O capabilities is the processing of natural language. An early attempt to implement a semantic grammar parser in Soar was only a limited success [44]. It worked, but did not appear to be the right long-term solution to language understanding in Soar. More recent work on NL-Soar has focused on the incremental construction of a model of the situation by applying comprehension operators to each incoming word [32]. Comprehension operators iteratively augment and refine the situation model, setting up expectations for the part of the utterance still to be seen, and satisfying earlier expectations. As a side effect of constructing the situation model, an utterance model is constructed to represent the linguistic structure of the sentence. This approach to language understanding has been successfully applied to acquiring task-specific problem spaces for three immediate reasoning tasks: relational reasoning [18], categorical syllogisms, and sentence verification [3]. It has also been used to process the input for these tasks as they are performed. Though NL-Soar is still far from providing a general linguistic capability, the approach has proven promising.

## 5. Conclusion

In this article we have taken a step towards providing an analysis of the Soar architecture as a basis for general intelligence. In order to increase understanding of the structure of the architecture we have provided a theoretical framework within which the architecture can be described, a discussion of methodological assumptions underlying the project and the system, and an illustrative example of its performance on a multi-column subtraction task. In order to facilitate comparisons between the capabilities of the current version of Soar and the capabilities required to achieve its ultimate goal as an architecture for general intelligence, we have described the natural tasks for the architecture, the sources of its power, and its scope and limits. If this article has succeeded, it should be clear that progress has been made, but that more work is still required. This applies equally to the tasks of developing Soar and analyzing it.

## Acknowledgement

This research was sponsored by the Defense Advanced Research Projects Agency (DOD) under contract N00039-86-C-0133 and by the Sloan Foundation. Computer facilities were partially provided by NIH grant RR-00785 to Sumex-Aim. The views and conclusions contained in this document are those of the authors and should not be interpreted as representing the official policies, either expressed or implied, of the Defense Advanced Research Projects Agency, the US Government, the Sloan Foundation, or the National Institutes of Health.

We would like to thank Beth Adelson, David Kirsh, and David McAllester for their helpful comments on an earlier draft of this article.

## References

[1] F.C. Bartlett, *Remembering: A Study in Experimental and Social Psychology* (Cambridge University Press, Cambridge, England, 1932).

[2] D. Chapman, Planning for conjunctive goals, *Artif. Intell.* **32** (1987) 333–377.

[3] H.H. Clark and W.G. Chase, On the process of comparing sentences against pictures, *Cogn. Psychol.* **3** (1972) 472–517.

[4] G. DeJong and R.J. Mooney, Explanation-based learning: an alternative view, *Mach. Learn.* **1** (1986) 145–176.

[5] T.G. Dietterich, Learning at the knowledge level, *Mach. Learn.* **1** (1986) 287–315.

[6] O. Etzioni and T.M. Mitchell, A comparative analysis of chunking and decision analytic control, in: *Proceedings AAAI Spring Symposium on Limited Rationality and AI*, Stanford, CA (1989).

[7] E.A. Feigenbaum and H.A. Simon, Epam-like models of recognition and learning, *Cogn. Sci.* **8** (1984) 305–336.

[8] D.H. Fisher and P. Langley, Approaches to conceptual clustering, in: *Proceedings IJCAI-85*, Los Angeles, CA (1985) 691–697.

[9] R. Flynn, Placing Soar on the connection machine, Prepared for and distributed at the AAAI Mini-Symposium "How Can Slow Components Think So Fast" (1988).

[10] J.A. Fodor, *The Modularity of Mind* (Bradford Books/MIT Press, Cambridge, MA, 1983).

[11] M.P. Georgeff and A.L. Lansky, Reactive reasoning and planning, in: *Proceedings AAAI-87*, Seattle, WA (1987) 677–682.

[12] A. Golding, P.S. Rosenbloom and J.E. Laird. Learning general search control from outside guidance, in: *Proceedings IJCAI-87*, Milan, Italy (1987).

[13] A. Gupta and M. Tambe, Suitability of message passing computers for implementing production systems, in: *Proceedings AAAI-88*, St. Paul, MN (1988) 687–692.

[14] C. Hewitt and D. Kirsh, Personal communication (1987).

[15] W.D. Hillis, *The Connection Machine* (MIT Press, Cambridge, MA, 1985).

[16] W. Hsu, M. Prietula and D. Steier, Merl-Soar: applying Soar to scheduling, in: *Proceedings Workshop on Artificial Intelligence Simulation, AAAI-88*, St. Paul, MN (1988) 81–84.

[17] T.R. Johnson, J.W. Smith Jr and B. Chandrasekaran, Generic Tasks and Soar, in: *Working Notes AAAI Spring Symposium on Knowledge System Development Tools and Languages*, Stanford, CA (1989) 25–28.

[18] P.N. Johnson-Laird, Reasoning by rule or model? in: *Proceedings 10th Annual Conference of the Cognitive Science Society*, Montreal, Que. (1988) 765–771.

[19] J.L. Kolodner, Maintaining order in a dynamic long-term memory, *Cogn. Sci.* **7** (1983) 243–280.

[20] J.L. Kolodner, ed., *Proceedings DARPA Workshop on Case-Based Reasoning*, Clearwater Beach, FL (1988).

[21] J.E. Laird, Universal subgoaling, Ph.D. thesis, Carnegie-Mellon University, Pittsburgh, PA (1983); also in: J.E. Laird, P.S. Rosenbloom and A. Newell, *Universal Subgoaling and Chunking: The Automatic Generation and Learning of Goal Hierarchies* (Kluwer, Hingham, MA, 1986).

[22] J.E. Laird, Soar user's manual (version 4), Tech. Rept. ISL-15, Xerox Palo Alto Research Center, Palo Alto, CA (1986).

[23] J.E. Laird, Recovery from incorrect knowledge in Soar, in: *Proceedings AAAI-88*, St. Paul, MN (1988) 618–623.

[24] J.E. Laird and K.A. McMahon, Destructive state modification in Soar, Draft V, Department of EECS, University of Michigan, Ann Arbor, MI (1989).

[25] J.E. Laird and A. Newell, A universal weak method, Tech. Rept. 83-141, Department of Computer Science, Carnegie-Mellon University, Pittsburgh, PA (1983).

[26] J.E. Laird, A. Newell and P.S. Rosenbloom, SOAR: an architecture for general intelligence, *Artif. Intell.* 33 (1987) 1–64.

[27] J.E. Laird, P.S. Rosenbloom and A. Newell, Towards chunking as a general learning mechanism, in: *Proceedings AAAI-84*, Austin, TX (1984) 188–192.

[28] J.E. Laird, P.S. Rosenbloom and A. Newell, Chunking in Soar: the anatomy of a general learning mechanism, *Mach. Learn.* 1 (1986) 11–46.

[29] J.E. Laird, P.S. Rosenbloom and A. Newell, Overgeneralization during knowledge compilation in Soar, in: T.G. Dietterich, ed., *Proceedings Workshop on Knowledge Compilation*, Otter Crest, OR (1986).

[30] J.E. Laird, E.S. Yager, C.M. Tuck and M. Hucka, Learning in tele-autonomous systems using Soar, in: *Proceedings NASA Conference on Space Telerobotics*, Pasadena, CA (1989).

[31] P. Langley, H.A. Simon, G.L. Bradshaw and J.M. Zytkow, *Scientific Discovery: Computational Explorations of the Creative Processes* (MIT Press, Cambridge, MA, 1987).

[32] R.L. Lewis, A. Newell and T.A. Polk, Toward a Soar theory of taking instructions for immediate reasoning tasks, in: *Proceedings 11th Annual Conference of the Cognitive Science Society*, Ann Arbor, MI (1989).

[33] M. Minsky, A framework for the representation of knowledge, in: P. Winston, ed., *The Psychology of Computer Vision* (McGraw-Hill, New York, 1975).

[34] M. Minsky, *The Society of Mind* (Simon and Schuster, New York, 1986).

[35] T.M. Mitchell, Generalization as search, *Artif. Intell.* 18 (1982) 203–226.

[36] T.M. Mitchell, R.M. Keller and S.T. Kedar-Cabelli, Explanation-based generalization: a unifying view, *Mach. Learn.* 1 (1986) 47–80.

[37] A. Newell, Reasoning, problem solving and decision processes: the problem space as a fundamental category, in: R. Nickerson, ed., *Attention and performance* 8 (Erlbaum, Hillsdale, NJ, 1980).

[38] A. Newell, *Unified Theories of Cognition* (Harvard University Press, Cambridge, MA, 1990).

[39] A. Newell and P.S. Rosenbloom, Mechanisms of skill acquisition and the law of practice, in: J.R. Anderson, ed., *Cognitive Skills and Their Acquisition* (Erlbaum, Hillsdale, NJ, 1981) 1–55.

[40] A. Newell, P.S. Rosenbloom and J.E. Laird, Symbolic architectures for cognition, in: M.I. Posner, ed., *Foundations of Cognitive Science* (Bradford Books/MIT Press, Cambridge, MA, 1989).

[41] A. Newell and H.A. Simon, *Human Problem Solving* (Prentice-Hall, Englewood Cliffs, NJ, 1972).

[42] N.J. Nilsson, *Principles of Artificial Intelligence* (Tioga, Palo Alto, CA, 1980).

[43] T.A. Polk and A. Newell, Modeling human syllogistic reasoning in Soar, in: *Proceedings 10th Annual Conference of the Cognitive Science Society*, Montreal, Que. (1988) 181–187.

[44] L. Powell, Parsing the picnic problem with a Soar3 implementation of Dypar-1, Department of Computer Science, Carnegie-Mellon University, Pittsburgh, PA (1984).

[45] J.R. Quinlan, Induction of decision trees, *Mach. Learn.* 1 (1986) 81–106.

[46] S. Rajamoney, G.F. DeJong, and B. Faltings, Towards a model of conceptual knowledge

acquisition through directed experimentation, in: *Proceedings IJCAI-85*, Los Angeles, CA (1985) 688–690.

[47] Y. Reich, Learning plans as a weak method for design, Department of Civil Engineering, Carnegie-Mellon University, Pittsburgh, PA (1988).

[48] P.S. Rosenbloom, Beyond generalization as search: towards a unified framework for the acquisition of new knowledge, in: G.F. DeJong, ed., *Proceedings AAAI Symposium on Explanation-Based Learning*, Stanford, CA (1988) 17–21.

[49] P.S. Rosenbloom, A symbolic goal-oriented perspective on connectionism and Soar, in: R. Pfeifer, Z. Schreter, F. Fogelman-Soulie and L. Steels, eds., *Connectionism in Perspective* (Elsevier, Amsterdam, 1989).

[50] P.S. Rosenbloom and J.E. Laird., Mapping explanation-based generalization onto Soar, in: *Proceedings AAAI-86*, Philadelphia, PA (1986) 561–567.

[51] P.S. Rosenbloom, J.E. Laird, J. McDermott, A. Newell and E. Orciuch, R1-Soar: an experiment in knowledge-intensive programming in a problem-solving architecture, *IEEE Trans. Pattern Anal. Mach. Intell.* **7** (1985) 561–569.

[52] P.S. Rosenbloom, J.E. Laird and A. Newell, Knowledge level leaning in Soar, in: *Proceedings AAAI-87*, Seattle, WA (1987) 499–504.

[53] P.S. Rosenbloom, J.E. Laird and A. Newell, The chunking of skill and knowledge, in: B.A.G. Elsendoorn and H. Bouma, eds., *Working Models of Human Perception* (Academic Press, London, 1988) 391–410.

[54] P.S. Rosenbloom, J.E. Laird and A. Newell, Meta-levels in Soar, in: P. Maes and D. Nardi, eds., *Meta-Level Architectures and Reflection* (North-Holland, Amsterdam, 1988) 227–240.

[55] P.S. Rosenbloom and A. Newell, The chunking of goal hierarchies: a generalized model of practice, in: R.S. Michalski, J.G. Carbonnell and T.M. Mitchell, eds., *Machine Learning: An Artificial Intelligence Approach* **2** (Morgan Kaufmann, Los Altos, CA, 1986) 247–288.

[56] P.S. Rosenbloom, A. Newell and J.E. Laird, Towards the knowledge level in Soar: the role of the architecture in the use of knowledge, in: K. VanLehn, ed., *Architectures for Intelligence* (Erlbaum, Hillsdale, NJ, 1990).

[57] E.D. Sacerdoti, Planning in a hierarchy of abstraction spaces, *Artif. Intell.* **5** (1974) 115–135.

[58] R.H. Saul, A Soar2 implementation of version-space inductive learning, Department of Computer Science, Carnegie-Mellon University, Pittsburgh, PA (1984).

[59] R. Schank and R. Ableson, *Scripts, Plans, Goals and Understanding* (Erlbaum, Hillsdale, NJ, 1977).

[60] D. Steier, Cypress-Soar: a case study in search and learning in algorithm design, in: *Proceedings IJCAI-87*, Milan, Italy (1987) 327–330.

[61] D.M. Steier, J.E. Laird, A. Newell, P.S. Rosenbloom, R. Flynn, A Golding, T.A. Polk, O.G. Shivers, A. Unruh and G.R. Yost, Varieties of learning in Soar: 1987, in: P. Langley, ed., *Proceedings Fourth International Workshop on Machine Learning*, Irvine, CA (1987) 300–311.

[62] D.M. Steier and A. Newell, Integrating multiple sources of knowledge in Designer-Soar: an automatic algorithm designer, in: *Proceedings AAAI-88*, St. Paul, MN (1988) 8–13.

[63] K.R. Swedlow and D.M. Steier, Soar 5.0 user's manual, School of Computer Science, Carnegie Mellon University, Pittsburgh, PA (1989).

[64] M. Tambe, Speculations on the computational effects of chunking, Department of Computer Science, Carnegie Mellon University, Pittsburgh, PA (1988).

[65] M. Tambe, A. Acharya and A. Gupta, Implementation of production systems on message passing computers: Simulation results and analysis, Tech. Rept. CMU-CS-89-129, School of Computer Science, Carnegie Mellon University, Pittsburgh, PA (1989).

[66] M. Tambe, D. Kalp, A. Gupta, C.L. Forgy, B. Milnes and A. Newell, Soar/PSM-E: Investigating match parallelism in a learning production system, in: *Proceedings ACM/SIGPLAN Symposium on Parallel Programming: Experience with Applications, Languages, and Systems* (1988) 146–161.

[67] M. Tambe and A. Newell, Some chunks are expensive, in: J. Laird, ed., *Proceedings Fifth International Conference on Machine Learning* Ann Arbor, MI (1988) 451–458.

[68] M. Tambe and P.S. Rosenbloom, Eliminating expensive chunks by restricting expressiveness, in: *Proceedings IJCAI-89*, Detroit, MI (1989).

[69] A. Unruh and P.S. Rosenbloom, Abstraction in problem solving and learning, in: *Proceedings IJCAI-89*, Detroit, MI (1989).

[70] A. Unruh, P.S. Rosenbloom and J.E. Laird, Dynamic abstraction problem solving in Soar, in: *Proceedings Third Annual Aerospace Applications of Artificial Intelligence Conference*, Dayton, OH (1987) 245–256.

[71] K. VanLehn, *Mind Bugs: The Origins of Procedural Misconceptions* (MIT Press, Cambridge, MA, 1990).

[72] K. VanLehn and W. Ball, Non-LIFO execution of cognitive procedures, *Cogn. Sci.* 13 (1989) 415–465.

[73] R. Washington and P.S. Rosenbloom, Applying problem solving and learning to diagnosis, Department of Computer Science, Stanford University, CA (1988).

[74] M. Wiesmeyer, Personal communication (1988).

[75] M. Wiesmeyer, Soar I/O reference manual, version 2, Department of EECS, University of Michigan, Ann Arbor, MI (1988).

[76] M. Wiesmeyer, New and improved Soar IO, Department of EECS, University of Michigan, Ann Arbor, MI (1989).

[77] G.R. Yost and A. Newell, A problem space approach to expert system specification, in: *Proceedings IJCAI-89*, Detroit, MI (1989).

Artificial Intelligence 47 (1991) 327–346
Elsevier

# Approaches to the study of intelligence

Donald A. Norman

*Department of Cognitive Science A-015, University of California, San Diego, La Jolla,
CA 92093, USA*

Received April 1990

*Abstract*

Norman, D.A., Approaches to the study of intelligence, Artificial Intelligence 47 (1991)
327–346.

How can human and artificial intelligence be understood? This paper reviews Rosenbloom,
Laird, Newell, and McCarl's overview of Soar, their powerful symbol-processing simulation
of human intelligence. Along the way, the paper addresses some of the general issues to be
faced by those who would model human intelligence and suggests that the methods most
effective for creating an artificial intelligence might differ from those for modeling human
intelligence. Soar is an impressive piece of work, unmatched in scope and power, but it is
based in fundamental ways upon Newell's "physical symbol system hypothesis"—any
weaknesses in the power or generality of this hypothesis as a fundamental, general
characteristic of human intelligence will affect the interpretation of Soar. But our understanding of the mechanisms underlying human intelligence is now undergoing rapid change
as new, neurally-inspired computational methods become available that are dramatically
different from the symbol-processing approaches that form the basis for Soar. Before we can
reach a final conclusion about Soar we need more evidence about the nature of human
intelligence. Meanwhile, Soar provides an impressive standard for others to follow. Those
who disagree with Soar's assumptions need to develop models based upon alternative
hypotheses that match Soar's achievements. Whatever the outcome, Soar represents a
major advance in our understanding of intelligent systems.

## Introduction

> Human intelligence . . . stands before us like a holy Grail—Rosen-
> bloom, Laird, Newell, and McCarl. [17]

How can human intelligence be understood? The question is an old one, but
age does not necessarily lead to wisdom, at least not in the sense that
long-standing interest has led to a large body of accumulated knowledge and
understanding. The work under discussion here, Soar, attempts to provide an
advance in our understanding by providing a tool for the simulation of thought,

thereby providing a theoretical structure of how human intelligence might operate.

Soar has a lofty mission: providing a critical tool for the study of human cognition. The goal is most clearly stated by Allen Newell in his William James lectures "Unified theories of cognition". Newell thought the statement important enough to present it twice, both as the first paragraph of the first chapter and then as the final paragraph of the final chapter:

> Psychology has arrived at the possibility of unified theories of cognition—theories that gain their power by having a single system of mechanisms that operate together to produce the full range of cognition.

> I do not say they are here. But they are within reach and we should strive to attain them. (Newell [11])

Soar represents the striving. Among other things, Soar hopes to provide a coherent set of tools that can then be used by the research community in a variety of ways. Soar is built upon a number of fundamental assumptions about the nature of human cognition: within the broad range of theories subsumed under these assumptions, Soar can provide powerful and important benefits. Prime among the assumptions is that the fundamental basis for intelligent behavior is a physical symbol system.

In this paper I examine the power and promise of Soar from the point of view of a cognitive scientist interested in human cognition. The emphasis, therefore, is not on Soar's capabilities as a system of artificial intelligence as much as its ability to simulate the behavior of humans and to enhance our understanding of human cognition. The goal is to provide a friendly, constructive critique, for the goal of Soar is one all cognitive scientists must share, even if there is disagreement about the underlying assumptions. Because of the wide scope and generality of Soar, it can only be examined by asking about fundamental issues in the study of intelligence, issues that lie at the foundations of artificial intelligence, of psychology, and of cognitive science.

## 1. Psychology and the study of human cognition

Psychology tends to be a critical science. It has grown up in a rich and sophisticated tradition of carefully controlled experimentation, the power of the analysis of variance as the statistical tool, and counterbalanced conditions as the experimental tool. Occam's Razor is held in esteem—no theory is allowed to be more complex than it need be. This is a reasonable criterion if several competing theories all attempt to account for the same phenomena. However, because of psychology's emphasis on a theory for every experimental result, the interpretation has caused a proliferation of very simple theories for very simple phenomena. There is a strong bias against theories such as Soar—they are more complex than the community is willing to accept, even when the range is extremely broad and comprehensive.

There is another negative tendency within psychology. Students are taught to be critics of experimental design: give students any experiment and they will find flaws. Graduate seminars in universities are usually devoted to detailed analyses of papers, ripping them apart point-by-point. Each paper provides the stimulation for new experimental work, each responding to the perceived flaws in the previous work. As a result, the field is self-critical, self-sustaining. Experiments seem mainly to be responses to other experiments. It is rare for someone to look back over the whole body of previous work in order to find some overall synthesis, rare to look over the whole field and ask where it is going.

With so much careful experimentation in psychology, surely there ought to be a place for compiling and understanding the systematic body of knowledge. This goal is shared by many, but it is especially difficult in psychology for there has been no systematic effort to compile these data, and the data are often collected through experimental methods different enough from one another to confound any simple compilation.

Why do we have this state of affairs? In part because of the extreme difficulties faced by those who study human behavior. The phenomena are subtle, for people are sensitive to an amazing range of variables. Experimental scientists over the years have found themselves fooled by apparent phenomena that turned out to be laboratory artifacts. We are trained to beware of "Clever Hans", the nineteenth century counting horse, certified as legitimate by a committee of eminent scientists. Alas, Hans couldn't count at all: he responded to subtle, unconscious cues from his audience. Modern experimental rigor is designed to avoid these and countless other pitfalls.

The resulting caution may, however, be an over-reaction. Complete control can only be found in the laboratory, but of necessity, a laboratory experiment has to simplify the conditions that are to be studied, both in order to control all the factors that are not of immediate interest and so that one can make precise measurements of behavior. But the simplification of the environment may have eliminated critical environmental structure, thereby changing the task that the person is performing. And the simplifications of the response measure may mean that the real behavior of interest is missed. Perhaps the emphasis on experimental rigor and control has led to measurements of the wrong variables?

Soar wades into the psychological arena by proposing a coherent, systematic way to evaluate the experimental data that now exist. It takes those data seriously and suggests that the difficulty in providing cohesion in the past has more to do with the limited theoretical tools available than with the nature of the data. Soar proposes to provide a "unified theory of cognition".

## 2. Toward a unified theory of cognition[1]

The lack of systematic, rich data in psychology has led many in AI to rely on introspection and "common sense" as evidence. But common sense is "folk-psychology" and it does not have a good reputation among behavioral scientists as a source of legitimate measures of behaviour. In order to improve the quality of theory in cognitive science in general, there needs to be a systematic, cumulative set of reliable and relevant experimental data. Yet in psychology, there has been surprisingly little building upon previous work, little "cumulative science". Why this lack? The developers of Soar suggest that the difficulty results from the lack of good theoretical tools that would allow one generation of researchers to build upon the work of the previous generation. One important gap is a set of modeling tools, tools that permit one to evaluate theoretical assumptions against empirical research in a systematic, constructive fashion.

Soar is really an attempt to do psychology differently than the way it has usually been done. It provides a set of general mechanisms that are postulated to range over all the relevant phenomena of cognition. The idea is to provide concrete mechanisms that can be tested against the known phenomena and data of psychology. When Soar fails, this will point to a deficiency in the theory, leading to refinement of the mechanisms: truly a cumulative approach to theory building. In this method, not only the data, but also the inner structure of the theory has its say (see Newell's famous analysis "You can't play 20 questions with nature and win" [9]).

The problem for such theory-building in psychology is that any given theory never quite gets the phenomenon right. That would normally be alright if there was agreement that the attempt provides useful information. But in the culture of modern day psychology, the response to such theories is "See, it doesn't account for Y, so it's wrong." The developers of Soar advocate the more constructive approach of using the misfits to guide the future development: "Yes, it accounts for X, but not for Y—I wonder what we would need to change to make it handle Y better?" "Don't bite my finger", says Allen Newell, "but look at where it is pointing."

In this review I follow the spirit of Newell's admonition: I do not bite at Soar, but rather, I examine the direction in which it points. Of course, I was also trained as a psychologist, so at times, the review may seem more critical than supportive. But the critiques are meant to be constructive, to state where I feel the more fundamental problems lie.

I do not examine the details of the (very) large number of papers and demonstrations of Soar that have now appeared. Rather I focus on the

---

[1] This section has gained much from discussions with Paul Rosenbloom, Allen Newell, and Stu Card. Some of the material was inspired by an e-mail interaction with Stu Card.

overriding philosophy and method of approach. I conclude that for those who travel in this direction, Soar provides the most systematic, most thoughtful approach to the terrain. However, I will also question whether the direction of travel is appropriate, or perhaps, whether it might not be important to examine several different paths along the terrain of human cognition.

## 3. Soar

### 3.1. An overview of Soar

The study of human intelligence requires the expertise of many disciplines ranging in level from that of the individual cell to that of societies and cultures. Soar aims at an in-between level, one that it calls the *cognitive band*. Soar is built upon a foundation of cognitive theory, and even the choice of levels at which it operates has a theoretical basis, in this case an analysis of the time-frame of intelligent systems. Newell ([10]; also see [12]) has argued that different levels of scientific disciplines study phenomena that lie within different time frames. According to this argument, cognitive events take place in the time bands that lie between 10 msec and 10 sec., and it is in this region that Soar aims to provide an appropriate theoretical basis (see [17, Fig. 1]). Not all events relevant to human intelligence lie within this band, of course. Events that occur with a time scale less than 10 msec. are relevant to the computational or neural base. Thus, this is the region studied by those interested in architecture; it is where the connectionist systems work. Events that take place with a time scale greater than 10 sec. are most relevant to rational cognition, to the use of logic or rule-following, as in expert systems where the system operates by following rules stated within its knowledge base.

Soar stakes out the middle ground, that of the cognitive band. At the lower levels of its operation it overlaps within studies of the neural band: Soar makes no claims about this level and tries to be compatible with all approaches, including (especially?) connectionist approaches (e.g., [16]). At the higher levels, Soar attempts to match up with the rational band and the logicist and expert system communities.

### 3.2. Soar's assumptions

Soar builds upon a number of assumptions and like all theories, how you evaluate it depends to a large extent upon how well you accept these basic premises. The basic premises are these:

(1) That psychological evidence should be taken seriously.
(2) That intelligence must be realized through a representational system based upon a physical symbol system.

(3) That intelligent activity is goal-oriented, symbolic activity.
(4) That all intelligent activity can be characterized as search through a problem space.
(5) That there is a single, universal architecture.
(6) That the architecture is uniform, with but a single form of long-term memory.
(7) That there is a single, universal learning mechanism.
(8) That much of the general power can come from an automatic subgoal mechanism.
(9) That the system derives its power from a combination of weak methods plus integration into a single system.

In addition, research on Soar is driven by four methodological assumptions:

(M1) That in the search for a general understanding of cognition, one should focus on the cognitive band, not on the neural or rational bands.
(M2) That general intelligence can be studied most usefully by not distinguishing between human and artificial intelligence.
(M3) That the architecture should consist of a small set of orthogonal mechanisms, with all intelligent behavior involving all or nearly all of these basic mechanisms.
(M4) Architectures should be pushed to the extreme to see how much general intelligence they can cover.

These assumptions arise for a combination of reasons. First, some are derived from behavioral evidence from psychology. Second, some are "natural" processing and representational decisions based on concepts from computer and information sciences. Thus, the assumptions of a physical symbol system drives the representations and processing. And third, some assumptions seem to be made for convenience, or personal preferences rather than for well-grounded reasons. An example of this is the exclusion of partial information, not even ubiquitous "activation values", or "connection strengths", concepts that have pervaded psychological theorizing for many decades, and that are the mainstay of connectionist modeling.

## 4. Soar as a model of human intelligence

### 4.1. Assessing the experimental evidence

Soar takes psychological data seriously. Its developers have culled the experimental literature for data in a form amenable to test. On the whole, Soar does pretty well at this, and a major portion of its claim to success is the ability to mimic psychological phenomena. But what are we to make of this claim?

The answer rests upon how well we think those phenomena get at the core issues of human intelligence and cognition.

There appear to be four assumptions that are critical:

(1) That there is a uniform computational architecture, including a single, uniform long-term memory structure.
(2) That there is a single form of learning (*chunking*).
(3) That all intelligent operations are performed by symbol manipulation—the physical symbol system hypothesis.
(4) That all reasoning and problem solving is done through search within a uniform problem space.

Assumption (1), the notion of uniform computational structure seems suspect. Now, this is simply not the sort of issue one can decide by experimental, behavioral observation. Whatever behavior is observed, one could postulate an underlying uniformity or non-uniformity: behavioral evidence can never distinguish between the two. But what of biological evidence? What do we know about the neurological basis of cognition? The brain is composed of different structures, each apparently specialized for different kinds of operations. The cortex is surely not the only place where cognitive operations take place, and although it is the largest relatively uniform structure in the brain, even it differs in appearance and structure from place to place. The cortex differs from the cerebellum which differs from the hippocampus and the thalmus, much as the liver differs from the pancreas and the kidney. We do not expect the organs of the body to have a common underlying chemical or biological structure, why would we expect uniformity in the biology of computational structures?

## 4.2. Semantic and episodic memory

The assumption of a single long-term memory seems unwarranted. Now, back in the days when all we had to go on was psychological, behavioral evidence, we talked of long-term memory, short-term memory, and various sensory (iconic) memories. I was even responsible for some of this. But now that we have a larger accumulation of evidence, especially evidence from neurologically impaired patients, this simple division no longer seems to apply.

A good example of the difficulty of assessing human cognitive architecture from behavioral data alone comes from the distinction in the psychological literature between semantic and episodic memory [25]. Tulving has suggested that we distinguish between semantic and episodic memory. Semantic memory is generalized, abstracted knowledge (e.g., "a dog has four legs, is a mammal, and is a member of the canine family"). Episodic memory is experiential in nature (e.g., the memory for the event when Sam, my family's dog, got stuck in the fence and it took three of us to extricate him). Tulving and other have claimed that these distinctions are more than simply a different representational format, but rather that they represent separate memory systems [26]. This, of course, would violate a basic postulate of Soar, and so, in his William James lectures, Newell reports upon a test of this idea [11, Chapter 6].

Soar passes the test, for the existing mechanisms of Soar seem quite capable of producing behavior of the sort seen for both episodic and semantic memory, and although the test is not made, it probably produces the right behavior under the right conditions. Newell is justifiably proud of this performance: "a unified theory contains the answer to a question, such as the episodic/semantic distinction. One does not add new information to the theory to obtain it. One simply goes to the theory and reads out the solution."

This demonstration is an excellent example of the power of Soar (or any other unified theory of cognition, Newell is careful to point out), but it also shows the weaknesses. For the scientific judgment on the distinction of memory types cannot rest on behavioral evidence alone: in fact, I believe the behavioral evidence will almost always be too weak to distinguish among theoretical variants. Much stronger evidence comes by combining behavioral observations with neuropsychological evidence, both by examining patients with brain abnormalities and through measurements of neural activity in the human brain. Neurological studies (see [23, 27]) strongly support the notion of separate memory structures. Tulving points out that some forms of brain damage produce amnesiacs that are more damaged in episodic memory than semantic; and measurement of regional cerebral blood flow in normal humans doing two different memory tasks that involve the two classes of memory activate different regions of the brain. Tulving uses these studies to argue specifically for the distinct neurological, psychological, and functional nature of episodic and semantic memory. Squire and Zola-Morgan [23] suggest that in addition to the differences found by Tulving, declarative and nondeclarative memories reside in different brain areas (both episodic and semantic memories are forms of declarative memory). If these studies are verified, they provide persuasive evidence against the uniform memory hypothesis, even though the behavioral performance of Soar is just fine.

These studies illustrate the difficulty faced by the theorist in this area: Behavioral studies are really not precise enough to distinguish among different biological mechanisms. Any theory that attempts to model the functional behavior of the human must also take into account different biological bases for these mechanisms. Presumably different biological mechanisms will also lead to different kinds of observable behavior, but the distinctions may not be noticed until one knows what to look for.

## 4.3. Learning

Is there a single form of learning—assumption (2)? Today's answer is that we do not know. Many psychologists distinguish among several kinds. Rumelhart and I claimed there were three: accretion, structuring, and tuning

[19]. Anderson [2] has claimed a similar three. What about the fundamental distinction between operant and classical learning, or any of the many forms of learning identified within the animal literature? Of course, it is quite possible that all these forms of learning rely upon a single primitive mechanism, so that something like "chunking" could be the substratum upon which all of these apparently disparate properties of the learning system are created. My personal opinion is that there probably is a simple primitive of learning, but that it is apt to be very low-level, more like a mechanism for strengthening a bond or link in an association than like the higher-level concept of chunking.

Note that other systems have other assumptions about the nature of learning. Connectionist models use one or another variant of hill climbing to adjust their weights, most frequently guided by a teacher, but under appropriate circumstances guided by other criteria. Weight adjustment provides an excellent mechanism for handling constraint-satisfaction tasks, for performing generalizations, and for systems that do not require exact matches, but will accept closest matches. There really is still not enough work exploring connectionist architectures with the sort of tasks done by Soar. However, connectionist architectures are especially well suited for skill learning, and at least one system does also produce the power law of performance [8].

Holland, Holyoak, Nisbett and Thagard's system of genetic algorithms provides another form of learning mechanism, one more rapid and efficient than the simple weight adjustment of connectionist systems [5]. This system is well-suited for a wide range of cognitive tasks, especially that of induction.

Explanation-based learning systems use several procedures: generalization, chunking, operationalization, and analogy (an excellent review and comparison of systems is provided by Ellman [4]). Soar, which is a form of explanation-based system, only uses chunking, which appears to limit its powers, especially in its lack of ability to learn from observation and to perform induction.

What of the power of Soar's learning? Learning is impasse-driven: new operators result when an impasse in processing occurs, forcing the generation of new subgoals or other mechanisms. New operators are created through chunking, when a sequence of operators reaches some desired state, the sequence can be "chunked" together into one new operator, creating the appropriate establishing conditions and output conditions to working memory. Chunking has obvious problems in forming just the right level of generalization. It can easily construct a chunk appropriate to the exact conditions which started the sequence, but this would be too specific for future use. Deciding which variables to generalize, which to make explicit is a major problem faced by all such learning mechanisms, and Soar is no exception.

As a result, Soar chunks can be "expensive" (in that there will soon be multiple, highly specialized chunks requiring analysis and search): new procedures have overcome this expense, but they had to be added for the purpose [24].

Soar also has trouble with induction: If I say the series is 1, 2, 4, what is the next number? Humans have no trouble with this task. In fact, humans do it too often, including when it is inappropriate and when the induced information is wrong: if Soar is to be a model of human performance, it too must have the same biases. My preference would be for a system where these "natural" errors of people fall naturally out of the system, not one where special mechanisms have to be added to produce the behavior. Chunking is really a limited mechanism: learning takes place only after a satisfactory solution is reached, and the learning occurs by collapsing the operator sequence into a single operator that is more efficient.

What about dealing with impasses? The normal way leads to a fairly logical, orderly pursuit through subgoal space. VanLehn, Ball, and Kowalski [28] have presented experimental evidence against the last-in-first-out constraint on the selection of goals that is present in Soar (and many other problem-solving theories): this is the assumption that leads to the problem solver working only on the unsatisfied goal that was created most recently. Are the mechanisms of Soar flexible enough to get around this assumption? Probably.

What can one conclude? As usual, the jury is still out. Chunking is clearly a powerful mechanism and the range of problems to which it can be applied is broad. It is not the only possible mechanism, however, and it is clearly not so well suited for some tasks as for others. But a systematic comparison of learning mechanisms and tasks has yet to be performed.

### 4.4. Symbol processing

Assumption (3) is that of symbol processing and the unified nature of intelligent processing. Again, this is so fundamental that it is difficult to get evidence. Some of us believe it necessary to distinguish between two very different kinds of processing. One, subconscious, takes place by means of constraint-satisfaction, pattern-matching structures, perhaps implemented in the form of connectionist nets. These are non-symbolic modes of computation (often called sub-symbolic[2]). The other kind of processing is that of higher-level conscious mechanisms, and it is only here that we have the classical symbol processing mechanisms that Soar attempts to model because this higher, symbolic level of processing also exists within the brain, it too must be constructed from neural circuits. The well-known difficulties that neural networks have with symbol manipulation, for maintaining variables and bindings, and for even such basic symbolic distinctions as that between type and token, lead to strong limitations on the power of this symbolic level of processing: it is

---

[2] I am fully aware of the controversy over the term "sub-symbolic", with the critics saying it has no meaning. Either something is symbolic or it is not. The term is, therefore, vague and ill-defined. It gives the pretense of a well-defined sense, but in fact, means quite different things to different people. And, therefore, it exactly suits my purpose.

slow, serial, and with limited memory size. This suggestion of a dual processing structure is in accord with the experimental evidence. In particular, the limits in the symbolic processor are consistent with human data. Thus, human ability to do formal symbolic reasoning (e.g., logical reasoning) without the aid of external devices is extremely limited.

The view I just proposed, with both sub-conscious and conscious processing, is a minority one, shared neither by the strong connectionists nor the strong symbolists. Moreover, Soar may not need to take a stance: it could argue (and it has done so) that any sub-conscious processing that might take place lies in the neural band, beneath the region of its interest, that these operations take place within the time domains faster than 100 msec. where hardware issues dominate. Soar is concerned only with symbolic representations and if these are constructed on top of underlying, more primitive computational structures, that is quite compatible with its structures (see [16]).

But it may very well be that the physical symbol system hypothesis does not hold for much of human cognition. Perhaps much of our performance is indeed done "without representation" as Brooks [3], among others, have suggested. It will be quite a while before the various cognitive sciences have settled on any consensus, but this assumption is so fundamental to Soar, that if the evidence beneath it is weakened, Soar's claims to a general model of human cognition must suffer.

Where do I stand on this? Mixed. As I said, I believe we probably do lower-level processing in a sub-symbolic mode, with symbols restricted to higher-order (conscious?) processing. Conscious processing is heavily restricted by the limits of working memory. I give part of this argument in an early paper of connectionism [14] and another useful view of these distinctions is given by Smolensky [21]. The dual-view is probably consistent with Soar, or at least some modification of Soar that takes into account new developments about the borderline of lower-level (neural band?) processing and symbolic processing.

## 4.5. Search within a uniform problem space

Finally, we have assumption (4), that not only is there a uniform representational and processing structure, but that all reasoning and problem solving is done through search within a uniform problem space. Again, who knows? Can a single representational and a single processing structure handle the differences among perception, problem solving, motor control? Among language, reasoning, analogies, deduction and inference? Maybe, or maybe not. We simply do not know.

This assumption is the one that gives many of my colleagues in AI the most trouble. I am not so certain, for the problem space of Soar is very powerful, and by appropriate coding of the symbols, it can act as if it were partitioned and structured.

Is a problem space appropriate for all tasks? Again, it isn't clear, but I am not convinced that this poses any fundamental difficulty for Soar. Thus, many of us have argued that physical constraints and information in the environment plays a major role in human planning, decision making and problem solving. But if so, this information is readily accommodated by Soar. Thus, in the current version, the formulation of the problem space automatically encodes physical constraints [17, Section 2.3]. And when Soar gets the appropriate I/O sensors, it should be just as capable of using environmental information as any other model of behavior. Here the only restriction is the state of today's technology, but in principle, these factors are readily accounted for.

## 5. Soar as artificial intelligence

How well does Soar do as a mechanism for AI? Here, Soar falls between the cracks. It is neither logic, nor frames, nor semantic nets. Soar classifies itself as a production system, but it is not like the traditional forms that we have become used to and that fill the basic texts on AI. As theoretical AI, Soar has several weaknesses, many shared by other approaches as well. In particular, Soar suffers from:

- weak knowledge representation;
- unstructured memory;
- the characterization of everything as search through a problem space.

Weak knowledge representation certainly stands out as one of the major deficits. In this era of highly sophisticated representational schemes and knowledge representation languages, it is somewhat of a shock to see an AI system that has no inheritance, no logic, no quantification: Soar provides only triples and a general purpose processing structure. How does Soar handle reasoning that requires counterfactuals and hypotheticals and quantifiers? How will it fare with language, real language? What about other forms of learning, for example, learning by being told, learning by reflection, learning by restructuring, or learning by analogy? How will Soar recover from errors? All unanswered questions, but never underestimate the sophistication of a dedicated team of computer professionals. Soar will master many or even all of these areas. In fact, in the time that elapsed between the oral presentation of the Soar paper under review and now, the final writing of the review, Soar has made considerable progress in just these areas.

What about other methods of deduction and inference? We have already noted Soar's weaknesses in doing inference.

Technically, Soar has all the power it needs. It is, after all, Turing-equivalent, and with the basic structure of triples it can represent anything that it needs. In fact, one of the assumptions of Soar is that it should start with only the minimum of representation and process: everything else that might be needed is learned. It gains considerable speed with experience—through chunking—and in any event, speed was never a prerequisite of a theoretical structure.

Soar gets its main strength by virtue of its uniformity of architecture, representation, and learning. It can solve anything because it is so general, so unspecialized. It then gets its power through the learning mechanism: the assumption is:

- weak methods + chunking → strong methods;
- the tuning of preferences → strength.

Soar has many positive features. It is a production system, but with a major difference. Conflict resolution, a critical feature of traditional production systems, has disappeared. All relevant Soar productions are executed in parallel. The execution puts all their memory data into working memory, where the decision procedure selects a relevant action to be performed from the information in working memory. Soar can be both goal-driven and data-driven. And the strategy of action is flexibly determined by the kind of information available within working memory.

### 5.1. Soar and its competition

How does Soar compare to other AI systems? Restricting the consideration to those that aspire to a unified theory of intelligence, and then further restricting it to evaluate the systems in terms of their relevance to human cognition, the answer is that there really isn't much competition. Of the more traditional AI systems, only Soar is viable. Soar's principles and structure seem much more in harmony with what we know of human processing than systems such as the traditional expert system approach to reasoning, or the decision processes of knowledge representation languages, various database systems and truth-maintenance systems, and logic programming. Work on explanation-based learning [4] could potentially be compared, but for the moment, there are no unified, grand systems to come out of this tradition (with the exception of Soar itself, which is a variant of explanation-based learning).

Psychologists have a history of system building as well that should be considered. Thus, Soar could be compared to the approach followed by Anderson in his continual refinements of his computer models (e.g., ACT*, [1]), or by the earlier work of Norman, Rumelhart, and the LNR Research Group [15]. But of these, only ACT* is active today. Here, I would probably conclude that ACT* is superior in the way it models the finer details of the psychological processes that it covers, but that its scope is quite restricted: ACT* is an important influential theory, but it has never been intended as a general, unified theory of all cognitive behavior.

There are numerous small systems, each devoted to the detailed modeling of restricted phenomena. Connectionist modeling fits this description, with perhaps the largest and most detailed simulation studies being those of Rumelhart and McClelland in their simulation of a wide variety of data on word recognition and perception [6, 18, 20]. In all these cases, although the work provides major contributions to our understanding of the phenomena being modeled, they are restricted in scope, hand-crafted for the task (even if the underlying representational structures are learned) and no single system is intended to be taken as a unified theory, applicable to a wide range of phenomena.

There is one major system, however, which does attempt the same range of generality—the genetic algorithm approach of Holland, Holyoak, Nisbett, and Thagard [5]. This work comes from a strong interdisciplinary group examining the nature of cognition and its experimental and philosophical basis. Its computer modeling tools do provide an alternative, a kind of cross between connectionist modeling and symbolic representation, with an emphasis on learning. How do these two systems compare? So far, Soar has the edge, in part because of the immense amount of effort to the development of a wide-ranging, coherent model. But the approach of Holland et al. [5] has the capability to become a second unified theory of cognition, one that would allow more precise comparison with the assumptions of Soar. It will be a good day for science when two similar systems are available, for comparisons of the performance on the same tasks by these two systems with very different underlying assumptions can only be beneficial. Indeed, this is one of the hopes of the Soar enterprise: the development of competing models that can inform one another.

## 6. Reflections and summary

### 6.1. Soar's stengths and weaknesses

The strength of Soar is that it starts with fundamental ideas and principles and pushes them hard. It derives strength and generality from a uniform architecture, uniform methods, and uniform learning. Weak methods are general methods, and although they may be slow, they apply to a wide range of problems: the combination of weak methods plus a general learning mechanism gives Soar great power. The learning method allows for specialization, for the chunking of procedures into efficient steps, tuned for the problem upon which it is working.

Learning within Soar is impressive. I was prepared to see Soar gradually improve with practice, but I was surprised to discover that it could take advantage of learning even within its first experience with a problem: routines learned (chunked) in the early phases of a problem aided it in the solution of the later phases, even within its first exposure. Soar may indeed have taken advantage of both worlds of generality and specialization: an initial generality that gives it scope and breadth, at the tradeoff of being slow and inefficient, plus chunking that provides a learned specialization for speed and efficiency.

The weaknesses of Soar derive from its strengths. It has a weak knowledge representation language and a weak memory structure. It has no formalism for higher-order reasoning, for productions, for rules, or for preferences. It is not clear how well Soar will do with natural language (where reasoning and quantification seem essential), or with argumentation, or for that matter, with simple input and output control. Everything in Soar is search: how far can that be carried?

## 6.2. Soar as a theoretical tool for psychology

Soar claims to be grounded upon psychological principles, but the psychology is weak. As I have pointed out, this is no fault of Soar, but it reflects the general status of psychological theory, which in turn reflects the difficulty of that scientific endeavor. Still, unsettled science provides shaky grounds for construction. How can I, as a psychologist, complain when someone takes psychological data seriously?

The problem is the sort of psychological evidence that is considered. As I indicated at the start of this review, there are different ideas about the nature of the appropriate evidence from psychology. The Soar team takes the evidence much more seriously than do I.

One basic piece of psychological evidence offered as support for the chunking hypothesis is the power law of learning, that the relationship between speed of performance and number of trials of experience follows a power law of the form $Time = k(trials)^p$ over very many studies, and with the number of trials as large as 50,000 (or more: see [13]). Yes, the ability of Soar to produce the power law of learning is impressive. At the time, it was the only model that could do so (now however, Miyata [8] has shown how a connectionist model can also yield the power law of learning).

Soar handles well the data from the standard sets of problem-solving tasks, for inference, and for other tasks of think-aloud problem solving. But how much of real cognition do these tasks reflect? There is a growing body of evidence to suggest that these are the sorts of tasks done primarily within the psychological laboratory or the classroom, and that they may have surprisingly little transfer to everyday cognition. For example, consider the set of problems against which Soar tests its ability to mimic human problem solving: the Eight Puzzle, tic-tac-toe, Towers of Hanoi, missionaries and cannibals, algebraic equations, satisfying local constraint networks, logical syllogisms, balance beam problems, blocks world problems, monkey-and-bananas, and the water-jug problems. These are indeed the traditional problems studied in both the human and artificial intelligence literature. But, I contend, these are not the typical problems of everyday life. They are not problems people are particularly good at. One reason psychologists study them is that they do offer so many difficulties: they thereby provide us something to study.

But if this is not how people perform in everyday life, then perhaps these should not be the baseline studies on which to judge intelligent behavior. If I am right, this stands as an indictment of human psychology, not of Soar, except that Soar has based its case on data from the human experimental literature.

### 6.3. The choice of phenomena to be modeled

How has Soar chosen the set of phenomena that it wishes to consider? Not clear. Thus, there is a well-established and rich core of knowledge about human short-term memory, and although the current theoretical status of the concept is unclear, the phenomena and data are still valid. The literature is well known to the developers of Soar, and key items are summarized in Newell's William James lectures. One of the major developments over the years is the finding that items in STM decay: not that less and less items are available, but that only partial information is available from any given item. Two major methods have been developed for representing this decay, one to allow each item to have some "activation value" that decreases with time or interference from other items (thus decreasing its signal-to-noise ratio), the other that each item is composed of numerous "micro-features", and each of the features drops out probabilistically as a function of time or interference from other items, so the main item gets noisier and noisier with time.

Soar decides to use neither of these mechanisms of memory loss. Why? Loss of activation is rejected, probably because activation values are simply not within the spirit of representation chosen for Soar ("The simplest decay law for a discrete system such as Soar is not gradual extinction, but probabilistic decay", Chapter 6 of the William James lectures [11]). And loss of microfeatures is not possible because the Soar representation is wholistic: internal components cannot be lost.

Does this difference matter? It is always difficult to assess the impact of low-level decisions upon the resulting global behavior. Clearly, the choice rules out the simulation of recognition-memory operating characteristics (e.g., [29]). This kind of decision permeates the model-building activity, and it isn't always easy to detect where a basic assumption is absolutely forced by the phenomena or universal processing constraints, where selected for more arbitrary reasons.

In general Soar seems on strongest ground when it discusses the highest-order of the cognitive band: tasks that clearly make use of symbol processing, especially problem-solving tasks. At the lowest level, it is weak on time-ordered tasks, both on the effects of time and activity rate on performance and cognition, and also on the simulation of tasks that require controlled rates of production. At the middle level, it is weakest on issues related to knowledge representation: the existing representation has little overall structure and none of the common organizational structures or inference rules of knowledge representation languages.

Soar also espouses the software-independence approach to modeling. That is, psychological functions are assumed to be independent of hardware implementation, so it is safe to study the cognitive band without examination of the implementation methods of the neural band, without consideration of the physical body in which the organism is imbedded, and without consideration of non-cognitive aspects of behavior. How big a role does the biological implementation of cognition play? What constraints, powers, and weaknesses result? What of the body, does it affect cognition? How about motivation, culture, social interaction. What about emotions? The separation of these aspects into separate compartments is the common approach to cognition of the information processing psychologist of an earlier era, but the psychologist of the 1990s is very apt to think the separation cannot be maintained. Certainly the connectionist takes as given that:

(1) There is continuous activation.
(2) The implementation makes a major difference.
(3) Time is important.
(4) Major biases and processing differences can result from extra-cognitive influences.

How do we weigh these various considerations? The field is young, the amount of knowledge low. Soar may be right. But it does not implement the only possible set of alternatives.

And how does Soar react to criticisms of this sort? Properly: Soar aspires to set the framework for general models of cognition. It tests one set of operating assumptions. The goal, in part, is to inspire others to do similar tasks, perhaps with different sets of assumptions and mechanisms. But then they are all to be assessed with the same data. The goal is not to show Soar right or wrong, the goal is to advance the general state of knowledge. With this attitude, Soar— and the science of cognition—can only win.

### 6.4. Soar as a modeling tool for AI

Maybe Soar should be evaluated separately for its role as a tool for artificial intelligence and for psychological modeling. Personally, that is my view, but the Soar community has soundly rejected this idea. One of the basic methodological assumptions, (M2), is that general intelligence can be studied most usefully by not distinguishing between human and artificial intelligence. But I am not convinced. Human intelligence has evolved to meet the demands of the situations encountered through evolutionary history, where survival and reproduction were critical aims. The brain has a biological basis and the sensory, motor, and regulatory structures reflect the evolutionary history and the demands made upon them over a time course measured in millions of years. Human intelligence is powerful, but restricted, specialized for creativity, adaptivity, and robustness, with powerful perceptual apparatus that probably dominates the mechanisms of thought. Human language is also the product of an evolutionary struggle, and its properties are still not understood by the scientific community, even though virtually all humans master their native, spoken language. The properties of biological and artificial systems are so dramatically different at the hardware level (the neural band), that this must certainly also be reflected at the cognitive level (see [7]).

Good artificial intelligence may not be good psychology. Soar attempts to be both, but by so doing, I fear it weakens its abilities on all counts. By attempting to account for the known experimental results on cognition, it is forced to adopt certain computational strategies that may hamper its performance on traditional tasks of artificial intelligence. And by being developed from the traditional framework of information processing artificial intelligence, it may limit the scope of human mechanisms that it tries to duplicate.

### 6.5. How should Soar be judged?

How should Soar—or any other model of intelligence—be judged? On the criteria of practical and theoretical AI I think the answer is clear. One uses a standard set of benchmarks, probably similar to what Soar has done. Here the answer is given by how well the system performs. On the issue of the simulation of human cognition, the answer is far from clear. We don't have a set of benchmark problems. If I am to be a constructive critic (look where Soar is pointing), I have to conclude that what it does, it does well: in this domain it has no competiton.

Soar does not aspire to be *the* tool for human simulation. Rather, it hopes to set an example of what can be done. Others are urged to follow, either by building upon Soar or by providing their own, unified theory of cognition, to be tested and compared by attempting to account for exactly the same set of data.

One practical barrier stands in the way of the systematic use and evaluation of Soar by the research community: the difficulty of learning this system. Today, this is not an easy task. There is no standard system, no easy introduction. Programming manuals do not exist. Until Soar is as easy to master as, say, LISP or PROLOG, there will never be sufficient people with enough expertise to put it to the test. If Soar usage is to go beyond the dedicated few there needs to be a standard system, some tutorial methods, and a standard text.

## 6.6. Conclusion: Powerful and impressive

In conclusion, Soar is a powerful, impressive system. It is still too early to assess Soar on either theoretical or practical grounds, for either AI or psychology, but already it has shown that it must be taken seriously on both counts. The chunking mechanism is a major contribution to our understanding of learning. The exploitation of weak methods provides a valuable lesson for system builders. And the use of uniform structures may very well provide more benefits than deficits. I am not so certain that we are yet ready for unified theory, for there are many uncertainties in our knowledge of human behavior and of the underlying mechanisms—our understanding of the biological structure of processing is just beginning to be developed, but already it has added to and changed some of our ideas about the memory systems. But for those who disagree or who wish to explore the terrain anyway, Soar has set a standard for all others to follow.

### Acknowledgement

This article has benefited from the aid of several reviewers as well as through discussions and correspondence with Stu Card, David Kirsh, Allen Newell, Paul Rosenbloom, and Richard Young. My research was supported by grant NCC 2-591 to Donald Norman and Edwin Hutchins from the Ames Research Center of the National Aeronautics and Space Agency in the Aviation Safety/Automation Program. Everett Palmer served as technical monitor. Additional support was provided by funds from the Apple Computer Company and Digital Equipment Corporation to the Affiliates of Cognitive Science at UCSD.

### References

[1] J.R. Anderson, The Architecture of Cognition (Harvard University Press, Cambridge, MA, 1983).
[2] J.R. Anderson, Cognitive Psychology and Its Implications (Freeman, New York, 1985).
[3] R.A. Brooks, Intelligence without representation, Artif. Intell. 47 (1991) 139–159, this volume.
[4] T. Ellman, Explanation-based learning: a survey of programs and perspectives, ACM Comput. Surv. 21 (1989) 163–221.
[5] J.H. Holland, K.J. Holyoak, R.E. Nisbett and P.R. Thagard, Induction: Processes of Inference, Learning, and Discovery (MIT Press, Cambridge, MA, 1987).
[6] J.L. McClelland and D.E. Rumelhart, An interactive activation model of context effects in letter perception, Part I: An account of basic findings, Psychol. Rev. 88 (1981) 375–407.
[7] C. Mead, Analog VLSI and Neural Systems (Addison-Wesley, Reading, MA, 1989).
[8] Y. Miyata, A PDP model of sequence learning that exhibits the power law, in: Proceedings 11th Annual Conference of the Cognitive Science Society, Ann Arbor, MI (1989) 9–16.

[9] A. Newell, You can't play 20 questions with nature and win, in: W.G. Case, ed., *Visual Information Processing* (Academic Press, San Diego, CA, 1973).

[10] A. Newell, Scale counts in cognition, 1986 American Psychological Association Distinguished Scientific Award Lecture.

[11] A. Newell, *Unified Theories of Cognition* (Harvard University Press, Cambridge, MA, 1990); 1987 William James lectures at Harvard University.

[12] A. Newell and S.K. Card, The prospects for psychological science in human-computer interaction, *Hum.-Comput. Interaction* 1 (1985) 209–242.

[13] A. Newell and P.S. Rosenbloom, Mechanisms of skill acquisition and the law of practice, in: J.R. Anderson, ed., *Cognitive Skills and Their Acquisition* (Erlbaum, Hillsdale, NJ, 1981).

[14] D.A. Norman, Reflections on cognition and parallel distributed processing, in: J.L. McClelland, D.E. Rumelhart and the PDP Research Group, eds., *Parallel Distributed Processing: Explorations in the Microstructure of Cognition* 2: *Psychological and Biological Models* (MIT Press/Bradford, Cambridge, MA, 1986).

[15] D.A. Norman, and D.E. Rumelhart, The LNR Research Group, *Explorations in Cognition* (Freeman, New York, 1975).

[16] P.S. Rosenbloom, A symbolic goal-oriented perspective on connectionism and Soar, in: R. Pfeifer, Z. Schreter, F. Fogelman-Soulie and L. Steels, eds., *Connectionism in Perspective* (Elsevier, Amsterdam, 1989).

[17] P.S. Rosenbloom, J.E. Laird, A. Newell and R. McCarl, A preliminary analysis of the Soar architecture as a basis for general intelligence, *Artif. Intell.* 47 (1991) 289–325, this volume.

[18] D.E. Rumelhart and J.L. McClelland, An interactive activation model of context effects in letter perception, Part II: The contextual enhancement effect and some tests and extensions of the model, *Psychol. Rev.* 89 (1982) 60–94.

[19] D.E. Rumelhart and D.A. Norman, Accretion, tuning and restructuring: three modes of learning, in: J.W. Cotton and R. Klatzky, eds., *Semantic Factors in Cognition* (Erlbaum, Hillsdale, NJ, 1978).

[20] M.S. Siedenberg and J.L. McClelland, A distributed, developmental model of word recognition and naming, *Psychol. Rev.* 96 (1989) 523–568.

[21] P. Smolensky, On the proper treatment of connectionism, *Brain Behav. Sci.* 11 (1988) 1–74.

[22] L.R. Squire, *Memory and Brain* (Oxford University Press, New York, 1987).

[23] L.R. Squire, and S. Zola-Morgan, Memory: Brain systems and behavior, *Trends Neurosci.* 11 (4) (1988) 170–175.

[24] M. Tambe and P.S. Rosenbloom, Eliminating expensive chunks by restricting expressiveness, in: *Proceedings IJCAI-89*, Detroit, MI (1989).

[25] E. Tulving, Episodic and semantic memory, in: E. Tulving and W. Donaldson, eds., *Organization of Memory* (Academic Press, San Diego, 1969).

[26] E. Tulving, *Elements of Episodic Memory* (Oxford University Press, New York, 1983).

[27] E. Tulving, Remembering and knowing the past, *Am. Sci.* 77 (1989) 361–367.

[28] K. VanLehn, W. Ball and B. Kowalski, Non-LIFO execution of cognitive procedures, *Cogn. Sci.* 13 (1989) 415–465.

[29] W.A. Wickelgren and D.A. Norman, Stength models and serial position in short-term recognition memory, *J. Math. Psychol.* 3 (1966) 316–347.

Artificial Intelligence 59 (1993) 285–294
Elsevier

ARTINT 1010

# Book Review

# Allen Newell, *Unified Theories of Cognition* *

Daniel C. Dennett

*Center for Cognitive Studies, Tufts University, Medford, MA 02155-7068, USA*

Received August 1991
Revised September 1992

The time for unification in cognitive science has arrived, but who should lead the charge? The immunologist-turned-neuroscientist Gerald Edelman [6] thinks that neuroscientists should lead—or more precisely that he should (he seems to have a low opinion of everyone else in cognitive science). Someone might think that I had made a symmetrically opposite claim in *Consciousness Explained* [4]: philosophers (or more precisely, those that agree with me!) are in the best position to see how to tie all the loose ends together. But in fact I acknowledged that unifying efforts such as mine are proto- theories, explorations that are too metaphorical and impressionistic to serve as the model for a unified theory. Perhaps Newell had me in mind when he wrote in his introduction (p.16) that a unified theory "can't be just a pastiche, in which disparate formulations are strung together with some sort of conceptual bailing wire", but in any case the shoe more or less fits, with some pinching. Such a "pastiche" theory can be a good staging ground, however, and a place to stand while considering the strengths and weaknesses of better built theories. So I agree with him.

> It is not just philosophers' theories that need to be made honest by modeling at this level; neuroscientists' theories are in the same boat. For instance, Gerald Edelman's (1989) elaborate theory of

*Correspondence to*: D.C. Dennett, Center for Cognitive Studies, Tufts University, Medford, MA 02155-7068, USA. E-mail: ddennett@pearl.tufts.edu.
* (Harvard University Press, Cambridge, MA, 1990); xvi + 549 pages.

"re-entrant" circuits in the brain makes many claims about how such re-entrants can accomplish the discriminations, build the memory structures, coordinate the sequential steps of problem solving, and in general execute the activities of a human mind, but in spite of a wealth of neuroanatomical detail, and enthusiastic and often plausible assertions from Edelman, we won't know what his re-entrants can do—we won't know that re-entrants are the *right* way to conceive of the functional neuroanatomy—until they are fashioned into a whole cognitive architecture at the grain-level of Act* or Soar and put through their paces. [4, p. 268]

So I begin with a ringing affirmation of the central claim of Newell's book. Let's hear it for models like Soar. Exploring whole cognitive systems at roughly that grain-level is the main highway to unification. I agree, moreover, with the reasons he offers for his proposal. But in my book I also alluded to two reservations I have with Newell's program without spelling out or defending either of them. This is obviously the time to make good on those promissory notes or recant them. "My own hunch", I said, "is that, for various reasons that need not concern us here, the underlying medium of production systems is *still* too idealized and oversimplified in its constraints" [4, p. 267]. And a little further along I expressed my discomfort with Newell's support for the traditional division between working memory and long-term memory, and the accompanying notion of *distal access* via symbols, since it encourages a vision of "movable symbols" being transported here and there in the nervous system—an image that slides almost irresistibly into the incoherent image of the Cartesian Theater, the place in the brain where "it all comes together" for consciousness.

Preparing for this review, I re-read *Unified Theories of Cognition*, and read several old and recent Newell papers, and I'm no longer confident that my reservations weren't based on misunderstandings. The examples that Newell gives of *apparently* alternative visions that can readily enough be accommodated within Soar—semantic and episodic memory within the single, unified LTM, Koler's proceduralism, Johnson-Laird's mental models, for instance—make me wonder. It's not that Soar can be all things to all people (that would make it vacuous), but that it is easy to lose sight of the fact that Soar's level is a *low* or foundational architectural level, upon which quasi- architectural or firmware levels can be established, at which to render the features and distinctions that at first Soar seems to deny. But let's put my reservations on the table and see what we make of them.

On the first charge, that Soar (and production systems in general) are still too idealized and oversimplified, Newell might simply agree, noting that we must begin with oversimplifications and use our experience with them to uncover the complications that matter. Is Soar *the* way to organize cognitive science, or is it "just" a valiant attempt to impose order (via a decomposition) on an incredibly heterogeneous and hard-to-analyze tangle? There's a whole messy world of individualized and unrepeatable mental phenomena out there, and the right question to ask is not: "Does Soar idealize away from these?"—because the answer is obvious: "Yes, so what?" The right question is: "Can the *important* complications be reintroduced gracefully as elaborations of Soar?" And the answer to that question depends on figuring out which complications are really important and why. Experience has taught me that nothing short of considerable mucking about with an actual implementation of Soar, something I still have not done, would really tell me what I should think about it, so I won't issue any verdicts here at all, just questions.

First, to put it crudely, what about pleasure and pain? I'm not just thinking of high-urgency interrupts (which are easy enough to add, presumably), but a more subtle and encompassing focusing role. Newell recognizes the problem of focusing, and even points out—correctly, in my view—that the fact that this can be a problem for Soar is a positive mark of verisimilitude. "Thus the issue for the standard computer is how to be interrupted, whereas the issue for Soar and Act* (and presumably for human cognition) is how to keep focused" (Newell, Rosenbloom and Laird [10]). But the Soar we are shown in the book is presented as hyperfunctional.

> Soar's mechanisms are dictated by the functions required of a general cognitive agent. We have not posited detailed technological limitations to Soar mechanisms. There is nothing inappropriate or wrong with such constraints. They may well exist, and if they do, they must show up in any valid theory. (p. 354)

Doesn't this extreme functionalism lead to a seriously distorted foundational architecture? Newell provides an alphabetized list (Fig. 8.1, p. 434) of some mental phenomena Soar has not yet tackled, and among these are daydreaming, emotion and affect, imagery, and play. Soar is all business. Soar is either working or sound asleep, always learning-by-chunking, always solving problems, never idling. There are no profligate expenditures on dubious digressions, no along-for-the-ride productions cluttering up the problem spaces, and Soar is never too tired and cranky to take on yet another impasse. Or so it seems. Perhaps if we put just the right new menagerie of operators on stage, or the right items of supplementary knowledge in memory, a sprinkling of sub-optimal goals, etc., a lazy, mathophobic, lust-obsessed Soar could stand forth for all to see. That is what I mean about how easy it is to misplace the level of Soar; perhaps all this brisk, efficient problem solving should be viewed as the biological (rather than psychological) activities of elements too small to be visible to the naked eye of the folk-psychological observer.

But if so, then there is a large element of misdirection in Newell's advertising about his functionalism. "How very functional your teeth are, Grandma!" said Red Riding Hood. "The better to model dysfunctionality when the time comes, my dear!" replied the wolf. Moreover, even when Soar deals with "intendedly rational behavior" of the sort we engage in when we are good experimental subjects—comfortable, well-paid, and highly motivated—I am skeptical about the realism of the model. Newell acknowledges that it leaves out the "feelings and considerations" that "float around the periphery" (p. 369), but isn't there also lots of *non*-peripheral waste motion in human cognition? (There certainly seems to me to be a lot of it when I think hard—but maybe Newell's own mental life is as brisk and no-nonsense as his book!)

Besides, the hyperfunctionality is *biologically* implausible (as I argue in my book). Newell grants that Soar *did* not arise through evolution (Fig. 8.1), but I am suggesting that perhaps it *could* not. The Spock-like rationality of Soar is a very fundamental feature of the architecture; there is no room *at the architectural level* for some thoughts to be harder to think *because they hurt*, to put it crudely. But isn't that a fact just as secure as any discovered in the psychological laboratory? Shouldn't it be a primary constraint? Ever since Hume got associationism under way with his quasi-mechanical metaphors of combination and attraction between ideas, we have had the task of describing the dynamics of thought: what makes the next thought follow in the heels of the current thought? Newell has provided us, in Soar, with a wonderfully deep and articulated answer—the best ever—but it is an answer that leaves out what I would have thought was a massive factor in the dynamics of thought: pain and pleasure. Solving some problems is a joy; solving others is a bore and a headache, and there are still others that you would go mad trying to solve, so painful would it be to contemplate the problem space. Now it *may just be* that these facts are emergent properties at a higher level, to be discerned in special instances of Soar chugging along imperturbably, but that seems rather unlikely to me. Alternatively, it may be that the *Sturm und Drang* of affect can be piped in as a later low-level embellishment without substantially modifying the basic architecture, but that seems just as unlikely.

David Joslin has pointed out to me that the business-like efficiency we see in the book is largely due to the fact that the various implementations of Soar that we are shown are all special-purpose, truncated versions, with tailor-made sets of operators and productions. In a fully general-purpose Soar, with a vastly enlarged set of productions, we would probably see more hapless wandering than we would want, and have to cast about for ways to focus Soar's energies. And it is here, plausibly, that an affective dimension might be just what is needed, and it has been suggested by various people (Sloman and Croucher [13], de Sousa [5]) that it cannot be packaged within the contents of further knowledge, but must make a contribution orthogonal to the contribution of knowledge.

That was what I had in mind in my first reservation, and as one can see, I'm not sure how sharply it cuts. As I said in my book, we've come a long way from the original von Neumann architecture, and the path taken so far can be extrapolated to still brainier and more biological architectures. The way to find out how much idealization we can afford is not to engage in philosophical debates.

My second reservation, about symbols and distal access, opens some different cans of worms. First, there is a communication problem I want to warn other philosophers about, because it has bedeviled me up to the time of revising the draft of this review. I think I now understand Newell's line on symbols and semantics, and will try to explain it. (If I still don't get it, no harm done—other readers will set me straight.) When he introduces symbols he seems almost to go out of his way to commit what we philosophers call use–mention errors. He gives examples of symbol tokens in Fig. 2-9 (p. 73). He begins with words in sentences (and that's fine), but goes on to *numbers* in equations. We philosophers would say that the symbols were *numerals*—names for numbers. Numbers aren't symbols. He goes on: atoms in formulas. No. Atom-symbols in formulas; formulas are composed of symbols, not atoms; molecules are composed of atoms. Then objects in pictures. No. Object-depictions in pictures. I am sure Newell knows exactly what philosophers mean by a use–mention error, so what is his message supposed to be? "For the purposes of AI it doesn't matter"? Or "We AI-types never get confused about such an obvious distinction, so we can go on speaking loosely"? I don't believe it. There is a sort of willful *semantic descent* (the opposite of Quine's semantic ascent, in which we decide to talk about talk about things) that flavors many AI discussions. It arises, I think, largely because in computer science the expressions up for semantic evaluation do in fact refer very often to things inside the computer—to subroutines that can be called, to memory addresses, to data structures, etc. Moreover, because of the centrality of the domain of arithmetic in computers, the topic of "discussion" is often numbers, and arithmetical expressions for them. So it is easy to lose sight of the fact that when you ask the computer to "evaluate" an expression, and it outputs "3", it isn't *giving* you a number; it's *telling* you a number. But that's all right, since all we ever want from numbers is to have them identified—you can't eat 'em or ride 'em. (Compare "Gimme all your money!" "OK. $42.60, including the change in my pocket.") Can it be that this confusion of symbols and numbers is also abetted by a misappreciation of the fact that, for instance, the binary ASCII code for the *numeral* "9" is not the binary expression of the number 9?

Whatever its causes—or even its justifications—this way of speaking creates the impression that, for people in AI, semantics is something entirely internal to the system. This impression is presumably what led Jerry Fodor into such paroxysms in "Tom Swift and his Procedural Grandmother" [7]. It is too bad he didn't know how to put his misgivings constructively. I tried once:

> We get the idea [from Newell [9]] that a symbol designates if it gives access to a certain object or if it can affect a certain object. And this almost looks all right as long as what we're talking about is internal states .... But of course the real problem is that that isn't what reference is all about. If that were what reference was all about, then what would we say about what you might call my Julie Christie problem? I have a very good physically instantiated symbol for Julie Christie. I know it refers to her, I know it really designates her, but it doesn't seem to have either of the conditions that Professor Newell describes, alas. [2, p. 53] (See also Smith [14].)

Newell's answer:

> The criticisms seemed to me to be a little odd because to say that one has access to something does not mean that one has access to *all* of that thing; having some information about Julie Christie certainly doesn't give one complete access to Julie Christie. That is what polite society is all about .... The first stage is that there are symbols *which lead to internal structures.* I don't think this is obscure, and it is important in understanding where the aboutness comes from ... the data structures *contain knowledge about things in the outside world.* So you then build up further symbols which access things that you can think of as knowledge about something—knowledge about Julie Christie for instance. If you want to ask why a certain symbol says something about Julie Christie, you have to ask why the symbolic expression that contains the symbol says something about Julie Christie. And the answer may be ... because of processes that put it together which themselves have knowledge about Julie Christie .... Ultimately it may turn out to depend upon history, it may depend on some point in the history of the system when it came in contact with something in the world which provided it with that knowledge. ([2, p. 171], emphasis mine)

What we have here, I finally realize, is simply a two-stage (or *n*-stage) functional role semantics: *in the end* the semantics of symbols is anchored to the world via the knowledge that can be attributed to the whole system *at the knowledge level* in virtue of its capacity, exercised or not, for perspicuous

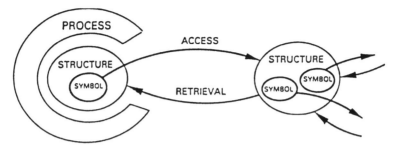

Fig. 1. Symbols provide distal access. (Originally, Fig. 2.10 (p. 75) in *Unified Theories of Cognition.*)

behavior vis-a-vis the items in the world its knowledge is about. And that's my view, too. What makes a data structure about Julie Christie is that it's the part of the system the presence of which explains my capacity to pick her out of a crowd, answer questions about her in quiz shows, etc., etc. That's all there is to it. But it is certainly misleading to say that the symbol gives one *any* "access" (partial access, in polite society!) to the object itself. (It turns out that Julie Christie and I have a mutual friend, who sent her an offprint of [2]. And what do you know, she ... sent me a Christmas card. "Getting closer", I thought. "Maybe Newell's right after all! You just have to be patient. Porsche, Porsche, Porsche.")

Newell's diagram in Fig. 1 makes it all clear (in retrospect) as long as you realize that it is not just that he concentrates (in his book and in his earlier writing) on the semantic link-arrows in the middle of the diagram—the access links tying symbols to their distal knowledge-stores—but that he simply *assumes* there is a solution to any problems that might arise about the interpretation of the arrows on the right-hand side of the diagram: those arrows, as I understand him now, lead one *either* to more data structures or eventually to something in the external world—but he is close to silent about this final, anchoring step. This is fine by me, but then I'm one of the few philosophers who thinks Twin-Earth and narrow content are artifactual philosophical conundrums of no importance to cognitive science [1,3]. Make no mistake, though: serious or not, Newell sweeps them under the rug right here.[1]

[1] In a more recent paper, he goes a bit further in defense of this interpretation: "The agent's knowledge is embodied in the knowledge of the four problem space components. However, this latter knowledge is about the problem space, states and operators; hence it cannot of itself be the knowledge of the agent, which is about the goal, actions and environment. It becomes the agent's knowledge by means of the relationships just described. That is, states are about the external world because of KL perception; operators are about the external world because of KL actions; the desired states are about the goal of the KL agent because of formulate-task; and the means-ends knowledge of select-operator is about performing tasks in the environment because it links environment-referring operators on environment-referring states to descriptions of environment-referring desired states." (Newell et al. [11, p. 23])

What concerns him is rather the interesting question of Plato's aviary: how does an intelligent agent with more knowledge than it can "contemplate" all at once get the right birds to come when it calls? (Dennett [4, p. 222–225]). And how do you do this without relying on a dubious *transportation* metaphor, which would require shipping symbol-tokens here and there in the system? I'm not sure I understand his answer entirely, but the crucial elements are given on p. 355:

> Functionally, working memory must be a short-term memory. It is used to hold the coded knowledge that is to be processed for the current task. It is necessary to replace that knowledge when the task changes. That replacement can be achieved in many ways, by moving the data [bad idea!—DCD], by moving the processes [better!—DCD], or by changing the access path [best!—DCD] .... Working memory for cognition has no continued functional existence outside these limits, however, since elements that are no longer linked to the goal stack become unavailable. Furthermore, problem spaces themselves have no existence independent of the impasses they are created to resolve.

I find these ideas some of the most difficult to understand in cognitive science, for they require setting aside, for once, what we might call the concrete crutch: the lazy picture of places (with boxes around them) and things moving to and fro. *That* vision, for all its utility at the symbol level, is a dangerous companion when we turn to the question of mapping computational processes onto brain processes. When Newell says "Search leads to the view that an intelligent agent is always operating within a *problem space.*" (p. 98) we should recognize that this is really being presented as an *a priori* constraint on how we shall interpret intelligent agents. Show me an intelligent agent, and whatever it does, I'll show you a way of interpreting it as setting up a problem space. Since the key term "distal" is defined relative to *that* space—that logical space—we should be cautious of interpreting it too concretely (cf. Fodor and Pylyshyn [8]).

So my second reservation is blunted as well. Two strikes, or maybe foul balls. There is one more issue I want to take a swing at as long as I'm up at bat. Newell's silence on the issue of natural language as a symbolic medium of cognition in human beings is uncanny. We know that Soar can (in principle) learn from taking *advice* (e.g., p. 312), and Newell sketches out the way Soar would or might handle language acquisition and comprehension (pp. 440–449; see especially his discussion of redundant encoding, p. 453), but I cannot figure out from these brief passages what Newell thinks happens to the overall shape of the competence of a cognitive system when it acquires a natural language, and I think his reticence on this score hides major issues. Early on he gives an eloquent survey of what he calls the "efflorescence of adaptation" by the human (and only the human) species (pp. 114–115), but does this paean to productive versatility proclaim that the symbols of an *internalized natural language* are necessary, or is it rather that one needs a pre-linguistic language of thought—in which case we may wonder why the human language of thought gives us such an edge over the other species, if it does not get most of its power from the external language we learn to speak. For instance, Newell's discussion of annotated models (pp. 393ff) is a fine perspective on the mental models debates, but I am left wondering: can a non-human intelligent agent—a dog or dolphin or ape, for instance—avail itself of an annotated model, or is that level of cognitive sophistication reserved for language-users? This is just one instance of a sort of empirical question that is left curiously burked by Newell's reticence.

This gap is all the more frustrating since in other regards I find Newell's treatment in Chapters 1 and 2 of the standard debating topics in the philosophy of cognitive science a refreshing challenge. These chapters are simply required reading henceforth for any philosophers of cognitive science. [2] Newell doesn't waste time surveying the wreckage; he gets down to business. He says, in effect: "Sit down and listen; I'll show you how to think about these topics." He simply *makes moves* in all the games we play, and largely leaves it to us to object or play along. This should be a model for all non-philosopher scientists who aspire (correctly!) to philosophical probity. Don't try to play the philosophers' games. Just make your moves, clearly and explicitly, and see if you can get away with them.

I very largely agree with his moves, and it will be a pity if philosophers who disagree with him don't rise to the bait. They may not, alas. At times Newell underestimates how ingrown his jargon is. I have pushed portions of his text on some very smart philosophers and neuroscientists, and they are often completely at sea. (These issues are awfully hard to communicate about, and I am well aware that the alternative expository tactics I have tried in my own writing run their own risks of massive misconstrual.)

It might seem odd, finally, for me not to comment at all on Newell's deliberate postponement of consideration of consciousness, which gets just a brief apology on p. 434. Is this not unconscionable? Not at all. Newell's

---

[2] Philosophers will find important material throughout the book, not just in the foundational chapters at the beginning. For instance, the discussion of the discovery of the data-chunking problem in Soar and its handling (pp. 326–345) can be interpreted as a sort of inverse version of Meno's paradox of inquiry. The problem is not how can I search for something if I don't already know what it is, but how can I set myself up so that when I confront a real Meno-problem, there will be a way I can solve it? (Alternatively, if Soar couldn't solve the data-chunking problem, Meno's claim would not be paradoxical when applied to Soar, but simply true.) I think the memory-management search control strategies that are adopted can be read as part of an explicit answer—much more explicit than any philosopher's answer—to Meno's challenge.

project is highly compatible with mine in *Consciousness Explained* [4]. For instance, I endorse without reservation his list of multiple constraints on mind in Fig. 1-7 (p. 19). How can he achieve this divorce of consciousness? Just look! The enabling insight, for Newell and for me, is that handsome is as handsome does; you don't need any *extra witnesses* in order to explain cognition. Newell modestly denies that he has yet touched on consciousness; I disagree. He's made a big dent.

# References

[1] D.C. Dennett, Beyond belief, in: A. Woodfield, ed., *Thought and Object* (Clarendon Press, Oxford, 1982).
[2] D.C. Dennett, Is there an autonomous "Knowledge Level"? in: Z.W. Pylyshyn and W. Demopoulos, eds., *Meaning and Cognitive Structure* (Ablex, Norwood, NJ, 1986) 51–54.
[3] D.C. Dennett, *The Intentional Stance* (MIT Press/Bradford Books, Cambridge, MA, 1987).
[4] D.C. Dennett, *Consciousness Explained* (Little Brown, Boston, 1991).
[5] R. de Sousa, *The Rationality of Emotion* (MIT Press, Cambridge, MA, 1987).
[6] G.M. Edelman, *The Remembered Present: A Biological Theory of Consciousness* (Basic Books, New York, 1989).
[7] J.A. Fodor, Tom Swift and his Procedural Grandmother, *Cognition* 6 (1978) 229–247.
[8] J.A. Fodor and Z.W. Pylyshyn, Connectionism and cognitive architecture: a critical analysis, *Cognition* 28 (1988) 3–71; also in: S. Pinker and J. Mehler, eds., *Connectionism and Symbol Systems* (MIT Press, Cambridge, MA, 1988) 3–71.
[9] A. Newell, The symbol level and the knowledge level, in: Z.W. Pylyshyn and W. Demopoulos, eds., *Meaning and Cognitive Structure* (Ablex, Norwood, NJ, 1986) 169–193.
[10] A. Newell, P.S. Rosenbloom and J.E. Laird, Symbolic architectures for cognition, in: M. Posner, ed., *Foundations of Cognitive Science* (MIT Press, Cambridge, MA, 1989).
[11] A. Newell, G. Yost, J.E. Laird, P.S. Rosenbloom and E. Altmann, Formulating the problem-space computational model, in: R. Rashid, ed., *Carnegie Mellon Computer Science: A 25-Year Commemorative* (ACM Press/Addison-Wesley, Reading, MA, 1992).
[12] Z.W. Pylyshyn and W. Demopoulos, eds., *Meaning and Cognitive Structure* (Ablex, Norwood, NJ, 1986).
[13] A. Sloman and M. Croucher, Why robots will have emotions, in: *Proceedings IJCAI-81*, Vancouver, BC (1981).
[14] B.C. Smith, The link from symbol to knowledge, in: Z.W. Pylyshyn and W. Demopoulos, eds., *Meaning and Cognitive Structure* (Ablex, Norwood, NJ, 1986) 40–50.

Artificial Intelligence 59 (1993) 265–283
Elsevier

ARTINT 1009

# Book Review

# Allen Newell, *Unified Theories of Cognition**

Michael A. Arbib

*Center for Neural Engineering, University of Southern California, Los Angeles,
CA 90089-2520, USA*

Received September 1991
Revised September 1992

## 1. Soar: a general cognitive architecture

Among the classics of AI is GPS, the General Problem Solver (Newell,
Shaw and Simon [17] in 1959). Its key notion was that solving a problem
consisted in finding a sequence of operators for transforming the present state
into some goal state. A given problem area would be characterized by a finite
set of *differences* and an *operator-difference table*. Given two states, one would
compute the differences to be reduced between them, and then, for each
difference, consult the table to find an operator that had proven fairly reliable
for reducing that difference in a variety of situations. However, the given
operator was not guaranteed to reduce the difference in all circumstances. GPS
then proceeds with search by a process called *means–end analysis*: pick a
difference, apply an operator, look at the new goal and the new state, look at
the new difference and so on until the goal is attained. The challenge is to keep
track of these states, operators, and differences to extract a "good" path, i.e.,
a relatively economical sequence of operators which will carry out the desired
transformation.

More than a decade after developing GPS, Newell and Simon (1972)
published a huge book called *Human Problem Solving* [18] in which they

---

*Correspondence to:* M.A. Arbib, Center for Neural Engineering, University of Southern
California, Los Angeles, CA 90089-2520, USA. E-mail: arbib@pollux.usc.edu.
* (Harvard University Press, Cambridge, MA, 1990); xvi + 549 pages.

0004-3702/93/$06.00 © 1993 — Elsevier Science Publishers B.V. All rights reserved

looked at protocols showing how people solve numerical puzzles or word problems. They used such studies to develop means–end analysis into a psychological model of how people solve problems. In this way, GPS contributed to work in both classic AI and cognitive psychology, with each state represented as a small structure of symbols, and with operators providing explicit ways of manipulating symbols in some serial fashion to search a space to find an answer.

Another two decades have passed and, in *Unified Theories of Cognition*, Allen Newell offers us a specific symbolic processing architecture called Soar which may be seen as the culmination of the GPS paradigm. Instead of just measuring a difference and reducing it, Soar can consult a *long-term memory* that has many productions of the form: "if $X$ is the problem, then try $Y$". It also has a *working memory* containing the current set of goals, the relationships between them, and information about what means have already been tried. Rather than relying on a single operator-difference table as in GPS, Soar can invoke a variety of *problem spaces*, each providing a set of tools appropriate for some subclass of problems (Fig. 1). Rather than always applying an operator to reduce a difference, Soar may recognize that attaining a particular goal suggests a specific problem space which then invokes a particular set of methods to be used. *Subgoal generation* remains a key issue. After applying an operator or using the methods in a particular space, Soar has either solved the problem or it has not—in which case further subgoals must be generated in the attempt to move towards the overall goal. Soar also offers a simple learning mechanism called *chunking*. In trying to achieve a goal, Soar may generate many subgoals and subsubgoals to yield a large tree of different subgoals. Eventually, Soar will grow the tree to the point where it can find a path leading from the present state to the goal state by applying a sequence of operators—at which stage the rest of the search tree can be discarded. Soar can then store this successful "chunk" of the search tree in memory so that when it next encounters a similar problem it can immediately use that sequence of subgoals without getting into extensive search. Soar can have multiple goals and these need not agree, and the system can be set either to pick any one goal and try to achieve it or to take some numerical measure and come up with the best possible result even if it must ignore some of the goals in the process.

I plan to address Newell's bold claim (see especially his Chapter 2, "Foundations of Cognitive Science") that the specific choices which he and his colleagues made in developing Soar are central to the study of cognitive science in general and of human cognitive architecture in particular. I will argue that those choices are so heavily rooted in the classic serial symbol-processing approach to computation that they lead to an architecture which, whatever its merits within AI, is ill-suited to serve as a model for human cognitive architecture. This critique will be grounded in the view that cognitive science is to be conducted in terms of a vocabulary of interacting functional units called

## LONG-TERM KNOWLEDGE

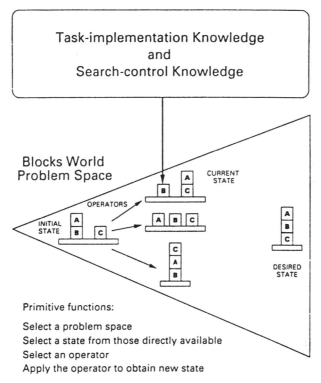

Task-implementation Knowledge
and
Search-control Knowledge

Blocks World
Problem Space

OPERATORS

Primitive functions:

Select a problem space
Select a state from those directly available
Select an operator
Apply the operator to obtain new state

Fig. 1. In Soar, the basic unit of processing is a problem space, as shown here. For different problem domains, different problem spaces may be invoked, each with its own representations and appropriate set of operators to carry out *problem search*. Part of Soar's knowledge is used to determine which is the appropriate knowledge to apply to attack a specific problem—this is *knowledge search*. Acting on a problem in one problem space may create subgoals which require the instantiation of new spaces for their attainment. (Figure 2-16 of Newell's *Unified Theories of Cognition*.)

*schemas* whose functional definition can in many (but not all) cases be constrained by neurological data. The review will then question the utility of Newell's use of a notion of knowledge akin to Chomsky's notion of competence by asserting that cognitive science must address data on human performance. However, the review closes on a more positive note, suggesting a research plan which links the schema-based approach to intelligence with some of Newell's key insights into the nature of problem solving. In particular, we will pay specific attention to Newell's notion of the "Great Move" from using specialized materials to support different schemas to using a medium in which it is possible to compose copies of whatever schemas are needed to form novel representations.

## 2. Differing criteria for a human cognitive architecture

What is an appropriate general framework for human cognitive architecture? Newell's approach to cognitive science is close to the following "extreme AI" position:

**Position (a).** Cognitive tasks rest on a set of basic processes, such as pattern recognition, search, memory, and inference, whose properties and interactions can be characterized in an abstract way independent of implementation. In particular, properties and interactions that we understand by implementing them on serial symbol processors are equally valid for the human mind.

Newell feels that problem spaces and the mechanisms that Soar provides to control them (Fig. 1) underlie any cognitive architecture. However, data may be employed to help constrain the specific problem spaces employed in any specific cognitive system. For a variety of human problem-solving tasks, Newell offers models which not only simulate *what* a human can do, but also have their structure constrained by data on the timing and errors of human performance. As such, these models certainly contribute to cognitive psychology, but in no way meet the demands of *cognitive neuroscience* which seeks to link cognitive capability to the brain mechanisms which subserve it. Timing data is not enough. In particular, Newell fails to make appropriate use of a wealth of data (experimental and clinical) about the effects of brain lesions on human and animal behavior. His approach also fails to connect gracefully with data and theories about instinctual behavior and the basis these provide for cognitive functions. Obviously, much useful work, including Newell's, can be done at a level of aggregation above that requiring the distribution of function over brain regions. I am not making the false claim that no good cognitive science can be done within the Soar framework. Rather, I am claiming that it is an approach that seems ill-suited to unify cognitive science if it is conceded that cognitive science must address, amongst other things, the data of clinical neurology.

Unfortunately, Newell's discussion of the "Foundations of Cognitive Science" (Chapter 2) offers neither an adequate concept of mind nor a well thought out characterization of cognitive science. He offers no "place to stand" from which to evaluate Soar, and takes no account of observations which suggest the importance of neurological data in dissecting cognitive processes. Newell takes "*mind* to be the control system that guides the behaving organism in its interactions with the dynamic real world" (p. 43). However, such a definition does not distinguish mind from brain, for it seems more correct to state that the *brain* is the control system that guides the behaving organism in its interactions with the dynamic real world. Again, he fails to address the notion that much of the control of such interactions is not mental, and that much of what is mental is subsymbolic and/or unconscious. Without offering a precise definition of "mental", let me just say that many people can agree on examples of mental activity (reading, thinking, etc.) even if they take the diametrically opposite philosophical positions of dualism (mind and brain are separate) or monism (mind is a function of brain). They would then agree that some mental activity (e.g., contemplation) need not result in overt "interactions with the dynamic real world", and that much of the brain's activity (e.g., controlling automatic breathing) is not mental. Face recognition seems to be a mental activity which we do not carry out through conscious symbol manipulation. And since Freud, even psychologists who reject his particular psychosexual theories accept his notion that much of our mental behavior is shaped by unconscious forces. (For an assessment of Freud and a schema-theoretic account of consciousness, see [5].)

Newell sees mind as providing *"response functions.* That is, the organism takes actions as a function of the environment. . . . However, many different response functions occur as the organism goes through time . . . such as one when you get yourself out of bed, one when you reach for your clothes, one when you face yourself in the mirror . . ." (p. 43). He then claims that "cognitive science needs a concept of knowledge that is used simply to describe and predict the response functions of a system" (p. 46). This ignores the issue of which response functions are cognitive and which are not. It also ignores the crucial distinction between being able to do something and having knowledge about it, a distinction related to "knowing how" versus "knowing that" which some (e.g., Squire [19]) take to underlie two kinds of human memory ("procedural" and "declarative") dissociable by brain lesions.

Despite his all too inclusive definition of "mind", when Newell (p. 61) charts the *Great Move* in evolution that distinguishes rational behavior from instinctive behavior, he gives the impression that he views rational behavior as the proper province of cognitive science, to the exclusion of instinctive behavior. By contrast, I believe it more fruitful to place human cognition in an evolutionary context rooted in mechanisms for instinctive behavior [1]. A famous example of this is provided by Humphrey's study [14] of "What the Frog's Eye Tells the Monkey's Brain". It had long been known that the role of tectum (the largest visual area in the midbrain) in directing whole body moments in frog is analogous to the role of superior colliculus (the mammalian homolog of tectum) in directing orienting movements in cat and monkey. It had also been believed by neurologists that a monkey (or human) without a visual cortex was blind. However, Humphrey argued that a monkey without visual cortex should have at least as much visual ability as a frog, but that such monkeys had not been taught to pay attention to available visual cues. After two years of attention training, the monkey without visual cortex that he worked with was able to use visual cues to grab at moving objects, and to use changes in luminance—such as an open door—for navigation, even though delicate processes of pattern recognition were never regained. Moreover, it was discovered that humans without visual cortex could also "see" in this sense—but, remarkably, they were not conscious that they could see. This phenomenon is referred to as *blindsight* (see Weiskrantz [21]). Clearly, blindsight is not in itself a rational behavior, being closely linked to the instinctive visually guided behavior of the frog. Yet, it seems to me that the above data are a crucial part of any theory of vision, and that anything that claims to be a "human cognitive architecture" must be able to address such data. This a Soar-based architecture does not do.

Many AI workers have used the slogan "aeroplanes don't flap their wings" to justify the claim that AI may be developed without reference to the study of biological systems. The same slogan equally justifies our skepticism that AI *per se* is adequate to address the needs of cognitive neuroscience. But if we reject Position (a) above (even for an AI informed by data on human performance but not on human neurology) must we go to the other extreme of what might be called "neurochemical reductionism"?:

**Position (b).** Any human cognitive architecture must take account of the way in which mood, emotion, and motivation affect human performance. We know that drugs can alter mood, and we know that the action of many of these drugs involves the way in which they bind to receptors in the cell membranes of neurons. Thus, no human cognitive architecture can be complete unless it incorporates the relevant specificities of neurochemistry.

Rather than discuss Position (b) explicitly, I will develop an intermediate position which encourages an interchange between *distributed* AI and cognitive neuroscience. To continue with the aeroplanes versus birds analogy, the bridging science of aerodynamics develops key concepts like lift, and then explains the different strategies of planes and birds in terms of the surface properties of the two kinds of wings and the way air is moved across them. Another discipline, materials science, has the task of understanding the surface properties. In the same way, we may hope (it is a research strategy which is yielding results but is by no means universally established) that the following approach may provide the right intermediate between Positions (a) and (b) above:

**Position (c).** Cognitive science is to be conducted in terms of a vocabulary of interacting functional units called *schemas*. Neuroscience then has the task of explaining the properties of these schemas in terms of neural circuitry or even the underlying neurochemistry and molecular biology. However, the functional definition of the schemas will in many cases be constrained by the data of clinical neurology and observations on modulation of behavior by variations in mood, emotion, and motivation.

To develop this argument, we must first turn to a brief exposition of schema theory, based on Arbib's [4].

## 3. Schema theory

Schema theory is an approach to knowledge representation that has been explicitly shaped by the need to understand how cognitive and instinctive functions can be implemented in a distributed fashion such as that involving the interaction of a multitude of brain regions. However, many of the concepts have been abstracted from biology to serve as "bringing" concepts which can be used in both distributed (DAI) and brain theory and thus can serve cognitive science whether or not the particular study addresses neurological or neurophysiological data:

(i) Schemas are ultimately defined by the execution of tasks within a physical environment. A set of *basic motor schemas* is hypothesized to provide simple, prototypical patterns of movement. These combine with *perceptual schemas* to form *assemblages* or *coordinated control programs* which interweave their activations in accordance with the current task and sensory environment to mediate more complex behaviors. Many schemas, however, may be abstracted from the perceptual-motor interface. Schema activations are largely task-driven, reflecting the goals of the organism and the physical and functional requirements of the task.

(ii) A schema is both a store of knowledge and the description of a process for applying that knowledge. As such, a schema may be instantiated to form multiple schema *instances* as active copies of the process to apply that knowledge. E.g., given a schema that represents generic knowledge about some object, we may need several active instances of the schema, each suitably tuned, to subserve our perception of a different instance of the object. Schemas can become *instantiated* in response to certain patterns of input from sensory stimuli or other schema instances that are already active.

(iii) Each instance of a schema has an associated *activity level*. That of a perceptual schema represents a "confidence level" that the object represented by the schema is indeed present; while that of a motor schema may signal its "degree of readiness" to control some course of action. The activity level of a schema instance may be but one of many parameters that characterize it. Thus the perceptual schema for "ball" might include parameters to represent size, color, and velocity.

(iv) The use, representation, and recall of knowledge is mediated through the activity of a network of interacting computing agents, the schema instances, which between them provide processes for going from a particular situation and a particular structure of goals and tasks to a suitable course of action (which may be overt or covert, as when learning occurs without action or the animal changes its state of readiness). This activity may involve passing of messages, changes of state (including activity level), instantiation to add new schema instances to the network, and deinstantiation to remove instances. Moreover, such activity may involve self-modification and self-organization.

(v) The key question is to understand how local schema interactions can integrate themselves to yield some overall result without explicit executive control, but rather through *cooperative computation*, a shorthand for "computation based on the competition and cooperation of concurrently active agents". For example, in VISIONS, a schema-based system for interpretation of visual scenes (Draper et al. [13]), schema instances represent hypotheses that particular objects occur at particular positions in a scene, so that instances may either represent conflicting hypotheses or offer mutual support. Cooperation yields a pattern of "strengthened alliances" between mutually consistent schema instances that allows them to achieve high activity levels to constitute the overall solution of a problem; competition ensures that instances which do not meet the evolving consensus lose activity, and thus are not part of this solution (though their continuing subthreshold activity may well affect later behavior). In this way, a schema network does not, in general, need a top-level executor, since schema instances can combine their effects by distributed processes of competition and cooperation, rather than the operation of an inference engine on a passive store of knowledge. This may lead to apparently emergent behavior, due to the absence of global control.

(vi) Learning is necessary because schemas are fallible. Schemas, and their connections within the schema network, must change so that over time they may well be able to handle a certain range of situations in a more adaptive way. In a general setting, there is no fixed repertoire of basic schemas. New schemas may be formed as assemblages of old schemas; but once formed a schema may be tuned by some adaptive mechanism. This tunability of schema assemblages allows them to become "primitive", much as a skill is honed into a unified whole from constituent pieces. Such tuning may be expressed at the level of schema theory itself, or may be driven by the dynamics of modification of unit interactions in some specific implementation of the schemas.

The words "brain" and "neural" do not appear in criteria (i)–(vi). We next spell out just what makes a schema-theoretical model part of brain theory:

(BTi) In brain theory, a given schema, defined functionally, may be distributed across more than one brain region; conversely, a given brain region may be involved in many schemas. A top-down analysis may advance specific hypotheses about the localization of (sub)-schemas in the brain and these may be tested by lesion experiments, with possible modification of the model (e.g., replacing one schema by several interacting schemas with different localizations) and further testing.

(BTii) Once a schema-theoretic model of some animal behavior has been refined to the point of hypotheses about the localization of schemas, we may then model a brain region by seeing if its known neural circuitry can indeed be shown to implement the posited schema. In some cases the model will involve properties of the circuitry that have not yet been tested, thus laying the ground for new experiments. In DAI, individual schemas may be implemented by artificial neural networks, or in some programming language on a "standard" (possibly distributed) computer.

Schema theory is far removed from serial symbol-based computation. Increasingly, work in AI now contributes to schema theory, even when it does not use this term. For example, Minsky [16] espouses a *Society of Mind* analogy in which "members of society", the agents, are analogous to schemas. Brooks [9] controls robots with layers of asynchronous modules that can be considered as a version of schemas (more of this later). Their work shares with schema theory, with its mediation of action through a network of schemas, the point that no single, central, logical representation of the world need link perception and action—the representation of the world is *the pattern of relationships between all its partial representations*. Another common theme, shared with Walter [20], Braitenberg [8], and Arbib [2], is the study of the "evolution" of simple "creatures" with increasingly sophisticated sensorimotor capacities.

We may now return to the claim of Position (c) that cognitive science is to be conducted in terms of a vocabulary of interacting schemas (or schema instances), and that neuroscience then has the task of explaining the properties of these schemas in terms of neural networks. Even though cognitive science itself is thus relieved of responsibility for explaining how schemas are implemented, it must still (a feathered flexible wing is different from a rigid metallic wing) be based, at least in part, on schemas which represent the functioning of hundreds of simultaneously active regions of the human brain. But there is nothing in the GPS tradition, or in Newell's book, that looks at distributed processing in any detail, let alone neurological data which constrains how the different parts of the computation might be located in the different parts of the brain. The point is *not* that all good cognitive science *must be* cognitive neuroscience. It is rather that a general framework for cognitive science must *include* cognitive neuroscience. In fact, given the current state of scientific knowledge, any current schema-level model of a cognitive system must be heterogeneous in that some schemas can be modeled in terms of detailed neural circuitry, some can be related to brain regions for which few details of circuitry are known, while others represent hypotheses about functional components for which little or no constraining neural data are available.

## 4. A cognitive architecture rooted in computer architecture

To understand why Newell's approach to cognitive science is so little adapted to the needs of cognitive neuroscience, we must see how his view of *cognitive architecture* is rooted in his 1971 work in *computer architecture* (Bell and Newell [6]), and in particular shaped by the hierarchy of computer systems in which the levels are (p. 47):

> *Bell–Newell computer hierarchy*
> program-level systems
> register-transfer systems
> logic circuits
> electrical circuits
> electronic devices

Newell states (p. 87) that such architectures emerged in the 1960s as the complexity of computer systems increased and that the enabling key was the development of the register-transfer level as an abstract description of the processing of bit vectors as a bridge between programs and the circuits that implement them. In developing his views of cognitive architecture, Newell makes three changes: he adds the knowledge level as an AI-motivated addition above the Bell–Newell hierarchy, he equates the symbol system level with the program level, and he does not specify the downward elaboration from the register-transfer level:

> *Newell cognitive hierarchy*
> knowledge-level systems
> symbol-level systems ($\approx$ programs)
> register-transfer systems

The knowledge level "abstracts completely from the internal processing and the internal representation. Thus, all that is left is the *content* of the representations and the *goals* toward which that content will be used" (p. 48). The program level in the Bell–Newell hierarchy is based on sequential operation of programs, and this feature of 1971-style computers (namely, seriality) has colored Newell's view of cognition:

> A knowledge system is embedded in an external environment, with which it interacts by a set of possible actions. The behavior of the system is the *sequence* of actions taken in the environment over time.... Its body of knowledge is about its environment, its goals, its actions, and the relations between them. It has a single law of behavior: the system takes actions to attain its goals, using *all* the knowledge that it has.... The system can obtain new knowledge from external knowledge sources via some of its actions.... Once knowledge is acquired, it is available *forever* after. The system is a single *homogeneous* body of knowledge, *all* of which is brought to bear on the determination of its actions. (p. 50, my italics)

The italicized *forever* and *all* stress the point that the knowledge level is an unattainable ideal, unconstrained by implementation limits of computing space or time (as in Chomsky's preference for theories of "competence" rather than "performance"). Newell's claim that "all the person's knowledge is always used to attain the goals of that person" (p. 50) is not even approximately true of normal human behavior—or even of highly aberrant behavior such as seeking to complete this review. The words *sequence* and *homogeneous* already predispose the theory against a distributed view of AI (coordinated problem solving by a network of heterogeneous schemas) let alone providing a conception of knowledge that can be related to the functioning of human brains. Moreover, Newell carries over from computer science the view that function at each level can be studied without attention to its implementation at lower levels:

> [Behavior at each level is] determined by the behavior laws, as formulated for that level, applying to its state as described at that level. The claim is that abstraction to the particular level involved still preserves all that is relevant for future behavior described at that level of abstraction.... Thus, to claim that humans can be described at the knowledge level is to claim there is a way of formulating them as agents that have knowledge and goals, such that their behavior is successfully predicted by the law that says: all the person's knowledge is always used to attain the goals of the person ... no details of the actual internal processing are required. This behavior of an existing system can be calculated if you know the system's goals and what the system knows about its environment. (pp. 49–50)

My point is not to throw away the idea of a level of abstract specifications (call it the knowledge level, if you will). Rather, it is my point that for cognitive science we need specifications which take timing and real-world interaction into account. Thus "hit the ball" is far removed from the level of retinal activity and muscle contractions, but the task imposes a concreteness of interaction that is far removed from the mere abstract knowledge that, e.g., a bat would serve the task better than a hand. The latter "knowledge" provides a useful annotation, but cannot provide a complete specification that can be refined level by level with logical exactness and without revision of the initial specification.

In Newell's cognitive science, symbol systems play the role of the program level. Newell (pp. 80–81) then defines an *architecture* as the fixed structure that realizes a symbol system. In the computer systems hierarchy it is the description of the system at the register-transfer level, below the symbol level, that provides the architecture. The architecture is the description of the system in whatever system description scheme exists next below the symbol level. This raises the question of what system description scheme exists next below the symbol level (i.e., what is the "register-transfer systems" level of the mind?). The "pure AI" approach of Position (a) would accept any system convenient for mapping symbol systems onto serial computers. However, the move towards brain function takes us away from seriality. We focus on competition and cooperation of concurrently active schema instances. More boldly, I claim that the schema level in the Position (c) approach to cognitive science replaces the symbol-system level in Newell's Position (a) approach, but I add that the Position (c) approach also dispenses with a knowledge level that is distinct from the schema level. The schema theorist may still want a "level" in which to talk about generic properties of schemas without reference to their particular specifications, but I view this as talk *about* cognitive systems, rather than a level of representation *of* those systems. On this account, symbols are replaced by schemas which, by combining representation and execution, are far richer than symbols are often taken to be.

Research in the neurophysiology of vision, memory, and action gives information a non-symbolic representation distributed in patterns that do not lend themselves immediately to a crisp description with a few symbols. It is thus a daunting, but exciting, challenge to show how the insights of Newell's approach can make contact with the study of neural networks and issues in cognitive neuroscience. Some members of the Soar community have begun to look at implementations on parallel computers, or at the use of artificial neural networks to implement Soar's memory functions (Cho, Rosenbloom, and Dolan [10]), but I know of no attempt to make extended contact between Soar and neuroscience.

## 5. Connectionism ≠ brain theory

In developing Soar and the various cognitive models in his book, Newell ignores the biological substrate save for some timing constraints in Chapter 3, and he emphasizes a serial symbol-computation perspective throughout. However, he does offer a few hints of possible changes. He states that "One of the major challenges in the development of massively parallel connectionist systems is whether they will find a different hierarchical organization. In any event, the computer-systems hierarchy is an important invariant structural characteristic, although its [*sic*] seems to be the only one" (p. 88); and he devotes Section 8.3 to some comparisons of Soar with connectionism. However, Section 8.3, "The Biological Band", is misnamed since the comparisons are with the artificial networks of connectionism, not with biological data on the (human) brain. The "neural networks" of connectionism are nets of abstract computing elements, rather than models of the actual circuitry of the brain.

Since our present focus is to determine the extent to which Soar can provide a framework for cognitive science broad enough to encompass cognitive neuroscience, it is thus important to know how relevant Newell's views are to this extension, and in particular to assess the extent to which the organization of "massively parallel connectionist systems" is the same as that of the brain. The connectionist comparison is, in fact, so undernourished and underconstrained by comparison with what is needed for a cognitive neuroscience that I need to emphasize the claim of the section title: *connectionism ≠ brain theory*.

For some "connectionists", all connectionist systems have the same structure, namely large randomly connected neural-like networks which become increasingly adapted to solve some problem through training and/or self-organization. In such an approach, there seem to be only two levels, the specification of what a network is to do (akin to the knowledge level?) and the tuned neural network itself (akin to the logic-circuit level), with nothing in between. However, brain theory is not connectionism, even though progress in connectionism may enrich our vocabulary of the computations that neural networks, viewed abstractly, can perform. Analysis of animal behavior or human cognition should yield a model of how that behavior is achieved through the *cooperative computation* of concurrently active regions or schemas of the brain (the two analyses are not equivalent: regions are structural units; schemas are functional units), rather than in terms of any simple one-way flow of information in a hierarchically organized system.

Items (BTi) and (BTii) of Section 3 embody the eventual goal of cognitive *neuro*science—that functional and structural analyses be rendered congruent. However, experience with brain modeling shows that a distribution of function across schemas that may seem psychologically plausible may not survive the test of neurological data which demand that the schemas be structured in such a way that their subschemas are allocatable across brain regions to yield a model that predicts the effects of various brain lesions.

For example, a model of our ability to make saccadic eye movements to one or more targets even after they are no longer visible requires a schema to inhibit reflex responses, as well as schemas for working memory (holding a "plan of action") and dynamic remapping (updating the "plan" as action proceeds). But this does not imply that a distinct *region* of the brain has evolved for each functionally distinct *schema*. More specifically, a neural refinement of the model (Dominey and Arbib [12]) distributes these three schemas across a variety of brain regions (parietal cortex, frontal eye fields, basal ganglia, and superior colliculus) in a way that responds to and explains a variety of neurophysiological data. (The reader may recall the data on blindsight, showing how the superior colliculus of monkeys can support a range of subconscious visual functions, but that these nonetheless seem to provide a basis for the totality, dependent on cerebral cortex, of our visual repertoire.)

To summarize, functions that appear well separated in an initial top-down analysis of some behavior or cognitive function may exhibit intriguing interdependencies as a result of shared circuitry in the neural model whose construction was guided by, but which also modifies, that initial analysis. I am thus sceptical of Newell's view (pp. 49–50, cited earlier) that each of the levels in his cognitive hierarchy can be operationally complete with no details of the actual internal processing being required. In particular, schema change may be driven by the dynamics of modification of unit interactions in some specific implementation of the schemas. The learning curve of two different neural networks may be dramatically different even though they come under the same symbolic description of their initial behavior.

As noted earlier, Newell's idea of architecture is rooted in the conceptually serial register-transfer level, and does not really come to terms with the possibility of a framework (cooperative computation) that *drastically* expands the concept of computation to embrace the style of the brain. Although Newell notes that massive parallelism can result in *qualitatively* different computations since real-time constraints reveal the effective amount of computation available within specified time limits, I do not find this issue returned to in the attempt to understand the nature of information processing in the human cognitive system, or in the brain that underlies it. By contrast, schema theory emphasizes the distributed, cooperative computation of multiple schema instances distributed across distinctive brain regions; it is delegation of schema functionality to neural networks that brings in massive parallelism. The hierarchy then becomes:

> *Schema-based cognitive hierarchy*
>     descriptions of behaviors
>     schemas ($\approx$ programs)
>     interacting brain regions
>     neural circuitry
>     neurons
>     sub-neural components (synapses, etc.)

We map schemas onto brain regions where possible, though accepting computer programs as a "default" when constraining neuroscience data are unavailable or inappropriate. In the brain, we might view successive refinements of the overall architecture as involving (i) the segregation into anatomically distinct regions, (ii) the classifications of different circuits and cell types in each region, and (iii) the overall specification of which cell type synapses on what other cell types and with what transmitter. Changes in the detailed pattern of, e.g., cell-by-cell synaptic weighting could then give the architecture its adaptability. The bulk of these changes will be seen as the dynamics of the "software", with changes in "architecture" corresponding only to overall shifts in "computing style" resulting from cooperative effects of myriad small changes.

### 6. The Great Move: searching for a conclusion

The tone of this review has been negative, in that it has emphasized the problems posed to those of us interested in the role of the brain in cognition by the use of a serial symbol-processing approach, or the use of the knowledge level as providing a performance-independent characterization of cognitive competence. I have not reviewed the many substantial contributions that Newell has made to AI and cognitive psychology, and which are well documented in his book. To somewhat redress the balance, this final section suggests a viable research plan which links the schema-based approach to intelligence with some of Newell's key insights into the nature of problem solving. We may start with Newell's discussion of ethology which sets the stage for his discussion of what he properly calls *the Great Move*:

> Finding feasible representations gets increasingly difficult with a richer and richer variety of things to be represented and richer and richer kinds of operational transformations that they undergo. More and more interlocking representation laws need to be satisfied. . . . [E]thologists have [studied] the adaptive character of lower organisms. . . . Unfortunately, not all adaptations require representations, and the examples, from the digger wasp to the stickleback, are not sorted out to make it easy to see exactly what is representation and what is not. . . . Instead of moving toward more and more specialized materials with specialized dynamics to support an increasingly great variety and intricacy of representational demands, an entirely different turn is possible. This is the move [the Great Move] to using a neutral, stable medium that is capable of registering variety and then *composing* whatever transformations are needed to satisfy the requisite representation law. Far from representational constriction, this path opens up the whole world of indefinitely rich representations. (p. 61)

The line between representation and non-representation is a sticky one. Does the stickleback lack a representation of males with which it is to compete, or is the representation too inclusive to discriminate the experimentalist's simulacrum from the actual opponent? Perhaps the key point is that the stickleback lacks the ability to recognize when it is mistaken and change its ways accordingly (and this is only the beginning of the necessary refinements— cf. Bennett [7] for all the ingredients that a bee would have to exhibit for its "language" to be a true index of rationality).

We may note here a controversy about the nature of AI fomented, e.g., by Brooks [9] which sets an ethologically inspired hierarchy of levels of control (mentioned earlier as being in the spirit of schema theory), each biasing rather than replacing the one below it, in opposition to the "classical" view of abstract operators applied to uniform representations. Newell offers a somewhat broader version of classical AI, since he allows a variety of problem spaces— but nonetheless sees these each as being implemented in some uniform medium, like that offered by the register-transfer level in the Bell–Newell hierarchy. However, it seems mistaken to see this as a sharp dichotomy in which one school or the other must prove triumphant. The schema theorist (as in our discussion of blindsight) explains a complex cognitive function through the interaction of "instinctive" schemas, implemented in specifically evolved circuitry, and "abstract" schemas that are developed through learning and experience in "general-purpose" (highly adaptive, post-Great-Move) circuitry. An intelligent system needs to combine the ability to react rapidly (jumping out of the way of an unexpected vehicle when crossing the street) with the ability to abstractly weigh alternatives (deciding on the best route to get to the next appointment).

In summary, a satisfactory account of Newell's "Great Move" should not seek a complete break from using specialized materials to support different schemas to using a medium in which it is possible to compose copies of whatever schemas are needed to form novel representations. Rather, we should provide—in the manner of schema theory—insight into how instinctive behavior provides a basis for, and is intertwined with, rational behavior. When I study frogs [2], I see the animal's behavior mediated by the dynamic interaction of multiple special-purpose schemas implemented in dedicated neural circuitry. But when I seek to understand human vision, I combine a model of low-level vision implemented across a set of dedicated brain regions (DeYoe and Van Essen [11]) with a general-purpose medium in which copies of schemas (schema instances) can be assembled, parameterized, and bound to regions of the image as they compete and cooperate in a process of distributed planning which creates an interpretation of a visual scene (recall item (v) of Section 3; cf. Arbib [3, esp. Sections 5.1, 5.2, 7.3, and 7.4]). The contrast between frog visuomotor coordination and the flexibility of human visual perception makes explicit the contrast between those schema assemblages that are "evolutionarily hardwired" into patterns of competition and cooperation between specific brain regions, and those which can, through multiple in- stantiations (both data- and hypothesis-driven), yield totally novel forms to develop new skills and represent novel situations. It is this latter form of "creative" representation that Newell espouses:

> The great move has forged a link between representations and composable response functions. If a system can compose functions and if it can do it internally in an arena under its own control, then that system can represent. How well it can represent depends on how flexible is its ability to compose functions that obey the needed representation laws—there can be limits to composability. How- ever, representation and composability are not inherently linked together. If the representations are realized in a special medium with appropriate . . . transformations, there need be no com- posability at all. (p. 63)

Such flexibility of composition, of being able to link in new problem spaces (recall Fig. 1) as the need arises to provide a complex problem-solving structure, is one of the great strengths of Soar. Even though I remain sceptical of Newell's sharp division between knowledge and its application, I feel that he advances our understanding when he makes the key distinction between *problem search* and *knowledge search*:

> There are two separate searches going on in intelligence. One is *problem search* which is the search of [a] problem space. . . . The other is *knowledge search*, which is the search in the memory of the system for the knowledge to guide the problem search. . . . [For] a special purpose intelligent system [only problem search need occur]. [For] agents that work on a wide range of tasks. . . [w]hen a new task arises, [their] body of knowledge must be searched for knowledge that is relevant to the task. . . . [K]nowledge search goes on continually—and the more problematical the situation, the more continuous is the need for it. (pp. 98–99)

All this suggests a rapprochement in which future work explores the integration of key insights from Soar with the distributed approach in which action is mediated through a network of schema instances in which no single, central, logical representation of the world need link perception and action. This would add to Newell's scheme the distinction between *off-line planning* which finds a sequence of operators to go all the way to the goal and *then* applies them in the world, and *dynamic planning* which chooses the next few (possibly concurrent) actions which may help achieve the goal, applies them, and then factors new sensory input into continued activity (cf. the "reactive planning" of Lyons and Hendriks [15]).

Perhaps a starting point is to regard a problem space as the analog of a schema, and the creation of a new problem space to meet a subgoal as the analog of schema instantiation. The key question then becomes: How do we restructure Soar when many problem spaces/schema instances can be simultaneously active, continually passing messages, both modulatory and symbolic, to one another? When this question is answered, the seriality that dominates Newell's book will be sundered, and the full-throated dialog between the Soar community and workers in cognitive neuroscience and distributed AI can truly begin.

## References

[1] M.A. Arbib, Perceptual motor processes and the neural basis of language, in: M.A. Arbib, D. Caplan and J.C. Marshall. eds., *Neural Models of Language Processes* (Academic Press, New York, 1982) 531–551.

[2] M.A. Arbib, Levels of modeling of mechanisms of visually guided behavior (with commentaries and author's response), *Behav. Brain Sci.* 10 (1987) 407–465.

[3] M.A. Arbib, *The Metaphorical Brain 2: Neural Networks and Beyond* (Wiley Interscience, New York, 1989).

[4] M.A. Arbib, Schema theory, in: S.C. Shapiro, ed., *The Encyclopedia of Artificial Intelligence* (Wiley Interscience, New York, 2nd ed., 1992).

[5] M.A. Arbib and M.B. Hesse, *The Construction of Reality* (Cambridge University Press, Cambridge, England, 1986).

[6] C.G. Bell and A. Newell, *Computer Structures: Readings and Examples* (McGraw-Hill, New York, 1971).

[7] J. Bennett, *Rationality: An Essay towards an Analysis* (Routledge & Kegan Paul, London, 1964).

[8] V. Braitenberg, *Vehicles: Experiments in Synthetic Psychology* (Bradford Books/MIT Press, Cambridge, MA, 1984).

[9] R.A. Brooks, A robust layered control system for a mobile robot, *IEEE J. Rob. Autom.* 2 (1986) 14–23.

[10] B. Cho, P.S. Rosenbloom and C.P. Dolan, Neuro-Soar: a neural-network architecture for goal-oriented behavior, in: *Proceedings 13th Annual Conference of the Cognitive Science Society*, Chicago, IL (1991).

[11] E.A. DeYoe and D.C. Van Essen, Concurrent processing streams in monkey visual cortex, *Trends Neurosci.* 11 (5) (1988) 219–226.

[12] P.F. Dominey and M.A. Arbib, A cortico-subcortical model for generation of spatially accurate sequential saccades, *Cerebral Cortex* 2 (1992) 153–175.

[13] B.A. Draper, R.T. Collins, J. Brolio, A.R. Hanson and E.M. Riseman, The schema system, *Int. J. Comput. Vision* 2 (1989) 209–250.

[14] N.K. Humphrey, What the frog's eye tells the monkey's brain, *Brain Behav. Evol.* 3 (1970) 324–337.

[15] D.M. Lyons and A.J. Hendriks, Planning, reactive, in: S.C. Shapiro, ed., *The Encyclopedia of Artificial Intelligence* (Wiley Interscience, New York, 2nd ed., 1992) 1171–1181.

[16] M.L. Minsky, *The Society of Mind* (Simon and Schuster, New York, 1985).

[17] A. Newell, J.C. Shaw and H.A. Simon, Report on a general problem-solving program, in: *Proceedings International Conference on Information Processing*, UNESCO House (1959) 256–264.

[18] A. Newell and H.A. Simon, *Human Problem Solving* (Prentice-Hall, Englewood Cliffs, NJ, 1972).

[19] L.R. Squire, *Memory and Brain* (Oxford University Press, Oxford, 1987).

[20] W.G. Walter, *The Living Brain* (Penguin Books, Harmondsworth, England, 1953).

[21] L. Weiskrantz, The interaction between occipital and temporal cortex in vision: an overview, in: F.O. Schmitt and F.G. Worden, eds., *The Neurosciences Third Study Program* (MIT Press, Cambridge, MA, 1974) 189–204.

Paul M. Churchland

# On the Nature of Theories:
# A Neurocomputational Perspective

## I. The Classical View of Theories

Not long ago, we all knew what a theory was: it was a set of sentences or propositions, expressible in the first-order predicate calculus. And we had what seemed to be excellent reasons for that view. Surely any theory had to be sta*table*. And after it had been fully stated, as a set of sentences, what residue remained? Furthermore, the sentential view made systematic sense of how theories could perform the primary business of theories, namely, prediction, explanation, and intertheoretic reduction. It was basically a matter of first-order deduction from the sentences of the theory conjoined with relevant premises about the domain at hand.

Equally important, the sentential view promised an account of the nature of learning, and of rationality. Required was a set of formal rules to dictate appropriate changes or updates in the overall set of believed sentences as a function of new beliefs supplied by observation. Of course there was substantial disagreement about which rules were appropriate. Inductivists, falsificationists, hypothetico-deductivists, and Bayesian subjectivists each proposed a different account of them. But the general approach seemed clearly correct. Rationality would be captured as the proper set of formal rules emerged from logical investigation.

Finally, if theories are just sentences, then the ultimate virtue of a theory is truth. And it was widely expected that an adequate account of rational methodol-

Several pages in section 4 are based on material from an earlier paper, "Reductionism, Connectionism, and the Plasticity of Human Consciousness," *Cultural Dynamics*, 1 (1): 1988. Three pages in section 5 are drawn from "Simplicity: The View from the Neuronal Level." In *Aesthetic Factors in Natural Science*, ed. N. Rescher (forthcoming, 1990). My thanks to the editors for permission to use that material here. For many useful discussions, thanks also to Terry Sejnowski, Patricia Churchland, David Zipser, Dave Rumelhart, Francis Crick, Stephen Stich, and Philip Kitcher.

ogy would reveal why humans must tend, in the long run, toward theories that are true.

Hardly anyone will now deny that there are serious problems with every element of the preceding picture—difficulties we shall discuss below. Yet the majority of the profession is not yet willing to regard them as fatal. I profess myself among the minority that does so regard them. In urging the poverty of 'sentential epistemologies' for over a decade now (Churchland 1975, 1979, 1981, 1986), I have been motivated primarily by the *pattern* of the failures displayed by that approach. Those failures suggest to me that what is defective in the classical approach is its fundamental assumption that languagelike structures of some kind constitute the basic or most important form of representation in cognitive creatures, and the correlative assumption that cognition consists in the manipulation of those representations by means of structure-sensitive rules.

To be sure, not everyone saw the same pattern of failure, nor were they prepared to draw such a strong conclusion even if they did. For any research program has difficulties, and so long as we lack a comparably compelling *alternative* conception of representation and computation, it may be best to stick with the familiar research program of sentences and rules for their manipulation.

However, it is no longer true that we lack a comparably compelling alternative approach. Within the last five years, there have been some striking theoretical developments and experimental results within cognitive neurobiology and 'connectionist' AI (artificial intelligence). These have provided us with a powerful and fertile framework with which to address problems of cognition, a framework that owes nothing to the sentential paradigm of the classical view. My main purpose in this essay is to make the rudiments of that framework available to a wider audience, and to explore its far-reaching consequences for traditional issues in the philosophy of science. Before turning to this task, let me prepare the stage by briefly summarizing the principal failures of the classical view, and the most prominent responses to them.

## II. Problems and Alternative Approaches

The depiction of learning as the rule-governed updating of a system of sentences or propositional attitudes encountered a wide range of failures. For starters, even the best of the rules proposed failed to reproduce reliably our preanalytic judgments of credibility, even in the artificially restricted or 'toy' situations in which they were asked to function. Paradoxes of confirmation plagued the H-D accounts (Hempel 1965; Scheffler 1963). The indeterminacy of falsification plagued the Popperian accounts (Lakatos 1970; Feyerabend 1970; Churchland 1975). Laws were assigned negligible credibility on Carnapian accounts (Salmon, 1966). Bayesian accounts, like Carnapian ones, presupposed a given probability space as the epistemic playground within which learning takes place, and they could not account for the rationality of major shifts from one probability space to another, which is what the most interesting and important cases of learning amount to. The rationality of large-scale *conceptual change*, accordingly, seemed beyond the reach of such approaches. Furthermore, simplicity emerged as a major determinant of theoretical credibility on most accounts, but none of them could provide an adequate definition of simplicity in syntactic terms, or give a convincing explanation of why it was relevant to truth or credibility in any case. One could begin to question whether the basic factors relevant to learning were to be found at the linguistic level at all.

Beyond these annoyances, the initial resources ascribed to a learning subject by the sentential approach plainly presupposed the successful completion of a good deal of sophisticated learning on the part of that subject already. For example, reliable observation judgments do not just appear out of nowhere. Living subjects have to *learn* to make the complex perceptual discriminations that make perceptual judgments possible. And they also have to *learn* the linguistic or propositional system within which their beliefs are to be constituted. Plainly, both cases of learning will have to involve some procedure quite distinct from that of the classical account. For that account presupposes antecedent possession of both a determinate propositional system and a capacity for determinate perceptual judgment, which is precisely what, prior to extensive learning, the human infant lacks. Accordingly, the classical story cannot possibly account for all cases of learning. There must exist a type of learning that is prior to and more basic than the process of sentence manipulation at issue.

Thus are we led rather swiftly to the idea that there is a level of representation *beneath* the level of the sentential or propositional attitudes, and to the correlative idea that there is a learning dynamic that operates primarily on sublinguistic factors. This idea is reinforced by reflection on the problem of cognition and learning in nonhuman animals, none of which appear to have the benefit of language, either the external speech or the internal structures, but all of which engage in sophisticated cognition. Perhaps their cognition proceeds entirely without benefit of any system for processing sentencelike representations.

Even in the human case, the depiction of one's knowledge as an immense set of individually stored 'sentences' raises a severe problem concerning the relevant retrieval or application of those internal representations. How is it one is able to retrieve, from the millions of sentences stored, exactly the handful that is relevant to one's current predictive or explanatory problem, and how is it one is generally able to do this in a few tenths of a second? This is known as the "Frame Problem" in AI, and it arises because, from the point of view of fast and relevant retrieval, a long list of sentences is an appallingly inefficient way to store information. And the more information a creature has, the worse its application problem becomes.

A further problem with the classical view of learning is that it finds no essential connection whatever between the learning of *facts* and the learning of *skills*. This is a problem in itself, since one might have hoped for a unified account of learning, but it is doubly a problem when one realizes that so much of the business of understanding a theory and being a scientist is a matter of the skills one has acquired. Memorizing a set of sentences is not remotely sufficient: one must learn to *recognize* the often quite various instances of the terms they contain; one must learn to *manipulate* the peculiar formalism in which they may be embedded; one must learn to *apply* the formalism to novel situations; one must learn to *control* the instruments that typically produce or monitor the phenomena at issue. As T. S. Kuhn first made clear (Kuhn 1962), these dimensions of the scientific trade are only artificially separable from one's understanding of its current theories. It begins to appear that even if we do harbor internal sentences, they capture only a small part of human knowledge.

These failures of the classical view over the full range of learning, both in humans and in nonhuman animals, are the more suspicious given the classical view's total disconnection from any theory concerning the structure of the biological *brain*, and the manner in which it might *implement* the kind of representations and computations proposed. Making acceptable contact with neurophysiological theory is a long-term constraint on any epistemology: a scheme of representation and computation that cannot be implemented in the machinery of the human brain cannot be an adequate account of human cognitive activities.

The situation on this score used to be much better than it now is: it was clear that the classical account of representation and learning could easily be realized in typical digital computers, and it was thought that the human brain would turn out to be relevantly like a digital computer. But quite aside from the fact that computer implementations of sentential learning chronically produced disappointing results, it has become increasingly clear that the brain is organized along computational lines radically different from those employed in conventional digital computers. The brain, as we shall see below, is a massively parallel processor, and it performs computational tasks of the classical kind at issue only very slowly and comparatively badly. To speak loosely, it does not appear to be designed to perform the tasks the classical view assigns to it.

I conclude this survey by returning to specifically philosophical matters. A final problem with the classical approach has been the failure of all attempts to explain why the learning process must tend, at least in the long run, to lead us toward *true* theories. Surprisingly, and perhaps distressingly, this Panglossean hope has proved very resistant to vindication (Van Fraassen 1980; Laudan 1981). Although the history of human intellectual endeavor does support the view that, over the centuries, our theories have become dramatically *better* in many dimensions, it is quite problematic whether they are successively 'closer' to 'truth'. Indeed, the notion of truth itself has recently come in for critical scrutiny (Putnam 1981; Churchland 1985; Stich 1990). It is no longer clear that there *is* any unique and unitary relation that virtuous belief systems must bear to the nonlinguistic world. Which leaves us free to reconsider the great many different dimensions of epistemic and pragmatic virtue that a cognitive system can display.

The problems of the preceding pages have not usually been presented in concert, and they are not usually regarded as conveying a unitary lesson. A few philosophers, however, have been moved by them, or by some subset of them, to suggest significant modifications in the classical framework. One approach that has captured some adherents is the 'semantic view' of theories (Suppe 1974; Van Fraassen 1980; Giere 1988). This approach attempts to drive a wedge between a theory and its possibly quite various linguistic formulations by characterizing a theory as a *set of models*, those that will make a first-order linguistic statement of the theory come out *true* under the relevant assignments. The models in the set all share a common abstract structure, and that structure is what is important about any theory, according to the semantic view, not any of its idiosyncratic linguistic expressions. A theory is true, on this view, just in case it includes the actual world, or some part of it, as one of the models in the set.

This view buys us some advantages, perhaps, but I find it to be a relatively narrow response to the panoply of problems addressed above. In particular, I think it strange that we should be asked, at this stage of the debate, to embrace an account of theories that has absolutely nothing to do with the question of how real physical systems might embody representations of the world, and how they might execute principled computations on those representations in such a fashion as to learn. Prima facie, at least, the semantic approach takes theories even farther into Plato's Heaven, and away from the buzzing brains that use them, than did the view that a theory is a set of sentences. This complaint does not do justice to the positive virtues of the semantic approach (see especially Giere, whose version does make some contact with current cognitive psychology). But it is clear that the semantic approach is a response to only a small subset of the extant difficulties.

A more celebrated response is embodied in Kuhn's *The Structure of Scientific Revolutions* (1962). Kuhn centers our attention not on sets of sentences, nor on sets of models, but on what he calls paradigms or exemplars, which are specific *applications* of our conceptual, mathematical, and instrumental resources. Mastering a theory, on this view, is more a matter of being able to perform in various ways, of being able to solve a certain class of problems, of being able to recognize diverse situations as relevantly similar to that of the original or paradigmatic application. Kuhn's view brings to the fore the historical, the sociological, and the psychological factors that structure our theoretical cognition. Of central importance is the manner in which one comes to perceive the world as one internalizes a theory. The perceptual world is redivided into new categories, and while the theory may be able to provide necessary and sufficient conditions for being an instance of any of its categories, the perceptual recognition of any instance of a category does not generally proceed by reference to those conditions, which often transcend perceptual experience. Rather, perceptual recognition proceeds by some inarticulable process that registers *similarity* to one or more perceptual *prototypes* of the category at issue. The recognition of new applications of the apparatus of the entire theory displays a similar dynamic. In all, a successful theory provides a prototypical beachhead that one attempts to expand by analogical extensions to new domains.

Reaction to this view has been deeply divided. Some applaud Kuhn's move toward naturalism, toward a performance conception of knowledge, and away from the notion of truth as the guiding compass of cognitive activity (Munevar 1981; Stich 1990). Others deplore his neglect of normative issues, his instrumentalism and relativism, and his alleged exaggeration of certain lessons from perceptual and developmental psychology (Fodor 1984). We shall address these issues later in the paper.

A third and less visible reaction to the classical difficulties has simply rejected the sentential or propositional attitudes as the most important form of representation used by cognitive creatures, and has insisted on the necessity of empirical and theoretical research into *brain* function in order to answer the question of what *are* the most important forms of representation and computation within cognitive creatures. Early statements can be found in Churchland 1975 and Hooker 1975; extended arguments appear in Churchland 1979 and 1981; and further arguments appear in Churchland, P.S., 1980 and 1986, and in Hooker 1987.

While the antisentential diagnosis could be given some considerable support, as the opening summary of this section illustrates, neuroscience as the recommended cure was always more difficult to sell, given the functional opacity of the biological brain. Recently, however, this has changed dramatically. We now have some provisional insight into the functional significance of the brain's microstructure, and some idea of how it represents and computes. What has been discovered so far appears to vindicate the claims of philosophical relevance and the expectations of fertility in this area, and it appears to vindicate some central elements in Kuhn's perspective as well. This neurofunctional framework promises to sustain wholly new directions of cognitive research. In the sections to follow I shall try to outline the elements of this framework and its applications to some familiar problems in the philosophy of science. I begin with the physical structure and the basic activities of the brainlike systems at issue.

## III. Elementary Brainlike Networks

The functional atoms of the brain are cells called neurons (figure 1). These have a natural or default level of activity that can, however, be modulated up or down by external influences. From each neuron there extends a long, thin output fiber called an *axon*, which typically branches at the far end so as to make a large number of *synaptic connections* with either the central cell body or the bushy *den-*

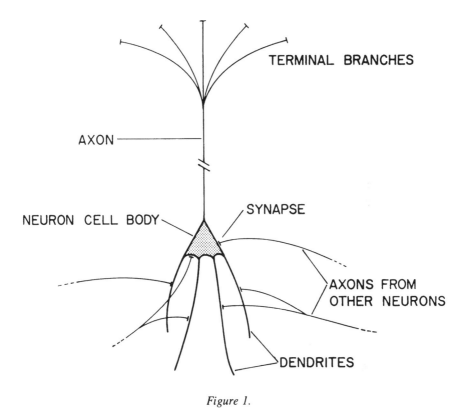

*Figure 1.*

*drites* of other neurons. Each neuron thus receives inputs from a great many other neurons, which inputs tend to excite (or to inhibit, depending on the type of synaptic connection) its normal or default level of activation. The level of activation induced is a function of the *number* of connections, of their size or *weight*, of their *polarity* (stimulatory or inhibitory), and of the *strength* of the incoming signals. Furthermore, each neuron is constantly emitting an output signal along its own axon, a signal whose strength is a direct function of the overall level of activation in the originating cell body. That signal is a train of pulses or *spikes*, as they are called, which are propagated swiftly along the axon. A typical cell can emit spikes along its axon at anything between zero and perhaps 200 Hz. Neurons, if you like, are humming to one another, in basso notes of varying frequency.

The networks to be explored attempt to simulate natural neurons with artifical units of the kind depicted in figure 2. These units admit of various levels of activation, which we shall assume to vary between 0 and 1. Each unit receives input signals from other units via 'synaptic' connections of various weights and polari-

## NEURON-LIKE PROCESSING UNIT

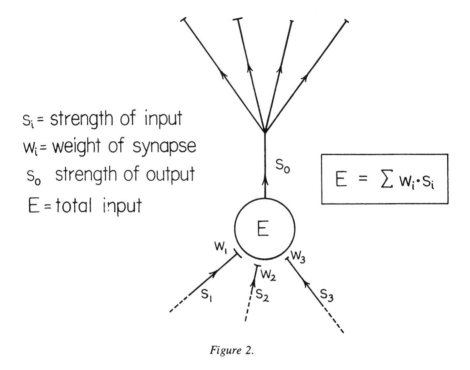

$s_i$ = strength of input
$w_i$ = weight of synapse
$s_o$  strength of output
$E$ = total input

$$E = \sum w_i \cdot s_i$$

*Figure 2.*

ties. These are represented in the diagram as small end-plates of various sizes. For simplicity's sake, we dispense with dendritic trees: the axonal end branches from other units all make connections directly to the 'cell body' of the receiving unit. The total modulating effect $E$ impacting on that unit is just the sum of the contributions made by each of the connections. The contribution of a single connection is just the product of its weight $w_i$ times the strength $s_i$ of the signal arriving at that connection. Let me emphasize that if for some reason the connection weights were to change over time, then the unit would receive a quite different level of overall excitation or inhibition in response to the very same configuration of input signals.

Turn now to the output side of things. As a function of the total input $E$, the unit modulates its activity level and emits an output signal of a certain strength $s_o$ along its 'axonal' output fiber. But $s_o$ is not a direct or *linear* function of $E$. Rather, it is an S-shaped function as in figure 3. The reasons for this small wrinkle will emerge later. I mention it here because its inclusion completes the

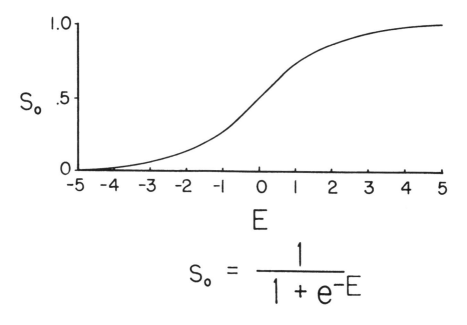

$$S_o = \frac{1}{1 + e^{-E}}$$

*Figure 3.*

story of the elementary units. Of their intrinsic properties, there is nothing left to tell. They are very simple indeed.

It remains to arrange them into networks. In the brain, neurons frequently consitute a population, all of which send their axons to the site of a second population of neurons, where each arriving axon divides into terminal end branches in order to make synaptic connections with many different cells within the target population. Axons from cells in this second population can then project to a third population of cells, and so on. This is the inspiration for the arrangement of figure 4.

The units in the bottom or input layer of the network may be thought of as 'sensory' units, since the level of activation in each is directly determined by aspects of the environment (or perhaps by the experimenter, in the process of simulating some environmental input). The activation level of a given input unit is designed to be a response to a specific aspect or dimension of the overall input stimulus that strikes the bottom layer. The assembled set of simultaneous activation levels in all of the input units is the network's *representation* of the input stimulus. We may refer to that configuration of stimulation levels as the *input vector*, since it is just an ordered set of numbers or magnitudes. For example, a given stimulus might produce the vector ⟨.5, .3, .9, .2⟩.

These input activation levels are then propagated upwards, via the output sig-

# A SIMPLE NETWORK

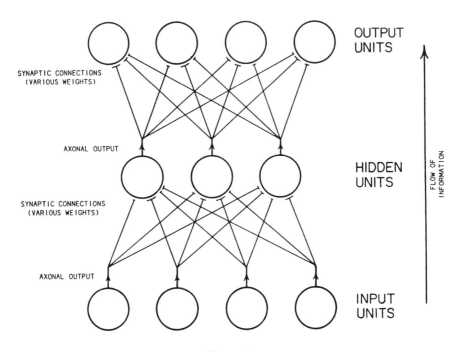

*Figure 4.*

nal in each unit's axon, to the middle layer of the network, to what are called the *hidden units*. As can be seen in figure 4, any unit in the input layer makes a synaptic connection of some weight or other with every unit at this intermediate layer. Each hidden unit is thus the target of several inputs, one for each cell at the input layer. The resulting activation level of a given hidden unit is essentially just the sum of all of the influences reaching it from the cells in the lower layer.

The result of this upward propagation of the input vector is a set of activation levels across the three units in the hidden layer, called the *hidden unit activation vector*. The values of that three-element vector are strictly determined by

(a) the makeup of the *input vector* at the input layer, and
(b) the various values of the *connection weights* at the ends of the terminal branches of the input units.

What this bottom half of the network does, evidently, is convert or transform one activation vector into another.

The top half of the network does exactly the same thing, in exactly the same way. The activation vector at the hidden layer is propagated upward to the output (topmost) layer of units, where an *output vector* is produced, whose character is determined by

(a)  the makeup of the activation vector at the hidden layer, and
(b)  the various values of the connection weights at the ends of the terminal branches of the hidden units.

Looking now at the whole network, we can see that it is just a device for transforming any given input-level activation vector into a uniquely corresponding output-level activation vector. And what determines the character of the global transformation effected is the peculiar set of values possessed by the many connection weights. This much is easy to grasp. What is not so easy to grasp, prior to exploring examples, is just how very powerful and useful those transformations can be. So let us explore some real examples.

## IV. Representation and Learning in Brainlike Networks

A great many of the environmental features to which humans respond are difficult to define or characterize in terms of their purely physical properties. Even something as mundane as being the vowel sound $\bar{a}$, as in "rain," resists such characterization, for the range of acoustical variation among acceptable and recognizable $\bar{a}$s is enormous. A female child at two years and a basso male at fifty will produce quite different sorts of atmospheric excitations in pronouncing this vowel, but each sound will be easily recognized as an $\bar{a}$ by other members of the same linguistic culture.

I do not mean to suggest that the matter is utterly intractable from a physical point of view, for an examination of the acoustical power spectrum of voiced vowels begins to reveal some of the similarities that unite $\bar{a}$s. And yet the analysis continues to resist a simple list of necessary and sufficient physical conditions on being an $\bar{a}$. Instead, being an $\bar{a}$ seems to be a matter of being *close enough* to a *typical $\bar{a}$* sound along a *sufficient* number of distinct *dimensions of relevance*, where each notion in italics remains difficult to characterize in a nonarbitrary way. Moreover, some of those dimensions are highly contextual. A sound type that would not normally be counted or recognized as an $\bar{a}$ when voiced in isolation may be unproblematically so counted if it regularly occurs, in someone's modestly accented speech, in all of the phonetic places that would normally be occupied by $\bar{a}$s. Evidently, what makes something an $\bar{a}$ is in part a matter of the entire linguistic surround. In this way do we very quickly ascend to the abstract and holistic level, for even the simplest of culturally embedded properties.

What holds for phonemes holds also for a great many other important features recognizable by us—colors, faces, flowers, trees, animals, voices, smells, feelings, songs, words, meanings, and even metaphorical meanings. At the outset, the categories and resources of physics, and even neuroscience, look puny and impotent in the face of such subtlety.

And yet it is a purely physical system that recognizes such intricacies. Short of appealing to magic, or of simply refusing to confront the problem at all, we must assume that some configuration of purely physical elements is capable of grasping and manipulating these features, and by means of purely physical principles. Surprisingly, networks of the kind described in the preceding section have many of the properties needed to address precisely this problem. Let me explain.

Suppose we are submarine engineers confronted with the problem of designing a sonar system that will distinguish between the sonar echoes returned from explosive mines, such as might lie on the bottom of sensitive waterways during wartime, and the sonar echoes returned from rocks of comparable sizes that dot the same underwater landscapes. The difficulty is twofold: echoes from both objects sound indistinguishable to the casual ear, and echoes from each type show wide variation in sonic character, since both rocks and mines come in various sizes, shapes, and orientations relative to the probing sonar pulse.

Enter the network of figure 5. This one has thirteen units at the input layer, since we need to code a fairly complex stimulus. A given sonar echo is run through a frequency analyzer, and is sampled for its relative energy levels at thirteen frequencies. These thirteen values, expressed as fractions of 1, are then entered as activation levels in the respective units of the input layer, as indicated in figure 5. From here they are propagated through the network, being transformed as they go, as explained earlier. The result is a pair of activation levels in the two units at the output layer. We need only two units here, for we want the network eventually to produce an output activation vector at or near $\langle 1, 0 \rangle$ when a mine echo is entered as input, and an output activation vector at or near $\langle 0, 1 \rangle$ when a rock echo is entered as input. In a word, we want it to *distinguish* mines from rocks.

It would of course be a miracle if the network made the desired discrimination immediately, since the connection weights that determine its transformational activity are initially set at random values. At the beginning of this experiment then, the output vectors are sure to disappoint us. But we proceed to *teach* the network by means of the following procedure.

We procure a large set of recorded samples of various (genuine) mine echoes, from mines of various sizes and orientations, and a comparable set of genuine rock echoes, keeping careful track of which is which. We then feed these echoes into the network, one by one, and observe the output vector produced in each case. What interests us in each case is the amount by which the actual output vector *differs* from what would have been the 'correct' vector, given the identity of the specific echo that produced it. The details of that error, for each element of the output vector, are then fed into a special rule that computes a set of small

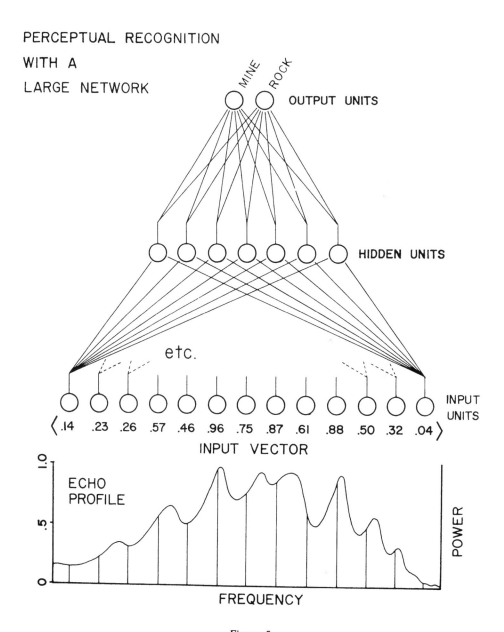

*Figure 5.*

changes in the values of the various synaptic weights in the system. The idea is to identify those weights most responsible for the error, and then to nudge their values in a direction that would at least reduce the amount by which the output vector is in error. The slighty modified system is then fed another echo from the training set, and the entire procedure is repeated.

This provides the network with a 'teacher'. The process is called "training up the network," and it is standardly executed by an auxiliary computer programmed to feed samples from the training set into the network, monitor its responses, and adjust the weights according to the special rule after each trial. Under the pressure of such repeated corrections, the behavior of the network slowly converges on the behavior we desire. That is to say, after several thousands of presentations of recorded echoes and subsequent adjustments, the network starts to give the right answer close to 90 percent of the time. When fed a mine echo, it generally gives something close to a $\langle 1, 0 \rangle$ output. And when fed a rock echo, it generally gives something close to a $\langle 0, 1 \rangle$.

A useful way to think of this is captured in figure 6. Think of an abstract space of many dimensions, one for each weight in the network (105 in this case), plus one dimension for representing the overall error of the output vector on any given trial. Any point in that space represents a unique configuration of weights, plus the performance error that that configuration produces. What the learning rule does is steadily nudge that configuration away from erroneous positions and toward positions that are less erroneous. The system inches its way down an 'error gradient' toward a global error minimum. Once there, it responds reliably to the relevant kinds of echoes. It even responds well to echoes that are 'similar' to mine echoes, by giving output vectors that are closer to $\langle 1, 0 \rangle$ than to $\langle 0, 1 \rangle$.

There was no guarantee the network would succeed in learning to discriminate the two kinds of echoes, because there was no guarantee that rock echoes and mine echoes would differ in any systematic or detectable way. But it turns out that mine echoes do indeed have some complex of relational or structural features that distinguishes them from rock echoes, and under the pressure of repeated error corrections, the network manages to lock onto, or become 'tuned' to, that subtle but distinctive weave of features.

We can test whether it has truly succeeded in this by now feeding the network some mine and rock echoes not included in the training set, echoes it has never encountered before. In fact, the network does almost as well classifying the new echoes as it does with the samples in its training set. The 'knowledge' it has acquired generalizes quite successfully to new cases. (This example is a highly simplified account of some striking results from Gorman and Sejnowski 1988.)

All of this is modestly amazing, because the problem is quite a difficult one, at least as difficult as learning to discriminate the phoneme $a$. Human sonar operators, during a long tour of submarine duty, eventually learn to distinguish the two kinds of echoes with some uncertain but nontrivial regularity. But they never per-

## LEARNING: GRADIENT DESCENT IN WEIGHT SPACE

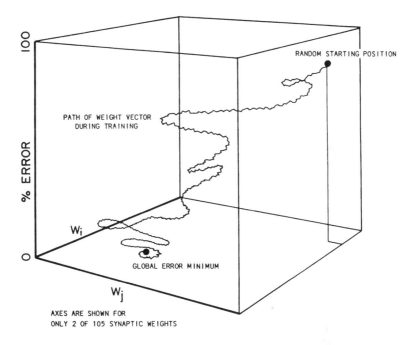

*Figure 6.*

form at the level of the artificial network. Spurred on by this success, work is currently underway to train up a network to distinguish the various phonemes characteristic of English speech (Zipser and Elman 1988). The idea is to produce a speech-recognition system that will not be troubled by the acoustic idiosyncracies of diverse speakers, as existing speech-recognition systems are.

The success of the mine/rock network is further intriguing because the 'knowledge' the network has acquired, concerning the distinctive character of mine echoes, consists of nothing more than a carefully orchestrated set of connection weights. And it is finally intriguing because there exists a learning algorithm – the rule for adjusting the weights as a function of the error displayed in the output vector – that will eventually produce the required set of weights, given sufficient examples on which to train the network (Rumelhart et al. 1986).

How can a set of connection weights possibly embody knowledge of the desired distinction? Think of it in the following way. Each of the thirteen input units represents one aspect or dimension of the incoming stimulus. Collectively, they give a simultaneous profile of the input echo along thirteen distinct dimensions. Now perhaps there is only one profile that is roughly characteristic of mine echoes; or perhaps there are many different profiles, united by a common relational feature (e.g., that the activation value of unit #6 is always three times the value of unit #12); or perhaps there is a disjunctive set of such relational features; and so forth. In each case, it is possible to rig the weights so that the system will respond in a typical fashion, at the output layer, to all and only the relevant profiles.

The units at the hidden layer are very important in this. If we consider the abstract space whose seven axes represent the possible activation levels of each of the seven hidden units, then what the system is searching for during the training period is a set of weights that *partitions* this space so that any mine input produces an activation vector across the hidden units that falls somewhere within one large subvolume of this abstract space, while any rock input produces a vector that falls somewhere into the complement of that subvolume (figure 7). The job of the top half of the network is then the relatively easy one of distinguishing these two subvolumes into which the abstract space has been divided.

Vectors near the center of (or along a certain path in) the mine-vector subvolume represent *prototypical* mine echoes, and these will produce an output vector very close to the desired $\langle 1, 0 \rangle$. Vectors nearer to the surface (strictly speaking, the *hyper*surface) that partitions the abstract space represent atypical or problematic mine echoes, and these produce more ambiguous output vectors such as $\langle .6, .4 \rangle$. The network's discriminative responses are thus graded responses: the system is sensitive to *similarities* along all of the relevant dimensions, and especially to rough conjunctions of these subordinate similarities.

So we have a system that learns to discriminate hard-to-define perceptual features, and to be sensitive to similarities of a comparably diffuse but highly relevant character. And once the network is trained up, the recognitional task takes only a split second, since the system processes the input stimulus in parallel. It finally gives us a discriminatory system that performs something like a living creature, both in its speed and in its overall character.

I have explained this system in some detail, so that the reader will have a clear idea of how things work in at least one case. But the network described is only one instance of a general technique that works well in a large variety of cases. Networks can be constructed with a larger number of units at the output layer, so as to be able to express not just two, but a large number of distinct discriminations.

One network, aptly called NETtalk by its authors (Rosenberg and Sejnowski 1987), takes vector codings for seven-letter segments of printed words as inputs, and gives vector codings for phonemes as outputs. These output vectors can be fed directly into a sound synthesizer as they occur, to produce audible sounds. What this network learns to do is to transform printed words into audible speech. Though it involves no understanding of the words that it 'reads', the network's feat

LEARNED PARTITION ON
HIDDEN UNIT ACTIVATION-VECTOR SPACE

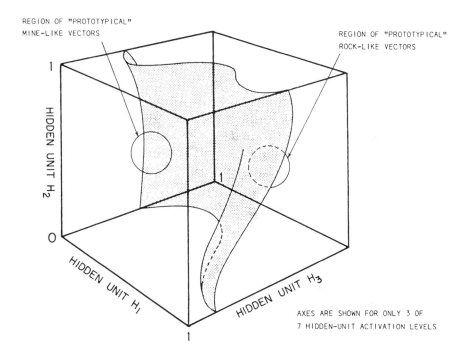

*Figure 7.*

is still very impressive, because it was given no rules whatever concerning the phonetic significance of standard English spelling. It began its training period by producing a stream of unintelligible babble in response to text entered as input. But in the course of many thousands of word presentations, and under the steady pressure of the weight-nudging algorithm, the set of weights slowly meanders its way to a configuration that reduces the measured error close to zero. After such training it will then produce as output, given arbitrary English text as input, perfectly intelligible speech with only rare and minor errors.

This case is significant for a number of reasons. First, the trained network makes a large number of discriminations (79, in fact), not just a binary one. Second, it contains no explicit representation of any *rules*, however much it might seem to be following a set of rules. Third, it has mastered an input/output transformation that is notoriously irregular, and it must be sensitive to lexical context in order to do so. (Specifically, the phoneme it assigns to the center or focal letter of its seven-letter input is in large part a function of the identity of the three letters on either side.) And fourth, it portrays some aspects of a 'sensori*motor*' skill, rather than a purely sensory skill: it is producing highly complex behavior.

NETtalk has some limitations, of course. Pronunciations that depend on specifically semantical or grammatical distinctions will generally elude its grasp (unless they happen to be reflected in some way in the corpus of its training words, as occasionally they are), since NETtalk knows neither meanings nor syntax. But such dependencies affect only a very small percentage of the transformations appropriate to any text, and they are in any case to be expected. To overcome them completely would require a network that actually understands the text being read. And even then mistakes would occur, for even humans occasionally misread words as a result of grammatical or semantical confusion. What is arresting about NETtalk is just how very much of the complex and irregular business of text-based pronunciation can be mastered by a simple network with only a few hundred neuronlike units.

Another rather large network (by Lehky and Sejnowski 1988a, 1988b) addresses problems in vision. It takes codings for smoothly varying gray-scale pictures as input, and after training it yields as outputs surprisingly accurate codings for the curvatures and orientations of the physical objects portrayed in the pictures. It solves a form of the 'shape from shading' problem long familiar to theorists in the field of vision. This network is of special interest because a subsequent examination of the 'receptive fields' of the trained hidden units shows them to have acquired some of the same response properties as are displayed by cells in the visual cortex of mature animals. Specifically, they show a maximum sensitivity to spots, edges, and bars in specific orientations. This finding echoes the seminal work of Hubel and Wiesel (1962), in which cells in the visual cortex were discovered to have receptive fields of this same character. Results of this kind are very important, for if we are to take these artificial networks as models for how the brain works, then they must display realistic behavior not just at the macro-level: they must also display realistic behavior at the microlevel.

Enough examples. You have seen something of what networks of this kind can do, and of how they do it. In both respects they contrast sharply with the kinds of representational and processing strategies that philosophers of science, inductive logicians, cognitive psychologists, and AI workers have traditionally ascribed to us (namely, sentencelike representations manipulated by formal rules). You can see also why this theoretical and experimental approach has captured the interest of those who seek to understand how the microarchitecture of the biological brain produces the phenomena displayed in human and animal cognition. Let us now explore the functional properties of these networks in more detail, and see how they bear on some of the traditional issues in epistemology and the philosophy of science.

## V. Some Functional Properties of Brainlike Networks

The networks described above are descended from a device called the *Perceptron* (Rosenblatt 1959), which was essentially just a two-layer as opposed to a three-layer network. Devices of this configuration could and did learn to discriminate a considerable variety of input patterns. Unfortunately, having the input layer connected directly to the output layer imposes very severe limitations on the range of possible transformations a network can perform (Minsky and Papert 1969), and interest in Perceptron-like devices was soon eclipsed by the much faster-moving developments in standard 'program-writing' AI, which exploited the high-speed general-purpose digital machines that were then starting to become widely available. Throughout the seventies, research in artificial 'neural nets' was an underground program by comparison.

It has emerged from the shadows for a number of reasons. One important factor is just the troubled doldrums into which mainstream or program-writing AI has fallen. In many respects, these doldrums parallel the infertility of the classical approach to theories and learning within the philosophy of science. This is not surprising, since mainstream AI was proceeding on many of the same basic assumptions about cognition, and many of its attempts were just machine implementations of learning algorithms proposed earlier by philosophers of science and inductive logicians (Glymour 1987). The failures of mainstream AI — unrealistic learning, poor performance in complex perceptual and motor tasks, weak handling of analogies, and snaillike cognitive performance despite the use of very large and fast machines — teach us even more dramatically than do the failures of mainstream philosophy that we need to rethink the style of representation and computation we have been ascribing to cognitive creatures.

Other reasons for the resurgence of interest in networks are more positive. The introduction of additional layers of intervening or 'hidden' units produced a dramatic increase in the range of possible transformations that the network could effect. As Sejnowski et al. (1986) describe it:

> . . . only the first-order statistics of the input pattern can be captured by direct connections between input and output units. The role of the hidden units is to capture higher-order statistical relationships and this can be accomplished if significant underlying features can be found that have strong, regular relationships with the patterns on the visible units. The hard part of learning is to find the set of weights which turn the hidden units into useful feature detectors.

Equally important is the S-shaped, nonlinear response profile (figure 3) now assigned to every unit in the network. So long as this response profile remains linear, any network will be limited to computing purely linear transformations. (A transformation $f(x)$ is *linear* just in case $f(n \bullet x) = n \bullet f(x)$, and $f(x + y) = f(x) + f(y)$.) But a nonlinear response profile for each unit brings the entire range of possible nonlinear transformations within reach of three-layer networks, a dramatic expansion of their computational potential. Now there are *no* transformations that lie beyond the computational power of a large enough and suitably weighted network.

A third factor was the articulation, by Rumelhart, Hinton, and Williams (1986a), of the *generalized delta rule* (a generalization, to three-layer networks, of Rosenblatt's original teaching rule for adjusting the weights of the Perceptron), and the empirical discovery that this new rule very rarely got permanently stuck in inefficient 'local minima' on its way toward finding the best possible configuration of connection weights for a given network and a given problem. This was a major breakthrough, not so much because "learning by the back-propagation of error," as it has come to be called, was just like human learning, but because it provided us with an efficient technology for quickly training up various networks on various problems, so that we could study their properties and explore their potential.

The way the generalized delta rule works can be made fairly intuitive given the idea of an abstract weight space as represented in figure 6. Consider any output vector produced by a network with a specific configuration of weights, a configuration represented by a specific position in weight space. Suppose that this output vector is in error by various degrees in various of its elements. Consider now a single synapse at the ouput layer, and consider the effect on the output vector that a small positive or negative change in its weight would have had. Since the output vector is a determinate function of the system's weights (assuming we hold the input vector fixed), we can calculate which of these two possible changes, if either, would have made the greater improvement in the output vector. The relevant change is made accordingly. (For more detail, see Rumelhart et al. 1986b.)

If a similar calculation is performed over every synapse in the network, and the change in its weight is then made accordingly, what the resulting shift in the position of the system's overall point in weight space amounts to is a small slide *down* the steepest face of the local 'error surface'. Note that there is no guarantee that this incremental shift moves the system directly towards the global position of zero error (that is why perfection cannot be achieved in a single jump). On the contrary, the descending path to a global error minimum may be highly circuitous. Nor is there any guarantee that the system must eventually reach such a global minimum. On the contrary, the downward path from a given starting point may well lead to a merely 'local' minimum, from which only a large change in the system's weights will afford escape, a change beyond the reach of the delta rule. But in fact this happens relatively rarely, for it turns out that the more dimensions (synapses) a system has, the smaller the probability of there being an intersecting local minimum in *every one* of the available dimensions. The global point is usually able to slide down some narrow cleft in the local topography. Empirically then, the back-propagation algorithm is surprisingly effective at driving the system to the global error minimum, at least where we can identify that global minimum effectively.

The advantage this algorithm provides is easily appreciated. The possible combinations of weights in a network increases exponentially with the size of the network. Assuming conservatively that each weight admits of only ten possible values, the number of distinct positions in 'weight space' (i.e., the number of possible weight configurations) for the simple rock/mine network of figure 5 is already $10^{105}$! This space is far too large to explore efficiently without something like the generalized delta rule and the back-propagation of error to do it for us. But with the delta rule, administered by an auxiliary computer, researchers have shown that networks of the simple kind described are capable of learning some quite extraordinary skills, and of displaying some highly intriguing properties. Let me now return to an exploration of these.

An important exploratory technique in cognitive and behavioral neuroscience is to record, with an implanted microelectrode, the electrical activity of a single neuron during cognition or behavior in the intact animal. This is relatively easy to do, and it does give us tantalizing bits of information about the cognitive significance of neural activity (recall the results of Hubel and Wiesel mentioned earlier). Single-cell recordings give us only isolated bits of information, however, and what we would really like to monitor are the *patterns* of simultaneous neural activation across large numbers of cells in the same subsystem. Unfortunately, effective techniques for simultaneous recording from large numbers of adjacent cells are still in their infancy. The task is extremely difficult.

By contrast, this task is extremely easy with the artificial networks we have been describing. If the network is real hardware, its units are far more accessible than the fragile and microscopic units of a living brain. And if the network is merely being simulated within a standard computer (as is usually the case), one can write the program so that the activation levels of any unit, or set of units, can be read out on command. Accordingly, once a network has been successfully trained up on some skill or other, one can then examine the collective behavior of its units during the exercise of that skill.

We have already seen the results of one such analysis in the rock/mine network. Once the weights have reached their optimum configuration, the activation vectors (i.e., the patterns of activation) at the hidden layer fall into two disjoint classes: the vector space is partitioned in two, as depicted schematically in figure 7. But a mere binary discrimination is an atypically simple case. The reader NETtalk, for example, partitions its hidden-unit vector space into fully seventy nine subspaces. The reason is simple. For each of the twenty six letters in the alphabet, there is at least one phoneme assigned to it, and for many letters there are several phonemes that might be signified, depending on the lexical context. As it happens, there are seventy nine distinct letter-to-phoneme associations to be learned if one is to master the pronunciation of English spelling, and in the successfully trained network a distinct hidden-unit activation vector occurs when each of these seventy nine possible transformations is effected.

In the case of the rock/mine network, we noted a similarity metric within each of its two hidden-unit subspaces. In the case of NETtalk, we also find a similarity metric, this time across the seventy nine functional hidden-unit vectors (by 'functional vector', I mean a vector that corresponds to one of the seventy nine desired letter-to-phoneme transformations in the trained network). Rosenberg and Sejnowski (1987) did a 'cluster analysis' of these vectors in the trained network. Roughly, their procedure was as follows. They asked, for every functional vector in that space, what other such vector is closest to it? The answers yielded about thirty vector pairs. They then constructed a secondary vector for each such pair, by averaging the two original vectors, and asked, for every such secondary vector, what other secondary vector (or so far unpaired primary vector) is closest to it? This produced a smaller set of secondary-vector pairs, on which the averaging procedure was repeated to produce a set of tertiary vectors. These were then paired in turn, and so forth. This procedure produces a hierarchy of groupings among the original transformations, and it comes to an end with a grand division of the seventy nine original vectors into two disjoint classes.

As it happens, that deepest and most fundamental division within the hidden-unit vector space corresponds to the division between the consonants and the vowels! Looking further into this hierarchy, into the consonant branch, for example, we find that there are subdivisions into the principal consonant types, and that within these branches there are further subdivisions into the most similar consonants. All of this is depicted in the tree diagram of figure 8. What the network has managed to recover, from its training set of several thousand English words, is the highly irregular phonological significance of standard English spelling, plus the hierarchical organization of the phonetic structure of English speech.

Here we have a clear illustration of two things at once. The first lesson is the capacity of an activation-vector space to embody a rich and well-structured hierarchy of categories, complete with a similarity metric embracing everything within it. And the second lesson is the capacity of such networks to embody representations of factors and patterns that are only partially or implicitly reflected in the corpus of inputs. Though I did not mention it earlier, the rock/mine network provides another example of this, in that the final partition made on its hidden-unit vector space corresponds in fact to the objective distinction between sonar targets made of *metal* and sonar targets made of *nonmetal*. That is the true uniformity that lies behind the apparently chaotic variety displayed in the inputs.

It is briefly tempting to suggest that NETtalk has the concept of a 'hard *c*', for example, and that the rock/mine network has the concept of 'metal'. But this won't really do, since the vector-space representations at issue do not play a conceptual

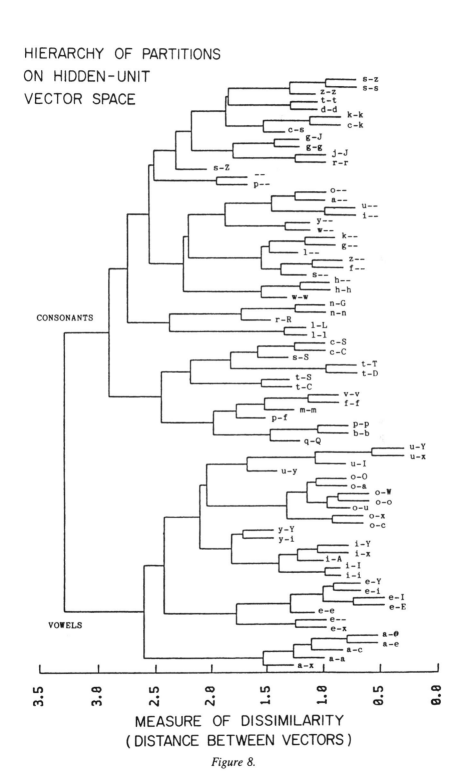

HIERARCHY OF PARTITIONS
ON HIDDEN-UNIT
VECTOR SPACE

MEASURE OF DISSIMILARITY
(DISTANCE BETWEEN VECTORS)

*Figure 8.*

161

or computational role remotely rich enough to merit their assimilation to specifically human concepts. Nevertheless, it is plain that both networks have contrived a system of internal representations that truly corresponds to important distinctions and structures in the outside world, structures that are not explicitly represented in the corpus of their sensory inputs. The value of those representations is that they and only they allow the networks to 'make sense' of their variegated and often noisy input corpus, in the sense that they and only they allow the network to respond to those inputs in a fashion that systematically reduces the error messages to a trickle. These, I need hardly remind, are the functions typically ascribed to *theories*.

What we are confronting here is a possible conception of 'knowledge' or 'understanding' that owes nothing to the sentential categories of current common sense. An individual's overall theory-of-the-world, we might venture, is not a large collection or a long list of stored symbolic items. Rather, it is a specific point in that individual's synaptic weight space. It is a configuration of connection weights, a configuration that partitions the system's activation-vector space(s) into useful divisions and subdivisions relative to the inputs typically fed the system. 'Useful' here means 'tends to minimize the error messages'.

A possible objection here points to the fact that differently weighted systems can produce the same, or at least roughly the same, partitions on their activation-vector spaces. Accordingly, we might try to abstract from the idiosyncratic details of a system's connection weights, and identify its global theory directly with the set of partitions they produce within its activation-vector space. This would allow for differently weighted systems to have the same theory.

There is some virtue in this suggestion, but also some vice. While differently weighted systems can embody the same partitions and thus display the same output performance on any given input, they will still *learn* quite differently in the face of a protracted sequence of new and problematic inputs. This is because the learning algorithm that drives the system to new points in weight space does not care about the relatively global partitions that have been made in activation space. All it cares about are the individual *weights* and how they relate to apprehended error. The laws of cognitive evolution, therefore, do not operate primarily at the level of the partitions, at least on the view of things here being explored. Rather, they operate at the level of the weights. Accordingly, if we want our 'unit of cognition' to figure in the *laws* of cognitive development, the point in weight space seems the wiser choice of unit. We need only concede that different global theories can occasionally produce identical short-term behavior.

The level of the partitions certainly corresponds more closely to the 'conceptual' level, as understood in common sense and traditional theory, but the point is that this seems not to be the most important dynamical level, even when explicated in neurocomputational terms. Knowing a creature's vector-space partitions may suffice for the accurate short-term prediction of its behavior, but that knowledge is inadequate to predict or explain the evolution of those partitions over the course of time and cruel experience. Knowledge of the weights, by contrast, *is* sufficient for this task. This gives substance to the conviction, voiced back in section II, that to explain the phenomenon of *conceptual change*, we need to unearth a level of subconceptual combinatorial elements within which different concepts can be articulated, evaluated, and then modified according to their performance. The connection weights provide a level that meets all of these conditions.

This general view of how knowledge is embodied and accessed in the brain has some further appealing features. If we assume that the brains of the higher animals work in something like the fashion outlined, then we can explain a number of puzzling features of human and animal cognition. For one thing, the speed-of-relevant-access problem simply disappears. A network the size of a human brain—with $10^{11}$ neurons, $10^3$ connections on each, $10^{14}$ total connections, and at least 10 distinct layers of 'hidden' units—can be expected, in the course of growing up, to partition its internal vector spaces into many billions of functionally relevant subdivisions, each responsive to a broad but proprietary range of highly complex stimuli. When the network receives a stimulus that falls into one of these classes, the network produces the appropriate activation vector in a matter of only tens or hundreds of milliseconds, because that is all the time it takes for the parallel-coded stimulus to make its way through only two or three or ten layers of the massively parallel network to the functionally relevant layer that drives the appropriate behavioral response. Since information is not stored in a long list that must somehow be searched, but rather in the myriad connection weights that configure the network, relevant aspects of the creature's total information are automatically accessed by the coded stimuli themselves.

A third advantage of this model is its explanation of the functional persistence of brains in the face of minor damage, disease, and the normal but steady loss of its cells with age. Human cognition degrades fairly gracefully as the physical plant deteriorates, in sharp contrast to the behavior of typical computers, which have a very low fault tolerance. The explanation of this persistence lies in the massively parallel character of the computations the brain performs, and in the very tiny contribution that each synapse or each cell makes to the overall computation. In a large network of 100,000 units, the loss or misbehavior of a single cell will not even be detectable. And in the more dramatic case of widespread cell loss, so long as the losses are more or less randomly distributed throughout the network, the gross character of the network's activity will remain unchanged: what happens is that the *quality* of its computations will be progressively degraded.

Turning now toward more specifically philosophical concerns, we may note an unexpected virtue of this approach concerning the matter of *simplicity*. This important notion has two problems. It is robustly resistant to attempts to define or measure it, and it is not clear why it should be counted an epistemic virtue in any case. There seems no obvious reason, either a priori or a posteriori, why the world should be simple rather than complex, and epistemic decisions based on the contrary assumption thus appear arbitrary and unjustified. Simplicity, conclude some (Van Fraassen 1980), is a merely pragmatic or aesthetic virtue, as opposed to a genuinely epistemic virtue. But consider the following story.

The rock/mine network of figure 5 displays a strong capacity for generalizing beyond the sample echoes in its training set: it can accurately discriminate entirely new samples of both kinds. But trained networks do not always generalize so well, and it is interesting what determines their success in this regard. How well the training generalizes is in part a function of *how many* hidden units the system possesses, or uses to solve the problem. There is, it turns out, an optimal number of units for any given problem. If the network to be trained is given more than the optimal number of hidden units, it will learn to respond appropriately to all of the various samples in its training set, but it will generalize to new samples only very poorly. On the other hand, with less than the optimal number, it never really learns to respond appropriately to all of the samples in its training set.

The reason is as follows. During the training period, the network gradually generates a set of internal representations at the level of the hidden units. One class of hidden-unit activation vectors is characteristic of rocklike input vectors; another class is characteristic of minelike input vectors. During this period, the system is *theorizing* at the level of the hidden units, exploring the space of possible activation vectors, in hopes of finding some partition or set of partitions on it that the output layer can then exploit in turn, so as to draw the needed distinctions and thus bring the process of error-induced synaptic adjustments to an end.

If there are far too many hidden units, then the learning process can be partially subverted in the following way. The lazy system cheats: it learns a set of *unrelated* representations at the level of the hidden units. It learns a distinct representation for each sample input (or for a small group of such inputs) drawn from the very finite training set, a representation that does indeed prompt the correct response at the output level. But since there is nothing common to all of the hidden-unit rock representations, or to all of the hidden-unit mine representations, an input vector from outside the training set produces a hidden-unit representation that bears no relation to the representations already formed. The system has not learned to see *what is common* within each of the two stimulus classes, which would allow it to generalize effortlessly to new cases that shared that common feature. It has just knocked together an *ad hoc* 'look-up table' that allows it to deal successfully with the limited samples in the training set, at which point the error messages cease, the weights stop evolving, and the system stops learning. (I am grateful to Terry Sejnowski for mentioning to me this wrinkle in the learning behavior of typical networks.)

There are two ways to avoid this *ad hoc*, unprojectible learning. One is to enlarge dramatically the size of the training set. This will overload the system's ability to just 'memorize' an adequate response for each of the training samples. But a more effective way is just to reduce the number of hidden units in the network, so that it lacks the resources to cobble together such wasteful and ungeneralizable internal representations. We must reduce them to the point where it has to find a *single* partition on the hidden-unit vector space, a partition that puts all of the sample rock representations on one side, and all of the sample mine representations on the other. A system constrained in this way will generalize far better, for the global partition it has been forced to find corresponds to something *common* to each member of the relevant stimulus class, even if it is only a unifying dimension of variation (or set of such dimensions) that unites them all by a similarity relation. It is the generation of that similarity relation that allows the system to respond appropriately to novel examples. They may be new to the system, but they fall on a spectrum for which the system now has an adequate representation.

Networks with only a few hidden units in excess of the optimal number will sometimes spontaneously achieve the maximally simple 'hypothesis' despite the excess units. The few unneeded units are slowly shut down by the learning algorithm during the course of training. They become zero-valued elements in all of the successful vectors. Networks will not always do this, however. The needed simplicity must generally be forced from the outside, by a progressive reduction in the available hidden units.

On the other hand, if the network has too few hidden units, then it lacks the resources even to express an activation vector that is adequate to characterize the underlying uniformity, and it will never master completely even the smallish corpus of samples in the training set. In other words, simplicity may be a virtue, but the system must command sufficient complexity at least to meet the task at hand.

We have just seen how forcing a neural network to generate a smaller number of distinct partitions on a hidden-unit vector space of fewer dimensions can produce a system whose learning achievements generalize more effectively to novel cases. *Ceteris paribus*, the simpler hypotheses generalize better. Getting by with fewer resources is of course a virtue in itself, though a pragmatic one, to be sure. But this is not the principal virtue here displayed. Superior generalization is a genuinely epistemic virtue, and it is regularly displayed by networks constrained, in the fashion described, to find the simplest hypothesis concerning whatever structures might be hidden in or behind their input vectors.

Of course, nothing guarantees successful generalization: a network is always hostage to the quality of its training set relative to the total population. And there may be equally simple alternative hypotheses that generalize differentially well. But from the perspective of the relevant microdynamics, we can see at least one clear reason why simplicity is more than a merely pragmatic virtue. It is an epistemic virtue, not principally because simple hypotheses avoid the vice of being complex, but because they avoid the vice of being *ad hoc*.

## VI. How Faithfully Do These Networks Depict the Brain?

The functional properties so far observed in these model networks are an encouraging reward for the structural assumptions that went into them. But just how accurate are these models, as depictions of the brain's microstructure? A wholly appropriate answer here is uncertain, for we continue to be uncertain about what features of the brain's microstructure are and are not functionally relevant, and we are therefore uncertain about what is and is not a 'legitimate' simplifying assumption in the models we make. Even so, it is plain that the models are *inaccurate* in a variety of respects, and it is the point of the present section to summarize and evaluate these failings. Let me begin by underscoring the basic respects in which the models appear to be correct.

It is true that real nervous systems display, as their principal organizing feature, layers or populations of neurons that project their axons *en masse* to some distinct layer or population of neurons, where each arriving axon divides into multiple branches whose end bulbs make synaptic connections of various weights onto many cells at the target location. This description captures all of the sensory modalities and their primary relations to the brain; it captures the character of the various areas of the central brain stem; and it captures the structure of the cerebral cortex, which in humans contains at least six distinct layers of neurons, where each layer is the source and/or the target of an orderly projection of axons to and/or from elsewhere.

It captures the character of the cerebellum as well (figure 9a), a structure discussed in an earlier paper (Churchland 1986) in connection with the problem of motor control. I there described the cerebellum as having the structure of a very large 'matrix multiplier', as schematized in figure 9b. Following Pellionisz and Llinas (1982), I ascribed to this neural matrix the function of performing sophisticated transformations on incoming activation vectors. This is in fact the same function performed between any two layers of the three-layered networks described earlier, and the two cases are distinct only in the superficial details of their wiring diagrams. A three-layered network of the kind discussed earlier is equivalent to a pair of neural matrices connected in series, as is illustrated in figures 10a and 10b. The only substantive difference is that in figure 10a the end branches synapse directly onto the receiving cell body itself, while in 10b they synapse onto some dendritic filaments extending out from the receiving cell body. The actual connectivity within the two networks is identical. The cerebellum and the motor end of natural systems, accordingly, seem further instances of the gross pattern at issue.

But the details present all manner of difficulties. To begin with small ones, note

SCHEMATIC SECTION: CEREBELLUM

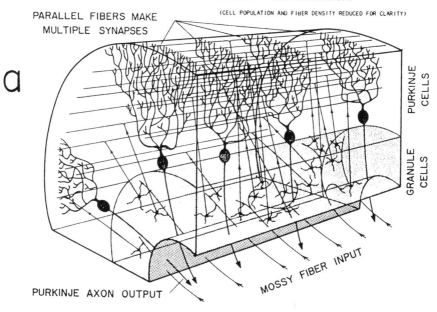

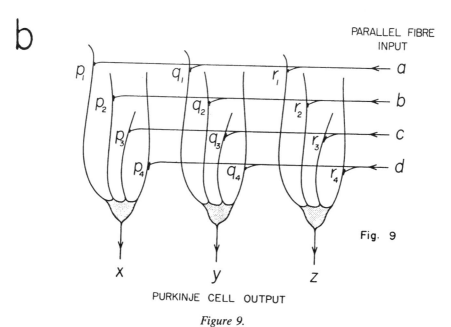

Fig. 9

Figure 9.

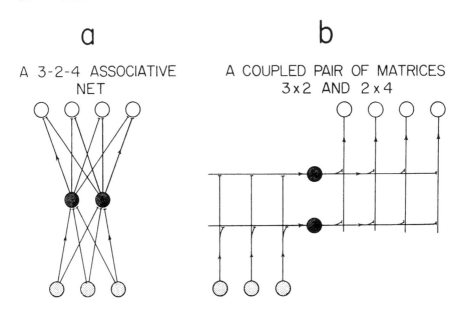

*Figure 10.*

that in real brains an arriving axon makes synaptic contact with only a relatively small percentage of the thousands or millions of cells in its target population, not with every last one of them as in the models. This is not a serious difficulty, since model networks with comparably pared connections still manage to learn the required transformations quite well, though perhaps not so well as a fully connected network.

More seriously, real axons, so far as is known, have terminal end bulbs that are uniformly inhibitory, or uniformly excitatory, depending on the type of neuron. We seem not to find a mixture of both kinds of connections radiating from the same neuron, nor do we find connections changing their sign during learning, as is the case in the models. Moreover, that mixture of positive and negative influences is essential to successful function in the models: the same input cell must be capable of inhibiting some cells down the line at the same time that it is busy exciting others. Further, cell populations in the brain typically show extensive 'horizontal' cell-to-cell connections *within* a given layer. In the models there are none at all (see, e.g., figure 4). Their connections join cells only to cells in distinct layers.

These last two difficulties might conceivably serve to cancel each other. One way in which an excitatory end bulb might serve to *inhibit* a cell in its target population is first to make an excitatory connection onto one of the many small *inter-*

*neurons* typically scattered throughout the target population of main neurons, which interneuron has made an inhibitory synaptic connection onto the target main neuron. Exciting the inhibitory interneuron would then have the effect of inhibiting the main neuron, as desired. And such a system would display a large number of short 'horizontal' intralayer connections, as is observed. This is just a suggestion, however, since it is far from clear that the elements mentioned are predominantly connected in the manner required.

More seriously still, there are several major problems with the idea that networks in the brain learn by means of the learning algorithm so effective in the models : the procedure of back-propagating apprehended errors according to the generalized delta rule. That procedure requires two things: 1) a computation of the partial correction needed for each unit in the output layer, and via these a computation of a partial correction for each unit in the earlier layers, and 2) a method of causally conveying these correction messages back through the network to the sites of the relevant synaptic connections in such a fashion that each weight gets nudged up or down accordingly. In a computer simulation of the networks at issue (which is currently the standard technique for exploring their properties), both the computation and the subsequent weight adjustments are easily done: the computation is done *outside* the network by the host computer, which has direct access to and control over every element of the network being simulated. But in the self-contained biological brain, we have to find some real source of adjustment signals, and some real pathways to convey them back to the relevant units. Unfortunately, the empirical brain displays little that answers to exactly these requirements.

Not that it contains nothing along these lines: the primary ascending pathways already described are typically matched by reciprocal or 'descending' pathways of comparable density. These allow higher layers to have an influence on affairs at lower layers. Yet the influence appears to be on the activity levels of the lower cells themselves, rather than on the myriad synaptic connections whose weights need adjusting during learning. There may be indirect effects on the synapses, of course, but it is far from clear that the brain's wiring diagram answers to the demands of the back-propagation algorithm.

The case is a little more promising in the cerebellum (figure 9a), which contains a second major input system in the aptly-named *climbing fibers* (not shown in the diagram for reasons of clarity). These fibers envelop each of the large Purkinje cells from below in the same fashion that a climbing ivy envelops a giant oak, with its filamentary tendrils reaching well up into the bushy dendritic tree of the Purkinje cell, which tree is the locus of all of the synaptic connections made by the incoming parallel fibers. The climbing fibers are thus at least roughly positioned to do the job that the back-propagation algorithm requires of them, and they are distributed one to each Purkinje cell, as consistent delivery of the error message requires. Equally, they might serve some other quite different learning algorithm, as advocated by Pellionisz and Llinas (1985). Unfortunately, there is as yet no compelling reason to believe that the modification of the weights of the parallel-fiber-to-Purkinje-dendrite synapses is even within the causal power of the climbing fibers. Nor is there any clear reason to see either the climbing fibers in the cerebellum, or the descending pathways elsewhere in the brain, as the bearers of any appropriately computed error-correction messages appropriate to needed synaptic change.

On the hardware side, therefore, the situation does not support the idea that the specific back-propagation procedure of Rumelhart et al. is the brain's central mechanism for learning. (Neither, it should be mentioned, did they claim that it is.) And it is implausible on some functional grounds as well. First, in the process of learning a recognition task, living brains typically show a progressive reduction in the reaction time required for the recognitional output response. With the delta rule, however, learning involves a progressive reduction in error, but reaction times are constant throughout. A second difficulty with the delta rule is as follows. A necessary element in its calculated apportionment of error is a representation of what would have been the *correct* vector in the output layer. That is why back-propagation is said to involve a global *teacher*, an information source that always knows the correct answers and can therefore provide a perfect measure of output error. Real creatures generally lack any such perfect information. They must struggle along in the absence of any sure compass toward the truth, and their synaptic adjustments must be based on much poorer information.

And yet their brains learn. Which means that somehow the configuration of their synaptic weights must undergo change, change steered in some way by error or related dissatisfaction, change that carves a path toward a regime of decreased error. Knowing this much, and knowing something about the microstructure and microdynamics of the brain, we can explore the space of possible learning procedures with some idea of what features to look for. If the generalized delta rule is not the brain's procedure, as it seems not to be, there remain other possible strategies for back-propagating sundry error measures, strategies that may find more detailed reflection in the brain. If these prove unrealizable, there are other procedures that do not require the organized distribution of any global error measures at all; they depend primarily on local constraints (Hinton and Sejnowski 1986; Hopfield and Tank 1985; Barto 1985; Bear et al. 1987).

One of these is worthy of mention, since something along these lines does appear to be displayed in biological brains. *Hebbian* learning (so-called after D. O. Hebb, who first proposed the mechanism) is a process of weight adjustment that exploits the temporal coincidence, on either side of a given synaptic junction, of a strong signal in the incoming axon and a high level of excitation in the receiving cell. When such conjunctions occur, Hebb proposed, some physical or chemical change is induced in the synapse, a change that increases its 'weight'. Of course, high activation in the receiving cell is typically caused by excitatory stimulation from many other incoming axons, and so the important temporal coincidence here is really between high activation among certain of the incoming axons. Those whose high activation coincides with the activation of many others have their subsequent influence on the cell increased. Crudely, those who vote with winners become winners.

A Hebbian weight-adjusting procedure can indeed produce learning in artificial networks (Linsker, 1986), although it does not seem to be as general in its effectiveness as is back-propagation. On the other hand, it has a major functional advantage over back-propagation. The latter has scaling problems, in that the process of calculating and distributing the relevant adjustments expands geometrically with the number of units in the network. But Hebbian adjustments are locally driven; they are independent of one another and of the overall size of the network. A large network will thus learn just as quickly as a small one. Indeed, a large network may even show a slight advantage over a smaller, since the temporal coincidence of incoming stimulations at a given cell will be better and better defined with increasing numbers of incoming axons.

We may also postulate 'anti-Hebbian' processes, as a means of reducing synaptic weights instead of increasing them. And we need to explore various possible flavors of each. We still have very little understanding of the functional properties of these alternative learning strategies. Nor are we at all sure that Hebbian learning, as described above, is really how the brain typically adjusts its weights. There does seem to be a good deal of activity-sensitive synaptic modification occurring in the brain, but whether its profile is specifically Hebbian is not yet established. Nor should we expect the brain to confine itself to only one learning strategy, for even at the behavioral level we can discern distinct types of learning. In sum, the problem of what mechanisms actually produce synaptic change during learning is an unsolved problem. But the functional success of the generalized delta rule assures us that the problem is solvable in principle, and other more plausible procedures are currently under active exploration.

While the matter of how real neural networks generate the right configuration of weights remains obscure, the matter of how they perform their various cognitive tasks once configured is a good deal clearer. If even small artifical networks can perform the sophisticated cognitive tasks illustrated earlier in this paper, there is no mystery that real networks should do the same or better. What the brain displays in the way of hardware is not radically different from what the models contain, and the differences invite exploration rather than disappointment. The brain is of course very much larger and denser than the models so far constructed. It has many layers rather than just two or three. It boasts perhaps a hundred distinct and highly specialized cell types, rather than just one. It is not a single $n$-layer network, but rather a large committee of distinct but parallel networks, interacting in sundry ways. It plainly commands many spaces of stunning complexity, and many skills in consequence. It stands as a glowing invitation to make our humble models yet more and more realistic, in hopes of unlocking the many secrets remaining.

## VII. Computational Neuroscience: The Naturalization of Epistemology

One test of a new framework is its ability to throw a new and unifying light on a variety of old phenomena. I will close this essay with an exploration of several classic issues in the philosophy of science. The aim is to reconstruct them within the framework of the computational neuroscience outlined above. In section 5 we saw how this could be done for the case of theoretical simplicity. We there saw a new way of conceiving of this feature, and found a new perspective on why it is a genuine epistemic virtue. The hope in what follows is that we may do the same for other problematic notions and issues.

A good place to begin is with the issue of foundationalism. Here the central bone of contention is whether our observation judgments must always be theory laden. The traditional discussion endures largely for the good reason that a great deal hangs on the outcome, but also for the less momentous reason that there is ambiguity in what one might wish to count as an 'observation judgment' (an explicitly uttered sentence? a covert assertion? a propositional attitude? a conscious experience? a sensation?), and a slightly different issue emerges depending on where the debate is located.

But from the perspective of this essay, it makes no difference at what level the issue might be located. If our cognitive activities arise from a weave of networks of the kind discussed above, and if we construe a global theory as a global configuration of synaptic weights, as outlined in section 5, then it is clear that no cognitive activity whatever takes place in the absence of vectors being processed by some specific configuration of weights. That is, no cognitive activity whatever takes place in the absence of some theory or other.

This perspective bids us see even the simplest of animals and the youngest of infants as possessing theories, since they too process their activation vectors with some configuration of weights or other. The difference between us and them is not that they lack theories. Rather, their theories are just a good deal simpler than ours, in the case of animals. And their theories are much less coherent and organized and informed than ours, in the case of human infants. Which is to say, they have yet to achieve points in overall weight space that partition their activation-vector spaces into useful and well-structured subdivisions. But insofar as there is cognitive activity at all, it exploits whatever theory the creature embodies, however useless or incoherent it might be.

The only place in the network where the weights need play no role is at the absolute sensory periphery of the system, where the external stimulus is transduced into a coded input vector, for subsequent delivery to the transforming layers of weights. However, at the first occasion on which these preconceptual states have any effect at all on the downstream cognitive system, it is through a changeable configuration of synaptic weights, a configuration that produces one set of partitions on the activation-vector space of the relevant layer of neurons, one set out of millions of alternative possible sets. In other words, the very first thing that happens to the input signal is that it gets conceptualized in one of many different possible ways. At subsequent layers of processing, the same process is repeated, and the message that finally arrives at the linguistic centers, for example, has been shaped at least as much by the partitional constraints of the embedded conceptual system(s) through which it has passed as by the distant sensory input that started things off.

From the perspective of computational neuroscience, therefore, cognition is constitutionally theory laden. Presumptive processing is not a blight on what would otherwise be an unblemished activity; it is just the natural signature of a cognitive system doing what it is supposed to be doing. It is just possible that some theories are endogenously specified, of course, but this will change the present issue not at all. Innateness promises no escape from theory ladenness, for an endogenous theory is still a *theory*.

In any case, the idea is not in general a plausible one. The visual system, for example, consists of something in the neighborhood of $10^{10}$ neurons, each of which enjoys better than $10^3$ synaptic connections, for a total of at least $10^{13}$ weights, each wanting specific genetic determination. That is an implausibly heavy load to place on the coding capacity of our DNA molecules. (The entire human genome contains only about $10^9$ nucleotides.) It would be much more efficient to specify endogenously only the general structural principles of a type of learning network that is then likely to learn in certain standard directions, given the standard sorts of inputs and error messages that a typical human upbringing provides. This places the burden of steering our conceptual development where it belongs – on the external world, an information source far larger and more reliable than the genes.

It is a commonplace that we can construct endlessly different theories with which to explain the familiar facts of the observable world. But it is an immediate consequence of the perspective here adopted that that we can also apprehend the 'observable world' itself in a similarly endless variety of ways. For there is no 'preferred' set of partitions into which our sensory spaces must inevitably fall. It all depends on how the relevant networks are *taught*. If we systematically change the pattern of the error messages delivered to the developing network, then even the very same history of sensory stimulations will produce a quite differently weighted network, one that partitions the world into classes that cross-classify those of current 'common sense', one that finds perceptual similarities along dimensions quite alien to the ones we currently recognize, one that feeds its outputs into a very differently configured network at the higher cognitive levels as well.

In relatively small ways, this phenomenon is already familiar to us. Specialists in various fields, people required to spend years mastering the intricacies of some domain of perception and manipulation, regularly end up being able to perceive facts and to anticipate behaviors that are wholly opaque to the rest of us. But there is no reason why such variation should be confined to isolated skills and specialized understanding. In principle, the human cognitive system should be capable of sustaining any one of an enormous variety of decidedly global theories concerning the character of its commonsense *Lebenswelt* as a whole. (This possibility, defended in Feyerabend 1965, is explored at some length via examples in Churchland 1979. For extended criticism of this general suggestion see Fodor 1984. For a rebuttal and counterrebuttal see Churchland 1988 and Fodor 1988.)

To appreciate just how great is the conceptual variety that awaits us, consider the following numbers. With a total of perhaps $10^{11}$ neurons with an average of at least $10^3$ connections each, the human brain has something like $10^{14}$ weights to play with. Supposing, conservatively, that each weight admits of only ten possible values, the total number of distinct possible configurations of synaptic weights (= distinct possible positions in weight space) is 10 for the first weight, times 10 for the second weight, times 10 for the third weight, etc., for a total of $10^{10^{14}}$, or $10^{100,000,000,000,000}$!! This is the total number of (just barely) distinguishable theories embraceable by humans, given the cognitive resources we currently command. To put this number into perspective, recall that the total number of elementary particles in the entire universe is only about $10^{87}$.

In this way does a neurocomputational approach to perception allow us to reconstruct an old issue, and to provide novel reasons for the view that our perceptual knowledge is both theory laden and highly plastic. And it will do more. Notice that the activation-vector spaces that a matured brain has generated, and the prototypes they embody, can encompass far more than the simple sensory types such as phonemes, colors, smells, tastes, faces, and so forth. Given high-dimensional spaces, which the brain has in abundance, those spaces and the prototypes they embody can encompass categories of great complexity, generality, and abstraction, including those with a temporal dimension, such as harmonic oscillator, projectile, traveling wave, Samba, twelve-bar blues, democratic election, six-course dinner, courtship, elephant hunt, civil disobedience, and stellar collapse. It may be that the input dimensions that feed into such abstract spaces will themselves often have to be the expression of some earlier level of processing, but that is no problem. The networks under discussion are hierarchically arranged to do precisely this as a matter of course. In principle then, it is no harder for such a system to represent types of *processes*, *procedures*, and *techniques* than to represent the 'simple' sensory qualities. From the point of view of the brain, these are just more high-dimensional vectors.

This offers us a possible means for explicating the notion of a *paradigm*, as used by T. S. Kuhn in his arresting characterization of the nature of scientific understanding and development (Kuhn 1962). A paradigm, for Kuhn, is a prototypical *application* of some set of mathematical, conceptual, or instrumental resources; an application expected to have distinct but similar instances, which it is the job of normal science to discover or construct. Becoming a scientist is less a matter of learning a set of laws than it is a matter of mastering the details of the prototypical applications of the relevant resources in such a way that one can recognize and generate further applications of a relevantly similar kind.

Kuhn was criticized for the vagueness of the notion of a paradigm, and for the unexplicated criterion of similarity that clustered further applications around it. But from the perspective of the neurocomputational approach at issue, he can be vindicated on both counts. For a brain to command a paradigm is for it to have settled into a weight configuration that produces some well-structured similarity space whose central hypervolume locates the prototypical application(s). And it is only to be expected that even the most reflective subject will be incompletely articulate on what dimensions constitute this highly complex and abstract space, and even less articulate on what metric distributes examples along each dimension. A complete answer to these questions would require a microscopic examination of the subject's brain. That is one reason why exposure to a wealth of examples is so much more effective in teaching the techniques of any science than is exposure to any attempt at listing all the relevant factors. We are seldom able to articulate them all, and even if we were able, listing them is not the best way to help a brain construct the relevant internal similarity space.

Kuhn makes much of the resistance typically shown by scientific communities to change or displacement of the current paradigm. This stubbornness here emerges as a natural expression of the way in which networks learn, or occasionally fail to learn. The process of learning by gradient descent is always threatened by the prospect of a purely *local* minimum in the global error gradient. This is a position where the error messages are not yet zero, but where every *small* change in the system produces even larger errors than those currently encountered. With a very high-dimensional space, the probability of there being a simultaneous local minimum in every dimension of the weight space is small: there is usually some narrow cleft in the canyon out which the configuration point can eventually trickle, thence to continue its wandering slide down the error gradient and toward some truly global minimum. But genuine local minima do occur, and the only way to escape them once caught is to introduce some sort of random noise into the system in hopes of bouncing the system's configuration point out of such tempting cul-de-sacs. Furthermore, even if a local quasi-minimum does have an escape path along one or more dimensions, the error gradient along them may there be quite shallow, and the system may take a very long time to find its way out of the local impasse.

Finally, and just as importantly, the system can be victimized by a highly biased 'training set'. Suppose the system has reached a weight configuration that allows it to respond successfully to all of the examples in the (narrow and biased) set it has so far encountered. Subsequent exposure to the larger domain of more diverse examples will not necessarily result in the system's moving any significant distance away from its earlier configuration, unless the relative frequency with which it encounters those new and anomalous examples is quite high. For if the encounter frequency is low, the impact of those examples will be insufficient to overcome the gravity of the false minimum that captured the initial training set. The system may require 'blitzing' by new examples if their collective lesson is ever to 'sink in'.

Even if we do present an abundance of the new and diverse examples, it is quite likely that the delta rule discussed earlier will force the system through a sequence of new configurations that perform very poorly indeed when re-fed examples from the original training set. This temporary loss of performance on certain previously 'understood' cases is the price the system pays for the chance at achieving a broader payoff later, when the system finds a new and deeper error minimum. In the case of an artificial system chugging coolly away at the behest of the delta rule, such temporary losses need not impede the learning process, at least if their frequency is sufficiently high. But with humans the impact of such a loss is often more keenly felt. The new examples that confound the old configuration may simply be ignored or rejected in some fashion, or they may be quarantined and made the target of a distinct and disconnected learning process in some adjacent network. Recall the example of sublunary and superlunary physics.

This raises the issue of explanatory unity. A creature thrown unprepared into a complex and unforgiving world must take its understanding wherever it can find it, even if this means generating a disconnected set of distinct similarity spaces, each providing the creature with a roughly appropriate response to some of the more pressing types of situation it typically encounters. But far better if it then manages to generate a single similarity space that unifies and replaces the variation that used to reside in two entirely distinct and smaller spaces. This provides the creature with an effective grasp on the phenomena that lay *between* the two classes already dealt with, but which were successfully comprehended by neither of the two old spaces. These are phenomena that the creature had to ignore, or avoid, or simply endure. With a new and more comprehensive similarity space now generating systematic responses to a wider range of phenomena, the creature has succeeded in a small piece of conceptual unification.

The payoff here recalls the virtue earlier discovered for simplicity. Indeed, it is the same virtue, namely, superior generalization to cases beyond those already encountered. This result was achieved, in the case described in section 5, by reducing the number of hidden units, thus forcing the system to make more efficient use of the representational resources remaining. This more efficient use is realized when the system partitions its activation-vector space into the minimal number of distinct similarity subspaces consistent with reducing the error messages to a minimum. When completed, this process also produces the maximal *organization* within and among those subspaces, for the system has found those enduring dimensions of variation that successfully unite the diversity confronting it.

Tradition speaks of developing a single 'theory' to explain everything. Kuhn (1962) speaks of extending and articulating a 'paradigm' into novel domains. Kitcher (1981, 1989) speaks of expanding the range of application of a given 'pattern of argument'. It seems to me that we might unify and illuminate all of these notions by thinking in terms of the evolving structure of a hidden-unit activation-vector space, and its development in the direction of representing all input vectors somewhere within a single similarity space.

This might seem to offer some hope for a Convergent Realist position within the philosophy of science, but I fear that exactly the opposite is the case. For one thing, nothing guarantees that we humans will avoid getting permanently stuck in some very deep but relatively local error minimum. For another, nothing guarantees that there exists a possible configuration of weights that would reduce the error messages to *zero*. A unique global error minimum relative to the human neural network there may be, but for us and for any other finite system interacting with the real world, it may always be nonzero. And for a third thing, nothing guarantees that there is only *one* global minimum. Perhaps there will in general be many quite different minima, all of them equally low in error, all of them carving up the world in quite different ways. Which one a given thinker reaches may be a function of the idiosyncratic details of its learning history. These considerations seem to remove the goal itself — a unique truth — as well as any sure means of getting there. Which suggests that the proper course to pursue in epistemology lies in the direction of a highly naturalistic and pluralistic form of pragmatism. For a running start on precisely these themes, see Munevar 1981 and Stich 1989.

## VIII. Concluding Remarks

This essay opened with a survey of the problems plaguing the classical or 'sentential' approach to epistemology and the philosophy of science. I have tried to sketch an alternative approach that is free of all or most of those problems, and has some novel virtues of its own. The following points are worth noting. Simple and relatively small networks of the sort described above have already demonstrated the capacity to learn a wide range of quite remarkable cognitive skills and capacities, some of which lie beyond the reach of the older approach to the nature of cognition (e.g., the instantaneous discrimination of subtle perceptual qualities, the effective recognition of similarities, and the real-time administration of complex motor activity). While the specific learning algorithm currently used to achieve these results is unlikely to be the brain's algorithm, it does provide an existence proof: by procedures of this general sort, networks can indeed learn with fierce efficiency. And there are many other procedures awaiting exploration.

The picture of learning and cognitive activity here painted encompasses the entire animal kingdom: cognition in human brains is fundamentally the same as cognition in brains generally. We are all of us processing activation vectors through artfully weighted networks. This broad conception of cognition puts cognitive theory firmly in contact with neurobiology, which adds a very strong set of constraints on the former, to its substantial long-term advantage.

Conceptual change is no longer a problem: it happens continuously in the normal course of all cognitive development. It is sustained by many small changes in the underlying hardware of synaptic weights, which changes gradually repartition the activation-vector spaces of the affected population of cells. Conceptual *simplicity* is also rather clearer when viewed from a neurocomputational perspective, both in its nature and in its epistemological significance.

The old problem of how to retrieve relevant information is transformed by the realization that it does not need to be 'retrieved'. Information is stored in brainlike networks in the global pattern of their synaptic weights. An incoming vector activates the relevant portions, dimensions, and subspaces of the trained network by virtue of its own vectorial makeup. Even an incomplete version of a given vector (i.e., one with several elements missing) will often provoke essentially the same response as the complete vector by reason of its relevant similarity. For example, the badly whistled first few bars of a familiar tune will generally evoke both its name and the rest of the entire piece. And it can do this in a matter of milliseconds, because even if the subject knows thousands of tunes, there are still no lists to be searched.

It remains for this approach to comprehend the highly discursive and linguistic dimensions of human cognition, those that motivated the classical view of cognition. We need not pretend that this will be easy, but we can see how to start. We can start by exploring the capacity of networks to manipulate the structure of existing language, its syntax, its semantics, its pragmatics, and so forth. But we might also try some novel approaches, such as allowing each of two distinct networks, whose principal concerns and activities are nonlinguistic, to try to learn from scratch some systematic means of manipulating, through a proprietary dimension of input, the cognitive activities of the other network. What system of mutual manipulation—what *language*—might they develop?

The preceding pages illustrate some of the systematic insights that await us if we adopt a more naturalistic approach to traditional issues in epistemology, an approach that is grounded in computational neuroscience. However, a recurring theme in contemporary philosophy is that normative epistemology *cannot* be 'naturalized' or reconstructed within the framework of any purely descriptive scientific theory. Notions such as 'justified belief' and 'rationality', it is said, cannot be adequately defined in terms of the nonnormative categories to which any natural science is restricted, since "oughts" cannot be derived from "ises". Conclusions are then drawn from this to the principled autonomy of epistemology from any natural science.

While it may be true that normative discourse cannot be replaced without remainder by descriptive discourse, it would be a distortion to represent this as the aim of those who would naturalize epistemology. The aim is rather to enlighten our normative endeavors by reconstructing them within a more adequate conception of what cognitive activity consists in, and thus to free ourselves from the burden of factual misconceptions and tunnel vision. It is only the *autonomy* of epistemology that must be denied.

Autonomy must be denied because normative issues are never independent of factual matters. This is easily seen for our judgments of instrumental value, as these always depend on factual premises about causal sufficiencies and dependencies. But it is also true of our most basic normative concepts and our judgments of intrinsic value, for these have factual presuppositions as well. We speak of *justification*, but we think of it as a feature of *belief*, and whether or not there are any beliefs and what properties they have is a robustly factual matter. We speak of *rationality*, but we think of it as a feature of *thinkers*, and it is a substantive factual matter what thinkers are and what cognitive kinematics they harbor. Normative concepts and normative convictions are thus always hostage to some background factual presuppositions, and these can always prove to be superficial, confused, or just plain wrong. If they are, then we may have to rethink whatever normative framework has been erected upon them. The lesson of the preceding pages is that the time for this has already come.

## References

Barto, A. G. 1985. Learning by Statistical Cooperation of Self-Interested Neuronlike Computing Elements. *Human Neurobiology* 4:229–56.

Bear, M. F., Cooper, L. N., and Ebner, F. F. 1987. A Physiological Basis for a Theory of Synapse Modification. *Science* 237 (no. 4810).

Churchland, P. M. 1975. Karl Popper's Philosophy of Science. *Canadian Journal of Philosophy* 5 (no. 1).

—— 1979. *Scientific Realism and the Plasticity of Mind*. Cambridge: Cambridge University Press.

——. 1981. Eliminative Materialism and the Propositional Attitudes. *Journal of Philosophy*. 78 *(no. 2)*.

——. 1985. The Ontological Status of Observables: In Praise of the Superempirical Virtues. In *Images of Science*, ed. P. M. Churchland and C. A. Hooker. Chicago, University of Chicago Press.

——. 1986. Some Reductive Strategies in Cognitive Neurobiology. *Mind* 95 (no. 379).

—— 1988. Perceptual Plasticity and Theoretical Neutrality: A Reply to Jerry Fodor. *Philosophy of Science* 55 (no. 2).

Churchland, P. S. 1980. A Perspective on Mind-Brain Research. *Journal of Philosophy* 77 (no. 4).

——. 1986. *Neurophilosophy: Toward a Unified Understanding of the Mind-Brain*. Cambridge, MIT Press.

Feyerabend, P. K. 1965. Reply to Criticism: Comments on Smart, Sellars, and Putnam. In *Boston*

*Studies in the Philosophy of Science*, ed. M. Wartofsky. Dordrecht: Reidel. Reprinted in *Realism, Rationalism & Scientific Method, Philosophical Papers, vol. 1*, Feyerabend, P. K. 1981. Cambridge: Cambridge University Press, 1981.

———. *1980. Consolations for the Specialist. In Criticism and the Growth of Knowledge*, eds. I. Lakatos and A. Musgrave. Cambridge: Cambridge University Press.

Fodor, J. A. 1984. Observation Reconsidered. *Philosophy of Science* 51 (no. 1).

———. 1988. A Reply to Churchland's "Perceptual Plasticity and Theoretical Neutrality." *Philosophy of Science* 55 (no. 2).

Giere, R. 1988. *Explaining Science: A Cognitive Approach*. Chicago: University of Chicago Press.

Glymour, C. 1987. "Artificial Intelligence is Philosophy". In *Aspects of Artificial Intelligence*, ed. J. Fetzer. Dordrecht: Reidel.

Gorman, R. P., and Sejnowski, T. J. 1988. Learned Classification of Sonar Targets Using a Massively-Parallel Network. *IEEE Transactions: Acoustics, Speech, and Signal Processing*. Forthcoming.

Hempel, K. 1965. "Studies in the Logic of Confirmation". In *Aspects of Scientific Explanation*. New York: The Free Press.

Hinton, G. E., and Sejnowski, T. J. 1986. "Learning and Relearning in Boltzmann Machines". In *Parallel Distributed Processing: Explorations in the Microstructure of Cognition*, eds. D. E. Rumelhart and J. L. McClelland. Cambridge: MIT Press. 1986.

Hooker, C. A. 1975. The Philosophical Ramifications of the Information-Processing Approach to the Mind-Brain. *Philosophy and Phenomenological Research* 36.

———. 1987. *A Realistic Theory of Science*. Albany: State University of New York Press.

Hopfield, J. J., and Tank, D. 1985. "Neural" Computation of Decisions in Optimization Problems. *Biological Cybernetics* 52:141–52.

Hubel, D. H., and Wiesel, T. N. 1962. Receptive Fields, Binocular Interactions, and Functional Architecture in the Cat's Visual Cortex. *Journal of Physiology* 160.

Kitcher, P. 1981. Explanatory Unification. *Philosophy of Science* 48 (no. 4).

———. 1989. "Explanatory Unification and the Causal Structure of the World". In *Minnesota Studies in the Philosophy of Science, vol. 13, Scientific Explanation*, ed. P. Kitcher. Minneapolis: University of Minnesota Press.

Kuhn, T. S. 1962. *The Structure of Scientific Revolutions*. Chicago: University of Chicago Press.

Lakatos, I. 1970. "Falsification and the Methodology of Scientific Research Programmes. In *Criticism and the Growth of Knowledge*, I. Lakatos and A. Musgrave. Cambridge University Press.

Laudan, L. 1981. A Confutation of Convergent Realism. *Philosophy of Science* 48 (no. 1).

Lehky, S., and Sejnowski, T. J. 1988a. "Computing Shape from Shading with a Neural Network Model". In *Computational Neuroscience*, ed. E. Schwartz. Cambridge: MIT Press.

———. 1988b. Network Model of Shape-From-Shading: Neural Function Arises from Both Receptive and Projective Fields. *Nature* 333 (June 2).

Linsker, R. 1986. From Basic Network Principles to Neural Architecture: Emergence of Orientation Columns. *Proceedings of the National Academy of Sciences, USA*, 83:8779–83.

Minsky, M., and Papert, S. 1969. *Perceptrons*. Cambridge: MIT Press.

Munevar, G. 1981. *Radical Knowledge*. Indianapolis: Hackett.

Pellionisz, A., and Llinas, R. 1982. Space-Time Representation in the Brain: The Cerebellum as a Predictive Space-Time Metric Tensor. *Neuroscience* 7 (no. 12):2949–70.

———. 1985. Tensor Network Theory of the Metaorganization of Functional Geometries in the Central Nervous System. *Neuroscience*. 16 (no. 2):245–74.

Putnam, H. 1981. *Reason, Truth, and History*. Cambridge: Cambridge University Press.

Rosenberg, C. R., and Sejnowski, T. J. 1987. Parallel Networks That Learn To Pronounce English Text. *Complex Systems, 1:145–68*.

Rosenblatt, F. 1959. *Principles of Neurodynamics*. New York: Spartan Books.

Rumelhart, D. E., Hinton, G. E., and Williams, R. J. 1986a. Learning Representations by Back-Propagating Errors. *Nature*, 323.

——. 1986b. "Learning Internal Representations by Error Propagation". In *Parallel Distributed Processing: Explorations in the Microstructure of Cognition*, ed. D. E. Rumelhart and J. L. McClelland. Cambridge: MIT Press.

Salmon, W. 1966. *The Foundations of Scientific Inference*. Pittsburgh: University of Pittsburgh Press.

Scheffler, I. 1963. *The Anatomy of Inquiry*. New York: Knopf.

Sejnowski, T. J., Kienker, P. K., and Hinton, G. E. 1986. Learning Symmetry Groups with Hidden Units: Beyond the Perceptron. *Physica D*: 22.

Stich, S. P. 1990. *The Fragmentation of Reason*. Cambridge: MIT Press.

Suppe, F. 1974. *The Structure of Scientific Theories*. Chicago: University of Illinois Press.

Van Fraassen, Bas 1980. *The Scientific Image*. Oxford: Oxford University Press.

Zipser, D., and Elman, J. D. 1988. Learning the Hidden Structure of Speech. *Journal of the Acoustical Society of America* 83(4):1615-25.

# Connectionism, Constituency, and the Language of Thought

## PAUL SMOLENSKY

I'm the only President you've got.

Lyndon Johnson[1]

In their paper, "Connectionism and cognitive architecture," Fodor and Pylyshyn (1988a) argue that connectionism cannot offer a cognitive architecture that is both viable and different from the Classical language of thought architecture: if it differs from the Classical architecture it is because it reinstantiates simple associationism, and is therefore not a viable candidate; if it is viable, it is because it implements the Classical view and therefore does not offer a new cognitive architecture – just a new implementation of the old one. It is my purpose here to expose the false dichotomy in this argument, to show that the space of connectionist cognitive architectures is much richer than this simple dichotomy presumes, and that in this space is a large region of architectures that are implementations neither of a Classical architecture nor of a simple associationist architecture; these architectures provide structured mental representations and structure-sensitive processes in a truly non-Classical way.

In section 1, I make a number of general remarks about connectionism, Fodor and Pylyshyn's argumentation, and the abuse of the term "implementation." In section 2, I focus on the crux of their argument, which turns on the compositional structure of mental states. I develop in some detail the argument that, unlike simple associationist models, connectionist models using *distributed representations* can embody compositionality at the same time as providing a new cognitive architecture that is not an implementation of a Classical language of thought. In section 3, I bring together the more technical discussion of section 2 back in contact with the more general issues raised in section 1. I argue that the debate surrounding compositionality illustrates the general point that by finding new formal instantiations of basic computational notions in the category of continuous mathematics, connectionism can open up genuinely new and powerful accounts of computation and cognition that go well beyond the limited progress that can be afforded by the kind of implementationalist strategy that Fodor and Pylyshyn advocate.

# 1  General Remarks

## 1.1  The True Commitment of Connectionism: PTC Version

In this paper I adopt a view of connectionism that was presented and discussed at some length in Smolensky (1988a,b), a view I call PTC (for the Proper Treatment of Connectionism). Oversimplifying a bit, according to PTC, the true commitment of connectionism is to a very general formalism for describing mental representations and mental processes. The Classical view is, of course, committed to the hypothesis that mental representations are elements of a *symbol system*, and that mental processes consist of symbol manipulation operations. PTC is committed to the hypothesis that mental representations are *vectors* partially specifying the state of a dynamical system (the activities of units in a connectionist network), and that mental processes are specified by the differential equations governing the evolution of that dynamical system.

The main point is this: under the influence of the Classical view, computation and cognition have been studied almost exclusively under the umbrella of discrete mathematics; the connectionist approach, on the other hand, brings the study of computation and cognition squarely in contact with the other half of mathematics – continuous mathematics. The true commitment, according to PTC, is to uncovering the insights this other half of mathematics can provide us into the nature of computation and cognition.

On the PTC account, simple associationism is a particularly impoverished and impotent corner of the connectionist universe. It may well be that the attraction a number of people feel to connectionism is an attraction to neo-associationism; but it is nonetheless a serious mistake to presume connectionism to be committed to simple associationist principles. To equate connectionism with simple associationism is no more appropriate than equating Classical symbolic theory with Aristotelean logic. (The temptation Fodor may provide his readers notwithstanding, I don't recommend the second identification any more than the first.)

In fact, the comparison with Aristotle is not wholly inappropriate. Our current understanding of the power of connectionist computation might well be compared with Aristotle's understanding of symbolic computation; before connectionists can take really serious shots at cognitive modeling, we probably have at least as far to go in developing connectionist computation as symbolic computation had to go between Aristotle and Turing. In giving up symbolic computation to undertake connectionist modeling, we connectionists have taken out an enormous loan, on which we are still paying nearly all interest: solving the basic problems we have created for ourselves rather than solving the problems of cognition. In my view, the loan is worth taking out for the goal of understanding how symbolic computation, or approximations to it, can emerge from numerical computation in a class of dynamical systems sharing the most general characteristics of neural computation.

Because cognitive modeling demands so much further progress in the development of connectionist computational techniques, I will argue here not for the superiority (nor even the plausibility) of a connectionist approach to cognitive modeling. Rather, I will argue that connectionism should be given a chance to progress unhampered by the misconception, fueled in significant part by Fodor and Pylyshyn (1988a; henceforth, F&P), that there is little point in pursuing the connectionist approach since it is doomed at the outset on fundamental grounds.

Given this characterization of the commitments of the Classical and connectionist approach, to claim, as F&P explicitly do, that any cognitive architecture that incorporates structured mental representations and processes sensitive to that structure is a Classical architecture, is to bloat the notion of "Classical architecture" well beyond reasonable bounds.

## 1.2   Implementation vs. Refinement

The bottom line of F&P can be paraphrased as follows. "*Standard* connectionism is just simple associationism wrapped in new jargon, and as such, is fatally flawed. Connectionists should pursue instead a *nonstandard* connectionism, embracing the principles of compositionality and structure-sensitive processing: they should accept the Classical view and should design their nets to be implementations of Classical architectures." Behind this moral is the assumption that connectionist models with compositionally structured representations must necessarily be implementations of a Classical architecture; it will be my major purpose to show that this is false. The connectionist systems I will advocate hypothesize models that are not an *implementation* but rather a *refinement* of the Classical symbolic approach; these connectionist models hypothesize a truly different cognitive architecture, to which the Classical architecture is a scientifically important approximation. The reader may suspect that I will be splitting hairs and that the difference between "implementation" and "refinement" will be of no philosophical significance. But in fact the new cognitive architecture I will hypothesize lacks the most crucial property of Fodor and Pylyshyn's Classical architecture: mental representations and mental processes are *not* supported by the same formal entities – there are no "symbols" that can do both jobs.[2] The new cognitive architecture is fundamentally two-level: formal, algorithmic specification of processing mechanisms, on the one hand, and semantic interpretation, on the other, must be done at two different levels of description.

There is a sense of "implementation" that cognitive science has inherited from computer science, and I propose that we use it. If there is an account of a computational system at one level and an account at a lower level, then the lower one is an *implementation* of the higher one if and only if the higher description is a complete, precise, algorithmic account of the behavior of that system. It is *not* sufficient that the higher-level account provide some sort of rough summary of the interactions at the lower level. It is *not* sufficient that the lower-level account involve some of the same basic ideas of how the problem is to be solved (for example, a decomposition of the problem into subproblems). Such weak usages of "implementation" abound in the literature, particularly in the numerous attempts to dismiss connectionism as "mere implementation." But in its correct usage, *implementation* requires that the higher-level account provide an exact, precise, algorithmic account of the system's behavior.

It's important to see that, unless this definition of implementation is adopted, it is impossible to legitimately argue to F&P's ultimate conclusion: as long as connectionists are doing implementation, they're not going to provide a new cognitive architecture. If it is shown only that connectionism "implements" the Classical architecture under a looser definition of the term, then the conclusion that follows is that the Classical account provides a rough, higher-level approximation to the connectionist account, or involves some of the same basic ideas about how information is represented and processed. This is a *much weaker* conclusion that what F&P are after. They want the conclusion that only true implementation will license: since the Classical account provides a complete, precise, algorithmic account of the cognitive system, there is nothing to be gained by going to the lower level account, as long as the phenomena of interest can be seen at the higher level; and, of course, it is exactly those phenomena that the Classicist will count as "truly cognitive." To account for intrinsically lower-level phenomena – in which category the Classicist will certainly include neural phenomena and may also include certain perceptual/motor phenomena – the Classicist will acknowledge the need to condescend to a lower level account; but within the domain of "pure cognition," Classicists won't need to get their hands so dirty. These are the sorts of conclusions that Classicists have pushed for decades on the basis of analogies to higher- and lower-level computer languages. But of course these languages, *by design*, satisfy the *correct* definition of implementation; none of these conclusions follows from weaker definitions, and none follows from the connectionist position I defend here. Far from the conclusion that "*nothing* can be gained from going to the lower level account," there is *plenty* to be gained: completeness, precision, and algorithmic accounts of processing, none of which is in general available at the higher level, according to PTC.

To see how the distributed connectionist architecture differs fundamentally from the Classical one – fails to provide an "implementation" using the correct definition of the term – I will now sketch how the connectionist architecture is intrinsically split over two levels of description. We'll consider the purest case: distributed connectionist models having the following two properties:

1. a Interpretation can be assigned to large-scale activity patterns but not to individual units;
   b The dynamics governing the interaction of individual units is sufficiently complex that the algorithm defining the interactions of individual units cannot be translated into a tractably-specified algorithm for the interaction of whole patterns.[3]

As a result of these two properties, we can see that there are two levels of analysis with very different characteristics. At the lower level, where the state variables are the activities of individual units, the processing is described by a complete, precise, and formal algorithm, but semantic interpretation cannot be done. At the higher level, where the system's state is described in terms of the presence of certain large-scale patterns, semantic interpretation can be done, but now complete, precise algorithms for the processing cannot be stated. As I have characterized this in Smolensky (1988a), the *syntax* or processing algorithm strictly resides at the lower level, while the *semantics* strictly resides at the upper level. Since both the syntax and the semantics are essential to the cognitive architecture, we have an intrinsically split-level cognitive architecture here: There is no account of the architecture in which the same elements carry both the syntax and the semantics. Thus we have a fundamentally new candidate for the cognitive architecture which is simply *not* an implementation of the Classical one.

Note that the conclusions of this section depend crucially on the assumption (1a) that connectionist representations are *distributed* (when viewed at the level of individual units, the level at which processing algorithms can be identified (1b)). Thus, while F&P attempt to give the impression that the issue of local vs. distributed representations is a little technical squabble between connectionists of no philosophical consequence, I believe this to be profound mistake. Distributed representations, when combined with (1b), entail that in the connectionist cognitive architecture, mental representations bear a fundamentally different relation to mental processes than is true in the Classical account. I will return to this crucial point in section 3.

## 2 Compositionality and Distributed Connectionist Representations

I shall not seek, and I will not accept, the nomination of my party for another term as your President.

Lyndon Johnson

In this section I consider the crux of F&P's argument, and argue that distributed connectionist architectures, without implementing the Classical architecture, can nonetheless provide structured mental representations and mental processes sensitive to that structure.

### 2.1 The Ultralocal Case

Here is a quick summary of what I take to be the central argument of F&P.

2  a  Thoughts have composite structure.

By this they mean things like: the thought that *John loves the girl* is not atomic; it's a composite mental state built out of thoughts about *John, loves* and *the girl*.

2  b  Mental processes are sensitive to this composite structure.

For example, from any thought of the form $p$ & $q$ – regardless of what $p$ and $q$ are – we can deduce $p$.

F&P elevate (2) to the status of defining the Classical View of Cognition, and claim that this is what is being challenged by connectionism. I am arguing that this is wrong, but for now we continue with F&P's argument.

Having identified claims (2) as definitive of the Classical View, F&P go on to argue that there are compelling arguments for these claims.[4] According to these arguments, mental states have the properties of productivity, systematicity, compositionality, and inferential coherence. Without going into all these arguments, let me simply state that for present purposes I'm willing to accept that they

187

are convincing enough to justify the conclusion that (2) must be taken quite seriously.

Now for F&P's analysis of connectionism. They assert that in (standard) connectionism, all representations are atomic; mental states have no composite structure, violating (2a). Furthermore, they assert, (standard) connectionist processing is association which is sensitive only to *statistics*, not to *structure* – in violation of (2b). Therefore, they conclude, (standard) connectionism is maximally non-Classical: it violates both the defining principles. Therefore connectionism is defeated by the compelling arguments in favor of the Classical view.

What makes F&P say that connectionist representations are atomic? The second figure of their paper (p. 16) says it all – it is rendered here as figure 1. This

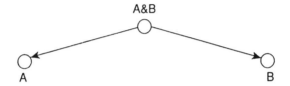

*Figure 1:* Fodor & Pylyshyn's network

network is supposed to illustrate the standard connectionist account of the inference from *A & B* to *A* and to *B*. It is true that Ballard and Hayes wrote a paper (Ballard and Hayes, 1984; also Ballard, 1986) about using connectionist networks to do automated resolution theorem proving in which networks like this appear. However it is a serious mistake to view this as the paradigmatic connectionist account for anything like human inferences of this sort. The kind of *ultralocal* connectionist representation, in which entire propositions are represented by individual nodes, is far from typical of connectionist models, and certainly not to be taken as *definitive* of the connectionist approach.[5]

A central claim in my response to F&P is that any critique of the connectionist approach must consider the consequences of using distributed representations, in which the representations of high level conceptual entities such as propositions are distributed over many nodes, and the same nodes simultaneously participate in the representation of many entities. Their response, in section 2.13 (p. 19), is as follows. The distributed/local representation issue concerns (they assume) whether each of the nodes in figure 1 refers to something complicated and lower level (the distributed case) or not (the local case). But, they claim, this issue is irrelevant, because it pertains to a *between-level* issue, and the compositionality of mental states is a *within level* issue.

My response is that they are correct that compositionality is a within-level issue, and correct that the distributed/local distinction is a between-level issue. Their argument presumes that because of this difference, one issue cannot influence the other. But that is a fallacy. It assumes that the between-level relation in distributed representations cannot have any consequences on the *within-level* structure of the relationships between the representations of *A & B* and the representation of *A*. And that's simply false. There are profound implications of distributed representations for compositionality; these are the subject of all of section 2 of this paper. In particular, it will turn out that figure 1 is exactly as relevant to a distributed connectionist account of inference as it is to a symbolic account. In the ultralocal case, figure 1 is relevant and their critique stands; in the distributed case, figure 1 is a bogus characterization of the connectionist account and their critique completely misses its target. It will further turn out that a valid analysis of the actual distributed case, based on suggestions of Pylyshyn himself, leads to quite the opposite conclusion: connectionist models using distributed representations describe mental states with a relevant kind of (within-level) constituent structure. The rather weak sense of constituent structure in generic distributed representations, identified in section 2.2, will be made much stronger in explicitly designed distributed representations, discussed in section 2.3, in which constituents can fill varying structural roles.

## 2.2   The Distributed (Weakly Compositional) Case

For now, the goal is to show that generic connectionist models using distributed representations ascribe to mental states the kind of compositional structure demanded by (2a), contrary to F&P's conclusion based on the ultralocal network of figure 1.

### 2.2.1   The Coffee Story

My argument consists primarily in carrying out an analysis that was suggested by Zenon Pylyshyn himself at the 1984 Cognitive Science Meeting in Boulder.[6]

We'll take a *distributed* representation of *cup with coffee* and subtract from it a distributed representation of *cup without coffee* and call what's left, following Pylyshyn, "the connectionist representation of *coffee*."

To generate these distributed representations I will use a set of "microfeatures" (Hinton, McClelland, and Rumelhart, 1986) that are not very micro – but that's always what happens in examples that are cooked up to be intuitively understandable in a nontechnical exposition. These microfeatures are shown in figure 2.

Figure 2 shows a distributed representation of *cup with coffee*: a pattern of activity in which those units that are active (black) are those that correspond to microfeatures present in the description of a cup containing coffee. Obviously, this is a crude, nearly sensory-level representation, but, again, that helps make the example more intuitive – it's not essential.

Given the representation of *cup with coffee* displayed in figure 2, Pylyshyn suggests we subtract the representation of *cup without coffee*. The representation of *cup without coffee* is shown in figure 3, and figure 4 shows the result of subtracting it from the representation of *cup with coffee*.

So what does this procedure produce as "the connectionist representation of *coffee*"? Reading off from figure 4, we have a burnt odor and hot brown liquid with curved sides and bottom surfaces contacting porcelain. This is indeed a representation of *coffee*, but in a very particular context: the context provided by *cup*.

| Units | Microfeatures |
|---|---|
| ● | upright container |
| ● | hot liquid |
| ○ | glass contacting wood |
| ● | porcelain curved surface |
| ● | burnt odor |
| ● | brown liquid contacting porcelain |
| ○ | oblong silver object |
| ● | finger-sized handle |
| ● | brown liquid with curved sides and bottom |

*Figure 2* Representation of cup with coffee.

What does this mean for Pylyshyn's conclusion that "the connectionist representation of *cup with coffee* is just the representation of *cup without coffee* combined with the representation of *coffee*"? What is involved in combining the representations of figures 3 & 4 back together to form that of figure 2? We

| Units | Microfeatures |
|---|---|
| ● | upright container |
| ○ | hot liquid |
| ○ | glass contacting wood |
| ● | porcelain curved surface |
| ○ | burnt odor |
| ○ | brown liquid contacting porcelain |
| ○ | oblong silver object |
| ● | finger-sized handle |
| ○ | brown liquid with curved sides and bottom |

*Figure 3* Representation of cup without coffee.

assemble the representation of *cup with coffee* from a representation of a *cup*, and a representation of *coffee*, but it's a rather strange combination. There's also the representation of the *interaction* of the cup with coffee – like *brown liquid contacting porcelain*. Thus the composite representation is built from coffee *extracted* from the situation *cup with coffee*, together with *cup* extracted from the situation *cup with coffee*, together with their interaction.

So the compositional structure is there, but it's there is an *approximate* sense. It's *not* equivalent to taking a context-indpendent representation of *coffee* and a context-independent representation of *cup* – and certainly not equivalent to taking a context-independent representation of the relationship *in* or *with* – and sticking them all together in a symbolic structure, concatenating them together to form the kind of syntactic compositional structures like with (cup, coffee) that F&P want connectionist nets to implement.

| Units | Microfeatures |
|-------|---------------|
| O | upright container |
| ● | hot liquid |
| O | glass contacting wood |
| O | porcelain curved surface |
| ● | burnt odor |
| ● | brown liquid contacting porcelain |
| O | oblong silver object |
| O | finger-sized handle |
| ● | brown liquid with curved sides and bottom |

*Figure 4* "Representation of coffee"

To draw this point out further, let's reconsider the representation of *coffee* once the cup has been subtracted off. This, suggests Pylyshyn, is the connectionist representation of *coffee*. But as we have already observed, this is really a representation of *coffee* in the particular context of being inside a cup. According to Pylyshyn's formula, to get the connectionist representation of *coffee* it should have been in principle possible to take the connectionist representation of *can with coffee* and subtract from it the connectionist representation of *can without coffee*. What would happen if we actually did this? We would get a representation of ground brown burnt smelling granules stacked in a cylindrical shape, together with granules contacting tin. This is the connectionist representation of *coffee* we get by starting with *can with coffee* instead of *cup with coffee*. Or we could start with the representation of *tree with coffee* and subtract off *tree without coffee*. We would get a connectionist representation for *coffee* which would be a representation of brown beans in a funny shape hanging suspended in mid-air. Or again we could start with *man with coffee* and get still another connectionist representation of *coffee*: one quite similar to the entire representation of *cup with coffee* from which we extracted our first representation of *coffee*.

The point is that the representation of *coffee* that we get out of the construction starting with *cup with coffee* leads to a different representation of *coffee* than we get out of other constructions that have equivalent a priori status. That means that if you want to talk about the connectionist representation of *coffee* in this distributed scheme, you have to talk about a *family of distributed activity patterns*. What knits together all these particular representations of *coffee* is nothing other than a type of family resemblance.

## 2.2.2   Morals of the Coffee Story

The first moral I want to draw out of this *coffee* story is this: unlike the ultralocal case of figure 1, with distributed representations, complex representations *are* composed of representations of constituents. The constituency relation here is a *within-level* relation, as F&P require: the pattern or *vector* representing *cup with coffee* is composed of a *vector* that can be identified as a distributed representation of *cup without coffee* together with a *vector* that can be identified as a particular distributed representation of *coffee*. In characterizing the constituent vectors of the vector representing the composite, we are *not* concerned with the fact that the vector representing *cup with coffee* is a vector comprised of the activity of individual microfeature units. The *between-level* relation between the vector and its individual numerical elements is *not* the constituency relation, and so section 2.1.4 (pp. 19–28) of F&P is irrelevant – it addresses a mistake that is not being made.

The second moral is that the constituency relation among distributed representations is one that is important for the analysis of connectionist models, and for explaining their behavior, but it is *not* a part of the information processing mechanism within the connectionist model. In order to process the vector representing *cup with coffee*, the network does not have to decompose it into constituents. For processing, it is the *between-level* relation, not the within-level relation, that matters. The processing of the vector representing *cup with coffee* is determined by the individual numerical activities that make up the vector: it is over these lower-level activities that the processes are defined. Thus the fact that there is considerable arbitrariness in the way the constituents of *cup with coffee* are defined introduced no ambiguities in the way the network processes that representation – the ambiguities exist only for us who analyze the model and try to explain its behavior. Any particular definition of constituency that gives us explanatory leverage is a valid definition of constituency; lack of uniqueness is not a problem.

This leads directly to the third moral: the decomposition of composite states into their constituents is not precise and uniquely defined. The notion of constituency is important but attempts to formalize it are likely to crucially involve *approximation*. As discussed at some length in Smolensky (1988a), this is the typical case: notions from symbolic computation provide important tools for constructing higher-level accounts of the behavior of connectionist models using distributed representation – but these notions provide approximate, not precise, accounts.

Which leads to the fourth moral: while connectionist networks using distributed representations *do* describe mental states with the type of constituency required by (2a), they do *not* provide an implementation – correctly defined – of a symbolic language of thought. The context-dependency of the constituents, the interactions that must be accommodated when they are combined, the inability to uniquely and precisely identify constituents, the imperative to take seriously the notion that the representation of *coffee* is a collection of vectors knit together by family resemblance – all these entail that the relation between connectionist constituency and syntactic symbolic constituency is *not* one of implementation. In particular, it would be absurd to claim that even if the connectionist story is correct then that would have no implications for the cognitive architecture, that it would merely fill in lower-level details without important implications for the higher-level account.

These conclusions all address compositional representation (2a) without explicitly addressing structure-sensitive processing (2b). Addressing structure -sensitivity to the depth necessary to grapple with real cognitive modeling is far beyond the scope of this paper; to a considerable extent, it is beyond the scope of current connectionism. However, let me simply state the fundamental hypothesis of PTC that weaves the statistical sensitivity characteristic of connectionist processing together with the notion of structure sensitivity: *the mind is a statistics-sensitive engine operating on structure-sensitive (numerical) representations.* The previous arguments have shown that distributed representations do possess constituency relations, and that, properly analyzed, these representations can be seen to encode structure. Extending this is grapple with the complexity of the kinds of rich structures implicated in complex cognitive processes is the topic of the next section. Here it suffices to observe that once we have complex structured information represented in distributed numerical patterns, statistics-sensitive processes can proceed to analyze the statistical regularities in a fully structure-sensitive way. Whether such processes can provide structure-sensitivity that is adequate to cope with the demands of linguistic and inferential processing is sure to be unknown for some time yet.

The conclusion, then, is that distributed models *can* satisfy (2). Whether (2) can be satisfied to the depth required by the full demands of cognitive modeling is of course an open empirical question – just as it is for the symbolic approach to satisfying (2). At the same time, distributed connectionist models do *not* amount to an implementation of the symbolic instantiations of (2) that F&P are committed to.

Before summing up, I'd like to return to figure 1. In what sense can figure 1 be said to describe the relation between the distributed representation of *A&B* and the distributed representations of *A* and *B*? It was the intent of the *coffee* story to show that the distributed representations of the constituents are, in an approximate but explanation-relevant sense, part of the representation of the composite. Thus, in the distributed case, the relation between the node of figure 1 labeled *A&B* and the others is one kind of whole/part relation. An inference mechanism that takes as input the vector representing *A&B* and produces as output the vector representing *A* is a mechanism that extracts a part from a whole. And in this sense it is no different from a symbolic inference mechanism that takes the syntactic structure A & B and extracts from it the syntactic constituent A. The connectionist mechanisms for doing this are of course quite different than the symbolic mechanisms, and the approximate nature of the whole/part relation gives the connectionist computation different overall characteristics: we don't have simply a new implementation of the old computation.

It is clear that, just as figure 1 offers a crude summary of the symbolic process of passing from A & B to A, a summary that uses the labels to encode hidden internal structures within the nodes, *exactly the same is true of the distributed connectionist case.* In the distributed connectionist case – *just as in the symbolic case* – the links in figure 1 are crude summaries of complex processes and not simple-minded causal channels that pass activity from the top node to the lower nodes. Such a simple causal story applies only to the ultralocal connectionist case, which is the only legitimate target of F&P's attack.

Let me be clear: there is no serious distributed connectionist model, as far as I know, of the kind of formal inference F&P have in mind here. Many proponents of connectionism would be content to claim that formal inference is a specially trained, poorly practiced skill that is far from central to cognition, and that therefore we can afford to put off worrying about providing a connectionist model of it for a long time. I prefer to say that, at root, the F&P argument concerns an important and central issue: the constituent structure of mental states; formal inference is just one setting in which to see the importance of that constituent structure. So the preceding discussion of the constituent structure of distributed representations does address the heart of their critique, even if a well-developed connectionist account of formal inference remains unavailable.


## 2.3   The Distributed (Strongly Compositional) Case

But, one might well argue, the sense in which the vector encoding the distributed representation of *cup with coffee* has constituent vectors representing *cup* and *coffee* is too weak to serve all the uses of constituent structure – in particular, too weak to support formal inference – because the vector representing *cup* cannot fill multiple structural roles. A true constituent can move around and fill any of a number of different roles in different structures. Can *this* be done with vectors encoding distributed representations, and be done in a way that doesn't amount to simply implementing symbolic syntactic constituency? The purpose of this section is to describe research showing that the answer is affirmative.

A large class of connectionist representations, which I call *tensor product representations*, is defined and analyzed in Smolensky (1987a), and applied in Dolan and Smolensky (1988). We generate various members of this class by variously specifying several parameters in a highly general method for creating connectionist representations of structured information. The resulting parametric variation in the representations is very broad, encompassing very simple representations such as the case of figure 1, as well as representations that are close to true implementations of a syntactic language of thought. This class of representations covers the spectrum from fully distributed representations to ultralocal ones, and includes representations with a full sense of constituency, where role-independent constituents are assigned to roles in a structure and the representation of the structure is built up systematically from the representation of the constituents.

The problem that motivates this work is mapping complex structure such as parse trees into vectors of activity in connectionist networks, in such a way that the constituent structure is available for connectionist processing. A general formal framework for stating this problem is to assume that there is a set of discrete structures $S$ (like parse trees) and a vector space $V$ – a space of activity states of a connectionist network. A connectionist representation is a mapping from $S$ to $V$; the theorist's job is to identify such mappings having various desirable properties. Tensor product representations can provide many of these properties.

A particular tensor product representation is constructed in two steps.

3   a   Specify a decompositional process whereby the discrete structures are explicitly broken down as a set of constituents, each filling a particular role in the structure as a whole. This step has nothing to do with connectionism *per se*; it just amounts to being specific about the kind of constituent structure we want to represent.

   b   Specify two connectionist representations: one for the structural roles and another for their fillers (the constituents). Thus, for every filler, we assign a vector in the state space of some network for representing fillers; similarly, we assign to every role a vector in the state space of some network for representing roles.

These two steps indicate the "parameters" in the general tensor product representational scheme that must be specified to individuate a particular representation. Once these parameters are specified, two very simple operations from the theory of vector spaces are used to generate the representation of a particular discrete structure. The representation of the whole is built from the representation of its constituent parts by the operation of *superposition* which is simply *vector addition*: the vector representing the whole is the sum of the vectors representing the parts. Step (3a) above specifies exactly what constituents are involved in this process. The vector representing a given constituent is actually a role-sensitive representation: a representation of that constituent *in the role it plays in the whole*. This vector is built by taking a particular vector product of the vector that represents the constituent independent of any role, and the vector representing the role in the structure that is filled by the constituent. Step (3b) specifies a set of vectors that represent individual structural roles and another set of vectors that represent individual fillers for those roles (constituents) independently of any role. The product operation here is a vector operation called the *tensor product* that takes two vectors and products a new vector; if the two vectors consist of $n$ and $m$ activity values, then their tensor product is a vector of $nm$ activity values, each one being a different product (using ordinary numerical multiplication) of two activity values, one from each of the original vectors.[7]

The tensor product provides a general solution to a problem that his been nagging the distributed connectionist representational world for a long time, the so-called *variable binding problem*. How can we take an activity pattern representing a variable and another pattern representing a value and generate a connectionist representation of their binding that has the right computational properties? The simplicity of the tensor product makes it possible to show it does in fact satisfy the computational demands of (distributed) connectionist variable binding. The tensor product technique is a generalization of specific tricks (especially, *conjunctive coding*: Hinton, McClelland, and Rumelhart, 1986; McClelland and Kawamoto, 1986; Smolensky, forthcoming) that have been used to solve this problem in particular instances in the past.

The tensor product representation of constituent structure considerably strengthens the notion of constituency brought out in the previous section through the *coffee* story. There we saw that the whole/part relation between *cup with coffee* and *coffee* is mirrored in a whole/part relation between their respective representations: the latter relation was not the whole/part relation between molecular symbolic structures and their atomic constituents, as in a symbolic language of thought, but rather the relation between a sum vector **w** and the component vectors that add up to it: $\mathbf{w} = \mathbf{c}_1 + \mathbf{c}_2 + \ldots$ The same is true here generally with respect to tensor product representations, but now in addition we can identify the representations of each constituent as a role-*dependent* representation built in a systematic way (through tensor product variable binding) from a role-*independent* representation of the filler and a filler-independent representation of its role.

Among the computational properties required of the variable binding mechanism is the possibility of *unbinding*: from the role-dependent representation of some constituent we must be able to extract the role-independent representation of that constituent. Similarly, given the vector representing a symbolic structure as a whole, it should be possible to extract the role-independent representation of the filler of any given role in the structure. Under a wide variety of conditions this is possible with the tensor product representation, although when so many roles are simultaneously filled that the capacity of the representing network is exceeded, corruptions, confusions, and errors can be introduced during unbinding. The conditions under which error-free unbinding can be performed, and characterization of the errors occurring when these conditions are violated, can be computed (Smolensky, 1987a). Thus, for example, if we have a tensor product representation for *P&Q*, and we wish to extract the first element *P* as part of a deductive process, then as long as the representing network is not trivially small, we can easily do so without error, using very simple (linear) connectionist processes.

So, returning to F&P's critique, let's see what the tensor product representational scheme can do for us in terms of the simple inference problems they talk about.

Using the tensor product technique, it is possible to define a family of representations of tree structures. We can consider a simple tree for *P&Q* consisting of *&* at the top, *P* as its left child, and *Q* as its right child; and we can view the roles as positions in the tree, the simplest kind of role decomposition. The tensor product representation of that tree structure is a vector $\mathbf{F}(P\&Q)$ which is related to the vectors representing the constituents, $\mathbf{F}(P)$ and $\mathbf{F}(Q)$, by a function $\mathbf{B}_{\&}$ that is particular to constructing conjunctions:

$$\mathbf{F}(P\&Q) = \mathbf{B}_{\&}\,[\mathbf{F}(P),\,\mathbf{F}(Q)]$$

The function $B_{\&}$ is defined by

$$\mathbf{B}_{\&}(\mathbf{u},\,\mathbf{v}) = \mathbf{c}_{\&} + \tau_0\mathbf{u} + \tau_1\mathbf{v}$$

where $\mathbf{c}_{\&}$ is a constant vector and $\tau_0$ and $\tau_1$ are linear operators (the most natural vector operators) that vary depending on how the parameters individuating the tensor product representation are chosen.

I have descended to this level of detail and used this notation because in footnote 9 (p. 14) of F&P, exactly this property is chosen to define $\mathbf{F}$ as a "physical instantiation mapping of combinatorial structure." In this sense the tensor product representation meets F&P's formal requirements for a representation of combinatorial structure.

But have we merely provided an implementation then of a symbolic language of thought? In general, the answer is "no." Depending on how we have chosen to set the parameters in specifying the tensor product representation (which determines the properties of $\tau_0$ and $\tau_1$), we can fail to have any of the following properties holding (Smolensky, 1987a):

4　a　*Uniqueness with respect to roles or fillers*. If we're not careful, even though the above equation is satisfied, we can end up with *P&Q* having the same representation as *Q&P*, or other more subtle ambiguities about what fills various roles in the structure.

b *Unbounded depth.* We may avoid the first problem (4a) for sufficiently small structures, but when representing sufficiently large or deep structures, these problems may appear. Unless the vector space in which we do our representation is infinite-dimensional (corresponding to a network with infinitely many units), we cannot solve (4a) for unbounded depth. (Of course, the same is true of Turing/von Neumann machines if they are only allowed bounded resources; but whereas the capacity limit in the symbolic case is a hard one, the tensor product representation allows for graceful degradation as resources are saturated.)

c *Nonconfusability in memory.* Even when problem (4a) is avoided, when we have representations with uniquely determined filler/role bindings, it can easily happen that we cannot simultaneously store many such structures in a connectionist memory without getting intrusions of undesired memories during the retrieval of a given memory.

d *Processing independence.* This is in a sense a generalization of the preceding point, concerning processing constraints that may arise even when problem (4a) is avoided. In simple associative processing, for example, we may find that we can associate two vectors representing symbolic structures with what we like, but then find ourselves unable to associate the representation of a third structure with what we like, because its associate is constrained by the other two.

With all these properties potentially failing to hold, it doesn't sound to me like we're dealing with an implementation of a symbolic language of thought. But at this point somebody's going to want to say, "Well, you've just got a *lousy* implementation of a symbolic language of thought." But it's not that simple. We may have lost some (superficially desirable, at least) features of a symbolic language of thought, but we've gained some (superficially desirable, at least) features of connectionist processing in return.

5 a *Massive parallelism.* Since we have a vector that represents an entire tree at once, we can feed it into the usual connectionist massively parallel processes. Unlike traditional AI programs, we don't have to spend all our time painfully traversing step-by-step long descending chains into the bowels of complex symbolic data structures: it's all there at once, all accessible in parallel.[8]

b *Content-addressable memory.* This is the usual distributed connectionist story, but now it applies to *structural information*.

c *Statistical inference.* F&P are among the first to attack connectionism for basing its processing mechanisms on statistical inference. One more reason for them to deny that the connectionist framework I am discussing truly constitutes an implementation of their preferred architecture. Yet their arguments *against* statistical processing are much less compelling than their arguments *for* structure-sensitive processing. We are now in a position to go after *both*, in a unified framework, dissolving a long-standing tension arising from a failure to see how to formally unify structure-sensitive and statistical processing. Rather than having to model the mind as *either* a structure cruncher *or* a number cruncher, we can now see it as a number cruncher in which the numbers crunched are in fact representing complex structures.[9]

d   *Statistical learning.* Since structure can now be brought fully into the world of connectionist learning research, we can move from declarations of dogma to actual empirical results about what structurally-rich representations and processes can and cannot be acquired from experience through statistically based learning. We can now foresee a time when it will be too late to put your money down on the fate of the "poverty of the stimulus" dogma.

The point is that the parametric variation in tensor product representations covers a rich territory, and an important item on the connectionist cognitive modeling agenda is to determine whether in that territory there is a set of representations that has the right mixture of the power of (5) and the limitations of (4) to capture real human behavior. This large space of tensor product representations extends from simple ultralocal representations of the sort F&P correctly dismiss towards – I hesitate to say all the way up to, but quite close to – a true implementation of a symbolic language of thought. If you want such an implementation, you have to go to a limit that includes the following characteristics:

6   a   *Orthogonality.* The angle between the vectors representing different roles needs to go to 90 degrees, and similarly for vectors representing the fillers, to eliminate non-uniqueness and minimize interference in memory.

b   *Infinite-dimensional representations.* Otherwise, we can't represent unboundedly deep structures without confusion.

c   *Simple operations.* If we happen to want an implementation of sequential algorithms, then in processing these representations we insist that the vector equivalent of the primitive symbolic operations (like Lisp's car, cdr, and cons) are all that can be done in one time step: We don't avail ourselves of the massively parallel operations that otherwise would be available to us.

I have talked so far mostly about representations and little about processing. If we are interested, as F&P are, in inferences such as that from $P\&Q$ to $P$, it turns out that with tensor product representations, this operation can be achieved by a simple linear transformation upon these representational vectors, the kind of transformation most natural in this category of representations.[10] Not only can this structure-sensitive process be achieved by connectionist mechanisms on connectionist representations, but it can be achieved through the simplest of all connectionist operations: linear mapping. All in an architecture that differs fundamentally from the Classical one; we have not implemented a symbolic language of thought.

## 3   Connectionism, Implementationalism, and Limitivism

I am not a crook.

Richard Nixon

Let me now bring the arguments of section 2 to bear on the general issues raised in section 1.

### 3.1 The methodological Implications of Implementationalism and Limitivism

It seems to me most likely that symbolic descriptions *will* provide scientifically important *approximate* higher level accounts of how the ultimate connectionist cognitive models compute – but that these distributed connectionist models will not implement a symbolic language of thought, under the relevant (and correct) definition of the word. The approximations involved demand a willingness to accept context-sensitive symbols and interactional components present in compositional structures, and the other funny business that came out in the *coffee* example. If we're willing to live with all those degrees of approximation, then we can usefully view these symbolic level descriptions as approximate higher level accounts of the processing in a connectionist network.

An important overall conclusion in the constituency issue, then, is that the Classical and connectionist approaches differ *not* in whether they accept principles (2), *but in how they formally instantiate them.* To really confront the Classical/connectionist dispute, one has to be willing to descend to the level of the particular formal instantiations they give to the nonformal principles (2). To fail to descend to this level of detail is to miss much of the issue. In the Classical approach, principles (2) are formalized using syntactic structures for mental representations and symbol manipulation for mental processes. In the distributed connectionist approach (2) are formalized using vectorial representations for mental representations, and the corresponding notion of compositionality, together with numerical mental processes that derive their structure sensitivity from the differential way that they treat the parts of vectors corresponding to different structural roles.

In terms of research methodology, this means that the agenda for connectionism should not be to develop a connectionist implementation of the symbolic language of thought, but rather to develop formal analysis of vectorial representations of complex structures and operations on those structures that are sufficiently structure-sensitive to do the required work. This is exactly the kind of research that, for example, tensor product representations are being used to support.

Thus the PTC position is that distributed representations provide a description of mental states with sematically interpretable constituents, but that there is no complete, precise formal account of the construction of composites or of mental processes in general that can be stated solely in terms of context-independent semantically interpretable constituents. On this account, there *is* a language of thought – but only approximately; the language of thought by itself does not provide a basis for an exact formal account of mental structure or processes – it cannot by itself support a precise formal account of the cognitive architecture.

Constituency is one illustration of a central component of the general PTC approach to connectionism: the relation hypothesized between connectionist models based on continuous mathematics and Classical models based on discrete, symbolic computation. That relationship might be called the *cognitive correspondence principle*: when powerful connectionist computational systems are appropriately analyzed at higher levels, elements of symbolic computation appear as emergent properties.

Figure 5 schematically illustrates the cognitive correspondence principle. At the top are nonformal notions: the central hypotheses that the principles of cognition consist in principles of memory, of inference, of compositionality and constituent structure, etc. In the F&P argument, the relevant nonformal principles are their compositionality principles (2).

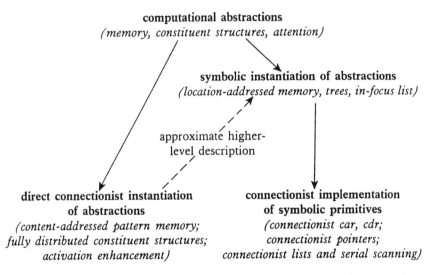

*Figure 5* PTC vs. implementationalism (Reprinted with permission of *The Behavioral and Brain Sciences.*)

The nonformal principles at the top of figure 5 have certain formalizations in the discrete mathematical category, which are shown one level down on the right branch. For example, memory is formalized as standard location-addressed memory or some appropriately more sophisticated related notion. Inference gets formalized in the discrete category as logical inference, a particular form of symbol manipulation. And so on.

The PTC research agenda consists in taking these kinds of cognitive principles and finding new ways to instantiate them in formal principles based on the continuous mathematics of dynamical systems; there are shown in figure 5 at the lowest level on the left branch. The concept of memory retrieval is reformalized in terms of the continuous evolution of a dynamical system towards a point attractor whose position in the state space is the memory; we naturally get content-addressed memory instead of location-addressed memory. (Memory storage becomes modification of the dynamics of the system so that its attractors are located where the memories are supposed to be; thus the principles of memory storage are even more unlike their symbolic counterparts than those of memory retrieval.) When reformalizing inference principles, the continuous formalism leads naturally to principles of statistical inference rather than logical inference. And so on.

The cognitive correspondence principle states that the general relationship between the connectionist formal principles and the symbolic formal principles – given that they are both instantiations of common nonformal notions, and to the extent that ultimately they are both scientifically valid descriptions of the same cognitive system – is that if we take a higher level analysis of what's going on in the connectionist systems we find that it matches, to some kind of approximation, what's going on in the symbolic formalism. This relation is indicated in figure 5 by the dotted arrow.

This is to be contrasted with an implementational view of connectionism such as that which F&P advocate. As portrayed in figure 5, the implementational methodology is to proceed from the top to the bottom not directly, via the left branch, but indirectly, via the right branch: connectionists should take the symbolic instantiations of the nonformal principles and should find ways of implementing *them* in connectionist networks.

The PTC methodology is to be contrasted not just with the implementational approach, but also with the eliminativist one. In terms of these methodological considerations, eliminativism has a strong and a weak form. The weak form advocates taking the left branch of figure 5 but ignoring altogether the symbolic formalizations, on the belief that the symbolic notions will confuse rather than enlighten us in our attempts to understand connectionist computation. The strong eliminativist position states that even viewing the nonformal principles at the top of figure 5 as a starting point for thinking about cognition is a mistake – that it is better, for example, to pursue a blind bottom-up strategy in which we take low-level connectionist principles from neuroscience and see where they lead us, without being prejudiced by archaic prescientifc notions such as those at the top of figure 5.

In rejecting both the implementationalist and eliminativist positions, PTC views connectionist accounts in significant part as reducing and explaining symbolic accounts. Connectionist accounts serve to refine symbolic accounts, to reduce the degree of approximation required, to enrich the computational notions from the symbolic and discrete world, to fill them out with notions of continuous computation. Primarily that's done by descending to a lower level of analysis, by exposing the hidden microstructure in these kinds of large-scale, discrete symbolic operations.

I have dubbed the PTC position *limitivism* because it views connectionism as delimiting the domain $D$ of validity of symbolic accounts, and explaining the validity of the symbolic approximation through passage to the "Classical limit," a general theoretical limit incorporating, e.g., the specifics described in (6), in which connectionist accounts admit, more and more exactly, higher-level symbolic accounts – at least in the limited domain $D$. This limitivist position on the relation between connectionism and symbolic theory is obviously modeled after a relation frequently observed in the refinement of physical theories, e.g., the relation between quantum and Newtonian mechanics.

The cognitive correspondence principle is so named because I believe that it has a role to play in the developing microtheory of cognition that's analogous to the role that the quantum correspondence principle played in the development of microtheory in physics. This case from physics instantiates the structure of figure 5 quite directly. There are certain fundamental physical principles that arch over both the classical and quantum formalisms: the notions of space and time and associated invariance principles, the principles of energy and momentum conservation, force laws, and so on. These principles at the top of figure 5 are instantiated in particular ways in the classical formalism, corresponding to the point one level down on the right branch. To go to a lower level of physical analysis requires the development of a new formalism. In this quantum formalism the fundamental principles are reinstantiated: they occupy the bottom of the left branch. The classical formalism can be looked at as a higher level description of the same principles operating at the lower quantum level: the dotted line of figure 5. Of course quantum mechanics does not *implement* classical mechanics: the accounts are intimately related, but classical mechanics provides an approximate, not an exact, higher-level account.[11] In a fundamental sense, the quantum and classical theories are quite incompatible: according to the ontology of quantum mechanics, the ontology of classical mechanics is quite impossible to realize in this world. But there is no denying that the classical ontology and the accompanying principles are theoretically essential, for at least two reasons: (a) to provide explanations (literally, perhaps, approximate ones) of an enormous range of classical phenomena for which direct explanation from quantum principles is hopelessly infeasible, and (b) historically, to provide the guidance necessary to discover the quantum principles in the first place. To try to develop lower-level principles without looking at the higher-level principles for guidance, given the insights we have gained from those principles, would seem – to put it mildly – inadvisable. It is basically this pragmatic consideration that motivates the cognitive correspondence principle and the PTC position it leads to.

### 3.2   Constituency via Vector Decomposition, Explanatory Relevance, and Causal Efficacy

As a final topic I would like to show how the previous methodological considerations relate specifically to the technical heart of this paper. I want to show that, if we take the general position advocated above that the research agenda of distributed connectionism is to find formal means within the continuous mathematics of dynamical systems for naturally and powerfully embodying central nonformal principles of computation and cognition, then the connectionist analysis of constituent structure I have described here is, if not inevitable, then at least perfectly natural. I take up this topic because it has been suggested that in my analysis, perhaps in order to cook up a refutation of F&P, I have seriously contorted the notion of constituency; that superposition of vectors, and tensor product binding, are just not appropriate means of instantiating constituency.

At the same time, I will consider the central question: "Is the sense in which vector decomposition constitutes a constituency relation adequate to make constituency *explanatorily relevant* to or *causally efficacious* in the account of the systematicity of thought, the basic problem motivating F&P's critique?"

Let me begin with a few words about the idea of decomposing a vector into a sum or superposition of component vectors: $\mathbf{w} = \mathbf{c}_1 + \mathbf{c}_2 + \ldots$. This technique is very commonly used to explain the behavior of dynamical systems; it works best for simple linear systems, where the equations governing the interaction between state variables are linear (such as the very simplest connectionist models). In that case – and the technique gets more complicated from there – the story is as follows.

We want to know, if we start the system off in some initial state described by the vector $\mathbf{w}$, what will the system's subsequent behavior be? (In the connectionist case, $\mathbf{w}$ characterizes the input, and we want to know what states the system will then go through; especially, what the later state that determines the output will be.) First we ask, how can the vector $\mathbf{w}$ be decomposed: $\mathbf{w} = \mathbf{c}_1 + \mathbf{c}_2 + \ldots$, so that the component vectors $\mathbf{c}_i$ are along certain special directions, determined by the linear interaction equations of the system; these directions $\mathbf{e}_i$ are called the "normal modes" of the system, and each $\mathbf{c}_i = c_i\mathbf{e}_i$, where the coefficient $c_i$ tells how strongly represented in this particular input $\mathbf{w}$ the $i^{th}$ normal mode is. Once we have decomposed the vector into components in the directions of the normal modes, we can write down in a closed form expression the state of the system at any later time: it is just the superposition of the states arising from each of the normal modes independently, and those normal modes are defined exactly so that it is possible to write down how they evolve in time.[12] Thus, knowing the interaction equations of the system, we can compute the normal modes and how they evolve in time, and then we can explain how *any* state evolves in time, simply be decomposing that state into components in the directions of the normal modes. To see an example of this technique applied to actual connectionist networks, see the general analysis of Smolensky (1986) and the specific analysis in Anderson and Mozer (1981) of the categorization performed in J. A. Anderson's "Brain-State-in-a-Box" model. (Both these analyses deal with what I call *quasi-linear* networks, a class covering many actual connectionist systems, in which the heart of the computation is linear, but a certain degree of non-linearity is also important.)

Thus, to explain the behavior of the system, we usually choose to decompose the state vector into components in the directions of the normal modes, which are conveniently related to the particular dynamics of this system. If there is change in how the system interacts with itself (as in connectionist networks that learn), over time we'll change the way we choose to break up the state in order to explain the behavior. There's no unique way to decompose a vector. That is to say, there are lots of ways that this input vector could be viewed as composed of constituents, but normal mode decomposition happens to enable a good explanation for behavior over time. In general, there may well be other compositions that are explanatorily relevant.

So, far from being an unnatural way to break up the part of a connectionist state vector that represents an input, decomposing the vector into components is exactly what we'd expect to need to do to explain the processing of that input.[13] If the connections that mediate processing of the vectors representing composite structures have the effect of sensible processing of the vector in terms of the task demands, it is very likely that in order to *understand and explain* the regularities in the network's behavior we will need to break the vector for the structure into the vectors for the constituents, and relate the processing of the whole to the processing of the parts. That this decomposition, and not arbitrary decompositions into meaningless component vectors, is useful for explaining the processing is a consequence of the connections that embody the process. Those particular components are useful for those particular connections. In general, what distinguishes one decomposition of a state vector that is useful for predicting behavior from other decompositions that are not is that the useful decomposition bears some special relation to the dynamics of the system. It may well turn out that to explain various aspects of the system's behavior (for example, various cognitive processes acting on a given input), we will want to exploit various decompositions.

Are the vector constituents in physical and connectionist systems causally efficacious? It would appear not, since the real mechanism driving the behavior of the system operates oblivious to our descriptive predilection to vector decomposition. It is the numerical values comprising the vector (in the connectionist case, the individual activity values) that really drive the machine.

As Fodor and Pylyshyn will, I believe, agree, caution in treating "causal efficacy" is required even for the Classical case. When we write a Lisp program, are the symbolic structures we think in terms of causally efficacious in the operation of the computer that runs the program? There is a sense in which they are: even though we normally think of the "real" causes as physical and far below the symbolic level, there is nonetheless a complete and precise algorithmic (temporal) story to tell about the states of the machine described at the level of symbols. Traditional computers (the hardware and especially the software) are designed to make that true, and it is the main source of their power.

The hypothesis I have attributed to distributed connectionism is that there is no comparable story at the symbolic level in the human cognitive architecture: no algorithm in terms of semantically interpretable elements that gives a precise formal algorithmic account of the system's behavior over time. That is a difference with the Classical view that I have made much of. It may be that a good way to characterize the difference is in terms of whether the constituents in mental structures are causally efficacious in mental processing.

Such causal efficacy was not my goal in developing the tensor product representation; rather, the goal was and is the design of connectionist systems that display the kinds of complex systematic behavior seen, for example, in language processing – and the mathematical explanation of that systematicity. As the examples from physics show, it is not only wrong to claim that to explain systematicity by reference to constituent structures requires that those constituents be causally efficacious: it is also wrong (but more honest) to claim (as Fodor often does) that such an explanatory strategy, while not provably unique, constitutes "the only game in town." There is an alternative explanatory strategy that has been practiced very effectively in physics for centuries, and that strategy can be applied in cognitive science as well. There are now at least two games in town, and rather than pretending otherwise, we should get on with the business of playing those games for all we can. Odds are, given how hard cognitive science is, we'll need to be playing other games before too long.

The Classical strategy for explaining the systematicity of thought is to hypothesize that there is a precise formal account of the cognitive architecture in which the constituents of mental representations have causally efficacious roles in the mental processes acting on them. The PTC view denies that such an account of the cognitive architecture exists,[14] and hypothesizes instead that, like the constituents of structures in quantum mechanics, the systematic effects observed in the processing of mental representations arises because the evolution of vectors can be (at least partially and approximately) explained in terms of the evolution of their components, even though the precise dynamical equations apply at the lower level of the individual numbers comprising the vectors and cannot be pulled up to provide a precise temporal account of the processing at the level of entire constituents – i.e., even though the constituents are not causally efficacious.[15]

## 4   Summary

Therefore, I shall resign the presidency effective at noon tomorrow.
Richard Nixon

Shifting attention away from the refutation of F&P's argument, let me summarize what I take to be the positive contributions of this paper.

7  a   As F&P plead, it *is* crucial for connectionism to separate itself from simplistic associationist psychology, and to accept the importance of a number of computational principles fundamental to traditional cognitive science, such as those relating to structure that F&P emphasize, which go beyond the computational repertoire of simple traditional connectionist networks.

b   The computational repertoire of connectionism should be extended by finding ways of directly, naturally, and powerfully realizing these computational principles within the continuous mathematics of dynamical systems.

c   Just as a set of symbolic structures offers a domain for modeling structured mental representation and processing, so do sets of vectors, once the appropriate notions (such as variable binding via tensor products) are recognized in the new mathematical category. Thus distributed connectionist representations provide a computational arena for structure processing.

d   The resulting connectionist model of mental processing is characterized by context-sensitive constituents, approximately (but not exactly) compositional semantics, massively parallel structure-sensitive processing, statistical inference and statistical learning with structured representations.

e   This connectionist cognitive architecture is intrinsically two-level: semantic interpretation is carried out at the level of patterns of activity while the complete, precise, and formal account of mental processing must be carried out at the level of individual activity values and connections. Mental processes reside at a lower level of analysis than mental representations.

f   Thus, not only is the connectionist cognitive architecture fundamentally different from the Classical one, so is the basic strategy for explaining the systematicity of thought. The systematic behavior of the cognitive system is to be explained by appealing to the systematic constituent structure of the representational vectors, and the connectivity patterns that give rise to and manipulate these vectors: but the mechanism responsible for that behavior does not (unlike in the Classical account) operate through laws or rules that are expressible formally at the level of the constituents.

The wind is changing

Mary Poppins

Only connect

E. M. Forster[16]

## Acknowledgments

I have benefited greatly from personal conversations with Jerry Fodor and Zenon Pylyshyn, conversations extending from February 1986, when Fodor presented an early version of the argument ("Against connectionism") at the Workshop on the Foundations of AI in Las Cruces, New Mexico, through a (surprisingly enjoyable) public debate held at MIT in March 1988. The concerns that drove my research to tensor product representations were kindled through that interaction. I have learned a tremendous amount from Georges Rey, thanks to his wonderful insight, open-mindedness, and patience; I would also like to thank him for the invitation to contribute to this volume and for his most helpful suggestions for this paper. Thanks, too, to Terry Horgan for very helpful discussions, as well as to the other participants of the Spindel Conference on Connectionism and the Philosophy of Mind (which resulted in the collection of papers in which Smolensky (1987b) appears). I thank Horgan, John Tienson, and the *Southern Journal of Philosophy* for permission to include a portion of Smolensky (1987b) here. Rob Cummins and Georg Schwarz have helped me enormously in sorting out a number of the issues discussed here, and I refer the reader to their papers for a number of important insights that have not been given their due here. Kevin Markey gets the credit for the crucial Presidential quotes. Finally I would like to thank Geoff Hinton, Jay McClelland, Dave Rumelhart, David Touretzky, and more recently, Alan Prince, for many helpful discussions on issues relating to connectionism and structure processing.

This work has been supported by NSF grants IRI-8609599 and ECE-8617947 to the author, by a grant to the author from the Sloan Foundation's computational neuroscience program, and by the Optical Connectionist Machine Program of the NSF Engineering Research Center for Optoelectronic Computing Systems at the University of Colorado at Boulder.

## NOTES

1  Quoted in Fodor, 1975a, p. 27.

2  This point is brought out nicely in Cummins and Schwarz (1987), Schwarz (1987), and Cummins (1989).

3  The complexity criterion here is very low: the interactions should be more complex than purely linear. A lengthy and hopefully accessible discussion may be found in Smolensky, (1986).

4  They admit up front that these arguments are a rerun updated for the 80's, a colorized version of a film that was shown in black and white some time ago – where the color comes mainly from replacing everywhere the word "behaviorism" by "connectionism."

5  The conception of connectionist representation and processing embodied in figure 1 is at the center of this entire argument, so it is important to properly locate this network and the Ballard and Hayes paper in the connectionist landscape; for those not well familiar with the territory, this may be facilitated by a sociogeographical digression. Hayes is a leading figure in the logic-based approach to symbolic AI, and (to my knowledge) this collaborative exercise is his only foray onto connectionist turf. Ballard is a leading connectionist of the "Rochester school," which tends to favor local representations over distributed ones, and which as a result represents a radically different set of foundational commitments (see Feldman and Ballard, 1982) from those of the "San Diego" or "PDP" school, as articulated for example in the PDP books (Rumelhart, McClelland, and the PDP Research Group, 1986; McClelland, Rumelhart, and the PDP Research Group, 1986); my version of the PDP framework is articulated as PTC in Smolensky (1988a, b), which explicitly address the contrast with Feldman and Ballard (1982). (Incidentally, the name "PDP" was coined to differentiate the approach from the "connectionist" approach already defined by Feldman and Ballard, 1982; the referent of "connectionist" subsequently expanded to engulf the PDP approach (e.g., *Cognitive Science*, 1985). This left what I have referred to as the "Rochester" approach without a distinctive name; the term "structured connectionist networks" is now sometimes used, but it is potentially quite misleading.) As already evidenced in section 1, it turns out that on foundational issues generally, the local vs. distributed issues forces the two schools of connectionism to take quite different positions; a response to F&P from the Feldman and Ballard (1982) perspective would have to differ completely from the one I offer here. While F&P argue that distributed representations make no difference, I now proceed to identify a crucial fallacy in that argument, which this paper as a whole shows to be quite inadequate.

6  A sort of debate about connectionism was held between Geoffrey Hinton and David Rumelhart on the one hand, and Zenon Pylyshyn and Kurt VanLehn on the other. While pursuing the nature of connectionist representations, Pylyshyn asked Rumelhart: "Look, can you guys represent a cup of coffee in these networks?" Rumelhart's reply was "Sure" so Pylyshyn continued: "And can you represent a cup without coffee in it?" Waiting for the trap to close, Rumelhart said "Yes," at which point Pylyshyn pounced: "Ah-hah, well, the difference between the two is just the representation of *coffee* – you've just built a representation of *cup with coffee* by combining a representation of *cup* with a representation of *coffee*."

7  As suggested to me by Georges Rey, the tensor product representation scheme can be understood by analogy to Gödel number encodings. In the Gödel encoding, the representation of a string ab . . . x . . . is the number $v = p_1{}^a p_2{}^b \cdots p_i{}^x \cdots$ where x is the $i$th symbol in the string. Each of the symbols in the alphabet, a, b, . . ., x, . . . is assigned a unique whole number code, $a, b, \ldots, x, \ldots$ To each possible position $i$ in the string corresponds a certain prime number $p_i$. Given $v$, it is possible to recover

the string it represents, provided we know both the set of primes used to code positions, $\{p_i\}$, and the encoding of the alphabet; this is because $v$ has a unique decomposition into powers of primes. In the tensor product scheme, this string would be represented by a vector $\mathbf{v} = \mathbf{p}_1 \otimes \mathbf{a} + \mathbf{p}_2 \otimes \mathbf{b} + \ldots + \mathbf{p}_i \otimes \mathbf{x} + \ldots$ Instead of numbers, each symbol is now encoded by a vector of activity values ($\mathbf{x}$ is represented by $\mathbf{x}$, etc.); instead of primes, each position $i$ is represented by an activity vector $\mathbf{p}_i$. In going from the Gödel scheme to the tensor product representation, numbers become vectors, the exponentiation used to bind symbols to their positions becomes the tensor product, and the multiplication used to combine the symbol/position bindings becomes vector addition. From $\mathbf{v}$ we can exactly recover the string if the vectors $\{\mathbf{p}_i\}$ are all linearly independent: if none can be expressed as a weighted sum of the others. This is the property that guarantees we can undo the vector addition operation, just as using primes ensures in the Gödel scheme that we can undo the multiplication operation (none of the $p_i$ can be expressed as a product of the others). Gödel numbering can be done recursively, so that the exponents representing consecutive objects (e.g. lines in a proof) can themselves be the Gödel numbers of strings; likewise, tensor product representations can be built recursively, so that the vector representing a filler (or role) can itself be the tensor product representation of a structure. This is possible because the tensor product takes two vectors and creates a new vector which can then be used in a subsequent tensor product. (This is the reason that tensor algebra is natural here; in matrix algebra, which is to some degree a subset of tensor algebra, the outer product of two vectors, which is the same set of numbers as the tensor product of those vectors, is treated as a new type object: a matrix – this blocks recursion.)

8    It's all well and good to say, as F&P do, that the Classical view has no commitment to serial processing. "We like parallel computation too." Fine, give me a massively parallel symbolic model that processes tree structures and I'll be happy to compare it to this. But I don't see it out there.

See Dolan & Smolensky (1988) for an actual distributed connectionist model, TPPS, that uses the tensor product to represent a symbolic structure and operate on it with massive parallelism. The system is an exercise in applying the tensor product representation to put on a somewhat more general and simple mathematical footing Touretzky & Hinton's (1985) Boltzmann machine implementation of a distributed connectionist production system, DCPS. Each production in TPPS does pattern matching against the whole symbolic structure in working memory in parallel, and does all parts of its action in parallel. Since it is an implementation of a traditional production system, however, productions are fired one at a time, although conflict resolution is done in parallel.

9    Like connectionist networks, traditional computers were originally viewed exclusively as number processors. Newell and Simon are credited with teaching us that traditional computers could also be used as powerful structure processors. I am essentially trying to make the same point about connectionist networks.

10    This is true provided the parameter values defining the representation satisfy the very weak constraint that the simplest possible confusions are avoided (such as confusing *P&Q* with *Q&P* or with *P or Q*).

11    Many cases analogous to "implementation" *are* found in physics: Newton's laws provide an "implementation" of Kepler's laws; Maxwell's theory "implements" Coulomb's law; the quantum principles of the hydrogen atom "implement" Balmer's formula.

12    For example, in a dynamical system that oscillates, the evolution of the normal modes in time is given by: $\mathbf{e}_n(t) = e^{i\omega_n t}\,\mathbf{e_n}$. Each particular normal mode $e_n$ consists of an oscillation with a particular frequency $\omega_n$.

13 How reasonable is it to view this decomposition process as a formalization of the notion of decomposing a "structure" into its "constituents"? (I am indebted to Tim van Gelder, personal communication, for very useful discussion of this issue; see also van Gelder, 1989.) I take it that it is a reasonable use of the term "constituent" to say that "electrons are constituents of atoms." In modern physics, what is the relation between the representation of the electron and the representation of the atom?

The state of the atom, like the states of all systems in quantum theory, is represented by a vector in an abstract vector space. Each electron has an internal state (its "spin"); it also has a role it plays in the atom as a whole: it occupies some "orbital," essentially a cloud of probability for finding it at particular places in the atom. The internal state of an electron is represented by a "spin vector"; the orbital or role of the electron (part) in the atom (whole) is represented by another vector, which describes the probability cloud. The vector representing the electron as situated in the atom is the tensor product of the vector representing the internal state of the electron and the vector representing its orbital. The atom as a whole is represented by a vector that is the sum or superposition of vectors, each of which represents a particular electron situated in its orbital. (There are also contributions of the same sort from nucleons.)

Thus the vector representing the whole is the sum of tensor products of pairs of vectors; in each pair, one vector represents the part independent of its role in the whole, and the other represent the role in the whole independent of the part that fills the role. This is exactly the way I have used tensor products to construct distributed connectionist representations for wholes from distributed connectionist representations of their parts (and from distributed representations of the roles of parts in the whole) – and this is exactly where the idea came from.

So someone who claims that the tensor product representational scheme distorts the notion of constituency has some explaining to do.

So does someone who claims that the sense in which the whole has parts is not explanatorily relevant. We explain the properties of atoms by invoking properties of their electronic configuration all the time. Quantum theory aside, physical systems whose states are described by vectors have for centuries had their behavior explained by viewing the state vector as a superposition of component vectors, and explaining the evolution of the total state in terms of the evolution of its component vectors – as I have indicated in the preceding discussion of normal modes.

Are the constituents of mental representations as I have characterized them in distributed connectionist systems causally efficacious in mental processing?

The term "causally efficacious" must be used with some caution. The equations that drive the atom do not work by first figuring out what the component particles are, and then working on each of them separately. The equations take the elements comprising the vector for the whole atom and change them in time. We can *analyze* the system by breaking up the vector for the whole into the vectors for the parts, and in general that's a good way to do the analysis; but nature doesn't do that in updating the state of the system from one moment to the next. So, in this case, are the constituents causally efficacious or not? The same question arises in the connectionist case.

14 Except for that limited part of the architecture I have called the "conscious rule interpreter"; see Smolensky, 1988a.

15 I use this characterization rather tentatively because I am not yet convinced that the notion of causal efficacy it presupposes is less problematic than what it is being invoked to elucidate.

16 Quoted in Fodor, 1975a; p. vi.

# Connectionism and the problem of systematicity: Why Smolensky's solution doesn't work

JERRY FODOR*

*Rutgers University and CUNY Graduate Center*

BRIAN P. McLAUGHLIN

*Rutgers University*

Received May 23, 1989, final revision accepted August 18, 1989

*Abstract*

Fodor, J., and McLaughlin, B.P., 1990. Connectionism and the problem of systematicity: Why Smolensky's solution doesn't work. Cognition, 35: 183–204.

*In two recent papers, Paul Smolensky responds to a challenge Jerry Fodor and Zenon Pylyshyn posed for connectionist theories of cognition: to explain the existence of systematic relations among cognitive capacities without assuming that mental processes are causally sensitive to the constituent structure of mental representations. Smolensky thinks connectionists can explain systematicity if they avail themselves of "distributed" mental representations. In fact, Smolensky offers two accounts of distributed mental representation, corresponding to his notions of "weak" and "strong" compositional structure. We argue that weak compositional structure is irrelevant to the systematicity problem and of dubious internal coherence. We then argue that strong compositional (tensor product) representations fail to explain systematicity because they fail to exhibit the sort of constituents that can provide domains for structure sensitive mental processes.*

## Introduction

In two recent papers, Paul Smolensky (1987, 1988b) responds to a challenge Jerry Fodor and Zenon Pylyshyn (Fodor & Pylyshyn, 1988) have posed for connectionist theories of cognition: to explain the existence of systematic relations among cognitive capacities without assuming that cognitive proces-

---

*Authors are listed alphabetically. Requests for reprints should be addressed to Jerry Fodor, Department of Philosophy, The Graduate Center, CUNY, 33 West 42nd Street, New York, NY 10036, U.S.A.

0010-0277/90/$7.10 © 1990, Elsevier Science Publishers B.V.

ses are causally sensitive to the constituent structure of mental representations. This challenge implies a dilemma: if connectionism can't account for systematicity, it thereby fails to provide an adequate basis for a theory of cognition; but if its account of systematicity requires mental processes that are sensitive to the constituent structure of mental representations, then the theory of cognition it offers will be, at best, an implementation architecture for a "classical" (language of thought) model. Smolensky thinks connectionists can steer between the horns of this dilemma if they avail themselves of certain kinds of distributed mental representation. In what follows, we will examine this proposal.

Our discussion has three parts. In section I, we briefly outline the phenomenon of systematicity and its Classical explanation. As we will see, Smolensky actually offers two alternatives to this Classical treatment, corresponding to two ways in which complex mental representations can be distributed; the first kind of distribution yields complex mental representations with "weak compositional structure", the second yields mental representations with "strong compositional structure". We will consider these two notions of distribution in turn: in section II, we argue that Smolensky's proposal that complex mental representations have weak compositional structure should be rejected both as inadequate to explain systematicity and on internal grounds; in section III, we argue that postulating mental representations with strong compositional structure also fails to provide for an explanation of systematicity. The upshot will be that Smolensky avoids only one horn of the dilemma that Fodor and Pylyshyn proposed. We shall see that his architecture is genuinely non-Classical since the representations he postulates are not "distributed over" constituents in the sense that Classical representations are; and we shall see that for that very reason Smolensky's architecture leaves systematicity unexplained.

## I. The systematicity problem and its Classical solution

The systematicity problem is that cognitive capacities come in clumps. For example, it appears that there are families of semantically related mental states such that, as a matter of psychological law, an organism is able to be in one of the states belonging to the family only if it is able to be in many of the others. Thus, you don't find organisms that can learn to prefer the green triangle to the red square but can't learn to prefer the red triangle to the green square. You don't find organisms that can think the thought that the girl loves John but can't think the thought that John loves the girl. You don't find organisms that can infer P from P&Q&R but can't infer P from P&Q.

And so on over a very wide range of cases. For the purposes of this paper, we assume without argument:

(i) that cognitive capacities are generally systematic in this sense, both in humans and in many infrahuman organisms;

(ii) that it is nomologically necessary (hence counterfactual supporting) that this is so;

(iii) that there must therefore be some psychological mechanism in virtue of the functioning of which cognitive capacities are systematic;

(iv) and that an adequate theory of cognitive architecture should exhibit this mechanism.

Any of i–iv may be viewed as tendentious; but, so far as we can tell, all four are accepted by Smolensky. So we will take them to be common ground in what follows.[1]

The Classical account of the mechanism of systematicity depends crucially on the idea that mental representation is language-like. In particular, mental representations have a combinatorial syntax and semantics. We turn to a brief discussion of the Classical picture of the syntax and semantics of mental representations; this provides the basis for understanding the Classical treatment of systematicity.

---

[1]Since the two are often confused. we wish to emphasize that taking *systematicity* for granted leaves the question of *compositionality* wide open. The systematicity of cognition consists of. for example. the fact that organisms that can think aRb can think bRa and vice versa. *Compositionality* proposes a certain explanation of systematicity: viz.. that the content of thoughts is determined. in a uniform way. by the content of the context-independent concepts that are their constituents: and that the thought that bRa is constituted of the same concepts as the thought that aRb. So the polemical situation is as follows. If you are a Connectionist who accepts systematicity. then you must argue either that systematicity can be explained without compositionality. or that connectionist architecture accommodates compositional representation. So far as we can tell. Smolensky vacillates between these options: what he calls "weak compositionality" favors the former and what he calls "strong compositionality" favors the latter.

We emphasize this distinction between systematicity and compositionality in light of some remarks by an anonymous *Cognition* reviewer: "By berating the [connectionist] modelers for their inability to represent the common-sense [uncontextualized] notion of 'coffee' ... Fodor and McLaughlin are missing a key point – the models are not supposed to do so. If you buy the ... massive context-sensitivity ... that connectionists believe in." Our strategy is *not*, however, to argue that there is something wrong with connectionism because it fails to offer an uncontextualized notion of mental (or, mutatis mutandis, linguistic) representation. Our argument is that if connectionists assume that mental representations are context sensitive, they will need to offer some explanation of systematicity that does not entail compositionality *and they do not have one*.

We do not, therefore, offer direct arguments for context-insensitive concepts in what follows; we are quite prepared that "coffee" should have a meaning only in context. Only, we argue, *if* it does, then some non-compositional account of the systematicity of coffee-throughts will have to be provided.

*Classical syntax and Classical constituents*

The Classical view holds that the syntax of mental representations is like the syntax of natural language sentences in the following respect: both include complex symbols (bracketing trees) which are constructed out of what we will call *Classical constituents*. Thus, for example, the English sentence "John loves the girl" is a complex symbol whose decomposition into Classical constituents is exhibited by some such bracketing tree as:

Sentence

• • • • •

•                    •

Subject        Predicate

                        •

•             •          Object

•             •               •

•             •               •

John        loves        the girl

Correspondingly, it is assumed that the mental representation that is entertained when one thinks the thought that John loves the girl is a complex symbol of which the Classical constituents include representations of John, the girl, and loving.

It will become clear in section III that it is a major issue whether the sort of complex mental representations that are postulated in Smolensky's theory have constituent structure. We do not wish to see this issue degenerate into a terminological wrangle. We therefore stipulate that, for a pair of expression types E1, E2, the first is a *Classical* constituent of the second *only if* the first is tokened whenever the second is tokened. For example, the English word "John" is a Classical constituent of the English sentence "John loves the girl" and every tokening of the latter implies a tokening of the former (specifically, every token of the latter *contains* a token of the former; you can't say "John loves the girl" without saying "John").[2] Likewise, it is assumed that a men-

---

[2]Though we shall generally consider examples where complex symbols literally *contain* their Classical constituents, the present condition means to leave it open that symbols may have Classical constituents that are not among their (spatio-temporal) parts. (For example, so far as this condition is concerned, it might be that the Classical constituents of a symbol include the values of a "fetch" operation that takes the symbol as an argument.)

talese symbol which names John is a Classical constituent of the mentalese symbol that means that John loves the girl. So again tokenings of the one symbol require tokenings of the other.

It is precisely because Classical constituents have this property that they are always accessible to operations that are defined over the complex symbols that contain them; in particular, it is precisely because Classical mental representations have Classical constituents that they provide domains for structure-sensitive mental processes. We shall see presently that what Smolensky offers as the "constituents" of connectionist mental representations are non-Classical in this respect, and that that is why his theory provides no account of systematicity.

*Classical semantics*

It is part of the Classical picture, both for mental representation and for representation in natural languages, that generally when a complex formula (e.g., a sentence) S expresses the proposition P, S's constituents express (or refer to) the elements of P.[3] For example, the proposition that John loves the girl contains as its elements the individuals John and the girl, and the two-place relation "loving". Correspondingly, the formula "John loves the girl", which English uses to express this proposition, contains as constituents the expressions "John", "loves" and "the girl". The sentence "John left and the girl wept", whose constituents include the formulas "John left" and "the girl wept", expresses the proposition that John left and the girl wept, whose elements include the proposition that John left and the proposition that the girl wept. And so on.

These assumptions about the syntax and semantics of mental representations are summarized by condition C:

C: If a proposition P can be expressed in a system of mental representation M, then M contains some complex mental representation (a "mental sentence") S, such that S expresses P and the (Classical) constituents of S express (or refer to) the elements of P.

---

[3]We assume that the elements of propositions can include, for example, individuals, properties, relations and other propositions. Other metaphysical assumptions are, of course, possible. For example, it is arguable that the constituents of propositions include *individual concepts* (in the Fregian sense) rather than individuals themselves; and so on. Fortunately, it is not necessary to enter into these abstruse issues to make the points that are relevant to the systematicity problem. All we really need is that propositions have internal structure, and that, characteristically, the internal structure of complex mental representations corresponds, in the appropriate way, to the internal structure of the propositions that they express.

*Systematicity*

The Classical explanation of systematicity assumes that C holds by nomological necessity; it expresses a *psychological law* that subsumes all systematic minds. It should be fairly clear why systematicity is readily explicable on the assumptions, first, that mental representations satisfy C, and, second, that mental processes have access to the constituent structure of mental representations. Thus, for example, since C implies that anyone who can represent a proposition can, ipso facto, represent its elements, it implies, in particular, that anyone who can represent the proposition that John loves the girl can, ipso facto, represent John, the girl and the two-place relation *loving*. Notice, however, that the proposition that *the girl loves John* is *also* constituted by these same individuals/relations. So, then, assuming that the processes that integrate the mental representations that express propositions have access to their constituents, it follows that anyone who can represent John's loving the girl can also represent the girl's loving John. Similarly, suppose that the constituents of the mental representation that gets tokened when one thinks that P&Q&R and the constituents of the mental representation that gets tokened when one thinks that P&Q both include the mental representation that gets tokened when one thinks that P. And suppose that the mental processes that mediate the drawing of inferences have access to the constituent structure of mental representations. Then it should be no surprise that anyone who can infer P from P&Q&R can likewise infer P from P&Q.

To summarize: the Classical solution to the systematicity problem entails that (i) systems of mental representation satisfy C (a fortiori, complex mental representations have Classical constituents); and (ii) mental processes are sensitive to the constituent structure of mental representations. We can now say quite succinctly what our claim against Smolensky will be: on the one hand, the cognitive architecture he endorses does not provide for mental representations with Classical constituents; on the other hand, he provides no suggestion as to how mental processes could be structure sensitive unless mental representations have Classical constituents; and, on the third hand (as it were) he provides no suggestion as to how minds could be systematic if mental processes aren't structure sensitive. So his reply to Fodor and Pylyshyn fails.

Most of the rest of the paper will be devoted to making this analysis stick.

## II. Weak compositionality

Smolensky's views about "weak" compositional structure are largely inexplicit and must be extrapolated from his "coffee story", which he tells in both of the papers under discussion (and also in 1988a). We turn now to considering this story.

Smolensky begins by asking how we are to understand the relation between the mental representation COFFEE and the mental representation CUP WITH COFFEE.[4] His answer to this question has four aspects that are of present interest:

(i) COFFEE and CUP WITH COFFEE are activity vectors (according to Smolensky's weak compositional account, this is true of the mental representations corresponding to all commonsense concepts; whether it also holds for (for example) technical concepts won't matter for what follows). A vector is, of course, a magnitude with a certain direction. A pattern of activity over a group of "units" is a state consisting of the members of the group each having an activation value of 1 or 0.[5] Activity vectors are representations of such patterns of activity.

(ii) CUP WITH COFFEE representations contain COFFEE representations as (non-Classical)[6] constituents in the following sense: they contain them as *component* vectors. By stipulation, $\mathbf{a}$ is a component vector of $\mathbf{b}$, if there is a vector $\mathbf{x}$ such that $\mathbf{a} + \mathbf{x} = \mathbf{b}$ (where "+" is the operation of vector addition). More generally, according to Smolensky, the relation between vectors and their non-Classical constituents is that the former are derivable from the latter by operations of vector analysis.

(iii) COFFEE representations and CUP WITH COFFEE representations are activity vectors over units which represent microfeatures (units like BROWN, LIQUID, MADE OF PORCELAIN, etc.).

---

[4]The following notational conventions will facilitate the discussion: we will follow standard practice and use capitalized English words and sentences as canonical names for mental representations. (Smolensky uses italicized English expressions instead.) We stipulate that the semantic value of a mental representation so named is the semantic value of the corresponding English word or sentence, and we will italicize words or sentences that denote semantic values. So, for example, COFFEE is a mental representation that expresses (the property of being) *coffee* (as does the English word "coffee"); JOHN LOVES THE GIRL is a mental representation that expresses the proposition that *John loves the girl*; and so forth. It is important to notice that our notation allows that the mental representation JOHN LOVES THE GIRL can be atomic and the mental representation COFFEE can be a complex symbol. That is, capitalized expressions should be read as the names of mental representations rather than as structural descriptions.

[5]Smolensky apparently allows that units may have continuous levels of activation from 0 to 1. In telling the coffee story, however, he generally assumes bivalence for ease of exposition.

[6]As we shall see below, when an activity vector is tokened, its component vectors typically are not. So the constituents of a complex vector are, ipso facto, non-Classical.

(iv) COFFEE (and, presumably, any other representation vector) is *context dependent*. In particular, the activity vector that is the COFFEE representation in CUP WITH COFFEE *is distinct from* the activity vector that is the COFFEE representation in, as it might be, GLASS WITH COFFEE or CAN WITH COFFEE. Presumably this means that the vector in question, with no context specified, does not give necessary conditions for being *coffee*. (We shall see later that Smolensky apparently holds that it doesn't specify sufficient conditions for being *coffee* either).

Claims i and ii introduce the ideas that mental representations are activity vectors and that they have (non-Classical) constituents. These ideas are neutral with respect to the distinction between strong and weak compositionality so we propose to postpone discussing them until section III. Claim iii, is, in our view, a red herring. The idea that there are microfeatures is orthogonal both to the question of systematicity and to the issues about compositionality. We therefore propose to discuss it only very briefly. It is claim iv that distinguishes the strong from the weak notion of compositional structure: a representation has weak compositional structure iff it contains context-dependent constituents. We propose to take up the question of context dependent-representation here.

We commence by reciting the coffee story (in a slightly condensed form).

Since, following Smolensky, we are assuming heuristically that units have bivalent activity levels, vectors can be represented by ordered sets of zeros (indicating that a unit is "off") and ones (indicating that a unit is "on"). Thus, Smolensky says, the CUP WITH COFFEE representation might be the following activity vector over microfeatures:

1–UPRIGHT CONTAINER
1–HOT LIQUID
0–GLASS CONTACTING WOOD[7]
1–PORCELAIN CURVED SURFACE
1–BURNT ODOR

---

[7]Notice that this microfeature is "off" in CUP WITH COFFEE, so it might be wondered why Smolensky mentions it at all. The explanation may be this: operations of vector combination apply only to vectors of the same dimensionality. In the context of the weak constituency story, this means that you can only combine vectors that are activity patterns *over the same units*. It follows that a component vector must contain the same units (though, possibly at different levels of activation) as the vectors with which it combines. Thus if GRANNY combines with COFFEE to yield GRANNY'S COFFEE, GRANNY must contain activation levels for all the units in COFFEE and vice versa. In the present example, it may be that CUP WITH COFFEE is required to contain a 0-activation level for GLASS CONTACTING WOOD to accommodate cases where it is a component of some other vector. Similarly with OBLONG SILVER OBJECT (below) since cups with coffee often have spoons in them.

1–BROWN LIQUID CONTACTING PORCELAIN
1–PORCELAIN CURVED SURFACE
0–OBLONG SILVER OBJECT
1–FINGER-SIZED HANDLE
1–BROWN LIQUID WITH CURVED SIDES AND BOTTOM[8]

This vector, according to Smolensky, contains a COFFEE representation as a constituent. This constituent can, he claims, be derived from CUP WITH COFFEE by subtracting CUP WITHOUT COFFEE from CUP WITH COF-FEE. The vector that is the remainder of this subtraction will be COFFEE.

The reader will object that this treatment presupposes that CUP WITH-OUT COFFEE is a constituent of CUP WITH COFFEE. Quite so. Smolensky is explicit in claiming that "the pattern or vector representing *cup with coffee* is composed of a vector that can be identified as a particular distributed representation of *cup without coffee* with a representation with the content *coffee*" (1988b: p. 10).

One is inclined to think that this must surely be wrong. If you combine a representation with the content *cup without coffee* with a representation with the content *coffee*, you get not a representation with the content *cup with coffee* but rather a representation with the self-contradictory content *cup without coffee with coffee*. Smolensky's subtraction procedure appears to con-fuse the representation of *cup without coffee* (viz. CUP WITHOUT COF-FEE) with the representation of *cup* without the representation of *coffee* (viz. CUP). CUP WITHOUT COFFEE expresses the content *cup without coffee*; CUP combines consistently with COFFEE. But nothing does both.

On the other hand, it must be remembered that Smolensky's mental rep-resentations are advertised as context dependent, hence non-compositional. Indeed, we are given *no clue at all* about what sorts of relations between the semantic properties of complex symbols and the semantic properties of their constituents his theory acknowledges. Perhaps in a semantics where con-stituents don't contribute their contents to the symbols they belong to, it's all right after all if CUP WITH COFFEE has CUP WITHOUT COFFEE (or, for that matter, PRIME NUMBER, or GRANDMOTHER, or FLYING SAUCER or THE LAST OF THE MOHICANS) among its constituents.

---

[8]Presumably Smolensky does not take this list to be exhaustive, but we don't know how to continue it. Beyond the remark that although the microfeatures in his examples correspond to "... nearly sensory-level representation[s] ..." that is "not essential", Smolensky provides no account at all of what determines which contents are expressed by microfeatures. The question thus arises why Smolensky assumes that COFFEE is not itself a microfeature. In any event, Smolensky repeatedly warns the reader not to take his examples of microfeatures very seriously, and we don't.

In any event, to complete the story, Smolensky gives the following features for CUP WITHOUT COFFEE:

1–UPRIGHT CONTAINER
0–HOT LIQUID
0–GLASS CONTACTING WOOD
1–PORCELAIN CURVED SURFACE
0–BURNT ODOR
0–BROWN LIQUID CONTACTING PORCELAIN
1–PORCELAIN CURVED SURFACE
0–OBLONG SILVER OBJECT
1–FINGER-SIZED HANDLE
0–BROWN LIQUID WITH CURVED SIDES AND BOTTOM etc.

Subtracting this vector from CUP WITH COFFEE, we get the following COFFEE representation:

0–UPRIGHT CONTAINER
1–HOT LIQUID
0–GLASS CONTACTING WOOD
0–PORCELAIN CURVED SURFACE
1–BURNT ODOR
1–BROWN LIQUID CONTACTING PORCELAIN
0–PORCELAIN CURVED SURFACE
0–OBLONG SILVER OBJECT
0–FINGER-SIZED HANDLE
1–BROWN LIQUID WITH CURVED SIDES AND BOTTOM

That, then, is Smolensky's "coffee story".

*Comments*

*(i) Microfeatures*
It's common ground in this discussion that the explanation of systematicity must somehow appeal to relations between complex mental representations and their constituents (on Smolensky's view, to combinatorial relations among vectors). The issue about whether there are microfeatures is entirely orthogonal; it concerns only the question *which properties the activation states of individual units express*. (To put it in more Classical terms, it concerns the question which symbols constitute the *primitive vocabulary* of the system of mental representations.) If there are microfeatures, then the activation states of individual units are constrained to express only (as it might be) "sensory" properties (1987: p. 146). If there aren't, then activation states of individual units can express not only such properties as *being brown* and *being hot*, but

also such properties as *being coffee*. It should be evident upon even casual reflection that, whichever way this issue is settled, the constituency question—viz., the question how the representation COFFEE relates to the representation CUP WITH COFFEE—remains wide open. We therefore propose to drop the discussion of microfeatures in what follows.

*(iv) Context-dependent representation*

As far as we can tell, Smolensky holds that the representation of *coffee* that he derives by subtraction from CUP WITH COFFEE is context dependent in the sense that it need bear no more than a "family resemblance" to the vector that represents *coffee* in CAN WITH COFFEE, GLASS WITH COFFEE, etc. There is thus no single vector that counts as *the* COFFEE representation, hence no single vector that is a component of all the representations which, in a Classical system, would have COFFEE as a Classical constituent.

Smolensky himself apparently agrees that this is the wrong sort of constituency to account for systematicity and related phenomena. As he remarks, "a true constituent can move around and fill any of a number of different roles in different structures" (1988b: p. 11) and the connection between constituency and systematicity would appear to turn on this. For example, the solution to the systematicity problem mooted in section I depends exactly on the assumption that tokens of the representation type JOHN express the same content in the context LOVES THE GIRL that they do in the context THE GIRL LOVES; (viz., that they pick out *John*, who is an element both of the proposition *John loves the girl* and of the proposition *the girl loves John.*) It thus appears, prima facie, that the explanation of systematicity requires context-independent constituents.

How, then, does Smolensky suppose that the assumption that mental representations have weak compositional structure, that is, that mental representation is context dependent, bears on the explanation of systematicity? He simply doesn't say. And we don't have a clue. In fact, having introduced the notion of weak compositional structure, Smolensky to all intents and purposes drops it in favor of the notion of strong compositional structure, and the discussion of systematicity is carried out entirely in terms of the latter. What, then, he takes the relation between weak and strong compositional structure to be,—and, for that matter, which kind of structure he actually thinks that mental representations have[9]—is thoroughly unclear.

---

[9]They can't have both; either the content of a representation is context dependent or it's not. So, if Smolensky does think that you need strong compositional structure to explain systematicity, and that weak compositional structure is the kind that Connectionist representations have, then it would seem that he *thereby* grants Fodor and Pylyshyn's claim that Connectionist representations can't explain systematicity. We find this all very mysterious.

In fact, quite independent of its bearing on systematicity, the notion of weak compositional structure as Smolensky presents it is of very dubious coherence. We close this section with a remark or two about this point.

It looks as though Smolensky holds that the COFFEE vector that you get by subtraction from CUP WITH COFFEE is not a COFFEE representation when it stands alone. "This representation is indeed a representation of coffee, but [only?] in a very particular context: the context provided by *cup* [i.e. CUP]" (1987: p. 147). If this is the view, it has bizarre consequences. Take a liquid that has the properties specified by the microfeatures that comprise COFFEE in isolation, but that isn't coffee. Pour it into a cup, et voila! it *becomes* coffee by semantical magic.

Smolensky explicitly doesn't think that the vector COFFEE that you get from CUP WITH COFFEE gives necessary conditions for being coffee, since you'd get a different COFFEE vector by subtraction from, say, GLASS WITH COFFEE. And the passage just quoted suggests that he thinks it doesn't give sufficient conditions either. But, then, if the microfeatures associated with COFFEE are neither necessary nor sufficient for being *coffee*[10] the question arises what, according to this story, *does* makes a vector a COFFEE representation; when does a vector have the content *coffee*?

As far as we can tell, Smolensky holds that what makes the COFFEE component of CUP WITH COFFEE a representation with the content *coffee* is that it is distributed over units representing certain microfeatures *and* that it figures as a component vector of a vector which is a CUP WITH COFFEE representation. As remarked above, we are given no details at all about this reverse compositionality according to which the embedding vector determines the contents of its constituents; how it is supposed to work isn't even discussed in Smolensky's papers. But, in any event, a regress threatens since the question now arises: if being a component of a CUP OF COFFEE representation is required to make a vector a *coffee* representation, what is required to make a vector a *cup of coffee* representation? Well, presumably CUP OF COFFEE represents *cup of coffee* because it involves the microfeatures it does *and* because it is a component of still another vector; perhaps one that is a THERE IS A CUP OF COFFEE ON THE TABLE representation. Does this go on forever? If it doesn't, then presumably there are some vectors which aren't constituents of any others. But now, what determines *their* contents? Not the contents of their constituents because, by assumption, Smolensky's semantics isn't compositional (CUP WITHOUT COFFEE is a constituent of CUP WITH COFFEE, etc.). And not the vectors that they

---

[10]If they were necessary and sufficient, COFFEE wouldn't be context dependent.

are constituents of, because, by assumption, there aren't any of those.

We think it is unclear whether Smolensky has a coherent story about how a system of representations could have weak compositional structure.

What, in light of all this, leads Smolensky to embrace his account of weak compositionality? Here's one suggestion: perhaps Smolensky confuses being a representation of a cup with coffee with being a CUP WITH COFFEE representation. Espying some cup with coffee on a particular occasion, in a particular context, one might come to be in a mental state that represents it as having roughly the microfeatures that Smolensky lists. That mental state would then be a representation of a cup with coffee in this sense: there is a cup of coffee that it's a mental representation of. But it wouldn't, of course, follow, that it's a CUP WITH COFFEE representation; and the mental representation of that cup with coffee might be quite different from the mental representation of the cup with coffee that you espied on some other occasion or in some other context. So *which mental representation a cup of coffee gets is context dependent*, just as Smolensky says. But that doesn't give Smolensky what he needs to make mental representations themselves context dependent. In particular, from the fact that cups with coffee get different representations in different contexts, it patently doesn't follow that the mental symbol that represents something as *being* a cup of coffee in one context might represent something as being something else (a giraffe say, or The Last of The Mohicans) in some other context. We doubt that anything will give Smolensky that, since we know of no reason to suppose that it is true.

In short, it is natural to confuse the true but uninteresting thought that how you mentally represent some coffee depends on the context, with the much more tendentious thought that the mental representation COFFEE is context dependent. Assuming that he is a victim of this confusion makes sense of many of the puzzling things that Smolensky says in the coffee story. Notice, for example, that all the microfeatures in his examples express more or less perceptual properties (cf. Smolensky's own remark that his microfeatures yield a "nearly sensory level representation"). Notice, too, the peculiarity that the microfeature "porcelain curved surface" occurs *twice* in the vector for CUP WITH COFFEE, COFFEE, CUP WITHOUT COFFEE and the like. Presumably, what Smolensky has in mind is that, when you look at a cup, you get to see two curved surfaces, one going off to the left and the other going off to the right.

Though we suspect this really is what's going on, we won't pursue this interpretation further since, if it's correct, then the coffee story is completely irrelevant to the question of what kind of constituency relation a COFFEE representation bears to a CUP WITH COFFEE; and that, remember, is the question that bears on the issues about systematicity.

## III. Strong compositional structure

So much, then, for "weak" compositional structure. Let us turn to Smolensky's account of "strong" compositional structure. Smolensky says that:

> A true constituent can move around and fill any of a number of different roles in different structures. Can *this* be done with vectors encoding distributed representations, and be done in a way that doesn't amount to simply implementing symbolic syntactic constituency? The purpose of this section is to describe research showing that the answer is affirmative. (1988b: p. 11)

The idea that mental representations are activity vectors over units, and the idea that some mental representations have other mental representations as components, is common to the treatment of both weak and strong compositional structure. However, Smolensky's discussion of the latter differs in several respects from his discussion of the former. First, units are explicitly supposed to have continuous activation levels between 0 and 1; second, he does not invoke the idea of microfeatures when discussing strong compositional structure; third, he introduces a new vector operation (multiplication) to the two previously mentioned (addition and subtraction); fourth, and most important, strong compositional structure does not invoke—indeed, would appear to be incompatible with—the notion that mental representations are context dependent. So strong compositional structure does not exhibit the incoherences of Smolensky's theory of context-dependent representation.

We will proceed as follows. First we briefly present the notion of strong compositional structure. Then we shall turn to criticism.

Smolensky explains the notion of strong compositional structure, in part, by appeal to the ideas of a tensor product representation and a superposition representation. To illustrate these ideas, consider how a connectionist machine might represent four-letter English words. Words can be decomposed into roles (viz., ordinal positions that letters can occupy) and things that can fill these roles (viz., letters). Correspondingly, the machine might contain activity vectors over units which represent the relevant roles (i.e., over the *role units*) and activity vectors over units which represent the fillers (i.e., over the *filler units*). Finally, it might contain activity vectors over units which represent *filled roles* (i.e., letters in letter positions); these are the *binding units*. The key idea is that the activity vectors over the binding units might be tensor products of activity vectors over the role units and the filler units. The representation of a word would then be a superposition vector over the binding units; that is, a vector that is arrived at by superimposing the tensor product vectors.

The two operations used here to derive complex vectors from component vectors are vector multiplication in the case of tensor product vectors and vector addition in the case of superposition vectors. These are iterative operations in the sense that activity vectors that result from the multiplication of role vectors and filler vectors might themselves represent the fillers of roles in more complex structures. Thus, a tensor product which represents the word "John" as *"J" in first position, "o" in second position ... etc.* might itself be bound to the representation of a syntactical function to indicate, for example, that "John" has the role subject-of in "John loves the girl". Such tensor product representations could themselves be superimposed over yet another group of binding units to yield a superposition vector which represents the bracketing tree (John) (loves (the girl)).

It is, in fact, unclear whether this sort of apparatus is adequate to represent all the semantically relevant syntactic relations that Classical theories express by using bracketing trees with Classical constituents. (There are, for example, problems about long-distance binding relations, as between quantifiers and bound variables.) But we do not wish to press this point. For present polemical purposes, we propose simply to assume that each Classical bracketing tree can be coded into a complex vector in such fashion that the constituents of the tree correspond in some regular way to components of the vector.

But this is not, of course, to grant that either tensor product or superposition vectors *have* Classical constituent structure. In particular, from the assumptions that bracketing trees have Classical constituents and that bracketing trees can be coded by activity vectors, it does *not* follow that activity vectors have Classical constituents. On the contrary, a point about which Smolensky is himself explicit is vital in this regard: the components of a complex vector need not even correspond to patterns of activity over units actually in the machine. As Smolensky puts it, the activity states of the filler and role units can be "imaginary" even though the ultimate activity vectors— the ones which do not themselves serve as filler or role components of more complex structures—must be actual activity patterns over units in the machine. Consider again our machine for representing four-letter words. The superposition pattern that represents, say, the word "John" will be an activity vector actually realized in the machine. However, the activity vector representing "J" will be merely imaginary, as will the activity vector representing *the first letter position.* Similarly for the tensor product activity vector representing *"J" in the first letter position.* The only pattern of activity that will be *actually tokened* in the machine is the superposition vector representing "John".

These considerations are of central importance for the following reason. Smolensky's main strategy is, in effect, to invite us to consider the components of tensor product and superposition vectors to be analogous to the Classical constituents of a complex symbol; hence to view them as providing a means by which connectionist architectures can capture the causal and semantic consequences of Classical constituency in mental representations. However, the components of tensor product and superposition vectors differ from Classical constituents in the following way: when a complex Classical symbol is tokened, its constituents are tokened. When a tensor product vector or superposition vector is tokened, its components are not (except per accidens). The implication of this difference, from the point of view of the theory of mental processes, is that whereas the Classical constituents of a complex symbol are, ipso facto, available to contribute to the causal consequences of its tokenings—in particular, they are available to provide domains for mental processes—the components of tensor product and superposition vectors can have no causal status as such. What is merely imaginary can't make things happen, to put this point in a nutshell.

We will return presently to what all this implies for the treatment of the systematicity problem. There is, however, a preliminary issue that needs to be discussed.

We have seen that the components of tensor product/superposition vectors, unlike Classical constituents, are not, in general, tokened whenever the activity vector of which they are the components is tokened. It is worth emphasizing, in addition, the familiar point that there is, in general, no *unique* decomposition of a tensor product or superposition vector into components. Indeed, given that units are assumed to have continuous levels of activation, there will be *infinitely* many decompositions of a given activity vector. One might wonder, therefore, what sense there is in talk of *the* decomposition of a mental representation into significant constituents given the notion of constituency that Smolensky's theory provides.[11]

Smolensky replies to this point as follows. Cognitive systems will be dynamical systems; there will be dynamic equations over the activation values of individual units, and these will determine certain regularities over activity vectors. Given the dynamical equations of the system, certain decompositions can be especially useful for "explaining and understanding" its behavior. In this sense, the dynamics of a system may determine "normal modes" of decomposition into components. So, for example, though a given superposition vector can, in principle, be taken to be the sum of many different sets of vectors, yet it may turn out that we get a small group of sets—even a unique

---

[11]The function of the brackets in a Classical bracketing tree is precisely to exhibit its decomposition into constituents; and when the tree is well formed this decomposition will be unique. Thus, the bracketing of "(John) (loves) (the girl)" implies, for example, both that "the girl" is a constituent and that "loves the" is not.

set—when we decompose in the direction of normal modes; and likewise for decomposing tensor product vectors. The long and short is that *it could, in principle, turn out* that, given the (thus far undefined) normal modes of a dynamical cognitive system, complex superposition vectors will have it in common with Classical complex symbols that they have a unique decomposition into semantically significant parts. Of course, it also could turn out that they don't, and no ground for optimism on this point has thus far been supplied.

Having noted this problem, however, we propose simply to ignore it. So here is where we now stand: by assumption (though quite possibly contrary to fact), tensor product vectors and superposition vectors can code constituent structure in a way that makes them adequate vehicles for the expression of propositional content; and, by assumption (though again quite possibly contrary to fact), the superposition vectors that cognitive theories acknowledge have a unique decomposition into semantically interpretable tensor product vectors which, in turn, have a unique decomposition into semantically interpretable filler vectors and role vectors; so it's determinate which proposition a given complex activity vector represents.

Now, assuming all this, what about the systematicity problem?

The first point to make is this: if tensor product/superposition vector representation solves the systematicity problem, the solution must be quite different from the Classical proposal sketched in section I. True tensor product vectors and superposition vectors "have constituents" in some suitably extended sense: tensor product vectors have semantically evaluable components, and superposition vectors are decomposable into semantically evaluable tensor product vectors. But the Classical solution to the systematicity problem assumes that *the constituents of mental representations have causal roles*; that they provide domains for mental processes. The Classical constituents of a complex symbol thus contribute to determining the causal consequences of the tokening of that symbol, and it seems clear that the "extended" constituents of a tensor product/superposition representation can't do that. On the contrary, the components of a complex vector are typically not even tokened when the complex vector itself is tokened; they are simply constituents into which the complex vector *could be* resolved consonant with decomposition in the direction of normal modes. But, to put it crudely, the fact that six *could be* represented as "3 × 2" cannot, in and of itself, affect the causal processes in a computer (or a brain) in which six *is* represented as "6". Merely counterfactual representations have no causal consequences; only actually tokened representations do.

Smolensky is, of course, sensitive to the question whether activity vectors really do have constituent structure. He defends at length the claim that he has not contorted the notion of constituency in claiming that they do. Part of this defense adverts to the role that tensor products and superpositions play in physical theory:

> The state of the atom, like the states of all systems in quantum theory, is represented by a vector in an abstract vector space. Each electron has an internal state (its "spin"); it also has a role it plays in the atom as a whole: it occupies some "orbital", essentially a cloud of probability for finding it at particular places in the atom. The internal state of an electron is represented by a "spin vector"; the orbital or role of the electron (part) in the atom (whole) is represented by another vector, which describes the probability cloud. The vector representing the electron as situated in the atom is the tensor product of the vector representing the internal state of the electron and the vector representing its orbital. The atom as a whole is represented by a vector that is the sum or superposition of vectors, each of which represents a particular electron in its orbital ... (1988b: pp. 19–20)

"So," Smolensky adds, "someone who claims that the tensor product representational scheme distorts the notion of constituency has some explaining to do" (1988b: p. 20).

The physics lesson is greatly appreciated; but it is important to be clear on just what it is supposed to show. It's not, at least for present purposes, in doubt that tensor products *can represent* constituent structure. The relevant question is whether tensor product representations *have* constituent structure; or, since we have agreed that they may be said to have constituent structure "in an extended sense", it's whether they have the kind of constituent structure to which causal processes can be sensitive, hence the kind of constituent structure to which an explanation of systematicity might appeal.[12] But we have already seen the answer to *this* question: the constituents of complex activity vectors typically aren't "there", so if the causal consequences of tokening a complex vector are sensitive to its constituent structure, that's a miracle.

We conclude that assuming that mental representations are activation vectors does not allow Smolensky to endorse the Classical solution of the systematicity problem. And, indeed, we think Smolensky would grant this since he admits up front that mental processes will not be causally sensitive to the strong compositional structure of mental representations. That is, he acknowledges that the constituents of complex mental representations play no causal

---

[12]It's a difference between psychology and physics that whereas psychology is about the casual laws that govern tokenings *of (mental) representations*, physics is about the causal laws that govern (not mental representations but) atoms, electrons and the like. Since *being a representation* isn't a property in the domain of physical theory, the question whether mental representations have constituent structure has no analog in physics.

role in determining what happens when the representations get tokened. "... Causal efficacy was not my goal in developing the tensor product representation ..." (1988b: p. 21). What are causally efficacious according to connectionists are the activation values of individual units; the dynamical equations that govern the evolution of the system will be defined over these. It would thus appear that Smolensky must have some *non*-Classical solution to the systematicity problem up his sleeve; some solution that does *not* depend on assuming mental processes that are causally sensitive to constituent structure. So then, after all this, what *is* Smolensky's solution to the systematicity problem?

Remarkably enough, *Smolensky doesn't say*. All he does say is that he "hypothesizes ... that ... the systematic effects observed in the processing of mental representations arise because the evolution of vectors can be (at least partially and approximately) explained in terms of the evolution of their components, even though the precise dynamical equations apply [only] to the individual numbers comprising the vectors and [not] at the level of [their] constituents—i.e. even though the constituents are not causally efficacious" (1988b: p. 21).

It is left unclear how the constituents ("components") of complex vectors are to explain their evolution (even partially and approximately) when they are, by assumption, at best causally inert and, at worst, merely imaginary. In any event, what Smolensky clearly does think is causally responsible for the "evolution of vectors" (and hence for the systematicity of cognition) are unspecified processes that affect the states of activation of the individual units (the neuron analogs) out of which the vectors are composed. So, then, as far as we can tell, the proposed connectionist explanation of systematicity (and related features of cognition) comes down to this: Smolensky "hypothesizes" that systematicity is somehow a consequence of underlying neural processes.[13] Needless to say, if that *is* Smolensky's theory, it is, on the one hand, certainly true, and, on the other hand, not intimately dependent upon his long story about fillers, binders, tensor products, superposition vectors and the rest.

By way of rounding out the argument, we want to reply to a question raised by an anonymous *Cognition* reviewer, who asks: "... couldn't Smolensky easily build in mechanisms to accomplish the matrix algebra oper-

---

[13]More precisely: we take Smolensky to be claiming that there is some property D, such that if a dynamical system has D its behavior is systematic, and such that human behavior (for example) is caused by a dynamical system that has D. The trouble is that this is a platitude since it is untendentious that human behavior is systematic, that its causation by the nervous system is lawful, and that the nervous system is dynamical. The least that has to happen if we are to have a substantive connectionist account of systematicity is: first, it must be made clear what property D is, and second it must be shown that D is a property that connectionist systems can have by law. Smolensky's theory does nothing to meet either of these requirements.

ations that would make the necessary vector explicit (or better yet, from his point of view, ... mechanisms that are sensitive to the imaginary components without literally making them explicit in some string of units)?"[14] But this misses the point of the problem that systematicity poses for connectionists, which is not to show that systematic cognitive capacities are *possible* given the assumptions of a connectionist architecture, but to explain how systematicity could be *necessary*—how it could be a *law* that cognitive capacities are systematic—given those assumptions.[15]

No doubt it is possible for Smolensky to wire a network so that it supports a vector that represents aRb if and only if it supports a vector that represents bRa; and perhaps it is possible for him to do that without making the imaginary units explicit[16] (though there is, so far, no proposal about how to ensure this for *arbitrary* a, R and b). The trouble is that, although the architecture permits this, it equally permits Smolensky to wire a network so that it supports a vector that represents aRb if and only if it supports a vector that represents zSq; or, for that matter, if and only if it supports a vector that represents The Last of The Mohicans. The architecture would appear to be absolutely indifferent as among these options.

Whereas, as we keep saying, in the Classical architecture, if you meet the conditions for being able to represent aRb, *YOU CANNOT BUT MEET THE CONDITIONS FOR BEING ABLE TO REPRESENT bRa*; the architecture won't let you do so because (i) the representation of a, R and b

---

[14]Actually, Smolensky is forced to choose the second option. To choose the first would, in effect, be to endorse the Classical requirement that tokening a symbol implies tokening its constituents; in which case, the question arises once again why such a network isn't an implementation of a language of thought machine. Just as Smolensky mustn't allow the representations of roles, fillers and binding units to be subvectors of superposition vectors if he is to avoid the "implementation" horn of the Fodor/Pylyshyn dilemma, so too he must avoid postulating mechanisms that make role, filler and binding units explicit (specifically, accessible to mental operations) whenever the superposition vectors are tokened. Otherwise he again has symbols with Classical constituents and raises the question why the proposed device isn't a language of thought machine. Smolensky's problem is that the very feature of his representations that make them wrong for explaining systematicity (viz., that their constituents are allowed to be imaginary) is the one that they have to have to assure that they aren't Classical.

[15]Fodor and Pylyshyn were very explicit about this. See, for example, 1988: p. 48.

[16]Terence Horgan remarks (personal communication) "... often there are two mathematically equivalent ways to calculate the time-evolution of a dynamical system. One is to apply the relevant equations directly to the numbers that are elements of a single total vector describing the initial state of the system. Another way is to mathematically decompose that vector into component normal-mode vector, then compute the time-evolution of each [of these] ... and then take the later state of the system to be described by a vector that is the superposition of the resulting normal-mode vectors." Computations of the former sort are supposed to be the model for operations that are "sensitive" to the components of a mental representation vector without recovering them. (Even in the second case, it's the theorist who recovers them in the course of the computations by which he makes his predictions. This does not, of course, imply that the constituents thus "recovered" participate in causal processes in the system under analysis.)

are constituents of the representation of aRb, and (ii) you have to token the constituents of the representations that you token, so Classical constituents can't be just imaginary. So then: it is *built into* the Classical picture that you can't think aRb unless you are able to think bRa, but the Connectionist picture is *neutral* on whether you can think aRb even if you can't think bRa. But it is a law of nature that you can't think aRb if you can't think bRa. So the Classical picture explains systematicity and the Connectionist picture doesn't. So the Classical picture wins.

**Conclusion**

At one point in his discussion, Smolensky makes some remarks that we find quite revealing: he says that, even in cases that are paradigms of Classical architectures (LISP machines and the like), "... we normally think of the 'real' causes as physical and far below the symbolic level ..." Hence, even in Classical machines, the sense in which operations at the symbol level are real causes is just that "... there is ... a complete and precise algorithmic (temporal) story to tell about the states of the machine described ..." at that level (1988b: p. 20). Smolensky, of course, denies that there is a "... comparable story at the symbolic level in the human cognitive architecture ... that is a difference with the Classical view that I have made much of. *It may be that a good way to characterize the difference is in terms of whether the constituents in mental structure are causally efficacious in mental processing*" (1988b: p. 20; our emphasis).

We say that this is revealing because it suggests a diagnosis: it would seem that Smolensky has succumbed to a sort of generalized epiphenomenalism. The idea is that even Classical constituents participate in causal processes solely by virtue of their physical microstructure, so even on the Classical story it's what happens at the neural level that *really* counts. Though the evolution of vectors can perhaps be explained in a predictively adequate sort of way by appeal to macroprocesses like operations on constituents, still if you want to know what's *really* going on — if you want the *causal* explanation — you need to go down to the "precise dynamical equations" that apply to activation states of units. That intentional generalizations can only approximate these precise dynamical equations is among Smolensky's recurrent themes. By conflating the issue about "precision" with the issue about causal efficacy, Smolensky makes it seem that to the extent that macrolevel generalizations are imprecise, to that extent macrolevel processes are epiphenomenal.

It would need a philosophy lesson to say all of what's wrong with this. Suffice it for present purposes that the argument iterates in a way that

Smolensky ought to find embarrassing. No doubt, we do get greater precision when we go from generalizations about operations on constituents to generalizations about operations on units. But if that shows that symbol-level processes aren't really causal, then it must be that unit-level processes aren't really causal either. After all, we get *still more* precision when we go down from unit-sensitive operations to molecule-sensitive operations, and more precision yet when we go down from molecule-sensitive operations to quark-sensitive operations. The moral is not, however, that the causal laws of psychology should be stated in terms of the behavior of quarks. Rather, the moral is that whether you have a level of causal explanation is a question, not just of how much precision you are able to achieve, but also of *what generalizations you are able to express*. The price you pay for doing psychology at the level of units is that you lose causal generalizations that symbol-level theories are able to state. Smolensky's problems with capturing the generalizations about systematicity provide a graphic illustration of these truths.

It turns out, at any event, that there is a crucial caveat to Smolensky's repeated claim that connectionist mechanisms can reconstruct everything that's interesting about the notion of constituency. Strictly speaking, he claims only to reconstruct whatever is interesting about constituents *except their causes and effects*. The explanation of systematicity turns on the causal role of the constituents of mental representations and is therefore among the casualties. Hilary Putnam, back in the days when he was still a Metaphysical Realist, used to tell a joke about a physicist who actually managed to build a perpetual motion machine; all except for a part that goes back and forth, back and forth, back and forth, forever. Smolensky's explanation of systematicity has very much the character of this machine.

We conclude that Fodor and Pylyshyn's challenge to connectionists has yet to be met. We still don't have *even a suggestion* of how to account for systematicity within the assumptions of connectionist cognitive architecture.

## References

Fodor, J., & Pylyshyn, P. (1988). Connectionism and cognitive architecture: A critical analysis. *Cognition*, *28*, 3–71.

Smolensky, P. (1987). The constituent structure of mental states: A reply to Fodor and Pylyshyn. *Southern Journal of Philosophy*, *26*, 137–160.

Smolensky, P. (1988a). On the proper treatment of connectionism. *Behavioral and Brain Sciences*, *11*, 1–23.

Smolensky, P. (1988b). Connectionism, constituency and the language of thought. University of Colorado Technical report; also forthcoming in Loewer, B., & Rey, G. (Eds.), *Meaning in mind: Fodor and his critics*. Oxford: Blackwell.

*by* **Daniel C. Dennett**
*Department of Philosophy, Tufts University, Medford, Mass. 02155*

*Why not the whole iguana?* I have no disagreements worth mentioning with Pylyshyn's paper, but would like to explore two comments of his.

"There have been grand theoreticians in psychology in the past (e.g., Freud, James, Hull) who have sought . . . general principles with very limited success," Pylyshyn suggests, because they lacked "a powerful technical tool to discipline and extend the power of the imagination." And now for the first time we have the tool that might permit us to express and test at least *sketches* of unified cognitive theories of whole creatures, the sort of theories to which Freud et al. aspired. Moreover, as Pylyshyn observes, the users of that tool have come to a consensus of sorts that theories of the whole creature are what is needed:

"The recurrence of major problems of organization and representation of knowledge, and the organization and distribution of responsibility or control . . . have produced the growing conviction among cognitive scientists that intelligence is not to be had by putting together language abilities, sensory abilities, visual abilities, memory, motivation, and reasoning (as the chapters of typical psychology textbooks suggest) but by bringing a large base of knowledge to bear in a disciplined way in all cognitive tasks "

Very true, but then why have cognitive scientists persisted in attempting to model sub-subsystems with artificially walled-off boundaries (not just language understanders, but nursery-story-only understanders, for instance)? Why are they not trying to model whole cognitive creatures? Because a model of a whole human being would be too big to handle; people know too much about too many topics, have too many interests, capacities, modalities of perception and action. One has to restrict oneself to a "toy" problem in a particular domain in order to keep the model "small" enough to be designed and tested at a reasonable cost in time and money. But faced with the conclusions quoted above, why not obtain one's simplicity and scaling down by attempting to model a whole cognitive creature of much less sophistication than a human being? Why not try to do a *whole* starfish, for instance? It has no eyes or ears, only rudimentary pattern-discrimination capacities, few modes of action, few needs or intellectual accomplishments. That could be a warm-up exercise for something a bit more challenging: a turtle, perhaps, or a mole. A turtle must organize its world knowledge, such as it is, so that it can keep life and limb together by making real time decisions based on that knowledge, so while a turtle-simulation would not need a natural language parser, for instance, it would need just the sorts of efficient organization and flexibility of control distribution you have to provide in the representation of world knowledge behind a natural language parsing system of a simulated human agent such as SHRDLU.

Perhaps there are good reasons for not pursuing such projects. I suspect that one of the *real* reasons such projects are not pursued is that in order to design a computer simulation of a turtle one would have to learn all about turtles, and who wants to go to all that trouble, when you already know enough about yourself and your friends (you think) to have all the performance data you need for the human mini-task of your choice? Moreover, only people who also knew a great deal about turtles would be knowledgeable enough to be impressed by your results.

Considering the abstractness of the problems properly addressed in A.I. (Dennett, 1978), one can put this attitude in a better light: one does not want to get bogged down with technical problems in modeling the cognitive eccentricities of turtles if the point of the exercise is to uncover *very* general, *very* abstract principles that will apply as well to the cognitive organization of the most sophisticated human beings. So why not then *make up* a whole cognitive creature, a Martian three-wheeled iguana, say, and an environmental niche for it to cope with? I think such a project *could* teach us a great deal about the deep principles of human cognitive psychology, but if it could not, I am quite sure that most of the current A.I. modeling of familiar human mini-tasks could not either.

REFERENCES

Dennett, D. C. Artificial Intelligence as Philosophy and as Psychology. In: M. Ringle (ed.), *Philosophical Perspectives in Artificial Intelligence.* New York, The Humanities Press, 1978.

234

Artificial Intelligence 47 (1991) 139–159
Elsevier

# Intelligence without representation*

Rodney A. Brooks

*MIT Artificial Intelligence Laboratory, 545 Technology Square, Rm. 836, Cambridge, MA 02139, USA*

Received September 1987

*Abstract*

Brooks, R.A., Intelligence without representation. Artificial Intelligence 47 (1991) 139–159.

Artificial intelligence research has foundered on the issue of representation. When intelligence is approached in an incremental manner, with strict reliance on interfacing to the real world through perception and action, reliance on representation disappears. In this paper we outline our approach to incrementally building complete intelligent Creatures. The fundamental decomposition of the intelligent system is not into independent information processing units which must interface with each other via representations. Instead, the intelligent system is decomposed into independent and parallel activity producers which all interface directly to the world through perception and action, rather than interface to each other particularly much. The notions of central and peripheral systems evaporate—everything is both central and peripheral. Based on these principles we have built a very successful series of mobile robots which operate without supervision as Creatures in standard office environments.

## 1. Introduction

Artificial intelligence started as a field whose goal was to replicate human level intelligence in a machine.

Early hopes diminished as the magnitude and difficulty of that goal was appreciated. Slow progress was made over the next 25 years in demonstrating isolated aspects of intelligence. Recent work has tended to concentrate on commercializable aspects of "intelligent assistants" for human workers.

* This report describes research done at the Artificial Intelligence Laboratory of the Massachusetts Institute of Technology. Support for the research is provided in part by an IBM Faculty Development Award, in part by a grant from the Systems Development Foundation, in part by the University Research Initiative under Office of Naval Research contract N00014-86-K-0685 and in part by the Advanced Research Projects Agency under Office of Naval Research contract N00014-85-K-0124.

0004-3702/91/$03.50 © 1991 — Elsevier Science Publishers B.V.

No one talks about replicating the full gamut of human intelligence any more. Instead we see a retreat into specialized subproblems, such as ways to represent knowledge, natural language understanding, vision or even more specialized areas such as truth maintenance systems or plan verification. All the work in these subareas is benchmarked against the sorts of tasks humans do within those areas. Amongst the dreamers still in the field of AI (those not dreaming about dollars, that is), there is a feeling that one day all these pieces will all fall into place and we will see "truly" intelligent systems emerge.

However, I, and others, believe that human level intelligence is too complex and little understood to be correctly decomposed into the right subpieces at the moment and that even if we knew the subpieces we still wouldn't know the right interfaces between them. Furthermore, we will never understand how to decompose human level intelligence until we've had a lot of practice with simpler level intelligences.

In this paper I therefore argue for a different approach to creating artificial intelligence:

- We must incrementally build up the capabilities of intelligent systems, having complete systems at each step of the way and thus automatically ensure that the pieces and their interfaces are valid.
- At each step we should build complete intelligent systems that we let loose in the real world with real sensing and real action. Anything less provides a candidate with which we can delude ourselves.

We have been following this approach and have built a series of autonomous mobile robots. We have reached an unexpected conclusion (C) and have a rather radical hypothesis (H).

(C) When we examine very simple level intelligence we find that explicit representations and models of the world simply get in the way. It turns out to be better to use the world as its own model.

(H) Representation is the wrong unit of abstraction in building the bulkiest parts of intelligent systems.

Representation has been the central issue in artificial intelligence work over the last 15 years only because it has provided an interface between otherwise isolated modules and conference papers.

## 2. The evolution of intelligence

We already have an existence proof of the possibility of intelligent entities: human beings. Additionally, many animals are intelligent to some degree. (This is a subject of intense debate, much of which really centers around a definition of intelligence.) They have evolved over the 4.6 billion year history of the earth.

It is instructive to reflect on the way in which earth-based biological evolution spent its time. Single-cell entities arose out of the primordial soup roughly 3.5 billion years ago. A billion years passed before photosynthetic plants appeared. After almost another billion and a half years, around 550 million years ago, the first fish and vertebrates arrived, and then insects 450 million years ago. Then things started moving fast. Reptiles arrived 370 million years ago, followed by dinosaurs at 330 and mammals at 250 million years ago. The first primates appeared 120 million years ago and the immediate predecessors to the great apes a mere 18 million years ago. Man arrived in roughly his present form 2.5 million years ago. He invented agriculture a mere 19,000 years ago, writing less than 5000 years ago and "expert" knowledge only over the last few hundred years.

This suggests that problem solving behavior, language, expert knowledge and application, and reason, are all pretty simple once the essence of being and reacting are available. That essence is the ability to move around in a dynamic environment, sensing the surroundings to a degree sufficient to achieve the necessary maintenance of life and reproduction. This part of intelligence is where evolution has concentrated its time—it is much harder.

I believe that mobility, acute vision and the ability to carry out survival-related tasks in a dynamic environment provide a necessary basis for the development of true intelligence. Moravec [11] argues this same case rather eloquently.

Human level intelligence has provided us with an existence proof but we must be careful about what the lessons are to be gained from it.

## 2.1. A story

Suppose it is the 1890s. Artificial flight is the glamor subject in science, engineering, and venture capital circles. A bunch of AF researchers are miraculously transported by a time machine to the 1980s for a few hours. They spend the whole time in the passenger cabin of a commercial passenger Boeing 747 on a medium duration flight.

Returned to the 1890s they feel vigorated, knowing that AF is possible on a grand scale. They immediately set to work duplicating what they have seen. They make great progress in designing pitched seats, double pane windows, and know that if only they can figure out those weird "plastics" they will have their grail within their grasp. (A few connectionists amongst them caught a glimpse of an engine with its cover off and they are preoccupied with inspirations from that experience.)

## 3. Abstraction as a dangerous weapon

Artificial intelligence researchers are fond of pointing out that AI is often denied its rightful successes. The popular story goes that when nobody has any

good idea of how to solve a particular sort of problem (e.g. playing chess) it is
known as an AI problem. When an algorithm developed by AI researchers
successfully tackles such a problem, however, AI detractors claim that since
the problem was solvable by an algorithm, it wasn't really an AI problem after
all. Thus AI never has any successes. But have you ever heard of an AI
failure?

I claim that AI researchers are guilty of the same (self) deception. They
partition the problems they work on into two components. The AI component,
which they solve, and the non-AI component which they don't solve. Typically,
AI "succeeds" by defining the parts of the problem that are unsolved as not
AI. The principal mechanism for this partitioning is abstraction. Its application
is usually considered part of good science, not, as it is in fact used in AI, as a
mechanism for self-delusion. In AI, abstraction is usually used to factor out all
aspects of perception and motor skills. I argue below that these are the hard
problems solved by intelligent systems, and further that the shape of solutions
to these problems constrains greatly the correct solutions of the small pieces of
intelligence which remain.

Early work in AI concentrated on games, geometrical problems, symbolic
algebra, theorem proving, and other formal systems (e.g. [6, 9]). In each case
the semantics of the domains were fairly simple.

In the late sixties and early seventies the blocks world became a popular
domain for AI research. It had a uniform and simple semantics. The key to
success was to represent the state of the world completely and explicitly.
Search techniques could then be used for planning within this well-understood
world. Learning could also be done within the blocks world; there were only a
few simple concepts worth learning and they could be captured by enumerating
the set of subexpressions which must be contained in any formal description of
a world including an instance of the concept. The blocks world was even used
for vision research and mobile robotics, as it provided strong constraints on the
perceptual processing necessary [12].

Eventually criticism surfaced that the blocks world was a "toy world" and
that within it there were simple special purpose solutions to what should be
considered more general problems. At the same time there was a funding crisis
within AI (both in the US and the UK, the two most active places for AI
research at the time). AI researchers found themselves forced to become
relevant. They moved into more complex domains, such as trip planning, going
to a restaurant, medical diagnosis, etc.

Soon there was a new slogan: "Good representation is the key to AI" (e.g.
*conceptually efficient programs in* [2]). The idea was that by representing only
the pertinent facts explicitly, the semantics of a world (which on the surface
was quite complex) were reduced to a simple closed system once again.
Abstraction to only the relevant details thus simplified the problems.

Consider a chair for example. While the following two characterizations are
true:

(CAN (SIT-ON PERSON CHAIR)), (CAN (STAND-ON PERSON CHAIR)),

there is much more to the concept of a chair. Chairs have some flat (maybe) sitting place, with perhaps a back support. They have a range of possible sizes, requirements on strength, and a range of possibilities in shape. They often have some sort of covering material, unless they are made of wood, metal or plastic. They sometimes are soft in particular places. They can come from a range of possible styles. In particular the concept of what is a chair is hard to characterize simply. There is certainly no AI vision program which can find arbitrary chairs in arbitrary images; they can at best find one particular type of chair in carefully selected images.

This characterization, however, is perhaps the correct AI representation of solving certain problems; e.g., a person sitting on a chair in a room is hungry and can see a banana hanging from the ceiling just out of reach. Such problems are never posed to AI systems by showing them a photo of the scene. A person (even a young child) can make the right interpretation of the photo and suggest a plan of action. For AI planning systems however, the experimenter is required to abstract away most of the details to form a simple description in terms of atomic concepts such as PERSON, CHAIR and BANANAS.

But this abstraction is the essence of intelligence and the hard part of the problems being solved. Under the current scheme the abstraction is done by the researchers leaving little for the AI programs to do but search. A truly intelligent program would study the photograph, perform the abstraction and solve the problem.

The only input to most AI programs is a restricted set of simple assertions deduced from the real data by humans. The problems of recognition. spatial understanding, dealing with sensor noise, partial models, etc. are all ignored. These problems are relegated to the realm of input black boxes. Psychophysical evidence suggests they are all intimately tied up with the representation of the world used by an intelligent system.

There is no clean division between perception (abstraction) and reasoning in the real world. The brittleness of current AI systems attests to this fact. For example, MYCIN [13] is an expert at diagnosing human bacterial infections, but it really has no model of what a human (or any living creature) is or how they work, or what are plausible things to happen to a human. If told that the aorta is ruptured and the patient is losing blood at the rate of a pint every minute, MYCIN will try to find a bacterial cause of the problem.

Thus, because we still perform all the abstractions for our programs. most AI work is still done in the blocks world. Now the blocks have slightly different shapes and colors, but their underlying semantics have not changed greatly.

It could be argued that performing this abstraction (perception) for AI programs is merely the normal reductionist use of abstraction common in all good science. The abstraction reduces the input data so that the program experiences the same perceptual world (*Merkwelt* in [15]) as humans. Other (vision) researchers will independently fill in the details at some other time and place. I object to this on two grounds. First, as Uexküll and others have pointed out, each animal species, and clearly each robot species with their own distinctly non-human sensor suites, will have their own different *Merkwelt*. Second, the *Merkwelt* we humans provide our programs is based on our own introspection. It is by no means clear that such a *Merkwelt* is anything like what we actually use internally—it could just as easily be an output coding for communication purposes (e.g., most humans go through life never realizing they have a large blind spot almost in the center of their visual fields).

The first objection warns of the danger that reasoning strategies developed for the human-assumed *Merkwelt* may not be valid when real sensors and perception processing is used. The second objection says that even with human sensors and perception the *Merkwelt* may not be anything like that used by humans. In fact, it may be the case that our introspective descriptions of our internal representations are completely misleading and quite different from what we really use.

## 3.1. A continuing story

Meanwhile our friends in the 1890s are busy at work on their AF machine. They have come to agree that the project is too big to be worked on as a single entity and that they will need to become specialists in different areas. After all, they had asked questions of fellow passengers on their flight and discovered that the Boeing Co. employed over 6000 people to build such an airplane.

Everyone is busy but there is not a lot of communication between the groups. The people making the passenger seats used the finest solid steel available as the framework. There was some muttering that perhaps they should use tubular steel to save weight, but the general consensus was that if such an obviously big and heavy airplane could fly then clearly there was no problem with weight.

On their observation flight none of the original group managed to get a glimpse of the driver's seat, but they have done some hard thinking and think they have established the major constraints on what should be there and how it should work. The pilot, as he will be called, sits in a seat above a glass floor so that he can see the ground below so he will know where to land. There are some side mirrors so he can watch behind for other approaching airplanes. His controls consist of a foot pedal to control speed (just as in these newfangled automobiles that are starting to appear), and a steering wheel to turn left and right. In addition, the wheel stem can be pushed forward and back to make the airplane go up and down. A clever arrangement of pipes measures airspeed of the airplane and displays it on a dial. What more could one want? Oh yes. There's a rather nice setup of louvers in the windows so that the driver can get fresh air without getting the full blast of the wind in his face.

An interesting sidelight is that all the researchers have by now abandoned the study of aerodynamics. Some of them had intensely questioned their fellow passengers on this subject and not one of the modern flyers had known a thing about it. Clearly the AF researchers had previously been wasting their time in its pursuit.

## 4. Incremental intelligence

I wish to build completely autonomous mobile agents that co-exist in the world with humans, and are seen by those humans as intelligent beings in their own right. I will call such agents *Creatures*. This is my intellectual motivation. I have no particular interest in demonstrating how human beings work, although humans, like other animals, are interesting objects of study in this endeavor as they are successful autonomous agents. I have no particular interest in applications; it seems clear to me that if my goals can be met then the range of applications for such Creatures will be limited only by our (or their) imagination. I have no particular interest in the philosophical implications of Creatures, although clearly there will be significant implications.

Given the caveats of the previous two sections and considering the parable of the AF researchers, I am convinced that I must tread carefully in this endeavor to avoid some nasty pitfalls.

For the moment then, consider the problem of building Creatures as an engineering problem. We will develop an *engineering methodology* for building Creatures.

First, let us consider some of the requirements for our Creatures.

- A Creature must cope appropriately and in a timely fashion with changes in its dynamic environment.
- A Creature should be robust with respect to its environment; minor changes in the properties of the world should not lead to total collapse of the Creature's behavior; rather one should expect only a gradual change in capabilities of the Creature as the environment changes more and more.
- A Creature should be able to maintain multiple goals and, depending on the circumstances it finds itself in, change which particular goals it is actively pursuing; thus it can both adapt to surroundings and capitalize on fortuitous circumstances.
- A Creature should do *something* in the world; it should have some purpose in being.

Now, let us consider some of the valid engineering approaches to achieving these requirements. As in all engineering endeavors it is necessary to decompose a complex system into parts, build the parts, then interface them into a complete system.

## 4.1. Decomposition by function

Perhaps the strongest traditional notion of intelligent systems (at least implicitly among AI workers) has been of a central system, with perceptual modules as inputs and action modules as outputs. The perceptual modules deliver a symbolic description of the world and the action modules take a symbolic description of desired actions and make sure they happen in the world. The central system then is a symbolic information processor.

Traditionally, work in perception (and vision is the most commonly studied form of perception) and work in central systems has been done by different researchers and even totally different research laboratories. Vision workers are not immune to earlier criticisms of AI workers. Most vision research is presented as a transformation from one image representation (e.g., a raw grey scale image) to another registered image (e.g., an edge image). Each group, AI and vision, makes assumptions about the shape of the symbolic interfaces. Hardly anyone has ever connected a vision system to an intelligent central system. Thus the assumptions independent researchers make are not forced to be realistic. There is a real danger from pressures to neatly circumscribe the particular piece of research being done.

The central system must also be decomposed into smaller pieces. We see subfields of artificial intelligence such as "knowledge representation", "learning", "planning", "qualitative reasoning", etc. The interfaces between these modules are also subject to intellectual abuse.

When researchers working on a particular module get to choose both the inputs and the outputs that specify the module requirements I believe there is little chance the work they do will fit into a complete intelligent system.

This bug in the functional decomposition approach is hard to fix. One needs a long chain of modules to connect perception to action. In order to test any of them they all must first be built. But until realistic modules are built it is highly unlikely that we can predict exactly what modules will be needed or what interfaces they will need.

## 4.2. Decomposition by activity

An alternative decomposition makes no distinction between peripheral systems, such as vision, and central systems. Rather the fundamental slicing up of an intelligent system is in the orthogonal direction dividing it into *activity* producing subsystems. Each activity, or behavior producing system individually connects sensing to action. We refer to an activity producing system as a *layer*. An activity is a pattern of interactions with the world. Another name for our activities might well be *skill*, emphasizing that each activity can at least post facto be rationalized as pursuing some purpose. We have chosen the word activity, however, because our layers must decide when to act for themselves, not be some subroutine to be invoked at the beck and call of some other layer.

The advantage of this approach is that it gives an incremental path from very simple systems to complex autonomous intelligent systems. At each step of the way it is only necessary to build one small piece, and interface it to an existing, working, complete intelligence.

The idea is to first build a very simple complete autonomous system, and *test it in the real world*. Our favourite example of such a system is a Creature, actually a mobile robot, which avoids hitting things. It senses objects in its immediate vicinity and moves away from them, halting if it senses something in its path. It is still necessary to build this system by decomposing it into parts, but there need be no clear distinction between a "perception subsystem", a "central system" and an "action system". In fact, there may well be two independent channels connecting sensing to action (one for initiating motion, and one for emergency halts), so there is no single place where "perception" delivers a representation of the world in the traditional sense.

Next we build an incremental layer of intelligence which operates in parallel to the first system. It is pasted on to the existing debugged system and tested again in the real world. This new layer might directly access the sensors and run a different algorithm on the delivered data. The first-level autonomous system continues to run in parallel, and unaware of the existence of the second level. For example, in [3] we reported on building a first layer of control which let the Creature avoid objects and then adding a layer which instilled an activity of trying to visit distant visible places. The second layer injected commands to the motor control part of the first layer directing the robot towards the goal, but independently the first layer would cause the robot to veer away from previously unseen obstacles. The second layer monitored the progress of the Creature and sent updated motor commands, thus achieving its goal without being explicitly aware of obstacles, which had been handled by the lower level of control.

## 5. Who has the representations?

With multiple layers, the notion of perception delivering a description of the world gets blurred even more as the part of the system doing perception is spread out over many pieces which are not particularly connected by data paths or related by function. Certainly there is no identifiable place where the "output" of perception can be found. Furthermore, totally different sorts of processing of the sensor data proceed independently and in parallel, each affecting the overall system activity through quite different channels of control.

In fact, not by design, but rather by observation we note that a common theme in the ways in which our layered and distributed approach helps our Creatures meet our goals is that there is no central representation.

- Low-level simple activities can instill the Creature with reactions to dangerous or important changes in its environment. Without complex representations and the need to maintain those representations and reason about them, these reactions can easily be made quick enough to serve their purpose. The key idea is to sense the environment often, and so have an up-to-date idea of what is happening in the world.
- By having multiple parallel activities, and by removing the idea of a central representation, there is less chance that any given change in the class of properties enjoyed by the world can cause total collapse of the system. Rather one might expect that a given change will at most incapacitate some but not all of the levels of control. Gradually as a more alien world is entered (alien in the sense that the properties it holds are different from the properties of the world in which the individual layers were debugged), the performance of the Creature might continue to degrade. By not trying to have an analogous model of the world, centrally located in the system, we are less likely to have built in a dependence on that model being completely accurate. Rather, individual layers extract only those *aspects* [1] of the world which they find relevant—projections of a representation into a simple subspace, if you like. Changes in the fundamental structure of the world have less chance of being reflected in every one of those projections than they would have of showing up as a difficulty in matching some query to a central single world model.
- Each layer of control can be thought of as having its own implicit purpose (or goal if you insist). Since they are *active* layers, running in parallel and with access to sensors, they can monitor the environment and decide on the appropriateness of their goals. Sometimes goals can be abandoned when circumstances seem unpromising, and other times fortuitous circumstances can be taken advantage of. The key idea here is to be using the world as its own model and to continuously match the preconditions of each goal against the real world. Because there is separate hardware for each layer we can match as many goals as can exist in parallel, and do not pay any price for higher numbers of goals as we would if we tried to add more and more sophistication to a single processor, or even some multiprocessor with a capacity-bounded network.
- The purpose of the Creature is implicit in its higher-level purposes, goals or layers. There need be no explicit representation of goals that some central (or distributed) process selects from to decide what is most appropriate for the Creature to do next.

## 5.1. No representation versus no central representation

Just as there is no central representation there is not even a central system. Each activity producing layer connects perception to action directly. It is only the observer of the Creature who imputes a central representation or central control. The Creature itself has none; it is a collection of competing behaviors. Out of the local chaos of their interactions there emerges, in the eye of an observer, a coherent pattern of behavior. There is no central purposeful locus of control. Minsky [10] gives a similar account of how human behavior is generated.

Note carefully that we are not claiming that chaos is a necessary ingredient of intelligent behavior. Indeed, we advocate careful engineering of all the interactions within the system (evolution had the luxury of incredibly long time scales and enormous numbers of individual experiments and thus perhaps was able to do without this careful engineering).

We do claim however, that there need be no explicit representation of either the world or the intentions of the system to generate intelligent behaviors for a Creature. Without such explicit representations, and when viewed locally, the interactions may indeed seem chaotic and without purpose.

I claim there is more than this, however. Even at a local level we do not have traditional AI representations. We never use tokens which have any semantics that can be attached to them. The best that can be said in our implementation is that one number is passed from a process to another. But it is only by looking at the state of both the first and second processes that that number can be given any interpretation at all. An extremist might say that we really do have representations, but that they are just implicit. With an appropriate mapping of the complete system and its state to another domain, we could define a representation that these numbers and topological connections between processes somehow encode.

However we are not happy with calling such things a representation. They differ from standard representations in too many ways.

There are no variables (e.g. see [1] for a more thorough treatment of this) that need instantiation in reasoning processes. There are no rules which need to be selected through pattern matching. There are no choices to be made. To a large extent the state of the world determines the action of the Creature. Simon [14] noted that the complexity of behavior of a system was not necessarily inherent in the complexity of the creature. but perhaps in the complexity of the environment. He made this analysis in his description of an Ant wandering the beach. but ignored its implications in the next paragraph when he talked about humans. We hypothesize (following Agre and Chapman) that much of even human level activity is similarly a reflection of the world through very simple mechanisms without detailed representations.

## 6. The methodology in practice

In order to build systems based on an activity decomposition so that they are truly robust we must rigorously follow a careful methodology.

## 6.1. Methodological maxims

First, it is vitally important to test the Creatures we build in the real world; i.e., in the same world that we humans inhabit. It is disastrous to fall into the temptation of testing them in a simplified world first, even with the best intentions of later transferring activity to an unsimplified world. With a simplified world (matte painted walls, rectangular vertices everywhere, colored blocks as the only obstacles) it is very easy to accidentally build a submodule of the system which happens to rely on some of those simplified properties. This reliance can then easily be reflected in the requirements on the interfaces between that submodule and others. The disease spreads and the complete system depends in a subtle way on the simplified world. When it comes time to move to the unsimplified world, we gradually and painfully realize that every piece of the system must be rebuilt. Worse than that we may need to rethink the total design as the issues may change completely. We are not so concerned that it might be dangerous to test simplified Creatures first and later add more sophisticated layers of control because evolution has been successful using this approach.

Second, as each layer is built it must be tested extensively in the real world. The system must interact with the real world over extended periods. Its behavior must be observed and be carefully and thoroughly debugged. When a second layer is added to an existing layer there are three potential sources of bugs: the first layer, the second layer, or the interaction of the two layers. Eliminating the first of these source of bugs as a possibility makes finding bugs much easier. Furthermore, there is only one thing possible to vary in order to fix the bugs—the second layer.

## 6.2. An instantiation of the methodology

We have built a series of four robots based on the methodology of task decomposition. They all operate in an unconstrained dynamic world (laboratory and office areas in the MIT Artificial Intelligence Laboratory). They successfully operate with people walking by, people deliberately trying to confuse them, and people just standing by watching them. All four robots are Creatures in the sense that on power-up they exist in the world and interact with it, pursuing multiple goals determined by their control layers implementing different activities. This is in contrast to other mobile robots that are given programs or plans to follow for a specific mission.

The four robots are shown in Fig. 1. Two are identical, so there are really three designs. One uses an offboard LISP machine for most of its computations, two use onboard combinational networks, and one uses a custom onboard parallel processor. All the robots implement the same abstract architecture, which we call the *subsumption architecture*, which embodies the fundamental ideas of decomposition into layers of task achieving behaviors, and incremental

Fig. 1. The four MIT AI laboratory Mobots. Left-most is the first built Allen, which relies on an offboard LISP machine for computation support. The right-most one is Herbert, shown with a 24 node CMOS parallel processor surrounding its girth. New sensors and fast early vision processors are still to be built and installed. In the middle are Tom and Jerry. based on a commercial toy chassis, with single PALs (Programmable Array of Logic) as their controllers.

composition through debugging in the real world. Details of these implementations can be found in [3].

Each layer in the subsumption architecture is composed of a fixed-topology network of simple finite state machines. Each finite state machine has a handful of states, one or two internal registers, one or two internal timers, and access to simple computational machines, which can compute things such as vector sums. The finite state machines run asynchronously, sending and receiving fixed length messages (1-bit messages on the two small robots, and 24-bit messages on the larger ones) over *wires*. On our first robot these were virtual wires; on our later robots we have used physical wires to connect computational components.

There is no central locus of control. Rather, the finite state machines are data-driven by the messages they receive. The arrival of messages or the expiration of designated time periods cause the finite state machines to change state. The finite state machines have access to the contents of the messages and might output them, test them with a predicate and conditionally branch to a different state, or pass them to simple computation elements. There is no possibility of access to global data, nor of dynamically established communications links. There is thus no possibility of global control. All finite state machines are equal, yet at the same time they are prisoners of their fixed topology connections.

Layers are combined through mechanisms we call *suppression* (whence the name subsumption architecture) and *inhibition*. In both cases as a new layer is added, one of the new wires is side-tapped into an existing wire. A pre-defined time constant is associated with each side-tap. In the case of suppression the side-tapping occurs on the input side of a finite state machine. If a message arrives on the net wire it is directed to the input port of the finite state machine as though it had arrived on the existing wire. Additionally, any new messages on the existing wire are suppressed (i.e., rejected) for the specified time period. For inhibition the side-tapping occurs on the output side of a finite state machine. A message on the new wire simply inhibits messages being emitted on the existing wire for the specified time period. Unlike suppression the new message is not delivered in their place.

As an example, consider the three layers of Fig. 2. These are three layers of control that we have run on our first mobile robot for well over a year. The robot has a ring of twelve ultrasonic sonars as its primary sensors. Every second these sonars are run to give twelve radial depth measurements. Sonar is

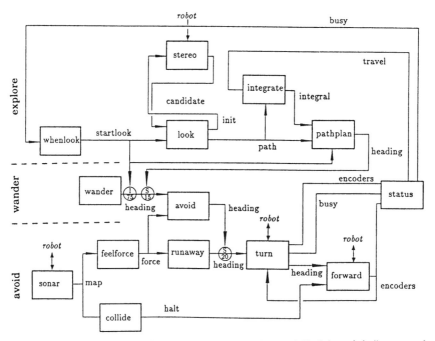

Fig. 2. We wire finite state machines together into layers of control. Each layer is built on top of existing layers. Lower level layers never rely on the existence of higher level layers.

extremely noisy due to many objects being mirrors to sonar. There are thus problems with specular reflection and return paths following multiple reflections due to surface skimming with low angles of incidence (less than thirty degrees).

In more detail the three layers work as follows:

(1) The lowest-level layer implements a behavior which makes the robot (the physical embodiment of the Creature) avoid hitting objects. It both avoids static objects and moving objects, even those that are actively attacking it. The finite state machine labelled *sonar* simply runs the sonar devices and every second emits an instantaneous map with the readings converted to polar coordinates. This map is passed on to the *collide* and *feelforce* finite state machine. The first of these simply watches to see if there is anything dead ahead, and if so sends a *halt* message to the finite state machine in charge of running the robot forwards—if that finite state machine is not in the correct state the message may well be ignored. Simultaneously, the other finite state machine computes a repulsive force on the robot, based on an inverse square law, where each sonar return is considered to indicate the presence of a repulsive object. The contributions from each sonar are added to produce an overall force acting on the robot. The output is passed to the *runaway* machine which thresholds it and passes it on to the *turn* machine which orients the robot directly away from the summed repulsive force. Finally, the *forward* machine drives the robot forward. Whenever this machine receives a halt message while the robot is driving forward, it commands the robot to halt.

This network of finite state machines generates behaviors which let the robot avoid objects. If it starts in the middle of an empty room it simply sits there. If someone walks up to it, the robot moves away. If it moves in the direction of other obstacles it halts. Overall, it manages to exist in a dynamic environment without hitting or being hit by objects.

(2) The next layer makes the robot wander about, when not busy avoiding objects. The *wander* finite state machine generates a random heading for the robot every ten seconds or so. The *avoid* machine treats that heading as an attractive force and sums it with the repulsive force computed from the sonars. It uses the result to suppress the lower-level behavior, forcing the robot to move in a direction close to what *wander* decided but at the same time avoid any obstacles. Note that if the *turn* and *forward* finite state machines are busy running the robot the new impulse to wander will be ignored.

(3) The third layer makes the robot try to explore. It looks for distant places, then tries to reach them. This layer suppresses the wander layer, and observes how the bottom layer diverts the robot due to obstacles (perhaps dynamic). It corrects for any divergences and the robot achieves the goal.

The *whenlook* finite state machine notices when the robot is not busy moving, and starts up the free space finder (labelled stereo in the diagram) finite state machine. At the same time it inhibits wandering behavior so that the observation will remain valid. When a path is observed it is sent to the *pathplan* finite state machine, which injects a commanded direction to the *avoid* finite state machine. In this way, lower-level obstacle avoidance continues to function. This may cause the robot to go in a direction different to that desired by *pathplan*. For that reason the actual path of the robot is monitored by the *integrate* finite state machine, which sends updated estimates to the *pathplan* machine. This machine then acts as a difference engine forcing the robot in the desired direction and compensating for the actual path of the robot as it avoids obstacles.

These particular layers were implemented on our first robot. See [3] for more details. Brooks and Connell [5] report on another three layers implemented on that particular robot.

## 7. What this is not

The subsumption architecture with its network of simple machines is reminiscent, at the surface level at least, with a number of mechanistic approaches to intelligence, such as connectionism and neural networks. But it is different in many respects for these endeavors, and also quite different from many other post-Dartmouth traditions in artificial intelligence. We very briefly explain those differences in the following sections.

### 7.1. It isn't connectionism

Connectionists try to make networks of simple processors. In that regard, the things they build (in simulation only—no connectionist has ever driven a real robot in a real environment, no matter how simple) are similar to the subsumption networks we build. However, their processing nodes tend to be uniform and they are looking (as their name suggests) for revelations from understanding how to connect them correctly (which is usually assumed to mean richly at least). Our nodes are all unique finite state machines and the density of connections is very much lower, certainly not uniform, and very low indeed between layers. Additionally, connectionists seem to be looking for explicit distributed representations to spontaneously arise from their networks. We harbor no such hopes because we believe representations are not necessary and appear only in the eye or mind of the observer.

### 7.2. It isn't neural networks

Neural networks is the parent discipline of which connectionism is a recent incarnation. Workers in neural networks claim that there is some biological significance to their network nodes, as models of neurons. Most of the models seem wildly implausible given the paucity of modeled connections relative to the thousands found in real neurons. We claim no biological significance in our choice of finite state machines as network nodes.

### 7.3. It isn't production rules

Each individual activity producing layer of our architecture could be viewed as an implementation of a production rule. When the right conditions are met in the environment a certain action will be performed. We feel that analogy is a little like saying that any FORTRAN program with IF statements is implementing a production rule system. A standard production system really is more—it has a rule base, from which a rule is selected based on matching preconditions of all the rules to some database. The preconditions may include variables which must be matched to individuals in the database. Our layers run in parallel and have no variables or need for matching. Instead, aspects of the world are extracted and these directly trigger or modify certain behaviors of the layer.

### 7.4. It isn't a blackboard

If one really wanted, one could make an analogy of our networks to a blackboard control architecture. Some of the finite state machines would be localized knowledge sources. Others would be processes acting on these knowledge sources by finding them on the blackboard. There is a simplifying point in our architecture however: all the processes know exactly where to look on the blackboard as they are hard-wired to the correct place. I think this forced analogy indicates its own weakness. There is no flexibility at all on where a process can gather appropriate knowledge. Most advanced blackboard architectures make heavy use of the general sharing and availability of almost all knowledge. Furthermore, in spirit at least, blackboard systems tend to hide from a consumer of knowledge who the particular producer was. This is the primary means of abstraction in blackboard systems. In our system we make such connections explicit and permanent.

### 7.5. It isn't German philosophy

In some circles much credence is given to Heidegger as one who understood the dynamics of existence. Our approach has certain similarities to work inspired by this German philosopher (e.g. [1]) but our work was not so inspired. It is based purely on engineering considerations. That does not preclude it from being used in philosophical debate as an example on any side of any fence, however.

## 8. Limits to growth

Since our approach is a performance-based one, it is the performance of the systems we build which must be used to measure its usefulness and to point to its limitations.

We claim that as of mid-1987 our robots, using the subsumption architecture to implement complete Creatures, are the most reactive real-time mobile robots in existence. Most other mobile robots are still at the stage of individual "experimental runs" in static environments, or at best in completely mapped static environments. Ours, on the other hand, operate completely autonomously in complex dynamic environments at the flick of their on switches, and continue until their batteries are drained. We believe they operate at a level closer to simple insect level intelligence than to bacteria level intelligence. Our goal (worth nothing if we don't deliver) is simple insect level intelligence within two years. Evolution took 3 billion years to get from single cells to insects, and only another 500 million years from there to humans. This statement is not intended as a prediction of our future performance, but rather to indicate the nontrivial nature of insect level intelligence.

Despite this good performance to date, there are a number of serious questions about our approach. We have beliefs and hopes about how these questions will be resolved, but under our criteria only performance truly counts. Experiments and building more complex systems take time, so with the caveat that the experiments described below have not yet been performed we outline how we currently see our endeavor progressing. Our intent in discussing this is to indicate that there is at least a plausible path forward to more intelligent machines from our current situation.

Our belief is that the sorts of activity producing layers of control we are developing (mobility, vision and survival related tasks) are necessary prerequisites for higher-level intelligence in the style we attribute to human beings.

The most natural and serious questions concerning limits of our approach are:

- How many layers can be built in the subsumption architecture before the interactions between layers become too complex to continue?
- How complex can the behaviors be that are developed without the aid of central representations?
- Can higher-level functions such as learning occur in these fixed topology networks of simple finite state machines?

We outline our current thoughts on these questions.

### 8.1. How many layers?

The highest number of layers we have run on a physical robot is three. In simulation we have run six parallel layers. The technique of completely debugging the robot on all existing activity producing layers before designing and adding a new one seems to have been practical till now at least.

## 8.2. How complex?

We are currently working towards a complex behavior pattern on our fourth robot which will require approximately fourteen individual activity producing layers.

The robot has infrared proximity sensors for local obstacle avoidance. It has an onboard manipulator which can grasp objects at ground and table-top levels, and also determine their rough weight. The hand has depth sensors mounted on it so that homing in on a target object in order to grasp it can be controlled directly. We are currently working on a structured light laser scanner to determine rough depth maps in the forward looking direction from the robot.

The high-level behavior we are trying to instill in this Creature is to wander around the office areas of our laboratory, find open office doors, enter, retrieve empty soda cans from cluttered desks in crowded offices and return them to a central repository.

In order to achieve this overall behavior a number of simpler task achieving behaviors are necessary. They include: avoiding objects, following walls, recognizing doorways and going through them, aligning on learned landmarks, heading in a homeward direction, learning homeward bearings at landmarks and following them, locating table-like objects, approaching such objects, scanning table tops for cylindrical objects of roughly the height of a soda can, serving the manipulator arm, moving the hand above sensed objects, using the hand sensor to look for objects of soda can size sticking up from a background. grasping objects if they are light enough, and depositing objects.

The individual tasks need not be coordinated by any central controller. Instead they can index off of the state of the world. For instance the grasp behavior can cause the manipulator to grasp any object of the appropriate size seen by the hand sensors. The robot will not randomly grasp just any object however, because it will only be when other layers or behaviors have noticed an object of roughly the right shape on top of a table-like object that the grasping behavior will find itself in a position where its sensing of the world tells it to react. If, from above, the object no longer looks like a soda can, the grasp reflex will not happen and other lower-level behaviors will cause the robot to look elsewhere for new candidates.

## 8.3. Is learning and such possible?

Some insects demonstrate a simple type of learning that has been dubbed "learning by instinct" [7]. It is hypothesized that honey bees for example are pre-wired to learn how to distinguish certain classes of flowers, and to learn routes to and from a home hive and sources of nectar. Other insects, butterflies, have been shown to be able to learn to distinguish flowers, but in an information limited way [8]. If they are forced to learn aout a second sort of flower, they forget what they already knew about the first, in a manner that suggests the total amount of information which they know, remains constant.

We have found a way to build fixed topology networks of our finite state machines which can perform learning, as an isolated subsystem, at levels comparable to these examples. At the moment of course we are in the very position we lambasted most AI workers for earlier in this paper. We have an isolated module of a system working, and the inputs and outputs have been left dangling.

We are working to remedy this situation, but experimental work with physical Creatures is a nontrivial and time consuming activity. We find that almost any pre-designed piece of equipment or software has so many preconceptions of how they are to be used built in to them, that they are not flexible enough to be a part of our complete systems. Thus, as of mid-1987, our work in learning is held up by the need to build a new sort of video camera and high-speed low-power processing box to run specially developed vision algorithms at 10 frames per second. Each of these steps is a significant engineering endeavor which we are undertaking as fast as resources permit.

Of course, talk is cheap.

### 8.4. The future

Only experiments with real Creatures in real worlds can answer the natural doubts about our approach. Time will tell.

### Acknowledgement

Phil Agre, David Chapman, Peter Cudhea, Anita Flynn, David Kirsh and Thomas Marill made many helpful comments on earlier drafts of this paper.

### References

[1] P.E. Agre and D. Chapman, Unpublished memo, MIT Artificial Intelligence Laboratory, Cambridge, MA (1986).
[2] R.J. Bobrow and J.S. Brown, Systematic understanding: synthesis, analysis, and contingent knowledge in specialized understanding systems, in: R.J. Bobrow and A.M. Collins, eds., Representation and Understanding (Academic Press, New York, 1975) 103–129.
[3] R.A. Brooks, A robust layered control system for a mobile robot, IEEE J. Rob. Autom. 2 (1986) 14–23.
[4] R.A. Brooks, A hardware retargetable distributed layered architecture for mobile robot control, in: Proceedings IEEE Robotics and Automation, Raleigh, NC (1987) 106–110.

[5] R.A. Brooks and J.H. Connell, Asynchronous distributed control system for a mobile robot, in: *Proceedings SPIE*, Cambridge, MA (1986) 77–84.

[6] E.A. Feigenbaum and J.A. Feldman, eds., *Computers and Thought* (McGraw-Hill, San Francisco, CA, 1963).

[7] J.L. Gould and P. Marler, Learning by instinct, *Sci. Am.* (1986) 74–85.

[8] A.C. Lewis, Memory constraints and flower choice in pieris rapae, *Science* **232** (1986) 863–865.

[9] M.L. Minsky, ed., *Semantic Information Processing* (MIT Press, Cambridge, MA, 1968).

[10] M.L. Minsky, *Society of Mind* (Simon and Schuster, New York, 1986).

[11] H.P. Moravec, Locomotion, vision and intelligence, in: M. Brady and R. Paul, eds., *Robotics Research* 1 (MIT Press, Cambridge, MA, 1984) 215–224.

[12] N.J. Nilsson, Shakey the robot, Tech. Note 323, SRI AI Center, Menlo Park, CA (1984).

[13] E.H. Shortliffe, *MYCIN: Computer-Based Medical Consultations* (Elsevier, New York, 1976).

[14] H.A. Simon, *The Sciences of the Artificial* (MIT Press, Cambridge, MA, 1969).

[15] J. Von Uexküll, *Umwelt und Innenwelt der Tiere* (Berlin, 1921).

## WHAT MIGHT COGNITION BE, IF NOT COMPUTATION?*

What is cognition? Contemporary orthodoxy maintains that it is computation: the mind is a special kind of computer, and cognitive processes are the rule-governed manipulation of internal symbolic representations. This broad idea has dominated the philosophy and the rhetoric of cognitive science—and even, to a large extent, its practice—ever since the field emerged from the postwar cybernetic melee. It has provided the general framework for much of the most well-developed and insightful research into the nature of mental operation. Yet, over the last decade or more, the computational vision has lost much of its lustre. Although work within it continues apace, a variety of difficulties and limitations have become increasingly apparent, and researchers across cognitive science and related disciplines have been casting around for other ways to understand cognitive processes. Partly as a result, there are now many research programs which, one way or another, stand opposed to the traditional computational approach; these include connectionism, neurocomputational approaches, ecological psychology, situated robotics, synergetics, and artificial life.

These approaches appear to offer a variety of differing and even conflicting conceptions of the nature of cognition. It is therefore an appropriate time to step back and reconsider the question: What general arguments are there in favor of the idea that cognitive processes must be specifically *computational* in nature? In order prop-

* Criticism and advice from numerous people helped improve this paper, but special acknowledgement is due to Robert Port, John Haugeland, and James Townsend. Audiences at the University of Illinois/Chicago, the New Mexico State University, Indiana University, the Australian National University, the University of New South Wales, Princeton University, Lehigh University, and the University of Skūvde were suitably and helpfully critical of earlier versions.

0022-362X/95/9207/345-81

erly to address this question, however, we must first address another: What are the alternatives? What *could* cognition be, if it were *not* computation of some form or other?

There are at least two reasons why this second question is important. First, arguments in favor of some broad hypothesis are rarely, if ever, completely general. They tend to be arguments not for *A* alone, but rather in favor of *A* as opposed to *B*, and such arguments often fail to support *A* as opposed to *C*. For example, one of the most powerful early considerations raised in favor of the computational conception of cognition was the idea that intelligent behavior requires sophisticated internal representations. While this clearly supported the computational conception against a behaviorism which eschewed such resources, however, it was no use against a connectionism which helped itself to internal representations, though rather different in kind than the standard symbolic variety.

The second reason we need to ask what alternatives there may be is that one of the most influential arguments in favor of the computational view is the claim that there is simply no alternative. This is sometimes known as the *"what else could it be?"* argument.[1] As Allen Newell[2] recently put it:

> ...although a small chance exists that we will see a new paradigm emerge for mind, it seems unlikely to me. Basically, there do not seem to be any viable alternatives. This position is not surprising. In lots of sciences we end up where there are no major alternatives around to the particular theories we have. Then, all the interesting kinds of scientific action occur inside the major view. It seems to me that we are getting rather close to that situation with respect to the computational theory of mind (*ibid.*, p. 56).

This paper describes a viable alternative. Rather than computers, cognitive systems may be dynamical systems; rather than computation, cognitive processes may be state-space evolution within these very different kinds of systems. It thus disarms the "what else could it be?" argument, and advances the broader project of evaluating competing hypotheses concerning the nature of cognition. Note that achieving these goals does not require decisively establishing that the dynamical hypothesis is true. That would require considerably more space than is available here, and to attempt it now would be hopelessly premature anyway. All that must be done is to describe

---

[1] This title may have been first used in print by John Haugeland in "The Nature and Plausibility of Cognitivism," *Behavioral and Brain Sciences*, I (1978): 215–26.

[2] "Are There Alternatives?" in W. Sieg, ed., *Acting and Reflecting* (Boston: Kluwer, 1990).

and motivate the dynamical conception sufficiently to show that it does in fact amount to an alternative conception of cognition, and one which is currently viable, as far as we can now tell.

A fruitful way to present the dynamical conception is to begin with an unusual detour, via the early industrial revolution in England, circa 1788.

### I. THE GOVERNING PROBLEM

A central engineering challenge for the industrial revolution was to find a source of power that was reliable, smooth, and uniform. In the latter half of the eighteenth century, this had become the problem of translating the oscillating action of the steam piston into the rotating motion of a flywheel. In one of history's most significant technological achievements, Scottish engineer James Watt designed and patented a gearing system for a rotative engine. Steam power was no longer limited to pumping; it could be applied to any machinery that could be driven by a flywheel. The cotton industry was particularly eager to replace its horses and water wheels with the new engines. High-quality spinning and weaving required, however, that the source of power be highly uniform, that is, there should be little or no variation in the speed of revolution of the main driving flywheel. This is a problem, since the speed of the flywheel is affected both by the pressure of the steam from the boilers, and by the total workload being placed on the engine, and these are constantly fluctuating.

It was clear enough how the speed of the flywheel had to be regulated. In the pipe carrying steam from the boiler to the piston there was a throttle valve. The pressure in the piston, and so the speed of the wheel, could be adjusted by turning this valve. To keep engine speed uniform, the throttle valve would have to be turned, at just the right time and by just the right amount, to cope with changes in boiler pressure and workload. How was this to be done? The most obvious solution was to employ a human mechanic to turn the valve as necessary. This had a number of drawbacks, however: mechanics required wages, and were often unable to react sufficiently swiftly and accurately. The industrial revolution thus confronted a second engineering challenge: design a device which can automatically adjust the throttle valve so as to maintain uniform speed of the flywheel despite changes in steam pressure or workload. Such a device is known as a *governor*.

Difficult engineering problems are often best approached by breaking the overall task down into simpler subtasks, continuing the process of decomposition until one can see how to construct devices that can directly implement the various component tasks. In the case of the governing problem, the relevant decomposition seems clear. A change need only be made to the throttle valve if the flywheel is not currently running at the correct speed. Therefore, the first subtask must be to measure the speed of the wheel, and the second subtask must be to calculate whether there is any discrepancy between the desired speed and the actual speed. If there is no discrepancy, no change is needed, for the moment at least. If there is a discrepancy, then the governor must determine by how much the throttle valve should be adjusted to bring the speed of the wheel to the desired level. This will depend, of course, on the current steam pressure, and so the governor must measure the current steam pressure and then on that basis calculate how much to adjust the valve. Finally, of course, the valve must be adjusted. This overall sequence of subtasks must be carried out as often as necessary to keep the speed of the wheel sufficiently close to the desired speed.

A device that can solve the governing problem would have to carry out these various subtasks repeatedly in the correct order, and so we can think of it as obeying the following algorithm:

1. Measure the speed of the flywheel.
2. Compare the actual speed against the desired speed.
3. If there is no discrepancy, return to step 1. Otherwise,
   a. measure the current steam pressure;
   b. calculate the desired alteration in steam pressure;
   c. calculate the necessary throttle valve adjustment.
4. Make the throttle valve adjustment.
   Return to step 1.

There must be some physical device capable of actually carrying out each of these subtasks, and so we can think of the governor as incorporating a tachometer (for measuring the speed of the wheel); a device for calculating the speed discrepancy; a steam pressure meter; a device for calculating the throttle valve adjustment; a throttle valve adjuster; and some kind of central executive to handle sequencing of operations. This conceptual breakdown of the components of the governor may even correspond to its actual breakdown; that is, each of these components may be implemented by a distinct, dedicated physical device. The engineering problem would then reduce to the (presumably much simpler) problem of constructing the various components and hooking them together so that the whole system functions in a coherent fashion.

Now, as obvious as this approach now seems, it was not the way the governing problem was actually solved. For one thing, it presupposes devices that can swiftly perform some quite complex calculations, and although some simple calculating devices had been invented in the seventeenth century, there was certainly nothing available in the late eighteenth century that could have met the demands of a practical governor.

The real solution, adapted by Watt from existing windmill technology, was much more direct and elegant. It consisted of a vertical spindle geared into the main flywheel so that it rotated at a speed directly dependent upon that of the flywheel itself (see figure 1). Attached to the spindle by hinges were two arms, and on the end of each arm was a metal ball. As the spindle turned, centrifugal force drove the balls outward and hence upward. By a clever arrangement, this arm motion was linked directly to the throttle valve. The result was that as the speed of the main wheel increased, the arms raised, closing the valve and restricting the flow of steam; as the speed decreased, the arms fell, opening the valve and allowing more steam to flow. The engine adopted a constant speed, maintained with extraordinary swiftness and smoothness in the presence of large fluctuations in pressure and load.

It is worth emphasizing how remarkably well the centrifugal governor actually performed its task. This device was not just an engineer-

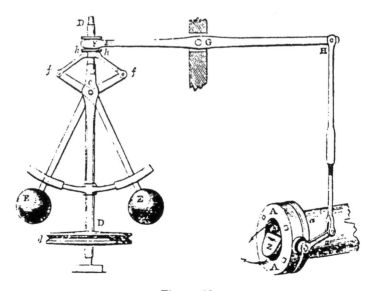

Figure 1[3]

[3] The Watt centrifugal governor for controlling the speed of a steam engine— from J. Farey, *A Treatise on the Steam Engine: Historical, Practical, and Descriptive* (London: Longman, Rees, Orme, Brown, and Green, 1827).

ing hack employed because computer technology was unavailable. *Scientific American* claimed in 1858 that an American variant of the basic centrifugal governor, "if not absolutely perfect in its action, is so nearly so, as to leave in our opinion nothing further to be desired."

But why should any of this be of any interest in the philosophy of cognitive science? The answer may become apparent as we examine a little more closely some of the differences between the two governors.

## II. TWO KINDS OF GOVERNORS

The two governors described in the previous section are patently different in construction, yet they both solve the same control problem, and we can assume (for purposes of this discussion) that they both solve it sufficiently well. Does it follow that, deep down, they are really the same kind of device, despite superficial differences in construction? Or are they deeply different, despite their similarity in overt performance?

It is natural to think of the first governor as a computational device; one which, as part of its operation computes some result, namely, the desired change in throttle valve angle. Closer attention reveals that there is in fact a complex group of properties here, a group whose elements are worth teasing apart.

Perhaps the most central of the computational governor's distinctive properties is its dependence on representation. Every aspect of its operation, as outlined above, deals with representations in some manner or other. The very first thing it does is measure its environment (the engine) to obtain a symbolic representation of current engine speed. It then performs a series of operations on this and other representations, resulting in an output representation, a symbolic specification of the alteration to be made in the throttle valve; this representation then causes the valve adjusting mechanism to make the corresponding change. This is why it is appropriately described as computational (now in a somewhat narrower sense): it literally computes the desired change in throttle valve by manipulating symbols according to a schedule of rules. Those symbols, in the context of the device and its situation, have meaning, and the success of the governor in its task is owed to its symbol manipulations being in systematic accord with those meanings. The manipulations are discrete operations which necessarily occur in a determinate sequence; for example, the appropriate change in the throttle valve can only be calculated after the discrepancy between current and desired speeds has been calculated. At the highest level, the whole device operates in a cyclic fashion: it first measures (or "perceives") its environment; it then internally computes an appropriate change in throttle valve; it then effects this change ("acts" on its environment). After the change has been made and given time to affect engine speed, the governor runs through whole the cycle again...and again.... Finally, notice that the governor is homuncular in construction. Homuncularity is a special kind of breakdown of a system into parts or components, each of which is responsible for a particular subtask. Homuncular components are ones that, like departments or committees within bureaucracies, interact by communication (that is, by passing meaningful messages). Obviously, the representational and computational nature of the governor is essential to its homuncular construction: if the system as a whole did not operate by manipulating representations, it would not be possible for its components to interact by communication.

These properties—representation, computation, sequential and cyclic operation, and homuncularity—form a mutually interdependent cluster; a device with any one of them will standardly possess others. Now, the Watt centrifugal governor does not exhibit this cluster of properties as a whole, nor any one of them individually. As obvious as this may seem, it deserves a little detailed discussion and argument, since it often meets resistance, and some useful insights can be gained along the way.

Since manipulable representations lie at the heart of the computational picture, the nonrepresentational nature of the centrifugal governor is a good place to start. There is a common and initially quite attractive intuition to the effect that the angle at which the arms are swinging is a representation of the current speed of the engine, and it is because the arms are related in this way to engine speed that the governor is able to control that speed. This intuition is misleading, however; arm angle and engine speed are of course intimately related, but the relationship is not representational. There are a number of powerful arguments favoring this conclusion. They are not based on any unduly restrictive definition of the notion of representation; they go through on pretty much any reasonable characterization, based around a core idea of some state of a system which, by virtue of some general representational scheme, stands in for some further state of affairs, thereby enabling the system to behave appropriately with respect to that state of affairs.[4]

---

[4] This broad characterization is adapted from Haugeland, "Representational Genera," in W. Ramsey, S.P. Stich, D.E. Rumelhart, eds., *Philosophy and Connectionist Theory* (Hillsdale, NJ: Erlbaum, 1991), pp. 61–89.

A useful criterion of representation—a reliable way of telling whether a system contains them or not—is to ask whether there is any explanatory utility in describing the system in representational terms. If you really can make substantially more sense of how a system works by concretely describing various identifiable parts or aspects of it as representations in the above sense, that is the best evidence you could have that the system really does contain representations. Conversely, if describing the system as representational lets you explain nothing over and above what you could explain before, why on earth suppose it to be so? Note that very often representational descriptions do yield substantial explanatory benefits. This is certainly true for pocket calculators, and mainstream cognitive science is premised on the idea that humans and animals are like that as well. A noteworthy fact about standard explanations of how the centrifugal governor works is, however, that they never talk about representations. This was true for the informal description given above, which apparently suffices for most readers; more importantly, it has been true of the much more detailed descriptions offered by those who have actually been in the business of constructing centrifugal governors or analyzing their behavior. Thus, for example, a mechanics manual for construction of governors from the middle of last century, Maxwell's original dynamical analysis (see below), and contemporary mathematical treatments all describe the arm angle and its role in the operation of the governor in nonrepresentational terms. The reason, one might reasonably conclude, is that the governor contains no representations.

The temptation to treat the arm angle as a representation comes from the informal observation that there is some kind of correlation between arm angle and engine speed; when the engine rotates at a certain speed, the arms will swing at a given angle. Now, supposing for the moment that this is an appropriate way to describe their relationship, it would not follow that the arm angle is a representation. One of the few points of general agreement in the philosophy of cognitive science is that mere correlation does not make something a representation. Virtually everything is correlated, fortuitously or otherwise, with something else; to describe every correlation as representation is to trivialize representation. For the arm angle to count, in the context of the governing system alone, as a representation, we would have to be told what else about it justifies the claim that it is a representation.

But to talk of some kind of correlation between arm angle and engine speed is grossly inadequate, and once this is properly understood, there is simply no incentive to search for this extra ingredient.

For a start, notice that the correlation at issue only obtains when the total system has reached its stable equilibrium point, and is immediately disturbed whenever there is some sudden change in, for example, the workload on the engine. At such times, the speed of the engine quickly drops for a short period, while the angle of the arms adjusts only at the relatively slow pace dictated by gravitational acceleration. Yet, even as the arms are falling, more steam is entering the piston, and hence the device is already working; indeed, these are exactly the times when it is most crucial that the governor work effectively. Consequently, no simple correlation between arm angle and engine speed can be the basis of the operation of the governor.

The fourth and deepest reason for supposing that the centrifugal governor is not representational is that, when we fully understand the relationship between engine speed and arm angle, we see that the notion of representation is just the wrong sort of conceptual tool to apply. There is no doubt that at all times the arm angle is in some interesting way related to the speed of the engine. This is the insight which leads people to suppose that the arm angle is a representation. Yet appropriately close examination of this dependence shows exactly why the relationship cannot be one of representation. For notice that, because the arms are directly linked to the throttle valve, the angle of the arms is at all times determining the amount of steam entering the piston, and hence at all times the speed of the engine depends in some interesting way on the angle of the arms. Thus, arm angle and engine speed are at all times both determined by, and determining, each other's behavior. As we shall see below, there is nothing mysterious about this relationship; it is quite amenable to mathematical description. Yet it is much more subtle and complex than the standard concept of representation can handle, even when construed as broadly as is done here. In order to describe the relationship between arm angle and engine speed, we need a more powerful conceptual framework than mere talk of representations. That framework is the mathematical language of dynamics, and in that language, the two quantities are said to be coupled. The real problem with describing the governor as a representational device, then, is that the relation of representing—something standing in for some other state of affairs—is too simple to capture the actual interaction between the governor and the engine.

If the centrifugal governor is not representational, then it cannot be computational, at least in the specific sense that its processing cannot be a matter of the rule-governed manipulation of symbolic representations. Its noncomputational nature can also be established another way. Not only are there no representations to be manipulated, there are no distinct manipulatings that might count as computational operations. There are no discrete, identifiable steps in which one representation gets transformed into another. Rather, the system's entire operation is smooth and continuous; there is no possibility of nonarbitrarily dividing its changes over time into distinct manipulatings, and no point in trying to do so. From this, it follows that the centrifugal governor is not sequential and not cyclic in its operation in anything like the manner of the computational governor. Since there are no distinct processing steps, there can be no sequence in which those steps occur. There is never any one operation that must occur before another one can take place. Consequently, there is nothing cyclical about its operation. The device has, to be sure, an "input" end (where the spindle is driven by the engine) and an "output" end (the connection to the throttle valve). But the centrifugal governor does not follow a cycle where it first takes a measurement, then computes a throttle valve change, then makes that adjustment, then takes a measurement, and so on. Rather, input, internal activity, and output are all happening continuously and at the very same time, much as a radio is producing music at the very same time as its antenna is receiving signals.

The fact that the centrifugal governor is not sequential or cyclic in any respect points to yet another deep difference between the two kinds of governor. There is an important sense in which time does not matter in the operation of the computational governor. There is, of course, the minimal constraint that the device must control the engine speed adequately, and so individual operations within the device must be sufficiently fast. There is also the constraint that internal operations must happen in the right sequence. Beyond these, however, there is nothing that dictates when each internal operation takes place, how long it takes to carry it out, and how long elapses between each operation. There are only pragmatic implementation considerations: which algorithms to use, what kind of hardware to use to run the algorithms, and so forth. The timing of the internal operations is thus essentially arbitrary relative to that of any wider course of events. It is as if the wheel said to the governing system: "Go away and figure out how much to change the valve to keep me spinning at 100 rpm. I don't care how you do it, how many steps you take, or how long you take over each step, as long as you report back within (say) 10 milliseconds."

In the centrifugal governor, by contrast, there is simply nothing that is temporally unconstrained in this way. There are no occurrences whose timing is arbitrary relative to the operation of the engine. All behavior in the centrifugal governor happens in the very same real time frame as change in the speed of the flywheel. We can sum up the point this way: the two kinds of governor differ fundamentally in their temporality, and the temporality of the centrifugal governor is essentially that of the engine itself.

Finally, it need hardly be labored that the centrifugal governor is not a homuncular system. It has parts, to be sure, and its overall behavior is the direct result of the organized interaction of those parts. The difference is that those parts are not modules interacting by communication; they are not like little bureaucratic agents passing representations among themselves as the system achieves the overall task.

### III. CONCEPTUAL FRAMEWORKS

In the previous section, I argued that the differences in nature between the two governors run much more deeply than the obvious differences in mechanical construction. Not surprisingly, these differences in nature are reflected in the kind of conceptual tools that we must bring to bear if we wish to understand the operation of these devices. That is, the two different governors require very different conceptual frameworks in order to understand how it is that they function as governors, that is, how they manage to control their environment.

In the case of the computational governor, the behavior is captured in all relevant detail by an algorithm, and the general conceptual framework we are bringing to bear is that of mainstream computer science. Computer scientists are typically concerned with what you can achieve by stringing together, in an appropriate order, some set of basic operations: either how best to string them together to achieve some particular goal (programming, theory of algorithms), or what is achievable in principle in this manner (computation theory). So we understand the computational governor as a device capable of carrying out some set of basic operations (measurings, subtractings, etc.), and whose sophisticated overall behavior results from nothing more than the complex sequencing of these basic operations. Note that there is a direct correspondence between elements of the governor (the basic processing steps it goes through) and elements of the algorithm which describes its operation (the basic instructions).

The Watt centrifugal governor, by contrast, cannot be understood this way at all. There is nothing in that device for any algorithm to lock onto. Very different conceptual tools have always been applied to this device. The terms in which it was described above, and indeed by Watt and his peers, were straightforwardly mechanical: rotations, spindles, levers, displacements, forces. Last century, more precise and powerful descriptions became available, but these also have nothing to do with computer science. In 1868, the physicist James Clerk Maxwell[5] made a pioneering extension of the mathematical tools of dynamics to regulating and governing devices. The general approach he established has been standard ever since. Though familiar to physicists and control engineers, it is less so to most cognitive scientists and philosophers of mind, and hence is worth describing in a little detail.

The key feature of the governor's behavior is the angle at which the arms are hanging, for this angle determines how much the throttle valve is opened or closed. Therefore, in order to understand the behavior of the governor, we need to understand the basic principles governing how arm angle changes over time. Obviously, the arm angle depends on the speed of the engine; hence we need to understand change in arm angle as a function of engine speed. If we suppose for the moment that the link between the governor and the throttle valve is disconnected, then this change is given by the differential equation:

$$\frac{d^2\theta}{dt^2} = (n\omega)^2 \cos\theta \sin\theta - \frac{g}{l}\sin\theta - r\frac{d\theta}{dt}$$

where $\theta$ is the angle of arms, $n$ is a gearing constant, $\omega$ is the speed of engine, $g$ is a constant for gravity, $l$ is the length of the arms, and $r$ is a constant of friction at hinges.[6] This nonlinear, second-order differential equation tells us the instantaneous acceleration in arm angle, as a function of what the current arm angle happens to be (designated by the state variable $\theta$), how fast arm angle is currently changing (the derivative of $\theta$ with respect to time, $d\theta/dt$) and the current engine speed ($\omega$). In other words, the equation tells us how change in arm angle is changing, depending on the current arm angle, the way it is changing already, and the engine speed. Note that in the system defined by this equation, change over time occurs only in arm angle $\theta$ (and its derivatives). The other quantities ($\omega$, $n$, $g$, $l$, and $r$) are assumed to stay fixed, and are called parameters. The particular values at which the parameters are fixed determine the precise shape of the change in $\theta$. For this reason, the parameter settings are said to fix the dynamics of the system.

This differential equation is perfectly general and highly succinct: it is a way of describing how the governor behaves for any arm angle and engine speed. This generality and succinctness comes at a price, however. If we happen to know what the current arm angle is, how fast it is changing, and what the engine speed is, then from this

---

[5] "On Governors," *Proceedings of the Royal Society*, XVI (1868): 270-83.
[6] Edward Beltrami, *Mathematics for Dynamical Modeling* (Boston: Academic, 1987), p. 163.

equation all we can figure out is the current instantaneous accelera-tion. If we want to know at what angle the arms will be in a half-sec-ond, for example, we need to find a solution to the general equation—that is, an equation that tells us what values $\theta$ takes as a function of time, which satisfies the differential equation. There are any number of such solutions, corresponding to all the different be-havioral trajectories that the governor might exhibit, but these solu-tions often have important general properties in common; thus, as long as the parameters stay within certain bounds, the arms will al-ways eventually settle into a particular angle of equilibrium for that engine speed; that angle is known as a *point attractor.*

Thus far I have been discussing the governor without taking into account its effect on the engine, and thereby indirectly on itself. Here, the situation gets a little more complicated, but the same math-ematical tools apply. Suppose we think of the steam engine itself as a dynamical system governed by a set of differential equations, one of which gives us some derivative of engine speed as a function of cur-rent engine speed and a number of other variables and parameters:

$$\frac{d^n \omega}{dt^n} = F(\omega, \ldots, \tau, \ldots)$$

One of these parameters is the current setting of the throttle valve, $\tau$, which depends directly on the governor arm angle $\theta$. We can thus think of $\theta$ as a parameter of the engine system, just as engine speed $\omega$ is a parameter of the governor system. (Alternatively, we can think of the governor and steam engine as comprising a single dynamical system in which both arm angle and engine speed are state vari-ables.) This relationship, known as *coupling,* is particularly interest-ing and subtle. Changing a parameter of a dynamical system changes its total dynamics (that is, the way its state variables change their val-ues depending on their current values, across the full range of values they may take). Thus, any change in engine speed, no matter how small, changes not the state of the governor directly, but rather the way the state of the governor *changes,* and any change in arm angle changes the way the state of the engine changes. Again, however, the overall system (coupled engine and governor) settles quickly into a point attractor, that is, engine speed and arm angle remain constant. Indeed, the remarkable thing about this coupled system is that under a wide variety of conditions it always settles swiftly into states at which the engine is running at a particular speed. This is of course exactly what is wanted: coupling the governor to the engine results in the engine running at a constant speed.

In this discussion, two very broad, closely related sets of conceptual resources have (in a modest way) been brought into play. The first is dynamical modeling, that branch of applied mathematics which attempts to describe change in real-world systems by describing the states of the system numerically and then writing equations that capture how these numerical states change over time. The second set of resources is dynamical systems theory, the general study of dynamical systems considered as abstract mathematical structures. Roughly speaking, dynamical modeling attempts to understand natural phenomena as the behavior of real-world realizations of abstract dynamical systems, whereas dynamical systems theory studies the abstract systems themselves. There is no sharp distinction between these two sets of resources, and for our purposes they can be lumped together under the general heading of dynamics.

### IV. MORALS

This discussion of the governing task suggests a number of closely related lessons for cognitive science:

(1) Various different kinds of systems, fundamentally different in nature and requiring very different conceptual tools for their understanding, can subserve sophisticated tasks—including interacting with a changing environment—which may initially appear to demand that the system have knowledge of, and reason about, its environment. The governing problem is one simple example of such a task; it can be solved either by a computational system or by a noncomputational dynamical system, the Watt centrifugal governor.

(2) In any given case, our sense that a specific cognitive task *must* be subserved by a (generically) computational system may be due to deceptively compelling preconceptions about how systems solving complex tasks must work. Many people are oblivious to the possibility of a noncomputational, dynamical solution to the governing problem, and so all-too-readily assume that it must be solved in a computational manner. Likewise, it may be that the basically computational shape of most mainstream models of cognition results not so much from the nature of cognition itself as it does from the shape of the conceptual equipment that cognitive scientists typically bring to bear in studying cognition.

(3) Cognitive systems may in fact be *dynamical* systems, and cognition the behavior of some (noncomputational) dynamical system. Perhaps, that is, cognitive systems are more relevantly similar to the centrifugal governor than they are similar either to the computational governor, or to that more famous exemplar of the broad category of computational systems, the Turing machine.

In what follows, the first and third of these points will be elaborated in just enough detail to substantiate the basic claim of this paper, that there is in fact a currently viable alternative to the computational conception of cognition. As a first step toward doing that, however, I shall briefly describe an example of dynamical research in cognitive science, in order to provide what might seem to be no more than rank speculation with a little healthy flesh.

## V. AN EXAMPLE OF DYNAMICAL RESEARCH

Consider the process of coming to make a decision between a variety of options, each of which has attractions and drawbacks. This is surely a high-level cognitive task, if anything is. Psychologists have done endless experimental studies determining how people choose, and produced many mathematical models attempting to describe and explain their choice behavior. The dominant approach in modeling stems from the classic expected-utility theory and statistical decision theory as originally developed by John von Neumann and Oskar Morgenstern. The basic idea here is that an agent makes a decision by selecting the option that has the highest expected utility, which is calculated in turn by combining some formal measure of the utility of any given possible outcome with the probability that it will eventuate if the option is chosen. Much of the work within the classical framework is mathematically elegant and provides a useful description of optimal reasoning strategies. As an account of the actual decisions people reach, however, classical utility theory is seriously flawed; human subjects typically deviate from its recommendations in a variety of ways. As a result, many theories incorporating variations on the classical core have been developed, typically relaxing certain of its standard assumptions, with varying degrees of success in matching actual human choice behavior. Nevertheless, virtually all such theories remain subject to some further drawbacks:

(1) They do not incorporate any account of the underlying motivations that give rise to the utility that an object or outcome holds at a given time.

(2) They conceive of the utilities themselves as static values, and can offer no good account of how and why they might change over time, and why preferences are often inconsistent and inconstant.

(3) They offer no serious account of the deliberation process, with its attendant vacillations, inconsistencies, and distress; and they have

nothing to say about the relationships that have been uncovered between time spent deliberating and the choices eventually made.

Curiously, these drawbacks appear to have a common theme; they all concern, one way or another, *temporal* aspects of decision making. It is worth asking whether they arise because of some deep structural feature inherent in the whole framework which conceptualizes decision-making behavior in terms of calculating expected utilities.

Notice that utility-theory based accounts of human decision making ("utility theories") are deeply akin to the computational solution to the governing task. That is, if we take such accounts as not just describing the outcome of decision-making behavior, but also as a guide to the structures and processes that underlie such behavior,[7] then there are basic structural similarities to the computational governor. Thus, utility theories are straightforwardly computational; they are based on static representations of options, utilities, probabilities, and so on, and processing is the algorithmically specifiable internal manipulation of these representations to obtain a final representation of the choice to be made. Consequently, utility theories are strictly sequential; they presuppose some initial temporal stage at which the relevant information about options, likelihoods, and so on, is acquired; a second stage in which expected utilities are calculated; and a third stage at which the choice is effected in actual behavior. And, like the computational governor, they are essentially atemporal; there are no inherent constraints on the timing of the various internal operations with respect to each other or change in the environment.

What we have, in other words, is a model of human cognition which, on one hand, instantiates the same deep structure as the computational governor, and on the other, seems structurally incapable of accounting for certain essentially temporal dimensions of decision-making behavior. At this stage, we might ask: What kind of model of decision-making behavior we would get if, rather, we took the *centrifugal* governor as a prototype? It would be a model with a relatively small number of continuous variables influencing each other in real time. It would be governed by nonlinear differential equations. And it would be a model in which the agent and the choice environment, like the governor and the engine, are tightly interlocked.

---

[7] See, for example, J.W. Payne, J.R. Bettman, and E.J. Johnson, "Adaptive Strategy Selection in Decision Making," *Journal of Experimental Psychology: Learning, Memory, Cognition*, XIV (1988): 534–52.

It would, in short, be rather like the *motivational oscillatory theory* (MOT) modeling framework described by mathematical psychologist James Townsend.[8] MOT enables modeling of various qualitative properties of the kind of cyclical behaviors that occur when circumstances offer the possibility of satiation of desires arising from more or less permanent motivations; an obvious example is regular eating in response to recurrent natural hunger. It is built around the idea that in such situations, your underlying motivation, transitory desires with regard to the object, distance from the object, and consumption of it are continuously evolving and affecting each other in real time; for example, if your desire for food is high and you are far from it, you will move toward it (that is, $z$ changes), which influences your satiation and so your desire. The framework thus includes variables for the current state of motivation, satiation, preference, and action (movement), and a set of differential equations describe how these variables change over time as a function of the current state of the system.[9]

[8] See "A Neuroconnectionistic Formulation of Dynamic Decision Field Theory," in D. Vickers and P.L. Smith, eds., *Human Information Processing: Measures, Mechanisms, and Models* (Amsterdam: North Holland, 1988); and "Don't Be Fazed by PHASER: Beginning Exploration of a Cyclical Motivational System," *Behavior Research Methods, Instruments and Computers*, xxiv (1992): 219–27.

[9] The equations, with rough and partial translations into English, are:

$$\frac{dx}{dt} = M - m - c$$

(The change in motivation depends on how the current levels of motivation and of consumption compare with some standard level of motivation, $M$.)

$$\frac{dx}{dt} = \left[ \frac{1}{z_1^2 + z_2^2 + a} + 1 \right] \cdot m$$

(The change in one's *preference* for the goal will depend on current motivation and one's distance from the object of preference.)

$$\frac{dc}{dt} = (x + C - c) \cdot \left[ \frac{b}{z_1^2 + z_2^2 + r} \right]$$

(The change in consumption will depend on the level of preference, the level of consumption, and the distance from the object of preference.)

$$\frac{dz_1}{dt} = -x \cdot z_1 \qquad \frac{dz_2}{dt} = -x \cdot z_2$$

(How one moves toward or away from the object depends on one's current level of preference for the object.) See "Don't Be Fazed by PHASER" for an accessible and graphic introduction to the behaviors defined by these equations.

MOT stands to utility theories in much the same relation as the centrifugal governor does to the computational governor. In MOT, cognition is not the manipulation of symbols, but rather state-space evolution in a dynamical system. MOT models produce behavior which, if one squints while looking at it, seems like decision making—after all, the agent will make the move which offers the most reward, which in this case means moving toward food if sufficiently hungry. But this is decision making without decisions, so to speak, for there never are in the model any discrete internal occurrences that one could characterize as decisions. In this approach, decision making is better thought of as the behavior of an agent under the influence of the pushes and pulls that emanate from desirable outcomes, undesirable outcomes, and internal desires and motivations; in a quasi-gravitational way, these forces act on the agent with strength varying as a function of distance.

The MOT modeling framework is a special case of a more general (and rather more complex) dynamical framework which Townsend and Jerome Busemeyer[10] call "decision field theory." That framework allows faithful modeling of a wide range of behaviors more easily recognizable as decision making as studied within the traditional research paradigm; indeed, their claim is that decision field theory "covers a broader range of phenomena in greater detail" than classical utility theories, and even goes beyond them by explaining in a natural way several important paradoxes of decision making, such as the so-called "common consequence effect" and "common ratio effect." The important point for immediate purposes, however, is that the general decision field theory works on the same fundamental dynamical principles as MOT. There is thus no question that at least certain aspects of human high-level cognitive functioning can be modeled effectively using dynamical systems of the kind that can be highlighted by reference to the centrifugal governor.

Thus far, all I have done is to use the governing problem as a means of exploring some of the deep differences between computational and noncomputational solutions to complex tasks, drawn out some suggestive implications for cognitive science, and used the Busemeyer and Townsend work to illustrate the claim that high-level cognitive processes can in fact be modeled using noncomputa-

---

[10] "Decision Field Theory: A Dynamic-Cognitive Approach to Decision Making in an Uncertain Environment," *Psychological Review,* c (1993): 432–59; an accessible overview is given in "Dynamic Representation of Decision Making," in R. Port and myself, eds., *Mind as Motion: Explorations in the Dynamics of Cognition* (Cambridge: MIT, 1995).

tional, dynamical systems. But these moves do not really describe an alternative to the computational conception so much as just gesture in that general direction. What we need now is a sharper characterization of the dynamical conception of cognition, and some reason to suppose that the dynamical conception really is viable as a general alternative.

### VI. THREE CONCEPTIONS OF COGNITIVE SYSTEMS

At the outset of this paper, I suggested that in order properly to evaluate the computational conception of cognition, we really need to know what viable alternatives there are (if any). Moreover, ideally, we would have some understanding of what the entire range of alternatives is, for only this way can we be sure that the candidates we are entertaining are in fact the most relevant. In other words, we need to be able to see the computational conception and its alternatives as options within a common field which contains all relevant possibilities.

Fortunately, the easiest way to present a sharpened characterization of the dynamical approach is in fact to sketch a common field within which can be situated, if not every conceivable option, at least the current main contenders—the computational, connectionist, and dynamical conceptions. The common field is the "space" of all state-dependent systems. A (concrete) state-dependent system is a set of features or aspects of the world which change over time interdependently, that is, in such a way that the nature of the change in any member of the system at a given time depends on the state of the members of the system at that time.[11] The most famous example from the history of science is, of course, the solar system: the positions and momentums of the sun and various planets are constantly changing in a way that always depends, in a manner captured in the laws first laid down by Newton, on what they happen to be. Another example is the Watt centrifugal governor, as described above: its future arm angles are determined by its current arm angle (and current rate of change of arm angle) according to its differential equation. And for our purposes, another particularly important category is that of computers: systems whose states are basically configurations of symbols and whose state at time $t + 1$ is always determined according to some rule by their state at time $t$.

Consider two centrifugal governors that are identical in all relevant physical detail. These devices will respond in exactly the same

---

[11] The notion of a *state-dependent* system is a generalization of that of a *state-determined* system (see Ross Ashby, *Design for a Brain* (London: Chapman and Hall, 1952)) to allow for systems in which the relation between change and current state is stochastic rather than deterministic.

way to a given engine speed; that is, their arm angles will pass through exactly the same sequences of positions over time. These two concrete systems share an abstract structure in their behavior. This structure can be distilled out, and its general properties studied, independently of any particular mechanical device. This mathematical structure is an example of an abstract state-dependent system. Generally speaking, concrete systems belong to the real world; they exist in time, and have states that change over time. Abstract systems, on the other hand, exist only in the timeless and changeless realm of pure mathematical form. They can be regarded as having three components: a set of entities (for example, the real numbers) constituting "states"; a set (for example, the integers) corresponding to points of "time," and a rule of evolution which pairs states with times to form sequences or trajectories. Thus, even if no centrifugal governor had ever been invented, mathematicians could study the abstract state-dependent system (or rather, family of systems)

$$\left\langle R^2,\ R,\ \frac{d^2\theta}{dt^2} = (n\omega)^2 \cos\theta \sin\theta - \frac{g}{l}\sin\theta - r\frac{d\theta}{dt} \right\rangle$$

where $(\theta,\ d\theta/dt)$ picks out points in $R^2$ (two dimensional Euclidean space) and the differential equation determines sequences of such points.

Abstract state-dependent systems can be realized ("made real") by particular parts (sets of aspects) of the real, physical world, as when a particular centrifugal governor realizes the abstract system just specified. An abstract system is realized by some part of the world when we can systematically classify its states (for example, by measurement) such that the sequences of states the concrete system undergoes is found to replicate the sequences specified by the abstract model. In fact, in order to count as a system at all, any concrete object must realize some abstract system or other (but not vice versa).

Now, when cognitive scientists come to study cognitive systems, whose basic nature is a matter for empirical investigation, they often proceed by providing models. Generally speaking, a model is another entity which is either better understood already, or somehow more amenable to exploration, and which is similar in relevant respects to the explanatory target. Scientific models are either concrete objects, or—more commonly—abstract mathematical entities; very often, they can be understood as state-dependent systems. If a model is sufficiently good, then we suppose that it somehow captures the nature of the explanatory target. What does this mean? Well, if the model is an abstract state-dependent system, then we suppose that the target system realizes the abstract system, or one relevantly like it. If the model is a concrete system, then we suppose that the model and the target system are systems of the same kind, in the sense that they both realize the same abstract system (or relevantly similar systems). Thus, even when providing a concrete model, what the scientist is really interested in determining is the abstract structure in the behavior of the target system.

There is a vast range of abstract state-dependent systems. Schools of thought which differ over the nature of cognition can be seen as differing over which of these abstract systems are realized by cognitive systems; or, put differently, as differing over *where* in the range of all possible systems the best models of cognition are to be found. So we can understand everyone as agreeing that cognitive systems are state-dependent systems of some kind, but as disagreeing as to which more particular category of state-dependent systems they belong. As will be explained below, this disagreement by no means exhausts the differences between the various schools of thought. Their differing commitments as to the relevant category of systems do, however, constitute a kind of core difference, around which their other differences can be organized.

1. *The computational hypothesis.* In one of the most well-known presentations of the computational conception of cognition, Newell and Herbert Simon[12] hypothesized that "physical symbol systems contain the necessary and sufficient means for general intelligent action," where a physical symbol system is "a machine that produces through time an evolving collection of symbol structures." Bearing this in mind, as well as other well-known characterizations of essentially the same target (for example, John Haugeland's definition of computers as interpreted automatic formal sytems, and various paradigm examples of computational systems such as Turing machines, pocket calculators, and classic AI systems such as Newell and Simon's GPS, Terry Winograd's SHRDLU, and Doug Lenat's CYC)[13] we can characterize the computational subcategory of state-dependent systems as follows: (ab-

[12] "Computer Science as Empirical Inquiry: Symbols and Search," in Haugeland, ed., *Mind Design* (Cambridge: MIT, 1981): pp. 35–66, here p. 40.
[13] See Haugeland, *Artificial Intelligence: The Very Idea* (Cambridge: MIT, 1985); Newell and Simon, "GPS, A Program That Simulates Human Thought," in E.A. Feigenbaum and J. Feldman, eds., *Computers and Thought* (New York: McGraw-Hill, 1963); Terry Winograd, *Understanding Natural Language* (New York: Academic, 1972); D.B. Lenat and R.V. Guha, *Building Large Knowledge-based Systems: Representation and Inference in the CYC Project* (Reading, MA: Addison-Wesley, 1990).

stract) computational systems are abstract state-dependent systems whose states are constituted in part by configurations of symbol types, whose time set is the integers (or some equivalent set), and whose rule of evolution specifies sequences of such configurations. A concrete computational system—a computer—is any system realizing an abstract computational system. In order to realize such a system, some chunk of the actual world must realize the sequences of configurations of symbol types specified by the abstract system. This means that, at any given time, it must contain an appropriate configuration of *tokens* of the symbol types, and it must change sequentially from one such configuration to another in accordance with the rule of evolution.

For example, consider a particular abstract Turing machine, Minsky's four symbol, seven head-state universal Turing machine defined by the following machine table:[14]

|   | 1 | 2 | 3 | 4 | 5 | 6 | 7 |
|---|---|---|---|---|---|---|---|
| Y | _L1 | _L1 | YL3 | YL4 | YR5 | YR6 | _R7 |
| _ | _L1 | YR2 | HALT | YR5 | YL3 | AL3 | YR6 |
| 1 | 1L2 | AR2 | AL3 | 1L7 | AR5 | AR6 | 1R7 |
| A | 1L1 | YR6 | 1L4 | 1L4 | 1R5 | 1R6 | _R2 |

This table dictates the specific symbol manipulations that take place in the machine. (Thus, the first square tells us that, if the head is currently in state 1 and the symbol in the cell over which the head is positioned is a 'Y', then change that symbol to a "_" (blank), move left, and "change" head state to state 1.) This machine constitutes the abstract state-dependent system, represented

$$< \{<s, p, h>\}, I, F>$$

where each total state of the system at a given time is itself a triple made up of a configuration of symbol types $s$ (corresponding to the contents of the entire tape), a head position with respect to that configuration ($p$), and a head state ($h$). The rule of evolution $F$ specifies sequences of total states of the system by specifying what the next (or successor) total state will be given the current total state; hence an appropriate time set for this system is the integers ($I$). $F$ is essentially equivalent to the machine table above, though the machine table specifies local manipulations rather than transformations from one total state to another. The rule can be obtained by reformulation of the machine table; the result is simple in form but too ungainly to be

---

[14] See Marvin Minsky, *Computation: Finite and Infinite Machines* (Englewood Cliffs, NJ: Prentice-Hall, 1967).

worth laying out here.[15] Note that a computation, from this perspective, is a sequence of transitions from one total state of the computational system to another; or, in other words, a matter of *touring* the system's symbolic state space.

A general form of the computational hypothesis, then, is that cognitive systems such as people are computational systems in the sense just defined, and that cognition is the behavior of such systems, that is, sequences of configurations of symbols. An alternative form is that for any given cognitive process, the best model of that process will be drawn from the computational subcategory of systems.

Although, as mentioned above, their primary interest is in the abstract structure of the target phenomenon, for various reasons researchers in this approach standardly provide a concrete model: an actual computer programmed so that (hopefully) it realizes the same (or a relevantly similar) abstract computational system as is realized by the cognitive systems under study. If the concrete model appears able to perform actual cognitive tasks in much the way people do, then the hypothesis that people are such systems is supported. One reason to provide a concrete model is that the abstract systems themselves are too complex to be studied by purely analytical means. In order to determine whether the model has the right properties, the theorist lets a concrete version run from a variety of starting points (initial conditions), and observes its behavior. Another reason for providing a concrete model is that, given the complexity of the abstract systems, it is very difficult actually to discover that structure except through an iterative procedure of constructing a concrete model, testing it, making improvements, and so on.

2. *The dynamical hypothesis.* Recall that one suggestion coming out of the discussion of the centrifugal governor was that an interesting alternative to the computational conception is that cognitive systems may be *dynamical* systems. In order to characterize this position as an alternative within the current framework, we need a definition of dynamical systems as a subcategory of state-dependent systems, a definition which is as useful as possible in clarifying differences among various approaches to the study of cognition.

The centrifugal governor is a paradigm example of a dynamical system. Perhaps the most pertinent contrast between it and the computational governor is that the states through which it evolves are not configurations of symbols but rather numerically measurable

---

[15] See Marco Giunti, *Computers, Dynamical Systems, Phenomena and the Mind*, Ph.D. Dissertation (Indiana University, 1991).

arm angles and rates of change of arm angle. Generalizing this feature, and, of course, looking over the shoulder at other textbook examples of dynamical systems and the kind of systems that are employed by dynamicists in cognitive science, we can define dynamical systems as state-dependent systems whose states are numerical (in the abstract case, these will be numbers, vectors, etc.; in the concrete case, numerically measurable quantities) and whose rule of evolution specifies sequences of such numerical states.

The rule of evolution in the case of the centrifugal governor was a differential equation. In general, a differential equation is any equation involving a function and one or more of its derivatives; informally, for current purposes, it can be thought of as an equation that tells you the instantaneous rate of change of some aspect of the system as a function of the current state of other aspects of the system. Since our interest is in cognition as processes that occur in time, we assume that the function is one of time (for example, $\theta(t)$) and that any derivative involved is with respect to time (for example, $d\theta/dt$). Because differential equations involve derivatives, they presuppose continuity; hence the "time" set in an abstract dynamical system is standardly $R$, the real numbers. Dynamical systems governed by differential equations are a particularly interesting and important subcategory, not least because of their central role in the history of science.[16] But dynamical systems in the general sense just defined might also be governed by difference equations, which specify the state of the system at time $t + 1$ in terms of its state at time $t$:

$$s_{t+1} = F(s_t)$$

and determine sequences of states, or trajectories, by repeated application or iteration. The "time" set for abstract systems defined by difference equations is standardly the integers. For example, one of the most-studied families of dynamical systems is that defined by the difference equation known as the logistic map.[17]

$$<R,\ I,\ x_{t+1} = ax_t(1 - x_t)>$$

where $a$ is a parameter; each possible value of $a$ makes the rule different and hence defines a distinct system.

A concrete dynamical system, of course, is any concrete system that realizes an abstract dynamical system. The realization relation-

[16] See M. Hirsch, "The Dynamical Systems Approach to Differential Equations," *Bulletin of the American Mathematical Society*, XI (1984): 1–64.

[17] For extensive discussion, see R.L. Devaney, *An Introduction to Chaotic Dynamical Systems* (Menlo Park, CA: Cummings, 1986).

ship here is quite different than in the computational case, however. Rather than configurations of tokens of symbol types, the concrete dynamical system is made up of quantities changing in a way that corresponds to the numerical sequences specified by the rule of evolution. This correspondence is set up by measuring the quantities, that is, by using some yardstick to assign a number to each quantity at any given point in time. For example, in the case of the centrifugal governor we set up a correspondence between the actual device and the abstract mathematical system by using the "degrees" yardstick to assign a number (for example, 45) to the angle of the arm at each point in time.

The dynamical hypothesis in cognitive science, then, is the exact counterpart to the computational hypothesis: cognitive systems such as people are *dynamical* systems in the sense just laid out, and cognition is state-space evolution in such systems. Alternatively, dynamicists are committed to the claim that the best model of any given cognitive process will turn out to be drawn from the dynamical subcategory of state-dependent systems.

As in the computational case, although the theorist's primary goal is to identify the relevant abstract structure, it is often necessary in practice to explore particular concrete models. It tends to be difficult, however, to set up and explore the behavior of a concrete dynamical system with the right properties. Fortunately, there is a convenient alternative: program (that is, physically configure) a computer (a concrete computational system) so that it produces sequences of symbol-configurations which *represent* points in the state trajectories of the abstract dynamical model under consideration. In such a situation, the computer does not itself constitute a model of the cognitive process, since it does not contain numerically measurable aspects changing over time in the way that aspects of the target system are hypothesized to be changing. That is, the computer does not realize the abstract dynamical model; rather, it *simulates* it.

3. *The connectionist hypothesis.* Broadly speaking, connectionists in cognitive science are those who try to understand cognition using connectionist models, which are typically characterized along something like the following lines:

Connectionist models are large networks of simple parallel computing elements, each of which carries a numerical *activation value* which it computes from the values of neighboring elements in the network, using some simple numerical formula. The network elements, or *units*, influence each other's values through connections that carry a numerical strength, or *weight*. The influence of each unit $i$ on unit $j$ is the activation value of unit $i$ times the strength of the connection from $i$ to $j$.[18]

In order to comprehend connectionism within the current framework, we need to characterize connectionist models as a particular subcategory of state-dependent systems. It is clear from the description just given, however, that all connectionist models are dynamical systems in the sense of the previous section. If the network has $n$ neural units, then the state of the system at any given time is just an $n$-dimensional vector of activation values, and the behavior of the network is a sequence of such vectors determined by the equations that update unit activation values. There are, of course, innumerable variations on this basic structure, and much connectionist work consists in exploring such variations in order to find a good model of some particular cognitive phenomenon.

Why then is connectionism not simply the same thing as the dynamical conception? There are two reasons, one discussed in this section, the other in the next. The first is that connectionist models are only a particular subcategory of the wider class of dynamical systems. The core connectionist hypothesis, that the best model of any given cognitive process will be a connectionist model, is thus best regarded as a more specific version of the wider dynamical hypothesis. There are plenty of dynamical systems that are *not* connectionist networks, and plenty of dynamicists in cognitive science who are not connectionists (for example, Busemeyer and Townsend in the work described above).

What then makes a dynamical system a connectionist system? Roughly, it should conform to the Smolensky characterization above. What this means in terms of species of dynamical state-dependent systems can be seen by examining a typical connectionist system, and noting those basic features which contrast with, for example, the centrifugal governor or the MOT model. Connectionist researchers Sven Anderson and Robert Port[19] used the following quite typical abstract connectionist dynamical system as a model of certain aspects of auditory pattern recognition:

$$\left\langle R^n, R, \frac{dy_i}{dt} = -\tau_i y_i(t) + \frac{1}{1 + e - \left( \sum_j w_{ij} y_j + I_i(t) + \theta_i \right)} \right\rangle$$

[18] Paul Smolensky, "On the Proper Treatment of Connectionism," *Behavioral and Brain Sciences*, XI (1988): 1–74, here p. 1.

[19] "A Network Model of Auditory Pattern Recognition," *Technical Report* XI (Indiana University Cognitive Science Program, 1990).

The network had $n$ neural units, each with a real activation value $y_i$. Hence its states were points in an $n$-dimensional space of real numbers, that is, elements of $R^n$; its time set was $R$, and its evolution equation was the differential equation given (in schema form) above, which specifies the instantaneous rate of change in each $y_i$ as a function of its current value, a decay parameter $(\tau_i)$, the activation of other units $(y_j)$, the connection weights $(w_{ij})$, any external input $(I_i)$, and a threshold or bias term $(\theta_i)$. For current purposes it is not necessary fully to understand this "simple numerical formula" or the behavior of the system as a whole. Of significance here are three closely related properties of connectionist systems that it illustrates. Connectionist systems are typically:

*High-dimensional*: connectionist networks standardly contain tens, or even hundreds or more, of neural units, each corresponding to a dimension of the state space. This makes them considerably larger in dimension than systems found in many other standard dynamical investigations in cognitive science, other sciences such as physics, and pure mathematics.

*Homogeneous*: connectionist networks are homogenous in the sense that they are made up of units that all have basically the same form; or, as Randy Beer has put the point, which are just parametric variations on a common theme. Thus, in the system above, a single equation schema suffices to describe the behavior of every unit in the network, with just the particular parameter values being specific to each unit.

*"Neural"*: connectionist systems are made up of units which are connected with others and which adjust their activation as a function of their total input, that is, of the summed weighted activations of other units. This structural property is reflected in the form of the evolution equations for connectionist models. Thus, the connectionist equation schema above includes the term $\Sigma w_{ij} y_j$ which stands for the summed input to a unit. The defining equations of connectionist systems always include a term of this general kind.

None of these properties obtains in the case of the centrifugal governor, nor in the case of the MOT model described above; both, therefore, count as good examples of nonconnectionist dynamical systems.

4. *Hypotheses and worldviews.* Thus far, the differences between the computationalist, dynamicist, and connectionist conceptions of cognition have been described simply in terms of differing commitments as to where in the space of state-dependent systems the best models of cognition are likely to be found. Yet each of these ap-

proaches is much more richly textured than this implies; they can and should be compared and contrasted in other ways as well.

At this point, the discussion of schools of thought in cognitive science connects with the earlier discussion of the governing problem. Recall that one suggestion emerging there was that cognitive systems may in fact be more similar to the centrifugal governor than to the computational governor. Recall also that the two kinds of governor were found to contrast at two distinct "levels"—that of basic properties (representation, computation, cyclic, etc.) and that of relevant conceptual framework; and that there was a kind of natural fit between these levels. It turns out that this fit is really three-way: if you have a computational state-dependent system, it naturally implements a system that is representational, sequential, cyclic, homuncular, and so on, and the most appropriate conceptual framework to bring to bear on a system that is computational at both these levels is, of course, that of computer science and mainstream computational cognitive science. Computationalists in cognitive science do not merely select models from a particular region of the space of abstract state-dependent systems; they also make strong presuppositions about the basic overall structure of cognitive systems and they use corresponding tools in thinking about how cognitive systems work.

In other words, taking cognitive systems to be state-dependent systems that proceed from one configuration of symbols to the next is part and parcel of a general vision of the nature of cognitive systems. For computationalists, the cognitive system is basically the brain, which is a kind of control unit located inside a body which in turn is located in an external environment. The cognitive system interacts with the outside world via its more direct interaction with the body. Interaction with the environment is handled by sensory and motor transducers, whose function is to translate between the purely physical events in the body and the environment and the symbolic states that are the medium of cognitive processing. The sense organs convert physical stimulation into elementary symbolic representations of events in the body and in the environment, and the motor system converts symbolic specifications of actions into movements of the muscles. Cognitive episodes take place in a cyclic and sequential fashion; first there is sensory input to the cognitive system, then the cognitive system algorithmically manipulates symbols, coming up with an output which then causes movement of the body; then the whole cycle then begins again. Internally, the cognitive system has a modular, hierarchical construction; at the highest level, there are modules corresponding to vision, language, planning, and so on, and each of these modules breaks down into simpler modules for more elementary tasks. Each module replicates in basic structure the cognitive system as a whole; thus, they take symbolic representations as inputs, algorithmically manipulate those representations, and deliver a symbolic specification as output. Note that because the cognitive system traffics only in symbolic representations, the human body and the physical environment can be dropped from consideration; it is possible to study the cognitive system as an autonomous, bodiless, and worldless system whose function is to transform input representations into output representations.

In short, in the computational vision, cognitive systems are the computational governor writ large. Of course, there are innumerable variants on the basic computational picture; any one might diverge from the standard picture in some respects, but still remain generically computational in nature (for example, symbolic models that utilize some measure of parallel processing).

The dynamical conception of cognition likewise involves interdependent commitments at three distinct levels, but stands opposed to the computational conception in almost every respect. The core dynamical hypothesis—that the best models of any given cognitive process will specify sequences, not of configurations of symbol types, but rather of numerical states—goes hand in hand with a conception of cognitive systems not as devices that transform symbolic inputs into symbolic outputs but rather as complexes of continuous, simultaneous, and mutually determining change, for which the tools of dynamical modeling and dynamical systems theory are most appropriate. In this vision, the cognitive system is not just the encapsulated brain; rather, since the nervous system, body, and environment are all constantly changing and simultaneously influencing each other, the true cognitive system is a single unified system embracing all three. The cognitive system does not interact with the body and the external world by means of the occasional static symbolic inputs and outputs; rather, interaction between the inner and the outer is best thought of as a matter of coupling, such that both sets of processes continually influencing each other's direction of change. At the level at which the mechanisms are best described, cognitive processing is not sequential and cyclic, for all aspects of the cognitive system are undergoing change all the time. Any sequential character in cognitive performance is the high-level, overall trajectory of change in a system whose rules of evolution specify not sequential change but rather simultaneous mutual coevolution.

Where does connectionism fit into all this? Perched somewhere in the middle. Recall that connectionist models are dynamical systems, but that there are reasons not simply to assimilate the connectionist and dynamical conceptions. The first was that connectionist models are really a quite specific kind of dynamical system. What we can now add is that although many connectionists are thoroughly dynamical in their general vision of the nature of cognitive systems, many others attempt to combine their connectionist dynamical substrates with an overall conception of the nature of cognitive systems which owes more to the computational worldview. Thus, consider "good old fashioned connectionism": standard, layered-network back-propagation connectionism of the kind that became fashionable with the well-known 1986 volumes. A classic exemplar is David Rumelhart and James McClelland's[20] past-tense learning model. In this kind of work, underlying systems that are basically dynamical in nature are configured so as sequentially to transform static input representations into output representations. They retain much of the basic structure of the computational picture, changing some ingredients (in particular, the nature of the representations) but retaining others. Connectionism of this kind can be regarded as having taken up a half-way house between the computational and dynamical conceptions, combining ingredients from both in what may well turn out to be an unstable mixture. If this is right, we should expect as time goes on that such connectionist models will increasingly give way either to implementations of generically computational conceptions of cognition, or to models that are more thoroughly dynamical.

### VII. IS THE DYNAMICAL CONCEPTION VIABLE?

In order soundly to refute the "what else could it be?" argument, a proposed alternative must be viable, that is, plausible enough that it is reasonably deemed an open empirical question whether the orthodox approach, or the alternative, is the more correct.

One measure of the viability of an approach is whether valuable research can be carried out within its terms. On this measure, the dynamical approach is certainly in good health. Dynamical theories and models have been or are being developed of a very wide range of aspects of cognitive functioning, from (so-called) low-level or peripheral aspects such as brain function, perception, and motor control, to (so-called) central or higher aspects such as language and

---

[20] "On Learning the Past Tenses of English Verbs," in McClelland and Rumelhart, eds., *Parallel Distributed Processing: Explorations in the Microstructure of Cognition, Volume II: Psychological and Biological Models* (Cambridge: MIT, 1986), pp. 216–68.

decision making, and through to related areas such as psychiatry and social psychology. As already mentioned, a good deal of connectionist work falls under the dynamical banner, and this work alone would qualify the dynamical approach as worth taking seriously. But there are nonconnectionist dynamical models of numerous aspects of cognition, and their ranks are swelling. In a number of fields under the broader umbrella of cognitive science, dynamics provides the dominant formal framework within which particular theories and models are developed: these include neural modeling, autonomous agent ("animat") research, ecological psychology, and, increasingly, developmental psychology.[21]

Of course, it is quite possible that a research program is flourishing, and yet there be deep reasons why it will eventually prove inadequate, either in general or with respect to particular aspects of cognition. (Consider behaviorism in its hey-day, for example.) In evaluating the plausibility of an alternative, we should also consider whether there are known *general* considerations that either strongly support—or, perhaps more importantly, stand opposed to—that approach.

Many considerations have been raised in favor of the computational conception of cognition, and, given the deep differences between the approaches, each might appear to constitute an argument against the dynamical alternative. It is not possible adequately to address all (or even any) such arguments here, but I shall briefly comment on two of the most powerful, in order to reveal not the weakness but rather something of the potential of the dynamical approach.

Cognition is distinguished from other kinds of complex natural processes (such as thunderstorms, subatomic processes, etc.) by at

---

[21] Rather than cite individual examples, I merely list here some overviews or collections that the interested reader can use as a bridge into the extensive realm of dynamical research on cognition. A broad sampling of current research is contained in *Mind as Motion: Explorations in the Dynamics of Cognition*; this book contains guides to a much larger literature. An excellent illustration of the power and scope of dynamical research, in a neural network guise, is S. Grossberg, ed., *Neural Networks and Natural Intelligence* (Cambridge: MIT, 1988). R. Serra and G. Zanarini, *Complex Systems and Cognitive Processes* (Berlin: Springer, 1990) presents an overview of a variety of dynamical systems approaches in artificial intelligence research. For the role of dynamics in developmental psychology, see Esther Thelen and Linda Smith, *A Dynamics Systems Approach to the Development of Cognition and Action* (Cambridge: MIT, 1993) and *Dynamic Systems in Development: Applications* (Cambridge: MIT, 1993). Hermann Haken, *Synergetic Computers and Cognition: A Top-down Approach to Neural Nets* (Berlin: Springer, 1991) provides an introduction and overview to the "synergetic" form of the dynamical approach.

least two deep features: on one hand, a dependence on knowledge; and distinctive kinds of complexity, as manifested most clearly in the structural complexity of natural languages. One challenge for cognitive scientists is to understand how a physical system might exhibit these features.

The usual approach to explaining the dependence on knowledge is to suppose that the system contains internal structures that represent that knowledge. Further, the most powerful known way of doing this is to use symbolic representations, manipulated by some computational system. Insofar as the dynamical approach abjures representation completely, or offers some less powerful representational substitute, it may seem doomed.

While the centrifugal governor is clearly a nonrepresentational dynamical system, and while it was argued above that representation figures in a natural cluster of deep features that are jointly characteristic of computational models, in fact there is nothing preventing dynamical systems from incorporating some form of representation; indeed, an exciting feature of the dynamical approach is that it offers opportunities for dramatically reconceiving the nature of representation in cognitive systems, even within a broadly noncomputational framework. A common strategy in dynamical modeling is to assign representational significance to some or all of the state variables or parameters (for example, see the Townsend and Busemeyer decision field theory model described above, or consider a connectionist network in which units stand for features of the domain). While representations of this kind may be exactly what is needed for some cognitive modeling purposes, they do not have the kind of combinatorial structure that is often thought necessary for other aspects of high-level cognition. Within the conceptual repertoire of dynamics, however, there is a vast range of entities and structures that might be harnessed into representational roles; individual state variables and parameters are merely the simplest of them. For example, it is known how to construct representational schemes in which complex contents (such as linguistic structures) are assigned in a recursive manner to points in the state space of a dynamical system, such that the representations form a fractal structure of potentially infinite depth, and such that the behavior of the system can be seen as transforming representations in ways that respect the represented structure.[22] Yet even these methods are doing little more than dipping a toe into the pool of possibilities. For ex-

[22] See, for example, Jordan Pollack, "Recursive Distributed Representations," *Artificial Intelligence*, XLVI (1990): 77–105.

ample, representations can be trajectories or attractors of various kinds, or even such exotica as transformations of attractor arrangements as a system's control parameters change.[23] Dynamicists are actively exploring how these and other representational possibilities might be incorporated into cognitive models, without buying the rest of the computational worldview. Consequently, while the dynamical approach is certainly a long way from having actual solutions to most concrete problems of knowledge representation, it clearly holds sufficient promise to maintain its current viability as an alternative.

What, then, about arguments that are based on the distinctive complexity of human cognition? Perhaps the most common, and probably the most persuasive argument of this kind focuses on the complexity of sentences of natural language. It begins from the observation that any proficient language user can understand and produce an effectively unbounded number of distinct sentences, and proceeds to note that these sentences can manifest phenomena such as repeated embedding and dependencies over arbitrarily long distances. If we attempt to describe languages with this kind of complexity by means of a grammar (a finite set of rules for combining a finite set of primitive elements into complex structures), we find they can only be compactly specified by grammars more powerful than so-called "regular" or "phrase-structure" grammars. If we then ask what kind of computational device is capable of following the rules of these grammars to recognize or produce such sentences, the answer is that they can only be implemented on machines more powerful than finite-state machines, such as push-down automata or linear-bounded automata. Therefore, human cognitive systems must be one of these more powerful computational systems.

A crucial question, then, is whether there is reason to believe that dynamical systems, with their numerical states and rules of evolution defined over them, are capable of exhibiting this order of complexity in behavior. The investigation of the "computational" power of dynamical systems, especially in the form of neural networks, is a relatively new topic, but there is already a sizable literature and results available indicate a positive answer. For example, J. P. Crutchfield and K. Young[24] have studied the complexity of the behavior in cer-

---

[23] See, for example, Jean Petitot, "Morphodynamics and Attractor Syntax," in *Mind as Motion: Explorations in the Dynamics of Cognition.*
[24] See J.P. Crutchfield and K. Young, "Computation at the Onset of Chaos," in W.H. Zurek, ed., *Complexity, Entropy, and the Physics of Information, SFI Studies in the Sciences of Complexity, Volume VIII* (Reading, MA: Addison-Wesley, 1990).

tain nonlinear dynamical systems "at the edge of chaos" (that is, at settings of parameters close to those settings which would produce genuinely chaotic behavior). If passing through a particular region of the state space is counted as producing a symbol, then allowing the system to run produces a sequence of symbols. It turns out that the complexity of these sequences is such that describing them requires an indexed context-free grammar. This means that the system is producing behavior of the same broad order of complexity as many believe natural language to possess.

Similarly, Jordan Pollack[25] has studied the ability of connectionist dynamical systems to recognize languages (that is, to indicate whether or not any given sequence belongs to the language). In his networks, the system bounces around its numerical state space under the influence of successive inputs corresponding to symbols in the sequence to be recognized. A well-formed sequence is regarded as successfully recognized if the system ends up in a particular region after exposure to the whole sentence, while ending up in some other region for non-well-formed sequences. Pollack (among others) has found that there are networks that can recognize nonregular languages, and in fact can learn to have this ability, via a novel form of induction in language learning, involving bifurcations in system dynamics which occur as the weights in the network gradually change.

More generally, it is clear that nonlinear dynamical systems can not only match but exceed the complexity of behavior of standard computational systems such as Turing machines.[26] Of course, this alone by no means establishes that cognitive systems are, or are more likely to be, dynamical systems than computational systems. It does establish that the dynamical approach is not automatically ruled out by these kinds of complexity considerations. What kind of system humans in fact are is therefore a question only to be resolved by means of patient and detailed modeling.

So much for defenses of viability. What positive reasons are there to think that the dynamical approach is actually on the right track? Again, space does not allow serious treatment of these arguments, but some are at least worth mentioning. In practice, an important part of the appeal of the dynamical approach is that it brings to the study of cognition tools that have proved so extraordinarily success-

---

[25] "The Induction of Dynamical Recognizers," *Machine Learning*, VII (1991): 227–52.

[26] See, for example, Hava Siegelmann and Eduardo Sontag, "Analog Computation via Neural Networks," *Theoretical Computer Science*, CXXX, 1 (1994): 331–60.

ful in so many other areas of science. But what is there about *cognition*, in particular, which suggests that it will be best understood dynamically?

One central fact about natural cognitive processes is that they always happen *in time*, which means not merely that, like any physical process including ordinary digital computation, they occupy some extent of actual time, but that details of *timing* (durations, rates, rhythms, etc.) are critical to a system that operates in a real body and environment. As we saw above, dynamics is all about describing how processes happen in time, while computational models are inherently limited in this respect. Cognition also has other general features for which a dynamical approach appears particularly well-suited. For example, it is a kind of complex behavioral organization that is emergent from the local interactions of very large numbers of (relatively) simple and homogenous elements. It is pervaded by both continuous and discrete forms of change. At every level, it involves multiple, simultaneous, interacting processes. Dynamics is a natural framework for developing theories that account for such features. Further, that within which cognition takes place (the brain, the body, and the environment) demand dynamical tools in their description. A dynamical account of cognition promises to minimize difficulties in understanding how cognitive systems are real biological systems in constant, intimate dependence on, or interaction with, their surrounds.[27]

A final way to underpin the viability of the dynamical conception is to place it and the computational conception in broad historical perspective. Computationalism, as cognitive science orthodoxy, amounts to a sophisticated instantiation of the basic outlines of a generically Cartesian picture of the nature of mind. Conversely, the prior grip that this Cartesian picture has on how most people think about mind and cognition makes the computational conception intuitively attractive to many people. This would be unobjectionable if the Cartesian conception was basically sound. But the upshot of philosophical evaluation of the Cartesian framework over the last three centuries, and especially this century, is that it seriously misconceives mind and its place in nature. Cognitive scientists tend to suppose that the primary respect in which Descartes was wrong about mind was in subscribing to an interactionist dualism, that is, that doctrine that mind and body are two distinct substances that

---

[27] For more detailed treatment of these and other arguments, see Port and my "It's about Time: An Overview of the Dynamical Approach to Cognition," in *Mind as Motion: Explorations in the Dynamics of Cognition.*

causally interact with one another. Already by the eighteenth century, however, the inadequacy of this particular aspect of Cartesianism had been repeatedly exposed, and thoroughgoing brain-based materialisms had been espoused by philosophers such as Thomas Hobbes and Julien Offray de La Mettrie. Some of the greatest achievements of twentieth-century philosophy of mind have been the exposing of various other, more subtle, pervasive, and pernicious epistemological and ontological misconceptions inherent in the Cartesian picture. These misconceptions are very often retained even when substance dualism is rejected in favor of some brain-based materialism, such as functionalism in its various guises.

For current purposes, one of the most important anti-Cartesian movements is the one spearheaded by Gilbert Ryle in Anglo-American philosophy and Martin Heidegger in "continental" philosophy.[28] Its target has been the generically Cartesian idea that mind is an inner realm of representations and processes, and that mind conceived this way is the causal underpinning of our intelligent behavior. This movement comprises at least three major components, all intimately interrelated. The first is a relocating of mind. The Cartesian tradition is mistaken in supposing that mind is an inner entity of any kind, whether mind-stuff, brain states, or whatever. Ontologically, mind is much more a matter of what we *do* within environmental and social possibilities and bounds. Twentieth-century anti-Cartesianism thus draws much of mind out, and in particular outside the skull. The second component is a reconceiving of our fundamental relationship to the world around us. In the Cartesian framework, the basic stance of mind toward the world is one of representing and thinking about it, with occasional, peripheral, causal interaction via perception and action. It has been known since Bishop Berkeley that this framework had fundamental epistemological problems. It has been a more recent achievement to show that escaping these epistemological problems means reconceiving the human agent as essentially embedded in, and skillfully coping with, a changing world; and that representing and thinking about the world is secondary to and dependent upon such embeddedness.[29] The third component is an attack on the supposition that the kind of behaviors we exhibit (such that we are embedded in our world and can

---

[28] See Ryle, *The Concept of Mind* (Chicago: University Press, 1984); Heidegger, *Being and Time*, John Macquarrie and Edward Robinson, trans. (New York: Harper, 1962); and Hubert Dreyfus, *Being-in-the-World: A Commentary on Heidegger's* Being and Time, *Division 1* (Cambridge: MIT, 1991).

[29] See Charles Guignon, *Heidegger and the Problem of Knowledge* (Indianapolis: Hackett, 1983).

be said to have minds) could ever be causally explained utilizing only the generically Cartesian resources of representations, rules, procedures, algorithms, and so on. A fundamental Cartesian mistake is, as Ryle variously put it, to suppose that practice is accounted for by theory; that knowledge how is explained in terms of knowledge that; or that skill is a matter of thought. That is, not only is mind not to be found wholly inside the skull; cognition, the inner causal underpinning of mind, is not to be explained in terms of the basic entities of the Cartesian conception of mind.

My concern here is not to substantiate these claims or the post-Cartesian conception of the person to which they point;[30] it is simply to make the computational conception of cognition seem less than inevitable by pointing out that serious doubt has been cast upon the philosophical framework in which it is embedded. Orthodox computational cognitive science has absorbed some of the important lessons of seventeenth-century reactions to Cartesianism, but so far has remained largely oblivious to the more radical twentieth-century critiques. Conversely, if we begin with a thoroughly post-Cartesian approach, the dynamical account of cognition will, in many ways, be immediately attractive. The post-Cartesian conception rejects the model of mind as an atemporal representer and, like the dynamical approach to cognition, emphasizes instead the ongoing, real-time interaction of the situated agent with a changing world. The post-Cartesian agent is essentially temporal, since its most basic relationship to the world is one of skillful coping; the dynamical framework is a therefore natural choice since it builds time in right from the very start. The post-Cartesian agent manages to cope with the world without necessarily representing it; a dynamical approach suggests how this might be possible by showing how the internal operation of a system interacting with an external world can be so subtle and complex as to defy description in representational terms—how, in other words, how cognition can *transcend* representation. In short, from the philosophical perspective that has managed to overcome the deep structures of the Cartesian world view, the dynamical approach looks distinctly appealing; the Watt governor is preferable to the Turing machine as a landmark for models of cognition.

TIM VAN GELDER

University of Melbourne

---

[30] Dreyfus, *What Computers* Still *Can't Do: A Critique of Artificial Reason* (Cambridge: MIT, 1992) is excellent in this regard.

# Radical Artificial Life: Some Trouble Spots

*Andy Clark* *
*Philosophy/Neuroscience/Psychology Program*
*Washington University in St Louis*
*St Louis 63105, USA*
andy@twinearth.wustl.edu

## Abstract

Has Cognitive Science reached a crucial conceptual juncture? Recent work in Dynamical Systems Theory (e.g. [1, 2]) and Artificial Life (e.g. [3]) claims to raise fundamental questions concerning the nature of internal representation and its role, if any, in a mature science of the mind. The emerging nexus of concerns looks set to fix the agenda for the most radical and innovative studies in the Philosophy of Cognitive Science of the coming decade (see e.g. [10]). Certain aspects of the Dynamical Systems/Artificial Life challenge, however, appear both problematic and less than crystal clear. In this short piece, I aim to highlight these murky areas, and to offer some preliminary critical responses. Despite these worries, I should stress at the outset that I believe the Dynamical Systems/Artificial Life research programme to be of the utmost interest and importance. For the notions upon which it is exerting such sustained and concrete pressure include some of the most fundamental yet least well understood ideas in the field.

I propose, then, to highlight and respond to just three issues:

1. The Coupling/Computation Distinction;

2. Representation and Intuitive Domain Decomposition;

3. Representational Interpretation Vs the Actual Existence of Internal Representations.

These issues all leak into one another, so the practice won't be as clean as the theory!

## 1 The Coupling/Computation Distinction

Environmental success, it is argued, largely depends on the appropriate coupling of complex dynamical systems (e.g. brain/body to local environment). But this coupling, it is then suggested, need not involve anything properly described as computation. Instead:

> Computational systems are properly viewed as special cases of dynamical systems more generally (namely, those whose internal states are systematically interpretable as referring to some semantic domain related to the system's function) whose relevance to autonomous agents in

general remains to be empirically demonstrated. Beer [2, p.39].

The reason for not depicting a given coupling as computation-dependent thus turns (in this passage) on the putative lack of semantic interpretability of the inner states of the target system. van Gelder [9] offers a slight twist on a similar argument, suggesting that even if we did cast the states of a delicately coupled system in representational terms we would nontheless often fail, using that vocabulary, to do justice to the full subtlety of the coupling.

The question whether a computational understanding is called for in a given case thus turns, it seems, on the questions:

- (a) whether there is any semantic interpretation of the states of the system available; and

- (b) whether a model of state-transitions defined over such (putative) representational structures is able to do justice to the full and fine-grained behaviours of the coupled system. (See also [2, p.40]).

The Computation Vs Coupling issue is thus really all about representation talk and its explanatory power. That seems correct, since there has to be a distinction between mere complex activity and computation, and it is hard to see in what else such a distinction might consist. So let's move on to look at representation.

## 2 Representation and Intuitive Domain De-composition

The radical Artificial Life/Dynamical Systems challenge depends, it seems to me, on a rather too rapid conflation of the notion of representation with notions of *explicit* representation, and of *familiar intuitive* representational contents. Thus both Beer [2] and Brooks [3] repeatedly stress that explicitly representing e.g. the environmental state may not constitute a fast, flexible means of engaging with that same environment. Such observations, however, do not rule out the kinds of fast, efficient coupling often achieved by neural network style solutions (e.g. P. M. Churchland's crab – see [4, ch.5]): solutions which are nonetheless recognised (e.g. [2, p.3]) as falling into a more generally representational camp.

But if *explicitness* of representation is not the real issue, what is? Beer is clear and to the point. He writes:

> I think that the notion of internal representation is best interpreted as an empirical hypothesis regarding the intelligibility of the organisation of an agent's internal dynamics. [2, p.39].

According to this story, then. it is the intelligibility of a system's internal dynamics *to us* that makes it the case that it does, or does not, rely on internal representations (and hence computation).

This is immediately discomforting for those of use (myself included) who are not inclined towards an in-principle anthropocentric understanding of the scope of notions like 'computation' and 'representation'. It seems to me fully intelligible to suppose that some sufficiently complex and alien system might *in fact* be engaging in the computational transformation of internal representations even though the content of such representational structures is way outside the ambit of humanly entertainable contents.

In addition, it remains unclear to what extent the notion of an 'intelligible inner organisation' is here identified with the rather narrower notion of an organisation which respects our initial *intuitions* concerning the semantic decomposition of a domain or of a task. Thus Beer writes that:

> I see no reason to expect the correspondence predicted by the representation hypothesis to be true in general. ... There is no ... requirement that we must find our own conceptualization of an agent's circumstances conveniently mirrored in its internal dynamics. [2, p.39].

There is no reason to suppose, however, that our finding certain internal states to be interpretable as bearing certain contents *depends on* our finding inner states which correlate with our initial intuitive understanding of the world. Neuroscience might conceivably identify groups of neurons which respond selectively to e.g. patterns which we had never previously regarded as in any way important or worth marking out. Connectionist networks might learn quite unexpected internal representations in order to perform a desired input-output mapping. In neither case does the ultimate fit with our initial conceptualization determine the *unintelligibility* of the internal organisation concerned.

In sum, neither explicitness nor fit with initial intuitions seems essential to the idea of an inner state being intelligible as a representational state. And it is not even clear that intelligibility to us (even once divorced from our initial intuitions) should be regarded as constitutive of an inner states being representational. Perhaps we could be warranted, on rather general scientific and observational grounds, in identifying a process as computational/representational while nontheless remaining forever ignorant of what, in detail, its representational content amounts to.

## 3  Representational Interpretation Vs the Actual Existence of Internal Representations

Here is a scenario which I find plausible. Cognitive Neuroscience marches on and identifies body upon body of neurons whose roles make some rough kind of sense to us; some circuits are said to represent properties such as *what* object is before us, others are said to help *locate* objects in space, still further circuits are said to perform control

operations, routeing and re-routeing signals around the brain and central nervous system, and so on and so on. (See e.g. [8]). In many cases, the interpretations of these states and processes fail to recapitulate our initial intuitions. But that, we saw, goes no way at all towards undermining their claim to representationality. Would such an unfolding of the cognitive scientific future vindicate a computational/representational vision against the radical Artificial Life/Dynamical Systems challenge?

The question is harder than it looks. For van Gelder (at least) does not deny the interpretability of system states as such. Instead his claim is that any such representational/computational description fails to do justice to the details of the rich couplings which (if the Dynamical System Theorist is correct) are the real source of adaptive success.

In a somewhat similar vein, Beer concedes both that advanced organisms will depend on lots of rich 'inner state' (they are not mere 'reactive systems' at the mercy of every environmental fluctuation), and that there will often be 'a principled relationship between an agent's sensory inputs and internal state on the one hand and its external behaviour on the other' [2, p.4]. Given this, it is clear that we could *depict* the inner states as representing and construct computer models of the processing involved. In fact, Beer explicitly allows as much, only pausing to add that:

> The mere fact that computational descriptions of autonomous agents are possible does not necessarily imply an underlying computational mechanism. Computer models of autonomous agents contain symbolic structures that represent theoretical entities *to the modeller*, while computational theories of autonomous agents claim that agents contain symbolic structures that represent their situation *to themselves*. [2, p.4, original emphasis].

Beer and van Gelder are thus agreed that the mere fact that rich inner states exist and can be given representational/computational interpretations is *not* sufficient to establish the correctness of a representational/computational understanding of mind. For Beer, this is because the designated symbolic structures may represent things only to the *modeller* and not to the system itself. For van Gelder, it is because the full story concerning the rich coupling between brain and world may not be capturable using *merely* the resources of a computational/representational theory and may instead require the putatively richer descriptive vocabulary of dynamical systems theory.

Both claims strike me as problematic. Beer's distinction between an inner state's having representational content for the modeller (only) and its having that content for the system itself is obscure. The full-blooded computational/representational approach is not *at all* committed to the existence of inner homunculi who read and understand the putatively representational inner items (see e.g.

[7]). But having given up on inner homunculi, there is no-one *except* the external modeller to whom the inner structures will *appear representational*. The system just *uses* the structures; they function within it in a purely causal way. To the extent that our (external, theoretic) best understanding of their cognitive role involves assigning representational contents to them, they are (it seems to me) as full-blooded and genuinely representational as any (non-homuncularist) adherent of a representational/computational theory of mind ever supposed.

van Gelder's claim is less obscure, but still hardly compelling. He simply *denies* that our (external, theoretic) best understanding of the brain/world coupling will be provided using the descriptive vocabulary of computation and representation. Using an example drawn from mechanics (the Watt Governor) he suggests that the subtle real-time interactions between two coupled dynamical systems may sometimes constitute richer, more intimately responsive and inter-connected problem solutions than a merely computational/representational description of the coupling could ever capture.

This is an important claim, and one I shall not confront head-on here. Instead, I would note only that *even if* that were true (and true as regards our understanding of the brain/world coupling in particular), it would not immediately follow that the computational/representational understanding was flawed or shallow, only that it was incomplete. It might be that certain aspects of the brain's engagement with the world are best understood in the terms van Gelder suggests while others positively require a computational/representational unpacking. Or that certain kinds of psychologically important generalization (e.g. concerning the logical structure of error profiles on a task) are best explained using a computational model, while others (e.g. errors of real-time response) require the pure dynamical system's perspective. In fact, van Gelder himself explicitly acknowledges just such a range of possibilities towards the end of his paper. The real issues thus become: first, just how *much* of cognition, as traditionally understood, requires a standard representational/computational understanding; and second, to what extent the very notion of internal representation may be capable of changing and evolving under the influence of these new perspectives. Both these issues are addressed at length in [6].

## 4  Conclusion

The Artificial Life/Dynamical Systems challenge is important but often overstated. There are two main reasons why this is so. First, it is too often assumed that demonstrating the poverty and/or unnecessaryness of highly classical representational solutions (involving e.g. explicit representations which are 'read' by a central processor and which exist as movable and re-creatable tokens in a type/token computational economy) is sufficient to undermine the representational/computationalist approach altogether. But in fact, as recent work in e.g. connectionism and neural networks (see e.g. [11, 5]) demonstrates, the space of representational/computational solutions is much larger and richer than the space of classical, read-and-write models. And second, it should not be assumed that all broadly-speaking cognitive phenomena will succumb to a single style of explanatory theorising. Some aspects of our fluent engagement with the world may indeed resist computational/representational explanation, while others may positively demand it.

From a philosophical perspective, the great virtue of these recent approaches lies in their ability to challenge received views of the nature and role of internal representation itself. But here, too, some caution is required. Anti-representationalist rhetoric is often confused about its target. Is it *explicit* representation, is it the interpretability of inner states or processes, or is it perhaps the idea of symbols which function as symbols *for the system* itself rather than for us? The last option is obscure (unless it is just another way of ruling out explicit, read-and-write computational models). The first is too narrow a target. The second would indeed be a *suitable* target, but interpretability is usually (and rightly) conceded by even radical anti-representationalists. So what *is* the claim, exactly?

The real challenge, perhaps, is for the fans of representationalism to now properly distinguish between:

- (a) *mere* interpretability; and

- (b) non-explicit but *genuine* representation.

Thus, as Beer points out, the behaviour of e.g. fluids, and planets, can be described by rule and symbol systems. But planets do not literally *compute* their orbits, nor fluids their flow. Superficially, this looks to be because the relevant rules are not *encoded* and *consulted* on the route to behaviour. But that only shows that planets and fluids do not use a read/write computational approach. Neither do most connectionist architectures. Yet we want to say that the connectionist solution is genuinely computational/representational (but inexplicit) whereas the planet/fluid case is non-computational and non-representational. The true thrust of the Artificial Life/Dynamical Systems challenge is, I believe, to force us to articulate and defend this intuitive distinction. And *that* will be a worthy legacy indeed.

## References

[1] R. Beer, *Intelligence as Adaptive Behavior: An experiment in Computational Neuroethology.* San Diego, CA: Academic Press, 1990.

[2] R. Beer, (to appear) A Dynamical Systems perspective on autonomous agents. in T. van Gelder (ed.) *Mind as Motion.* Cambridge, MA: MIT Press, in press.

[3] R. Brooks, Intelligence without representation *Artificial Intelligence* 47:139–59, 1991.

[4] P. M. Churchland, *A Neurocomputational Perspective*. Cambridge, MA: MIT Press, 1989.

[5] A. Clark, *Microcognition*. Cambridge, MA: MIT Press, 1989.

[6] A. Clark and J. Toribio. Doing Without Representing? *Synthese*, special issue on connectionism and the frontiers of artificial intelligence. Forthcoming.

[7] D. Dennett, *Brainstorms*. Cambridge, MA: MIT Press, 1981.

[8] D. van Essen, C. Anderson, and B. Olshausen, Dynamic routing strategies in sensory, motor and cognitive processing. In C. Koch and J. Davis (eds) *Large Scale Neuronal Theories of the Brain*. Cambridge, MA: MIT Press, in press.

[9] T. van Gelder, What might cognition be if not computation? In T. van Gelder (ed.) *Mind as Motion*. Cambridge, MA: MIT Press, in press.

[10] T. van Gelder, (ed.) *Mind as Motion*. Cambridge, MA: MIT Press, in press.

[11] J. McClelland and D. Rumelhart, editors, *Parallel Distributed Processing: Explorations in the Microstructure of Cognition*. Volumes I and II. Cambridge, MA: MIT Press, 1986.

# Autonomy and Artificiality

*Margaret A. Boden* *
*School of Cognitive and Computing Sciences,*
*University of Sussex, Brighton BN1 9QH, U.K.*
maggieb@cogs.susx.ac.uk

## Abstract

What science tells us about human autonomy is practically important, because it affects the way that ordinary people see themselves. Denials of one's ability for self-control are experiénced as threatening.

The sciences of the artificial (AI and A-Life) support two opposing intuitions concerning autonomy. One, characteristic of "classical" AI, is that determination of behaviour by the external environment lessens an agent's autonomy. The other, characteristic of A-Life and situated robotics, is that to follow a pre-conceived internal plan is to be a mere puppet (one can no longer say "a mere robot").

These intuitions can be reconciled, since autonomy is not an all-or-none property. Three dimensions of behavioural control are crucial: (1) The extent to which response to the environment is direct (determined only by the present state in the external world) or indirect (mediated by inner mechanisms partly dependent on the creature's previous history). (2) The extent to which the controlling mechanisms were self-generated rather than externally imposed. (3) The extent to which inner directing mechanisms can be reflected upon, and/or selectively modified. Autonomy is the greater, the more behaviour is directed by self-generated (and idiosyncratic) inner mechanisms, nicely responsive to the specific problem-situation, yet reflexively modifiable by wider concerns.

An A-Life worker has said: "The field of Artificial Life is unabashedly mechanistic and reductionist. However, this *new mechanism* ... is vastly different from the mechanism of the last century." One difference involves the emphasis on emergent properties. Even classical AI goes beyond what most think of as "machines". The "reductionism" of artificiality denies that the only respectable concepts lie at the most basic ontological level. AI and A-Life help us to understand how human autonomy is possible.

## 1   The Problem – And Why It Matters

Let us begin with a quotation – or, rather, several:

> For the many, there is hardly concealed discontent.... . "I'm a machine," says the spot welder. "I'm caged," says the bank teller, and echoes the hotel clerk. "I'm a mule," says the steel worker." "A monkey can do what I can do," says the receptionist. "I'm less than a farm implement," says the migrant worker. "I'm an object," says the high fashion model. Blue collar

and white call upon the identical phrase: "I'm a robot." Terkel, [31, p.xi].

Studs Terkel encountered these remarks during his study of American attitudes to employment. What relevance can they have here? Welders and fashion models are not best known for an interest in philosophy. Blue collar and white, surely, have scant interest in the abstract issue of scientific reductionism?

The "surely", here, is suspect. Admittedly, neither the blue nor the white feel much at ease with philosophical terminology. But ignorance of jargon does not imply innocence of issues.

These workers clearly took for granted, as most people do, that there is a clear distinction between humans on the one hand and animals – and machines – on the other. They took for granted, too, that this distinction is grounded in the variety of human skills and, above all, in personal autonomy. When their working-conditions gave no scope for their skills and autonomy, they experienced not merely frustration but also personal threat – not least, to their sense of worth, or human dignity.

"So much the worse for them, poor deluded fools!", some might retort, appealing not only to (scientific) truth but also to what they see as (humanistic) illusion – specifically, the illusion of freedom inherent in the notion of human dignity.

The behaviourist B. F. Skinner, for example, argued that "the literature of dignity ...stands in the way of further human achievements" [30, p.59], the main achievement he had in mind being the scientific understanding of human behaviour. "Dignity", he said. is a matter of giving people credit, of admiring them for their (self-generated) achievements. But his behaviourist principles implied that "the environment", not "autonomous man", is in control [30, p.21] No credit, then, to *us*, if we exercise some skill – whether bodily, mental, or moral. Spot welder and fashion model can no longer glory in their dexterity or gracefulness, nor clerk and cleric in their profession or vocation. Honesty and honest toil alike are de-credited, de-dignified.

Behaviourism, then, questions our notions of human worth. But it is at least concerned with life. Animals are living things, and *Rattus Norvegicus* a moderately merry mammal. Some small shred of our self-respect can perhaps be retained, if we are classed with rats, or even pigeons. But artificial intelligence, it seems, is another matter. For AI compares us with computers. and dead, automatic tincannery is all they are capable of. Sequential or connectionist, it makes no difference: machines are not even alive. The notion that they could help us to an adequate account of the mind seems quite absurd.

The absurdity is compounded with threat. For (on this view) it seems that if human minds were understood in AI-terms, everything we think of as distinctively human – freedom, creativity, morals – would be explained away. Ultimately, a computational psychology and neuroscience would reduce these matters to a set of chemical reactions and electrical pulses. No autonomy there ...and no dignity, either. We could not exalt human skills and personality above the dexterity of monkeys or the obstinacy of mules. As for honouring excellence in the human mind, this would be like preferring a Rolls Royce to a Mini: some basis in objectivity, no doubt, but merely a matter of ranking machines.

Given these widespread philosophical assumptions, it is no wonder if AI is feared by ordinary people. They think of it as even more threatening to their sense of personal worth than either industrial automation or "mechanical" work-practices, the subjects of the complaints voiced to Terkel.

What they think *matters*. Given the central constructive role in our personal life of the self-concept, we should expect that people who believe (or even half-believe) they are mere machines may behave accordingly. Similarly, people who feel they are being treated like machines, or caged animals, may be not only frustrated and insulted but also insidiously lessened by the experience. Such malign effects can indeed be seen, for instance in psychotherapists' consulting rooms. Thirty years ago, before the general public had even heard of AI, the therapist Rollo May remarked on some depersonalizing effects of behaviourism, and of reductionist science in general:

> I take very seriously ...the dehumanizing dangers in our tendency in modern science to make man over into the image of the machine, into the image of the techniques by which we study him.... A central core of modern man's 'neurosis' is the undermining of his experience of himself as responsible, the sapping of his willing and decision. [19, p.20].

I have used this quote elsewhere, but make no apology for repeating it. It shows the practical results of people's defining themselves as (what they think of as) machines, not only in a felt unhappiness but also in an observable decline of personal autonomy.

The upshot is that it is practically important, not just theoretically interesting, to examine the layman's philosophical assumptions listed above. Are they correct? Or are they mere sentimental illusion, a pusillanimous refusal to face scientific reality? In particular, are AI-concepts and AI-explanations compatible with the notion of human dignity?

## 2 AI and Ants

At first sight, the answer may appear to be "No". For it is not only behaviourists who see conditions in the external environment as causing apparently autonomous behaviour. Only a few years after May's complaint quoted above, Herbert Simon – a founding-father of AI – took much the same view [28].

Simon described the erratic path of the ant, as it avoided the obstacles on its way to nest or food, as the result of a series of simple and immediate reactions to the local details of the terrain. He did not stop with ants, but tackled

humans too. For over twenty years, Simon has argued that rational thought and skilled behaviour are largely triggered by specific environmental cues. The extensive psychological experiments and computer-modelling on which his argument is based were concerned with chess, arithmetic, and typing [25, 6]. But he would say the same of bank-telling and spot-welding.

Simon's ant was not taken as a model by most of his AI-colleagues. Instead, they were inspired by his earliest, and significantly different, work on the computer simulation of problem-solving [24, 23]. This ground-breaking theoretical research paid no attention to environmental factors, but conceived of human thought in terms of internal mental/computational processes, such as hierarchical means-end planning and goal-representations.

Driven by this "internalist" view, the young AI-community designed – and in some cases built – robots guided top-down by increasingly sophisticated internal planning and representation [1, ch.12]. Plans were worked out ahead of time. In the most flexible cases, certain contingencies could be foreseen, and the detailed movements, and even the sub-plans, could be decided on at the time of execution. But even though they inhabited the physical world, these robots were not real-world, real-time, creatures. Their environments were simple, highly predictable, "toy-worlds". They typically involved a flat ground-plane, polyhedral and/or pre-modelled shapes, white surfaces, shadowless lighting, and – by human standards – painfully slow movements. Moreover, they were easily called to a halt, or trapped into fruitless perseverative behaviour, by unforeseen environmental details.

Recently, however, the AI-pendulum has swung towards the ant. Current research in *situated robotics* sees no need for the symbolic representations and detailed anticipatory planning typical of earlier AI-robotics. Indeed, the earlier strategy is seen as not just unnecessary, but ineffective. Traditional robotics suffers from the brittleness of classical AI-programs in general: unexpected input can cause the system to do something highly inappropriate, and there is no way in which the problem-environment can help guide it back onto the right track. Accepting that the environment cannot be anticipated in detail, workers in situated robotics have resurrected the insight – often voiced within classical AI, but also often forgotten – that the best source of information about the real world is the real world itself.

Accordingly, the "intelligence" of these very recent robots is in the hardware, not the software [3, 4]. There is no high-level program doing detailed anticipatory planning. Instead, the creature is engineered in such a way that, within limits, it naturally does the right (adaptive) thing at the right time. Behaviour apparently guided by goals and hierarchical planning can, nevertheless, occur [18].

Situated robotics is closely related to two other recent forms of computer modelling, likewise engaged in studying "emergent" behaviours. These are *genetic algorithms* (GAs) and *artificial life* (A-Life).

GA-systems are self-modifying programs. which contin-

301

ually come up with new rules (new structures) [12, 13]. They use rule-changing algorithms modelled on genetic processes such as mutation and crossover, and algorithms for identifying and selecting the relatively successful rules. Mutation makes a change in a single rule; crossover brings about a mix of two, so that (for instance) the lefthand portion of one rule is combined with the righthand portion of the other. Together, these algorithms (working in parallel) generate a new system better adapted to the task in hand.

One example of a GA-system is a computer-graphics program written by Karl Sims [29]. This program uses genetic algorithms to generate new images, or patterns, from pre-existing images. Unlike most GA-systems, the selection of the "fittest" examples is not automatic, but is done by the programmer – or by someone fortunate enough to be visiting his office while the program is being run. That is, the human being selects the images which are aesthetically pleasing, or otherwise interesting, and these are used to "breed" the next generation. (Sims could provide automatic selection rules, but has not yet done so – not only because of the difficulty of defining aesthetic criteria, but also because he aims to provide an interactive graphics-environment, in which human and computer can cooperate in generating otherwise unimaginable images.)

In a typical run of the program, the first image is generated at random (but Sims can feed in a real image, such as a picture of a face, if he wishes). Then the program makes nineteen independent changes (mutations) in the initial image-generating rule, so as to cover the VDU-screen with twenty images: the first, plus its nineteen ("asexually" reproduced) offspring. At this point, the human uses the computer-mouse to choose either *one* image to be mutated, or *two* images to be "mated" (through crossover). The result is another screenful of twenty images, of which all but one (or two) are newly-generated by random mutations or crossovers. The process is then repeated, for as many generations as one wants.

(The details of this GA-system need not concern us. However, so as to distinguish it from magic, a few remarks may be helpful. It starts with a list of twenty very simple LISP-functions. A "function" is not an actual instruction, but an instruction-schema: more like "$x + y$" than "$2 + 3$". Some of these functions can alter parameters in pre-existing functions: for example, they can divide or multiply numbers, transform vectors, or define the sines or cosines of angles. Some can combine two pre-existing functions, or nest one function inside another (so multiply-nested hierarchies can eventually result). A few are basic image-generating functions, capable (for example) of generating an image consisting of vertical stripes. Others can process a pre-existing image, for instance by altering the light-contrasts so as to make "lines" or "surface-edges" more or less visible. When the program chooses a function at random, it also randomly chooses any missing parts. So if it decides to *add* something to an existing number (such as a numerical parameter inside an image-generating function), and the "something" has not been specified, it randomly chooses the amount to be added. Similarly, if it decides to *combine* the pre-existing function with some other function, it may choose that function at random.)

As for A-Life, this is the attempt to discover the abstract functional principles underlying life in general [15]. A-Life is closely related to AI (and uses various methods which are also employed in AI). One might define A-Life as the abstract study of life, and AI as the abstract study of mind. But if one assumes that life prefigures mind, that cognition is – and must be – grounded in self-organizing adaptive systems, then the whole of AI may be seen as a sub-class of A-Life. Work in A-Life is therefore potentially relevant to the question of how AI relates to human dignity.

Research in A-Life uses computer-modelling to study processes that start with relatively simple, locally interacting units, and generate complex individual and/or group behaviours. Examples of such behaviours include self-organization, reproduction, adaptation, purposiveness, and evolution.

Self-organization is shown, for instance, in the flocking behaviour of flocks of birds, herds of cattle, and schools of fish. The entire group of animals seems to behave as one unit. It maintains its coherence despite changes in direction, the (temporary) separation of stragglers, and the occurrence of obstacles – which the flock either avoids or "flows around". Yet there is no overall director working out the plan, no sergeant-major yelling instructions to all the individual animals, and no reason to think that any one animal is aware of the group as a whole. The question arises, then, how this sort of behaviour is possible.

Ethologists argue that communal behaviour of large groups of animals must depend on local communications between neighbouring individuals, who have no conception of the group-behaviour as such. But just what are these "local communications"?

Flocking has been modelled within A-Life, in terms of a collection of very simple units, called Boids [27]. Each Boid follows three rules: (1) keep a minumum distance from other objects, including other Boids; (2) match velocity to the average velocity of the Boids in the immediate neighbourhood; (3) move towards the perceived centre of mass of the Boids in the neighbourhood. These rules, depending as they do only on very limited, local, information, result in the holistic flocking behaviour just described. It does not follow, of course, that real birds follow just those rules: that must be tested by ethological studies. But this research shows that it is at least *possible* for group-behaviour of this kind to depend on very simple, strictly local, rules.

Situated robotics, GAs, and A-Life could be combined, for they share an emphasis on bottom-up, self-adaptive, parallel processing. At present, most situated robots are hand-crafted. In principle, they could be "designed" by evolutionary algorithms from the GA/A-Life stable. Fully-simulated robots have already been evolved, and real robots are now being constructed with the help of simulated evolution. The automatic evolution of real physical robots *without any recourse to simulation* is more difficult [5], but progress is being made in this area too.

Recent work in evolutionary robotics [10] has simulated insect-like robots, with simple "brains" controlling their behaviour. The (simulated) neural net controlling the (simulated) visuomotor system of the robot gradually adapts to its specific (simulated) task-environment. This automatic adaptation can result in some surprises. For instance, if – in the given task-environment – the creature does not actually need its (simulated) inbuilt whiskers as well as its eyes, the initial network-links to the whiskers may eventually be lost, and the relevant neural units may be taken over by the eyes. *Eyes* can even give way to *eye*: if the task is so simple that only one eye is needed, one of them may eventually lose its links with the creature's network-brain.

Actual (physical) robots of this type can be generated by combining simulated evolution with hardware-construction [10]. The detailed physical connections to, and within, the "brain" of the robot-hardware are adjusted every *n* generations (where *n* may be 100, or 1,000, or ...), mirroring the current blueprint evolved within the simulation. This acts as a cross-check: the real robot should behave as the simulated robot does. Moreover, the resulting embodied robot can roam around an actual physical environment, its real-world task-failures and successes being fed into the background simulation so as to influence its future evolution. The brain is not the only organ whose anatomy can be evolved in this way: the placement and visual angle of the creatures' eyes can be optimized, too. (The same research-team has begun work on the evolution of physical robots without any simulation. This takes much longer, because every single evaluation of every individual in the population has to be done using the real hardware.)

The three new research-fields outlined above have strong links with biology: with neuroscience, ethology, genetics, and the theory of evolution. As a result, animals are becoming theoretically assimilated to *animats* [21]. The behaviour of swarms of bees, and of ant-colonies, is hotly discussed at A-Life conferences, and entomologists are constantly cited in the A-Life and situated-robotics literatures [16]. Environmentally situated (and formally defined) accounts of apparently goal-seeking behaviour in various animals, including birds and mammals, are given by (some) ethologists [20]. And details of invertebrate psychology, such as visual tracking in the hoverfly, are modelled by research in connectionist AI [8, 9].

In short, Simon's ant is now sharing the limelight on the AI-stage. Some current AI is more concerned with artificial insects than with artificial human minds. But – what is of particular interest to us here – this form of AI sees itself as designing "autonomous agents" (as A-Life in general seeks to design "autonomous systems").

## 3  Autonomous Agency

Autonomy is ascribed to these artificial insects because it is their intrinsic physical structure, adapted as it is to the sorts of environmental problem they are likely to meet, which enables them to act appropriately. Unlike traditional robots, their behaviour is not directed by complex software written for a general-purpose machine. imposed on their bodies by some alien (human) hand. Rather, they are specifically constructed to adapt to the particular environment they inhabit.

We are faced, then, with two opposing intuitions concerning autonomy. Our (and Skinner's) original intuition was that response determined by the external environment lessens one's autonomy. But the nouvelle-AI intuition is that to be in thrall to an internal plan is to be a mere puppet. (Notice that one can no longer say "a mere robot".) How can these contrasting intuitions be reconciled?

Autonomy is not an all-or-nothing property. It has several dimensions, and many gradations. Three aspects of behaviour - or rather, of its control – are crucial. First, the extent to which response to the environment is direct (determined only by the present state in the external world) or indirect (mediated by inner mechanisms partly dependent on the creature's previous history). Second, the extent to which the controlling mechanisms were self-generated rather than externally imposed. And third, the extent to which inner directing mechanisms can be reflected upon, and/or selectively modified in the light of general interests or the particularities of the current problem in its environmental context. An individual's autonomy is the greater, the more its behaviour is directed by self-generated (and idiosyncratic) inner mechanisms, nicely responsive to the specific problem-situation, yet reflexively modifiable by wider concerns.

The first aspect of autonomy involves behaviour mediated, in part, by inner mechanisms shaped by the creature's past experience. These mechanisms may. but need not, include explicit representations of current or future states. It is controversial, in ethology as in philosophy, whether animals have explicit internal representations of goals [22]. And, as we have seen, AI includes strong research-programmes on both sides of this methodological fence. But this controversy is irrelevant here. The important distinction is between a response wholly dependent on the current environmental state (given the original, "innate", bodily mechanisms), and one largely influenced by the creature's experience. The more a creature's past experience differs from that of other creatures, the more "individual" its behaviour will appear.

The second aspect of autonomy, the extent to which the controlling mechanisms were self-generated rather than externally imposed, may seem to be the same as the first. After all, a mechanism shaped by experience is sensitive to the past of that particular individual - which may be very different from that of other, initially comparable, individuals. But the distinction, here, is between behaviour which "emerges" as a result of self-organizing processes, and behaviour which was deliberately prefigured in the design of the experiencing creature.

In computer-simulation studies within A-Life, and within situated robotics also, holistic behaviour – often of an unexpected sort – may emerge. It results, of course, from the initial list of simple rules concerning locally interacting units. But it was neither specifically mentioned in those rules, nor (often) foreseen when they were written.

A flock, for example, is a holistic phenomenon. A bird-watcher sees a flock of birds as a unit, in the sense that it shows behaviour that can be described only at the level of the flock itself. For instance, when it comes to an obstacle, such as a tall building, the flock divides and "flows" smoothly around it, reorganizing itself into a single unit on the far side. But no individual bird is divided in half by the building. And no bird has any notion of the flock as a whole, still less any goal of reconstituting it after its division.

Clearly, flocking behaviour must be described on its own level, even though it can be explained by (reduced to) processes on a lower level. This point is especially important if "emergence-hierarchies" evolve as a result of new forms of perception, capable of detecting the emergent phenomena *as such*. Once a holistic behaviour has emerged it, or its effects, may be detected (perceived) by some creature or other – including, sometimes, the "unit-creatures" making it up.

(This implies that a creature's perceptual capacities cannot be fully itemized for all time. In Gibsonian terms, one might say that evolution does not know what all the relevant affordances will turn out to be, so cannot know how they will be detected. The current methodology of AI and A-Life does not allow for "latent" perceptual powers, actualized only by newly-emerged environmental features. This is one of the ways in which today's computer-modelling is biologically unrealistic [14].)

If the emergent phenomenon can be detected, it can feature in rules governing the perceiver's behaviour. Holistic phenomena on a higher level may then result . . . and so on. Ethologists, A-Life workers, and situated roboticists all assume that increasingly complex hierarchical behaviour can arise in this sort of way. The more levels in the hierarchy, the less direct the influence of environmental stimuli – and the greater the behavioural autonomy.

Even if we can *explain* a case of emergence, however, we cannot necessarily *understand* it. One might speak of intelligible vs. unintelligible emergence.

Flocking gives us an example of the former. Once we know the three rules governing the behaviour of each individual Boid, we can see lucidly how it is that holistic flocking results.

Sims' computer-generated images give us an example of the latter. One may not be able to say just why *this* image resulted from *that* LISP-expression. Sims himself cannot always explain the changes he sees appearing on the screen before him, even though he can access the mini-program responsible for any image he cares to investigate, and for its parent(s) too. Often, he cannot even "genetically engineer" the underlying LISP-expression so as to get a particular visual effect. To be sure, this is partly because his system makes several changes simultaneously, with every new generation. If he were to restrict it to making only one change, and studied the results systematically, he could work out just what was happening. But when several changes are made in parallel, it is often impossible to understand the generation of the image *even though* the "explanation" is available.

Where real creatures are concerned, of course, we have multiple interacting changes, and no explanation at our finger-tips. At the genetic level, these multiple changes and simultaneous influences arise from mutations and crossover. At the psychological level, they arise from the plethora of ideas within the mind. Think of the many different thoughts which arise in your consciousness, more or less fleetingly, when you face a difficult choice or moral dilemma. Consider the likelihood that many more conceptual associations are being activated unconsciously in your memory, influencing your conscious musings accordingly. Even if we had a listing of all these "explanatory" influences, we might be in much the same position as Sims, staring in wonder at one of his *n*th-generation images and unable to say why *this* LISP-expression gave rise to it. In fact, we cannot hope to know about more than a fraction of the ideas aroused in human minds (one's own, or someone else's) when such choices are faced.

The third criterion of autonomy listed above was the extent to which a system's inner directing mechanisms can be reflected upon, and/or selectively modified, by the individual concerned. One way in which a system can adapt its own processes, selecting the most fruitful modifications, is to use an "evolutionary" strategy such as the genetic algorithms mentioned above. It may be that something broadly similar goes on in human minds. But the mutations and selections carried out by GAs are modelled on biological evolution, not conscious reflection and self-modification. And it is conscious deliberation which many people assume to be the crux of human autonomy.

For the sake of argument, let us accept this assumption at face-value. Let us ignore the mounting evidence, from Freud to social psychology (e.g. [26]), that our conscious thoughts are less relevant than we like to think. Let us ignore neuroscientists' doubts about whether our conscious intentions actually direct our behaviour (as the folk-psychology of "action" assumes) [17]. Let us even ignore the fact that *unthinking spontaneity* – the opposite of conscious reflection – is often taken as a sign of individual freedom. (Spontaneity may be based in the sort of multiple constraint satisfaction modelled by connectionist AI, where many of the constraints are drawn from the person's idiosyncratic experience.) What do AI, and AI-influenced psychology, have to say about conscious thinking and deliberate self-control?

Surprisingly, perhaps, the most biologically realistic (more accurately: the least biologically unrealistic) forms of AI cannot help us here. Ants, and artificial ants, are irrelevant. Nor can connectionism help. It is widely agreed, even by connectionists, that conscious thought requires a sequential "virtual machine", more like a von Neumann computer than a parallel-processing neural net. As yet, we have only very sketchy ideas about how the types of problem-solving best suited to conscious deliberation might be implemented in connectionist systems.

The most helpful AI approach so far, where conscious deliberation is involved, is GOFAI: good old-fashioned AI [11] – much of which was inspired by human introspection. Consciousness involves reflection on one level of processes going on at a lower level. Work in classical AI, such as the work on planning mentioned above, has studied multi-level problem-solving. Computationally-informed work in developmental psychology has suggested that flexible self-control, and eventually consciousness, result from a series of "representational redescriptions" of lower-level skills [7].

Representational redescriptions, many-levelled maps of the mind, are crucial to creativity [2, esp. ch.4]. Creativity is an aspect of human autonomy. Many of Terkel's workers were frustrated because their jobs allowed them no room for creative ingenuity. Our ability to think new thoughts in new ways is one of our most salient, and most valued, characteristics.

This ability involves someone's doing something which they not only *did not* do before, but which they *could not* have done before. To do this, they must either explore a formerly unrecognized area of some pre-existing "conceptual space", or transform some dimension of that generative space. Transforming the space allows novel mental structures to arise which simply could not have been generated from the initial set of constraints. The nature of the creative novelties depends on which feature has been transformed, and how. Conceptual spaces, and procedures for transforming them, can be clarified by thinking of them in computational terms. But this does not mean that creativity is predictable, or even fully explicable *post hoc*: for various reasons (including those mentioned above), it is neither [2, ch.9].

Autonomy in general is commonly associated with un-predictability. Many people feel AI to be a threat to their self-esteem because they assume that it involves a deterministic predictability. But they are mistaken. Some connectionist AI-systems include non-deterministic (stochastic) processes, and are more efficient as a result.

Moreover, determinism does not always imply predictability. Workers in A-Life, for instance, justify their use of computer-simulation by citing chaos theory, according to which a fully deterministic dynamic process may be theoretically unpredictable [15]. If there is no analytic solution to the differential equations describing the changes concerned, the process must simply be "run", and observed, to know what its implications are. The same is true of many human choices. We cannot always predict what a person will do. Moreover, predicting *one's own* choices is not always possible. One may have to "run one's own equations" to find out what one will do, since the outcome cannot be known until the choice is actually made.

## 4 Conclusion

One of the pioneers of A-Life has said: "The field of Artificial Life is unabashedly mechanistic and reductionist. However, this *new mechanism* – based as it is on multiplicities of machines and on recent results in the fields of nonlinear dynamics, chaos theory, and the formal theory of computation – is vastly different from the mechanism of the last century." Langton [15, p.6; italics in original].

Our discussion of A-Life and *nouvelle AI* has suggested just how vast this difference is. Similarly, the potentialities of classical AI systems go far beyond what most people – fashion-models, spot-welders, bank-tellers – think of as "machines". If this is reductionism, it is very different from the sort of reductionism which insists that the only scientifically respectable concepts lie at the most basic ontological level (neurones and biochemical processes, or even electrons, mesons, and quarks).

In sum, AI does not reduce our respect for human minds. If anything, it increases it. Far from denying human autonomy, it helps us to understand how it is possible. The autonomy of Terkel's informants was indeed compromised – but by inhuman working conditions, not by science. Science in general, and AI in particular, need not destroy our sense of human dignity.

## References

[1] M. A. Boden, *Artificial Intelligence and Natural Man* (2nd edn.). London: MIT Press, 1987.

[2] M. A. Boden. *The Creative Mind: Myths and Mechanisms.* London: Weidenfeld & Nicolson, 1990.

[3] V. Braitenberg, *Vehicles: Essays in Synthetic Psychology.* Cambridge, Mass.: MIT Press, 1984.

[4] R. A. Brooks, Intelligence Without Representation. *Artificial Intelligence,* 47:139-159, 1991.

[5] R. A. Brooks, Artificial Life and Real Robots. In F. J. Varela and P. Bourgine, eds., *Toward a Practice of Autonomous Systems: Proceedings of the First European Conference on Artificial Life,* Cambridge, Mass.: MIT Press, pp.3-10, 1992.

[6] S. K. Card, T. P. Moran, and A. Newell. *The Psychology of Human-Computer Interaction.* Hillsdale, N.J.: Erlbaum. 1983.

[7] A. Clark and A. Karmiloff-Smith. The Cognizer's Innards, *Mind and Language.* In press.

[8] D. Cliff, The Computational Hoverfly: A Study in Computational Neuroethology. In J.-A. Meyer and S. W. Wilson (eds.), *From Animals to Animats: Proceedings of the First International Conference on Simulation of Adaptive Behaviour.* Cambridge. Mass.: MIT Press, pp.87–96, 1990.

[9] D. Cliff, Neural Networks for Visual Tracking in an Artificial Fly. In F. J. Varela and P. Bourgine, eds., *Toward a Practice of Autonomous Systems: Proceedings of the First European Conference on Artificial Life*. Cambridge, Mass.: MIT Press, pp.78–87. 1992.

[10] D. Cliff, I. Harvey, and P. Husbands. Explorations in Evolutionary Robotics, *Adaptive Behavior*, 2(1):73–110. 1993.

[11] J. Haugeland, *Artificial Intelligence: The Very Idea*. Cambridge, Mass.: MIT Press, 1985.

[12] J. H. Holland, *Adaptation in Natural and Artificial Systems: An Introductory Analysis with Applications to Biology, Control, and Artificial Intelligence*. Ann Arbor: Univ. Michigan Press, 1975. (Reissued MIT Press, 1991.)

[13] J. H. Holland, K. J. Holyoak, R. E. Nisbet, and P. R. Thagard. *Induction: Processes of Inference, Learning, and Discovery*. Cambridge, Mass.: MIT Press, 1986.

[14] Kugler. Talk given at the Summer-School on "Comparative Approaches to Cognitive Science", Aix-en-Provence (organizers, J.-A. Meyer & H. L. Roitblat), 1992.

[15] C. G. Langton, Artificial Life. In C. G. Langton (ed.), *Artificial Life: Proceedings of an Interdisciplinary Workshop on the Synthesis and Simulation of Living Systems*. New York: Addison-Wesley, pp.1–47. 1989.

[16] D. Lestel, Fourmis Cybernetiques et Robots-Insectes: Socialite et Cognition a l'Interface de la Robotique et de l'Ethologie Experimentale, *Information Sur Les Sciences Sociales*, 31(2):179–211, 1992.

[17] B. Libet, Are the Mental Experiences of Will and Self-Control Significant for the Performance of a Voluntary Act?, *Behavioral and Brain Sciences*, 10:783–86, 1987.

[18] P. Maes, ed. *Designing Autononmous Agents*. Cambridge, Mass.: MIT Press, 1991.

[19] R. May, *Existential Psychology*. New York: Random House, 1961.

[20] D. McFarland, Goals, No-Goals, and Own-Goals. In A. Montefiore and D. Noble, eds., *Goals, No-Goals, and Own-Goals*, London: Unwin Hyman, pp.39–57, 1989.

[21] J.-A. Meyer and S. W. Wilson, eds. *From Animals to Animats: Proceedings of the First International Conference on Simulation of Adaptive Behaviour*. Cambridge, Mass.: MIT Press, 1991.

[22] A. Montefiore and D. Noble, eds. *Goals, No-Goals, and Own-Goals*. London: Unwin Hyman, 1989.

[23] A. Newell, J. C. Shaw, and H. A. Simon. Empirical Explorations with the Logic Theory Machine: A Case-Study in Heuristics. In E. A. Feigenbaum and J. Feldman (eds.), *Computers and Thought*. New York: McGraw-Hill, pp.109–133, 1963.

[24] A. Newell and H. A. Simon. GPS – A Program That Simulates Human Thought. In H. Billing (ed.), *Lernende Automaten*. Munich: Oldenbourg, pp.109–124, 1961. Reprinted in E. A. Feigenbaum and J. Feldman (eds.), *Computers and Thought*. New York: McGraw-Hill, pp.279–296, 1963.

[25] A. Newell and H. A. Simon. *Human Problem Solving*. Englewood Cliffs, N.J.: Prentice-Hall, 1972.

[26] R. E. Nisbett and L. Ross. *Human Inference: Strategies and Shortcomings in Social Judgment*. Englewood Cliffs, N.J.: Prentice-Hall, 1980.

[27] C. W. Reynolds. Flocks, Herds, and Schools: A Distributed Behavioral Model, *Computer Graphics* 21(4):25–34, 1987.

[28] H. A. Simon, *The Sciences of the Artificial*. Cambridge, Mass.: MIT Press, 1969.

[29] K. Sims, Artificial Evolution for Computer Graphics, *Computer Graphics*, 25(4):319–328, 1991.

[30] B. F. Skinner, *Beyond Freedom and Dignity*. New York: Alfred Knopf, 1971.

[31] S. Terkel, *Working*. New York: Pantheon, 1974.

# Acknowledgments

Newell, Allen. "Physical Symbol Systems." *Cognitive Science* 4 (1980): 135–83. Reprinted with the permission of Ablex Publishing.

Rosenbloom, Paul S., John E. Laird, Allen Newell, and Robert McCarl. "A Preliminary Analysis of the Soar Architecture as a Basis for General Intelligence." *Artificial Intelligence* 47 (1991): 289–325. Reprinted with the permission of North Holland.

Norman, Donald A. "Approaches to the Study of Intelligence." *Artificial Intelligence* 47 (1991): 327–46. Reprinted with the permission of North Holland.

Dennett, Daniel C. "Review of Allen Newell's *Unified Theories of Cognition.*" *Artificial Intelligence* 59 (1993): 285–94. Reprinted with the permission of North Holland.

Arbib, Michael A. "Review of Allen Newell's *Unified Theories of Cognition.*" *Artificial Intelligence* 59 (1993): 265–83. Reprinted with the permission of North Holland.

Churchland, Paul M. "On the Nature of Theories: A Neurocomputational Perspective." In *Scientific Theories,* edited by C. Wade Savage. *Minnesota Studies in the Philosophy of Science* vol. 14 (Minneapolis: University of Minnesota Press, 1990): 59–101. Reprinted with the permission of the University of Minnesota Press. Copyright 1990 by the Regents of the University of Minnesota.

Smolensky, Paul. "Connectionism, Constituency, and the Language of Thought." In *Meaning in Mind,* edited by B. Loewer and G. Rey (Oxford: Blackwell, 1991): 201–27. Reprinted with the permission of Blackwell Publishers.

Fodor, Jerry and Brian P. McLaughlin. "Connectionism and the Problem of Systematicity: Why Smolensky's Solution Doesn't Work." *Cognition* 35 (1990): 183–204. Reprinted with the permission of Elsevier Science B.V.

Dennett, Daniel C. "Why Not the Whole Iguana?" *Behavioral and Brain Sciences* 1 (1978): 103–104. Reprinted with the permission of Cambridge University Press.

Brooks, Rodney A. "Intelligence Without Representation." *Artificial Intelligence* 47 (1991): 139–59. Reprinted with the permission of North Holland.

van Gelder, Tim. "What Might Cognition Be, If Not Computation?" *Journal of Philosophy* 92 (1995): 345–81. Reprinted with the permission of the Journal of Philosophy, Inc., Columbia University, and the author.

Clark, Andy. "Radical Artificial Life: Some Trouble Spots." *AISB Quarterly* 87 (1994): 43–46. Reprinted with the permission of the author.

Boden, Margaret A. "Autonomy and Artificiality." *AISB Quarterly* 87 (1994): 22–28. Reprinted with the permission of the author.

Printed and bound by CPI Group (UK) Ltd, Croydon, CR0 4YY

17/10/2024

01775685-0007